Egon Schiele

M. Rassley.
'07

Grange
BOOKS

Text : Esther Selsdon,
Jeanette Zwingerberger and Ashley Bassie

Designed by:
Baseline Co Ltd
127-129A Nguyen Hue
Fiditourist 3rd Floor
District 1, Ho Chi Minh City
Vietnam

Published in 2007 by Grange Books
an imprint of Grange Books Plc
The Grange Kingsnorth Industrial Estate
Hoo, nr Rochester, Kent ME3 9ND
www.grangebooks.co.uk

ISBN: 978-1-84013-850-4

Printed in China

"Art cannot be modern… Art is primordially eternal."

– Egon Schiele

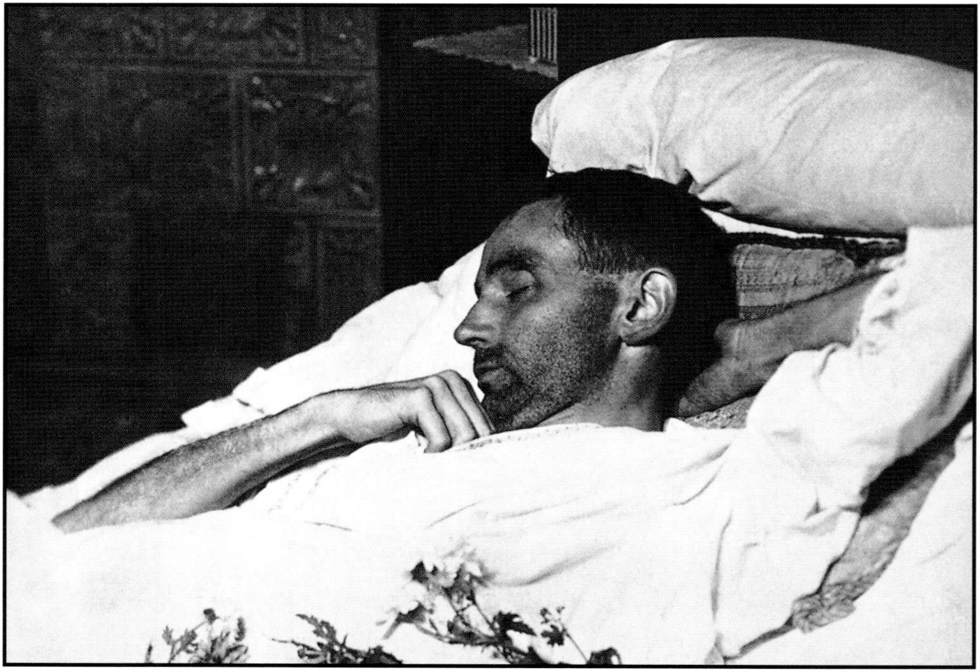

Schiele on his deathbed, 1918

Biography

1890 : Birth of Egon Schiele in Tulln, Austria

1890-1900 : Schiele devotes himself to drawing at a very young age, finding his first motifs in his native city and his surroundings.

1906 : Schiele enters the Vienna Academy of Fine Arts.

1907 : Meets Gustav Klimt. Klimt influenced Schiele's first works and never ceased to encourage the young artist.

1908 : Exhibition in Klosterneuburg.

1909 : Rebels against the teachings of his Academy professor and he writes, along with several colleagues, a list of demands asking for greater freedom of artistic expression. Because of this incident, he is forced to leave the Academy. Schiele then founds the New Art group (Neukunstgruppe) along with artists like Anton Peschka and Hans Massmann. The group will hold their first exhibition at Vienna's Pisko Salon. Thanks to Klimt, Schiele is invited to the prestigious International Exhibition of Vienna.

1910 : Meets with Arthur Roessler, an art critic who presents Schiele to many collectors.

1911 : Works in Krumau, Bavaria. He lives with one of his models, Wally Neuzil, offending the morality of the habitants of the small village. He then leaves for Neulengbach before settling down in Vienna in 1912.

1912 : He exhibits in Budapest with the Neukunstgruppe and in Munich. Publication of his first lithograph. He is accused of the corruption of a minor, and is sentenced to three weeks in prison between March and April, a penalty that profoundly affects him.

EGON SCHIELE

He then records his bitterness and revolts over his punishment in his Prison Journal, published by Arthur Roessler in 1922. In July, he presents at Cologne's Sonderbund Exhibition, one of the most outstanding events of Austrian expressionism.

1913 : He is admitted into the Bund Österreichischer Künstler (a league of Austrian artists) whose president is Gustav Klimt. In March, Schiele and the other artists in the league exhibit in Budapest. He then participates in the spring exhibition at the Munich Secession, at the Grosse Kunstausstellung in Berlin and at the forty-third exhibition at the Vienna Secession. He also contributes his writings and drawings to the Berlin review Die Aktion.

1915 : Marriage of Egon Schiele and Edith Harms. The effects of this lifestyle change on Schiele can be seen in his work as his eroticism became less violent. Even though he had escaped from mobilisation, the medical commission returned to its decision and declared him fit for the front. He is drafted into the Austrian army. His artistic production decreased considerably.

1916 : Schiele exhibits at the Berlin Secession and then at the Munich Secession. *Die Aktion* gives him a special issue.

1917 : He returns to Vienna where he sits on the Imperial Commission. From now on, Schiele can spend his time focusing on painting. He creates the Kunsthalle, a free association of artists. He participates in an exhibition at Vienna's Kaisergarten and then in various exhibitions in Amsterdam, Stockholm and Copenhagen. Schiele begins to contribute to the new Viennese movement, *Der Anbruch.*

1918 : Death of Gustav Klimt on 6 February. Schiele's participation in the Viennese Secession is a success for his financial and artistic plans. A number of Viennese personalities are interested in his ever-growing body of work and success. In the fall, his wife contracts the Spanish flu and dies on 28 October. Egon Schiele also contracts the virus, follows suit and falls ill, passing away on 31 October.

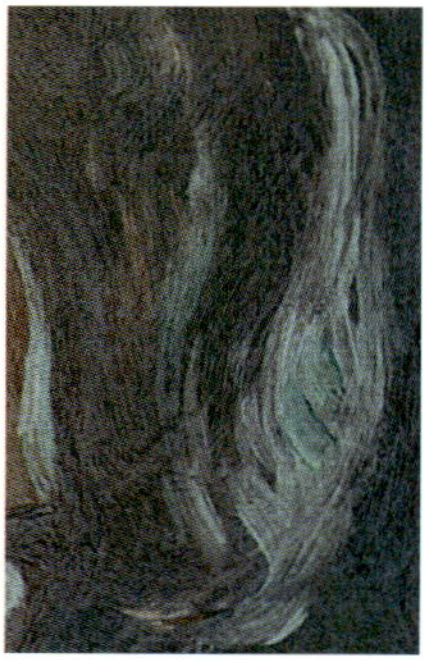

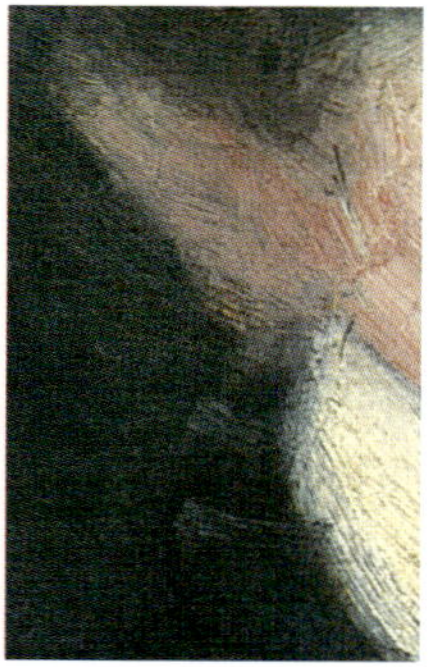

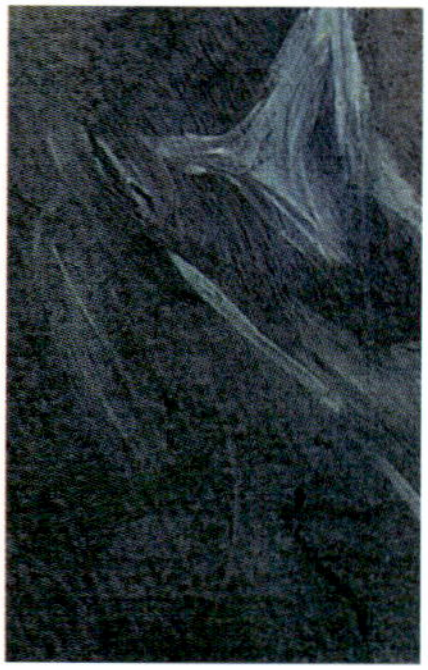

Foreword

Egon Schiele's work is so distinctive that it resists categorisation. Admitted to the Vienna Academy of Fine Arts at just sixteen, he was an extraordinarily precocious artist, whose consummate skill in the manipulation of line, above all, lent a taut expressivity to all his work. Profoundly convinced of his own significance as an artist, Schiele achieved more in his abruptly curtailed youth than many other artists achieved in a full lifetime.

Self-Portrait

1907
Oil on cardboard, 32.4 x 31.2 cm
Private collection

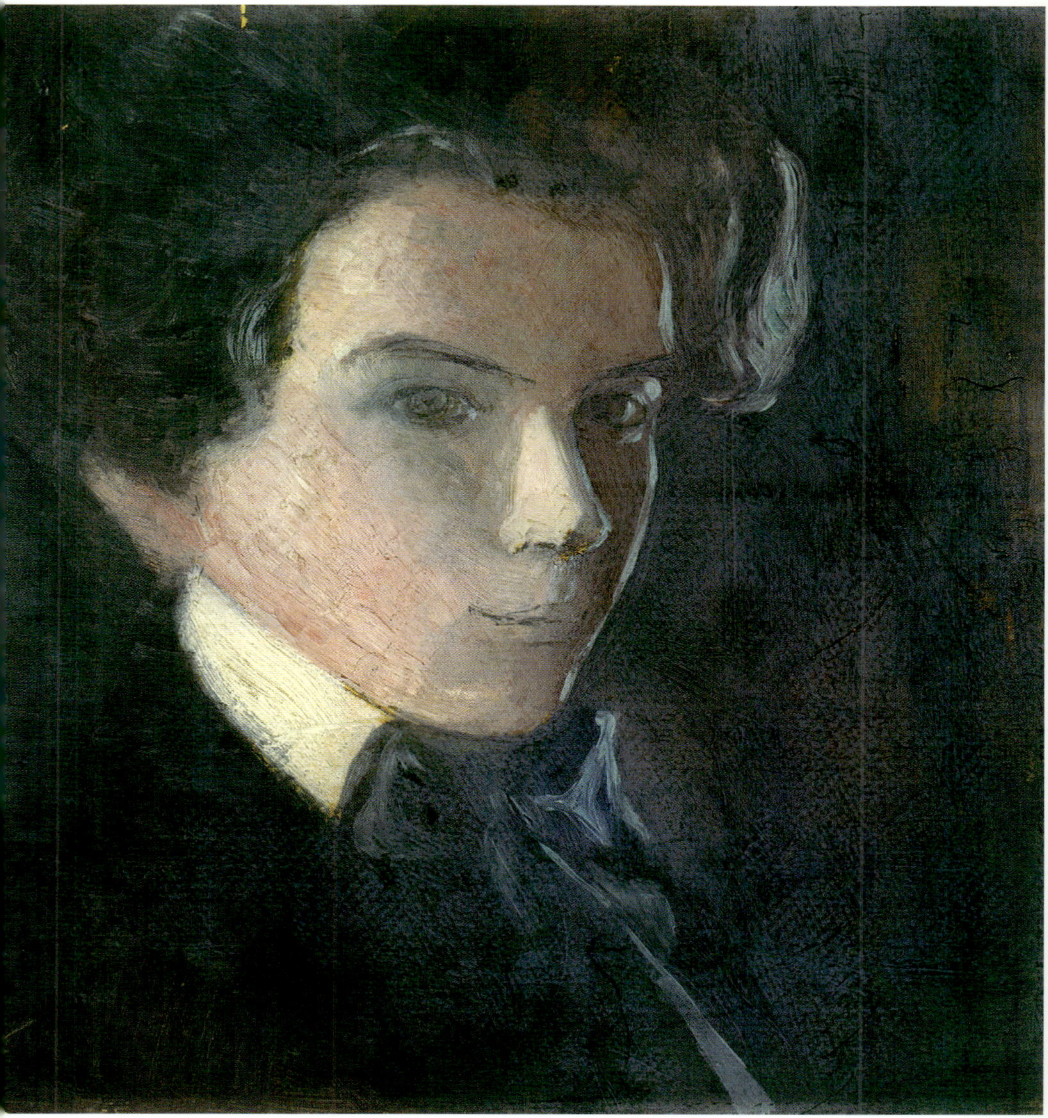

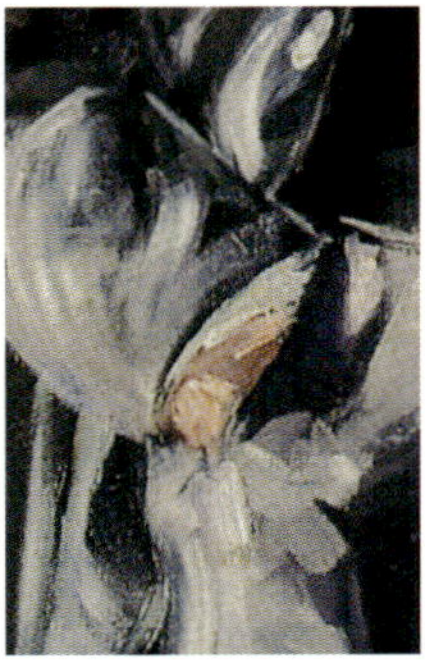

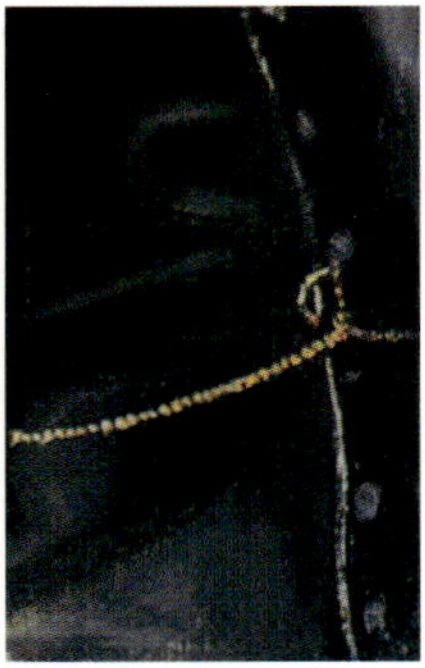

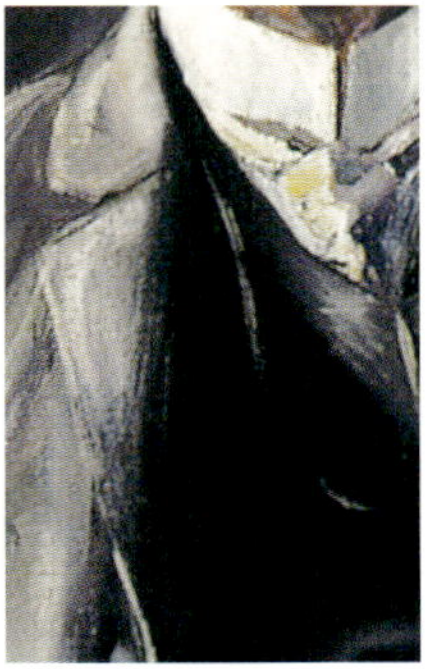

In the photograph of Schiele on his deathbed, the twenty-eight year old appears asleep, his gaunt body completely emaciated, his head resting on his bent arm; the similarity to his drawings is astounding. Because of the danger of infection, his last visitors were able to communicate with the Spanish flu-infected Schiele only by way of a mirror, which was set up on the threshold between his room and the parlour. During the same year, 1918, Schiele had designed a mausoleum for himself and his wife.

Portrait of Leopold Czihaczek, Standing

1907
Oil on canvas, 149.8 x 49.7 cm
Private collection

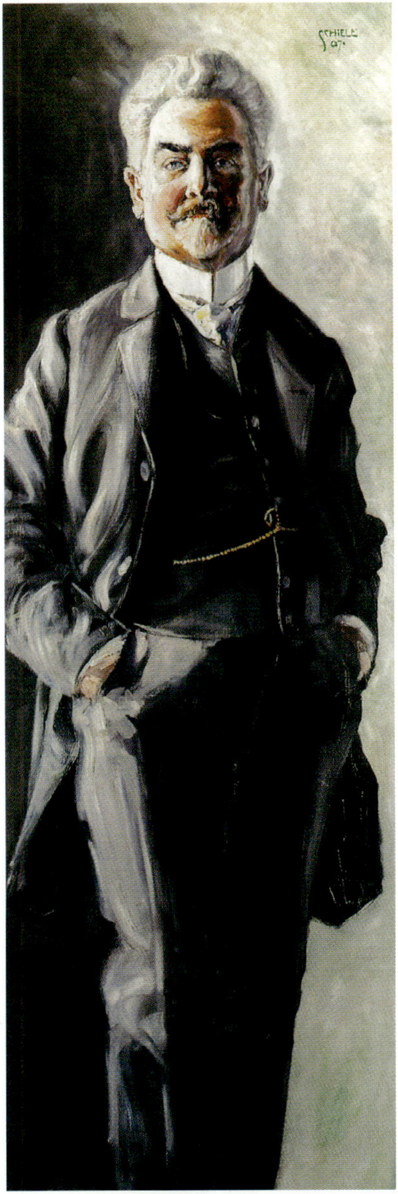
SCHIELE
07

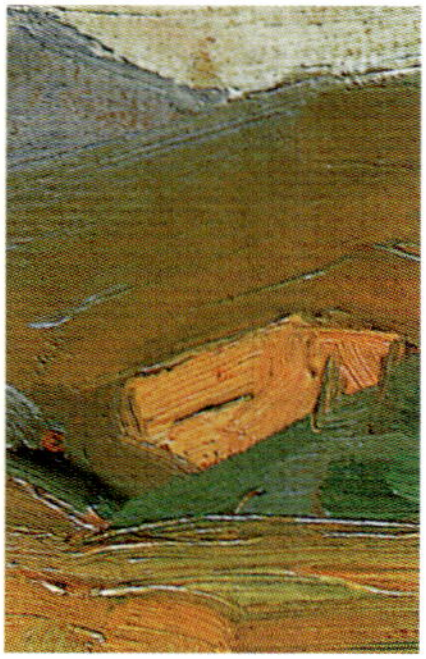

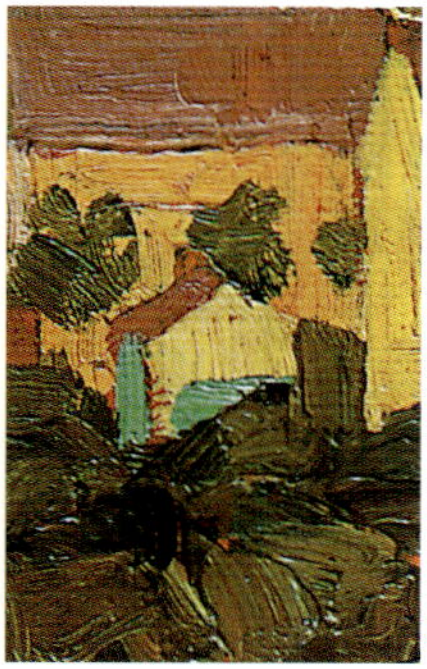

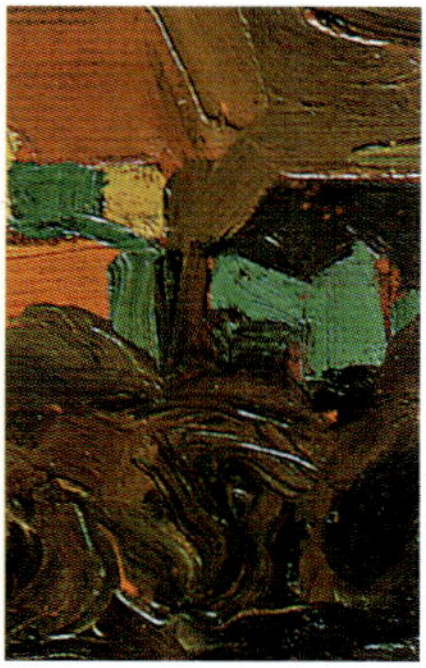

Did he know, he who had so often distinguished himself as a person of foresight, of his nearing death? Did his individual fate fuse collectively with the fall of the old system, that of the Habsburg Empire.

Schiele's productive life scarcely extended beyond ten years, yet during this time he produced 334 oil paintings and 2,503 drawings (Jane Kallir, New York, 1990). He painted portraits and still-lifes land and townscapes; however, he became famous for his draftsmanship.

Village with Mountains

1907
Oil on paper, 21.7 x 28 cm
Private collection

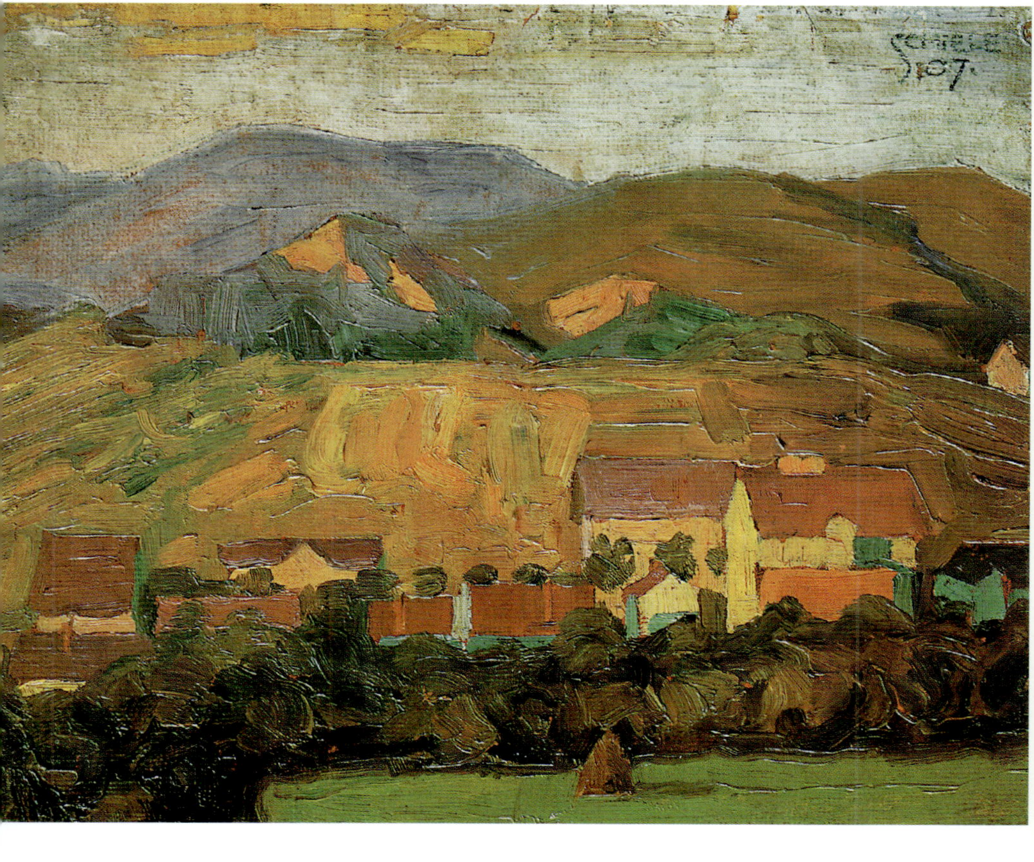
SCHIELE
S.07.

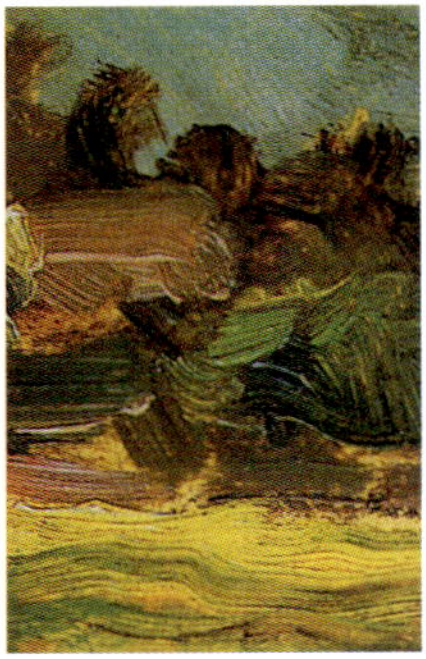
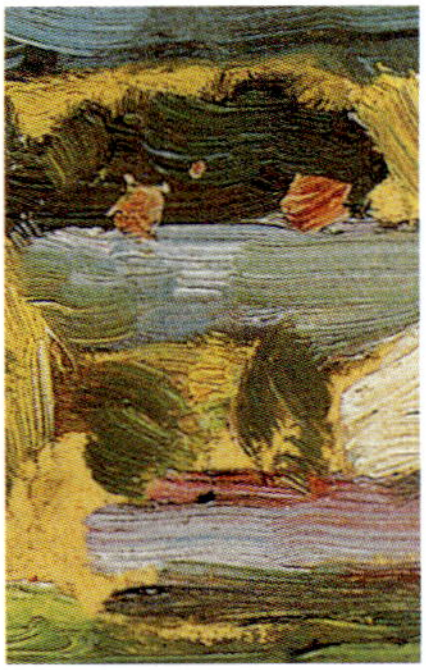
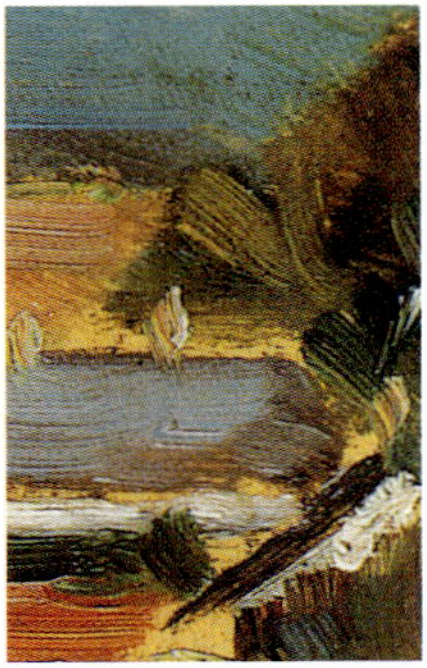

His sketches already demonstrated an astonishing sense of observation. Schiele, like many other expressionist artists of his times, looked into the innermost psychic life of his subjects as well as his own. According to the expressionists, this introspection was the purest definition of the process of artistic creation.

A potent aspect of Expressionism was the conviction held by its creators, that their endeavours were carrying art into a wholly new realm of experience. Expressionist art could display spectacular technical innovation. However, formal, surface qualities were a means, not an end.

Landscape in Lower Austria

1907
Oil on card, 17.5 x 22.5 cm
Private collection

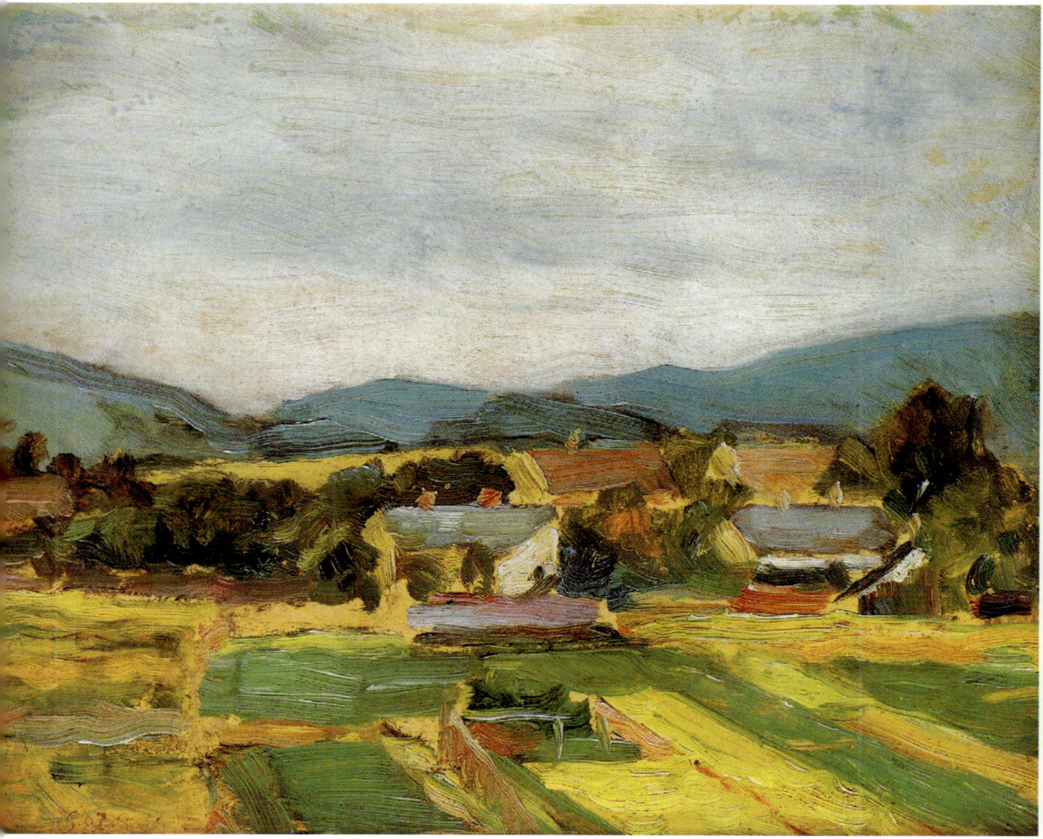

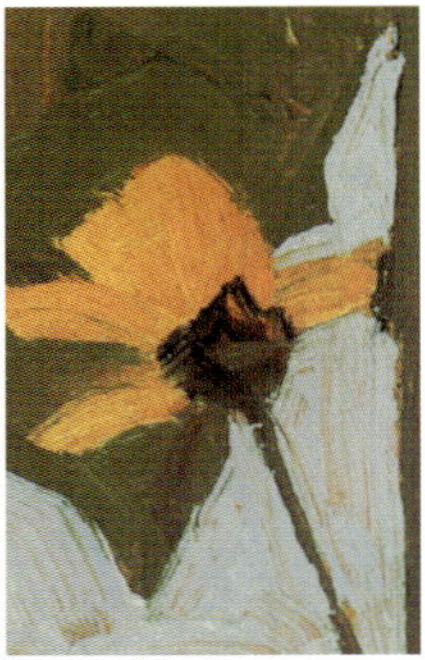

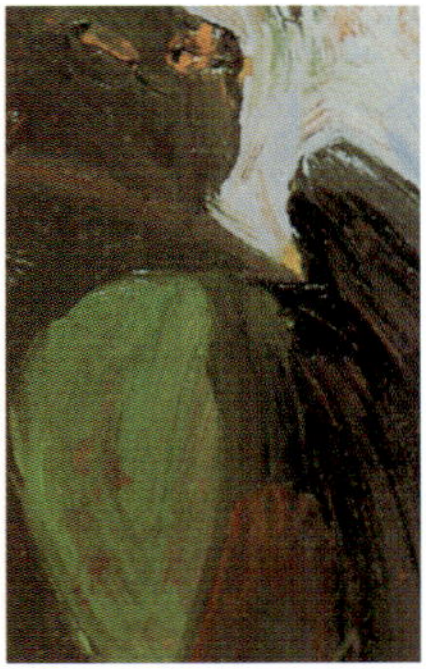

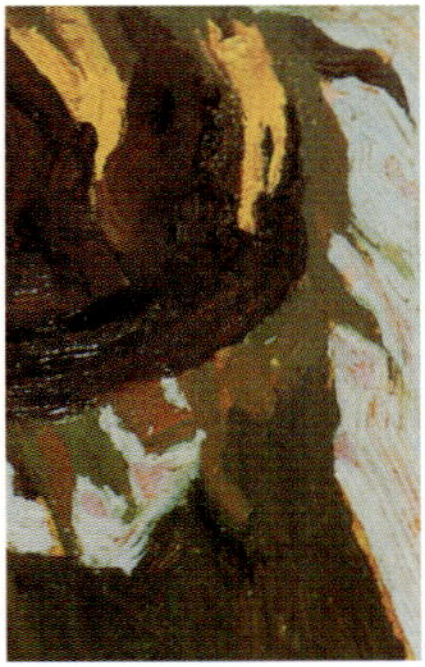

Expressionism aspired to give form to nothing less than a new kind of inward *vision*. It involved a heightened perception that appeared, to some viewers, to verge on clairvoyance. Expressionists sought an intimate, subjective, and deeply resonant communication between the artist and the viewer. Kokoschka described it as "form-giving to the experience, thus mediator and message from self to fellow human. As in love, two individuals are necessary. Expressionism does not live in an ivory tower; it calls upon a fellow being whom it awakens."

Sunflower I

1908
Oil on carboard, 44 x 33 cm
Niederösterreichisches Landesmuseum, Vienna

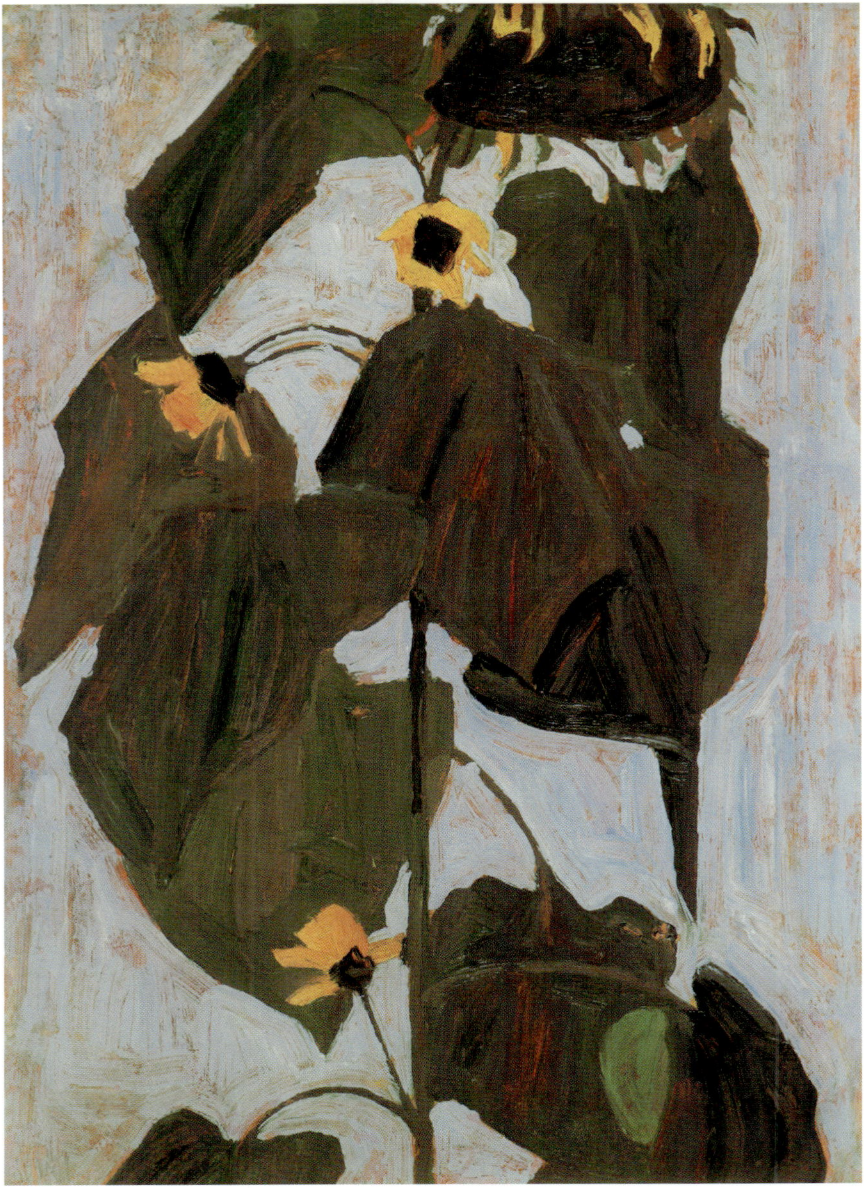

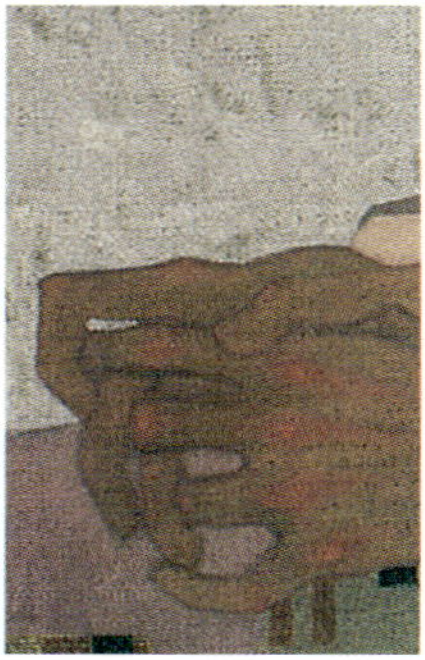

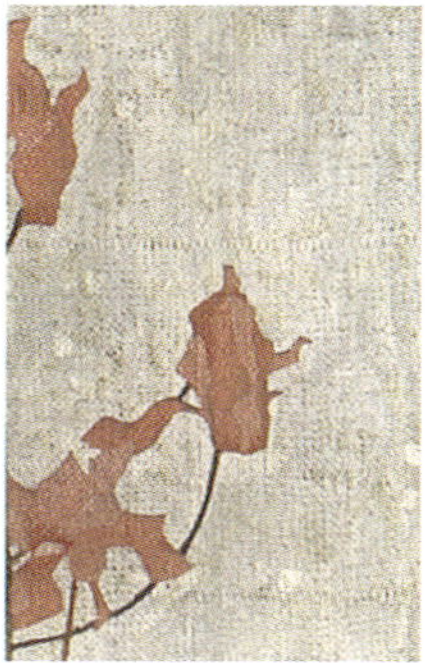

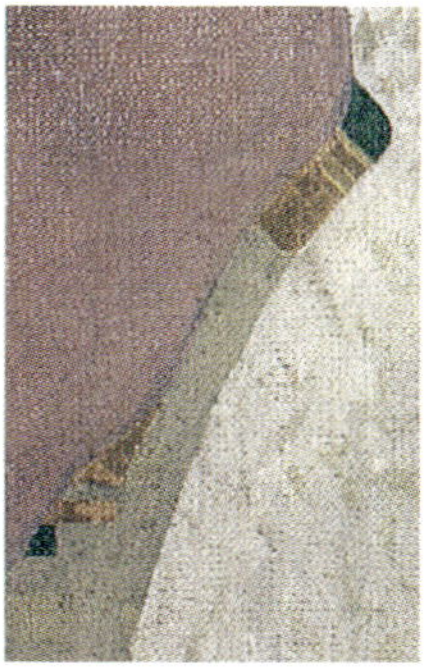

Straining against the moral grip of conventions of thought, speech and behaviour inherited from the nineteenth century, Expressionism was the means by which many artists and writers tried to give free expression to the instinctively, authentically wayward psyche – to break out of the straitjacket, as it were. Sigmund Freud's research into the unconscious and the processes of repression – whereby painful memories or unacceptable impulses are consigned to the unconscious – only appeared to confirm the existence of a powerful and conflict-ridden "inner life."

Portrait of the Painter Anton Peschka

1909
Oil and metallic paint, 110.2 x 100 cm
Private collection

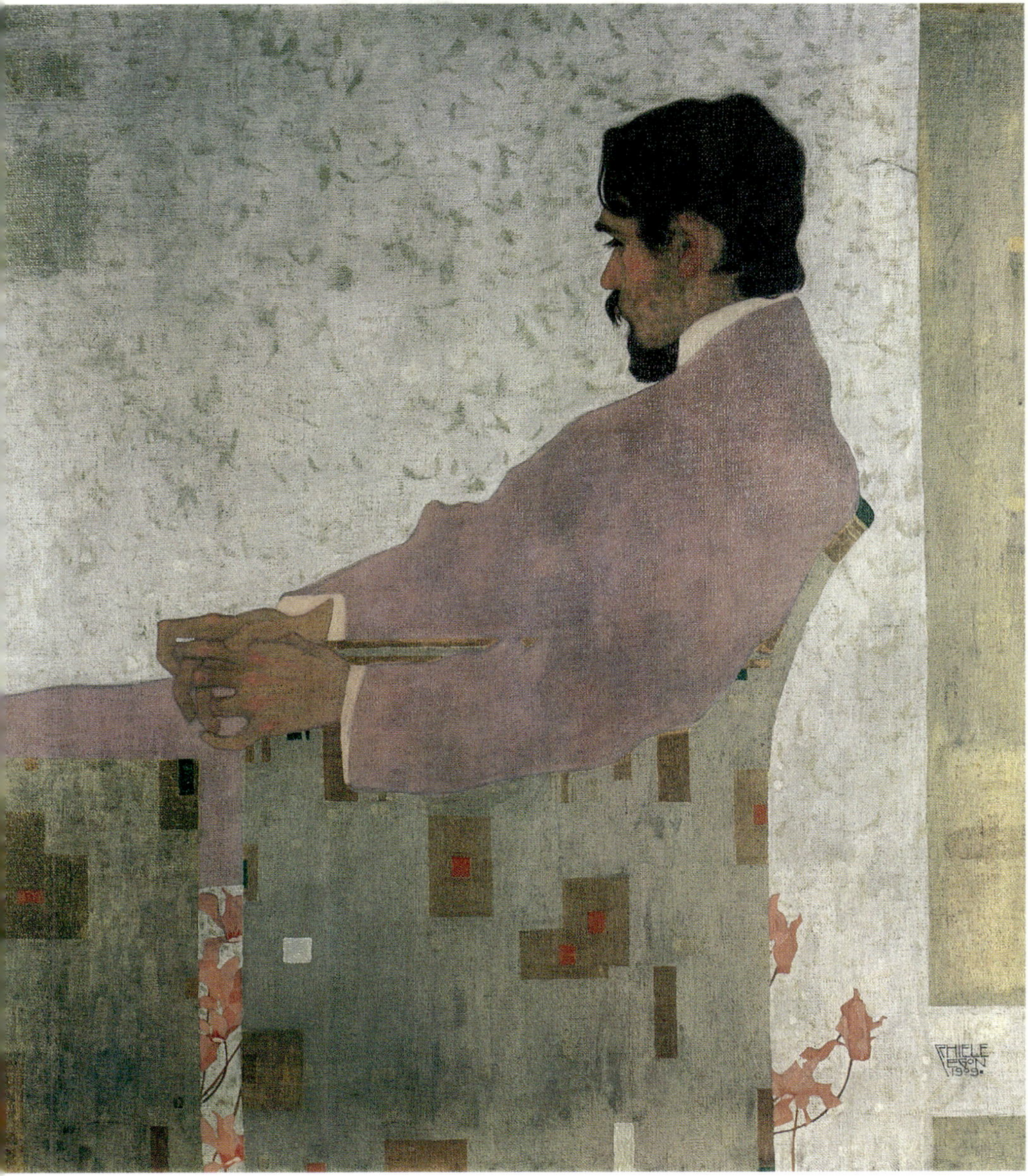
SCHIELE
EGON
1909

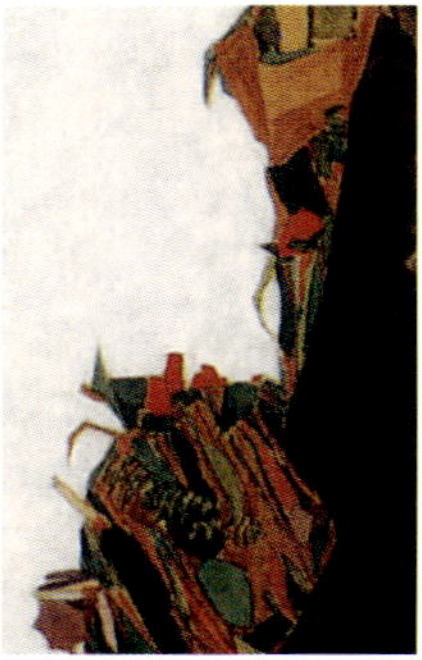

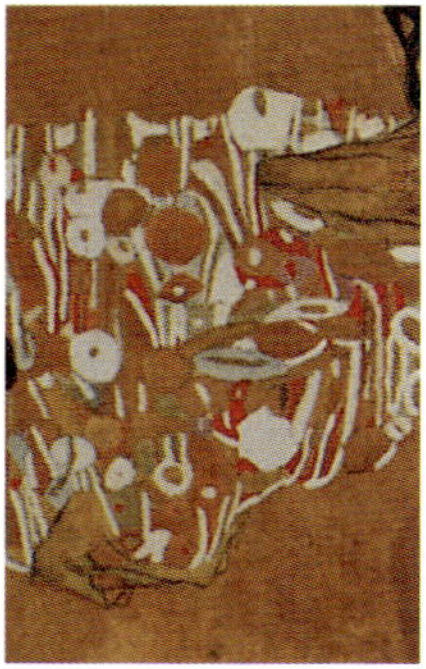

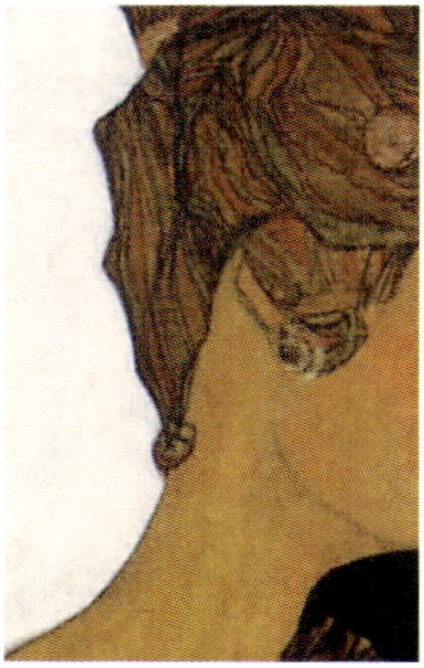

In attempting to give expression to repressed aspects of the psyche, Expressionist art, literature, theatre, dance and music therefore tended to emphasise what was unruly, violent, chaotic, ecstatic or even demonic. *Eros* and *Thanatos*, sex- and death-drives, were recurrent underlying themes. This kind of excavation of the psyche was especially marked in the radical new art that started to emerge from Austria around 1910. As Vienna's definitive satirist Karl Kraus, put it, "form is not the dress of thought, but its flesh."

Portrait of Gerti Schiele

1909
Oil, silver, gold-bronze paint and pencil on canvas,
139.5 x 140.5 cm
The Museum of Modern Art, New York
Purchase and partial gift of the Lauder family, New York

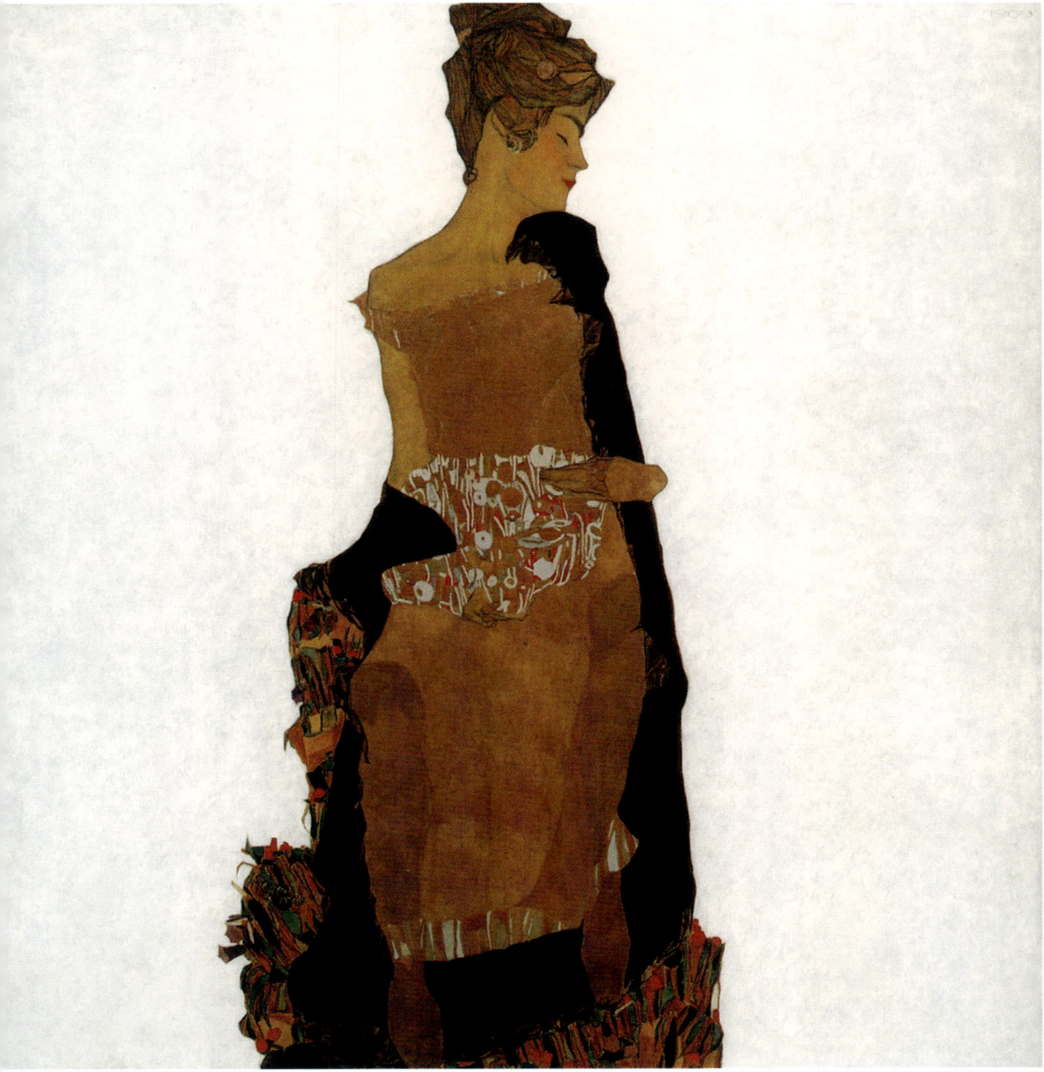

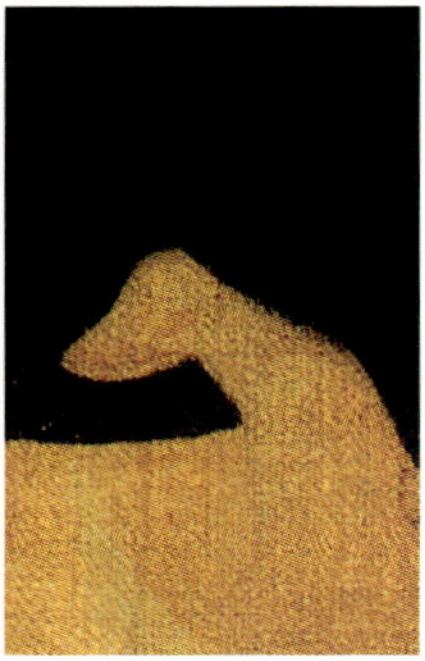
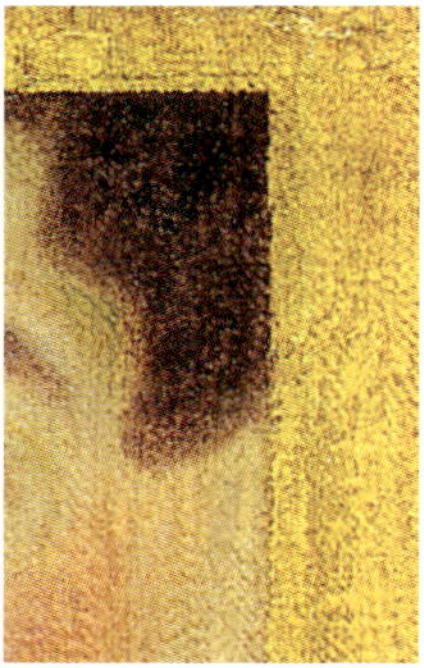
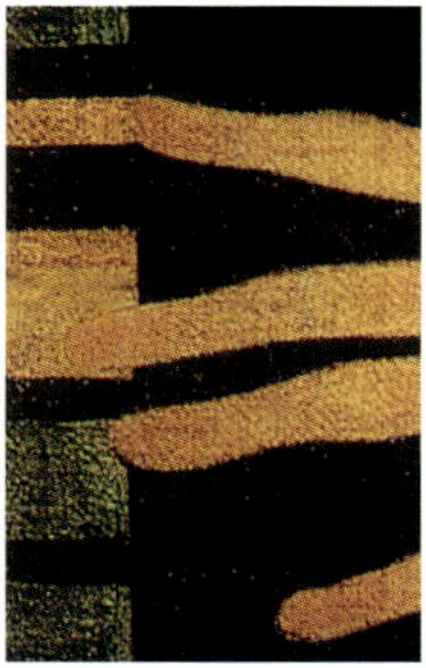

Thus, while Sigmund Freud exposed the repressed pleasure principles of upper-class Viennese society, which put its women into corsets and bulging gowns and granted them solely a role as future mothers, Schiele bares his models. His nude studies penetrate brutally into the privacy of his models and finally confront the viewer with his or her own sexuality.

Self-Portrait with Spread Fingers

1909
Oil and metallic paint on canvas, 71.5 x 27.5 cm
Private collection, New York

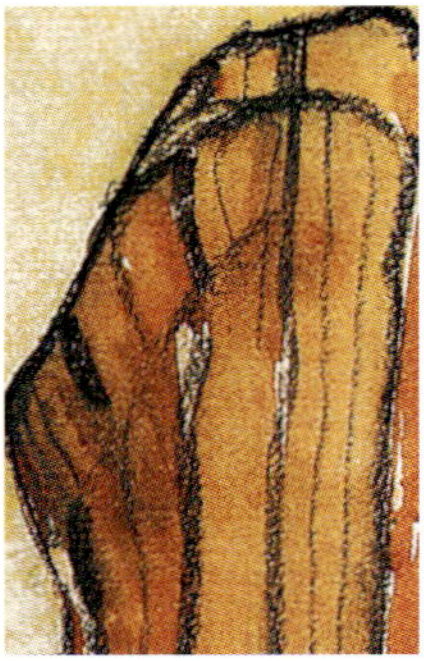
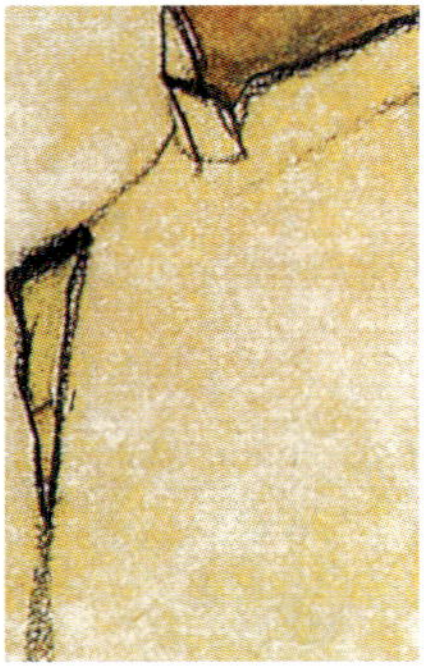
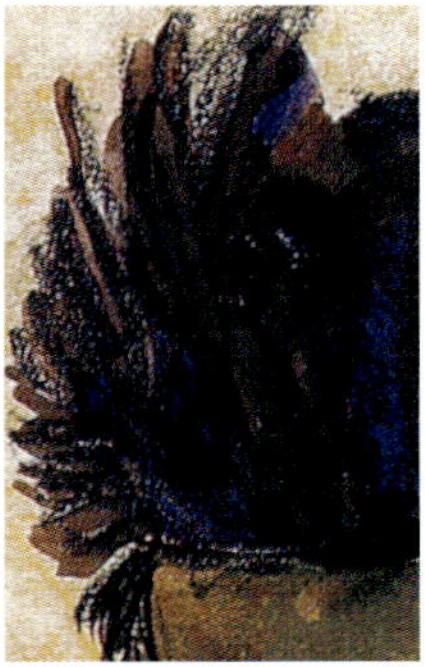

The German art encyclopaedia, compiled by *Thieme and Becker*, described Schiele as an eroticist because Schiele's art is an erotic portrayal of the human body. Futhermore, Schiele studied both male and female bodies. His models express an incredible freedom with respect to their own sexuality, self-love, homosexuality or voyeurism, as well as skilfully seducing the viewer. For Schiele, the clichéd ideas of feminine beauty did not interest him. He knew that the urge to look is interconnected with the mechanisms of disgust and allure. The body contains the power of sex and death within itself.

Self-Portrait

1910
Gouache, watercolour and black pencil
44.3 x 30.6 cm
Leopold Museum, Vienna

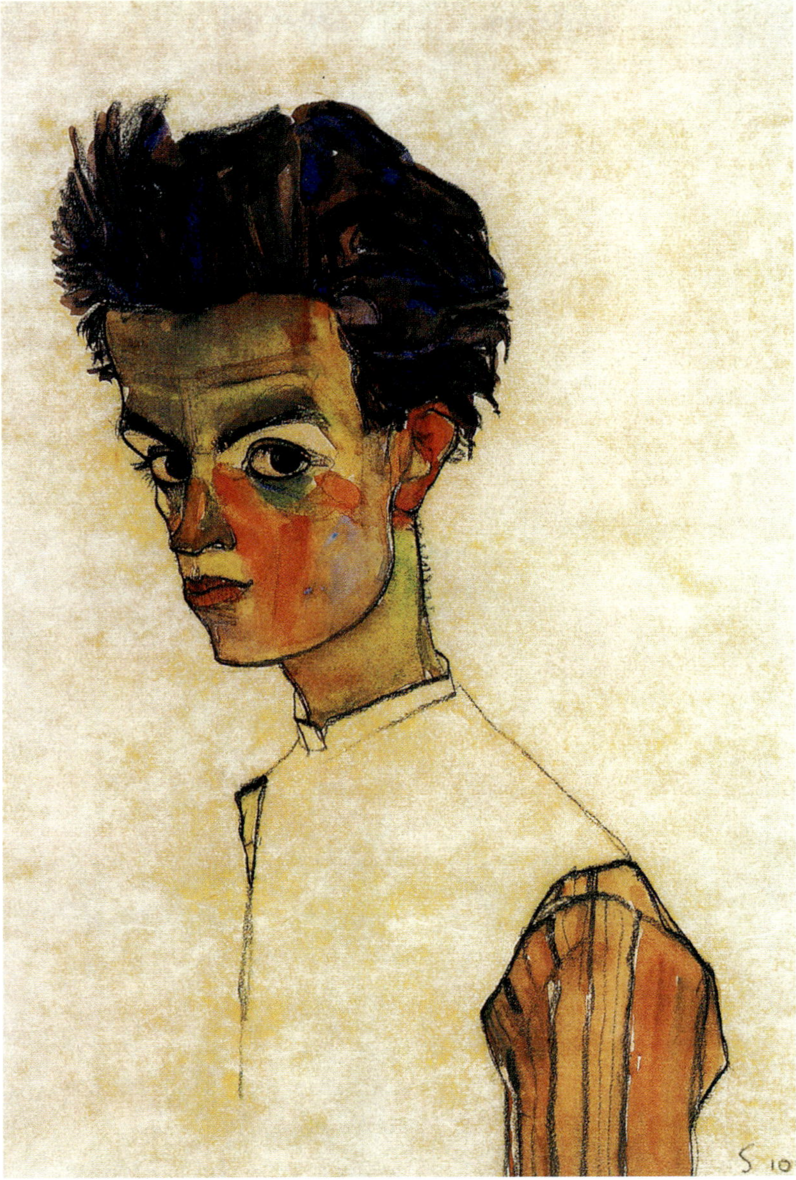
S 10

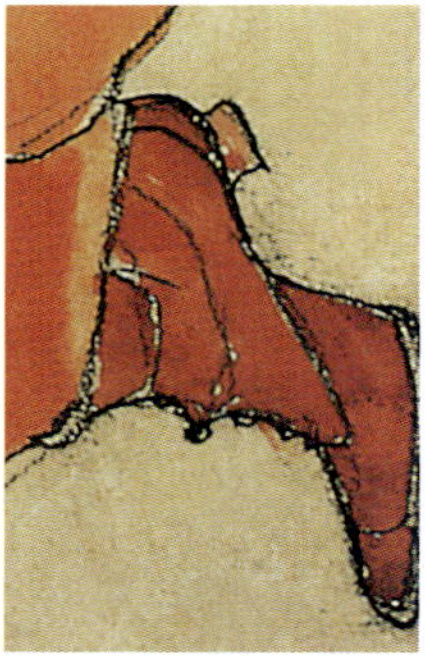

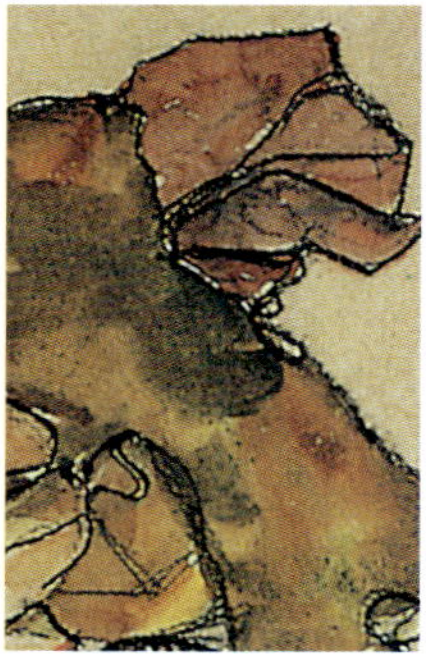

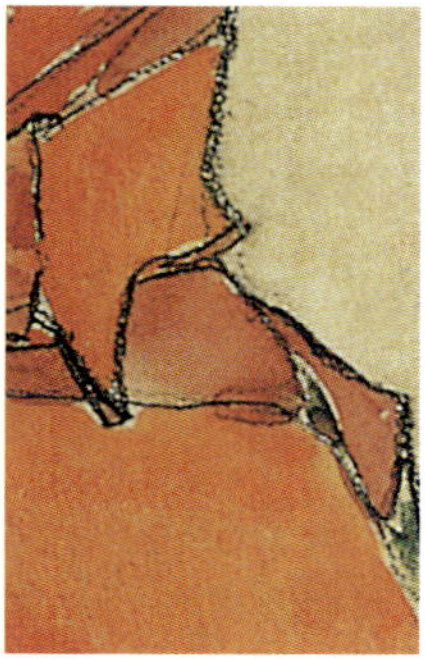

Schiele's Childhood

In modern industrial times, with the noise of racing steam engines and factories and the human masses working within in them, Egon Schiele was born in the railway station hall of Tulln, a small, lower Austrian town on the Danube on 12 June, 1890. After his older sisters Melanie (1886-1974) and Elvira (1883-1893), he was the third child of the railway director Adolf Eugen (1850-1905) and his wife Marie, (née Soukoup) (1862-1935).

Kneeling Girl in Orange-Red Dress

1910
Gouache, watercolour and black pencil on paper
44.6 x 31 cm
Leopold Museum, Vienna

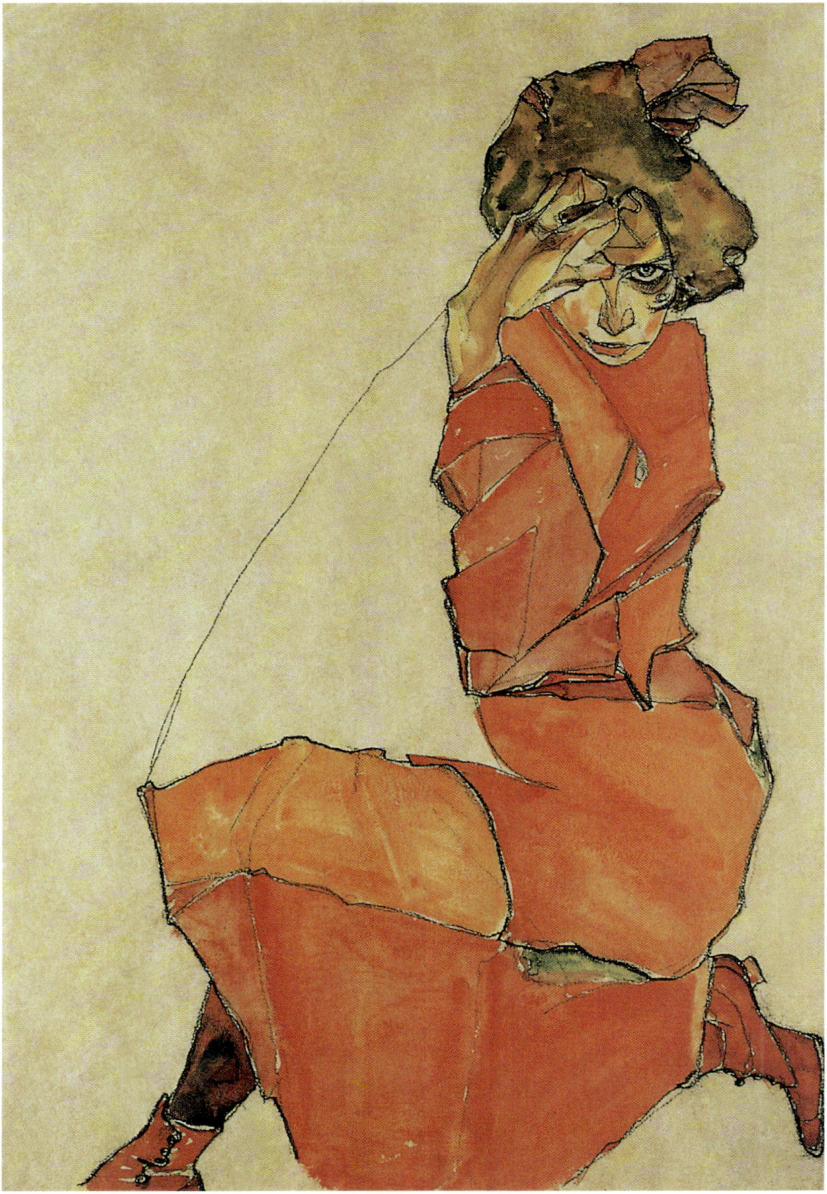

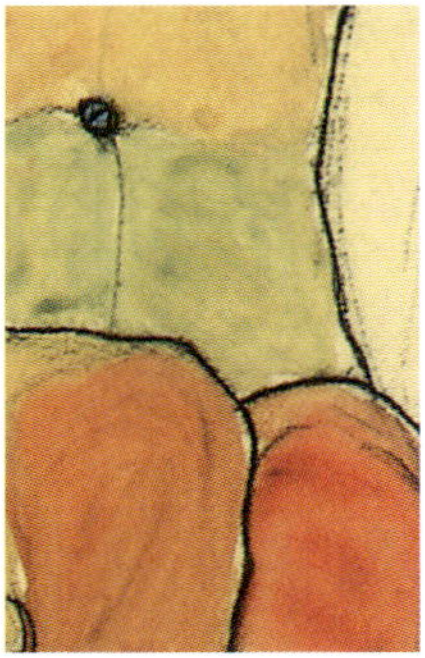

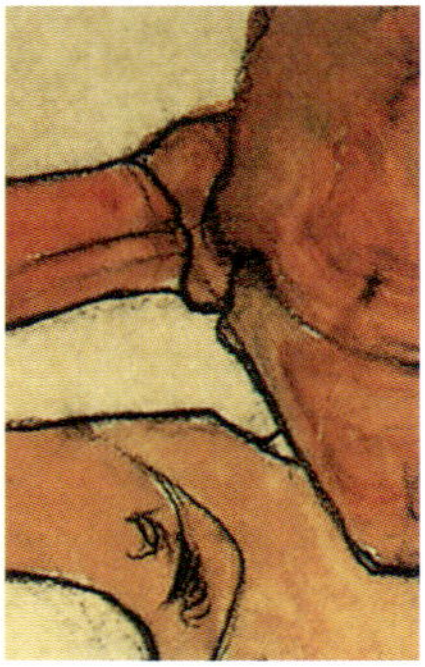

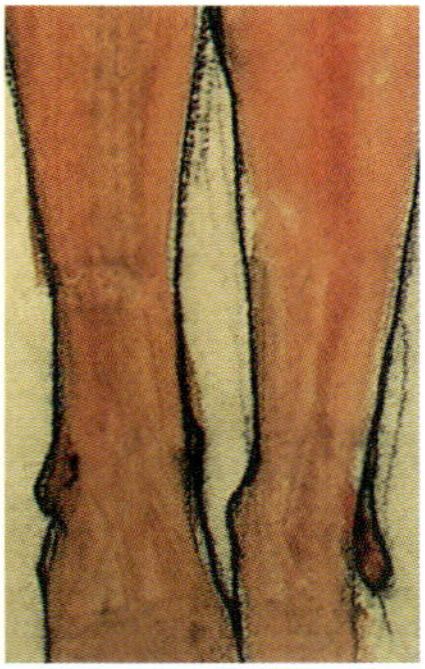

The shadows of three male stillbirths were a precursor for the only boy, who, in his third year of life would lose his ten-year-old sister Elvira. The high infant mortality rate was the lot of former times, a fate which Schiele's later work and his pictures of women would characterise. In 1900, he attended the grammar school in Krems. But he was a poor pupil, who constantly took refuge in his drawings, which his enraged father burned. In 1902, Schiele's father sent his son to the regional grammar and upper secondary school in Klosterneuburg.

Seated Female Nude with Raised Right Arm
(Gertrude Schiele)

1910
Gouache, watercolour and black pencil on paper
45 x 31,5 cm
Wien Museum, Vienna

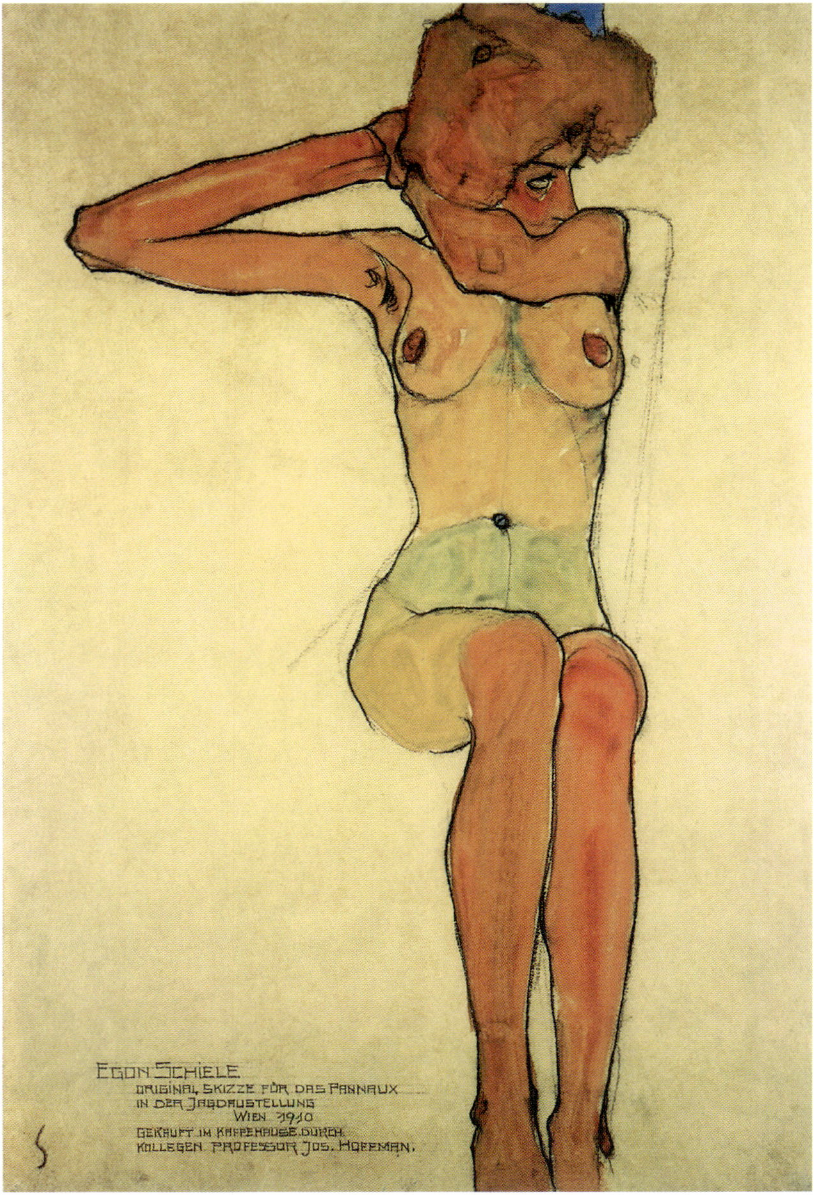
EGON SCHIELE
ORIGINAL SKIZZE FÜR DAS PANNAUX
IN DER JAGDAUSTELLUNG
WIEN 1910
GEKAUFT IM KAFFEHAUSE DURCH
KOLLEGEN PROFESSOR JOS. HOFFMAN.

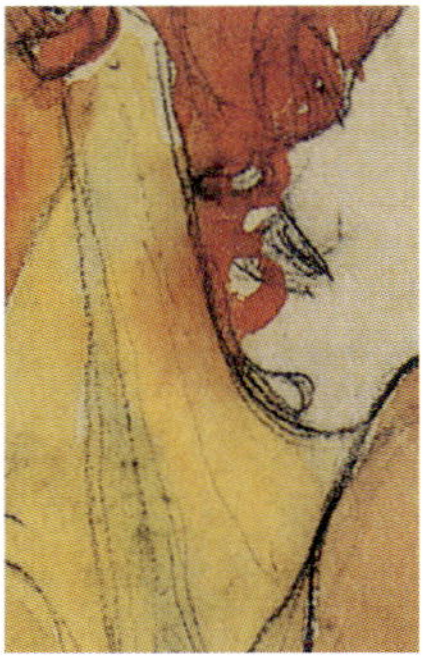

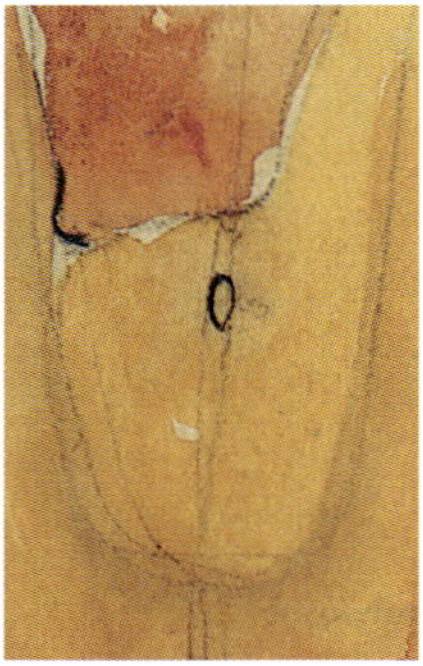

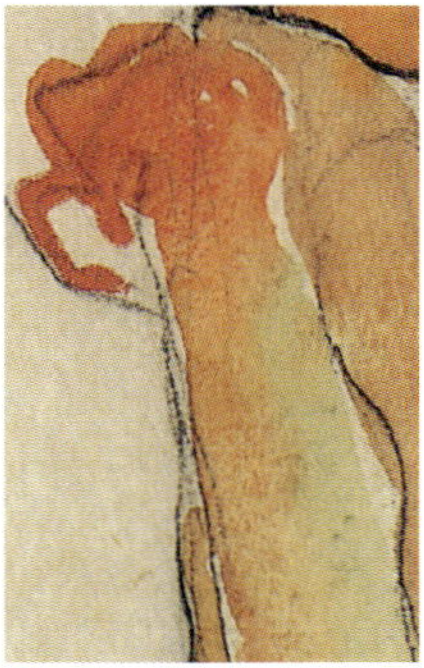

The young Schiele had a difficult childhood marked by his father's ill health. He suffered from syphilis, which, according to family chronicles, he is said to have contracted while on his honeymoon as a result of a visit to a bordello in Triest. His wife fled from the bedroom during the wedding night and the marriage was only consummated on the fourth day, on which he infected her also. Despair characterised Schiele's father, who, retired early and sat at home dressed in his service uniform, in a state of mental confusion. In the summer of 1904, stricken by increasing paralysis, he tried to throw himself out of a window.

Nude Girl with Folded Arms
(Gertrude Schiele)

1910
Watercolour and black pencil on paper, 48.8 x 28 cm
Albertina, Vienna

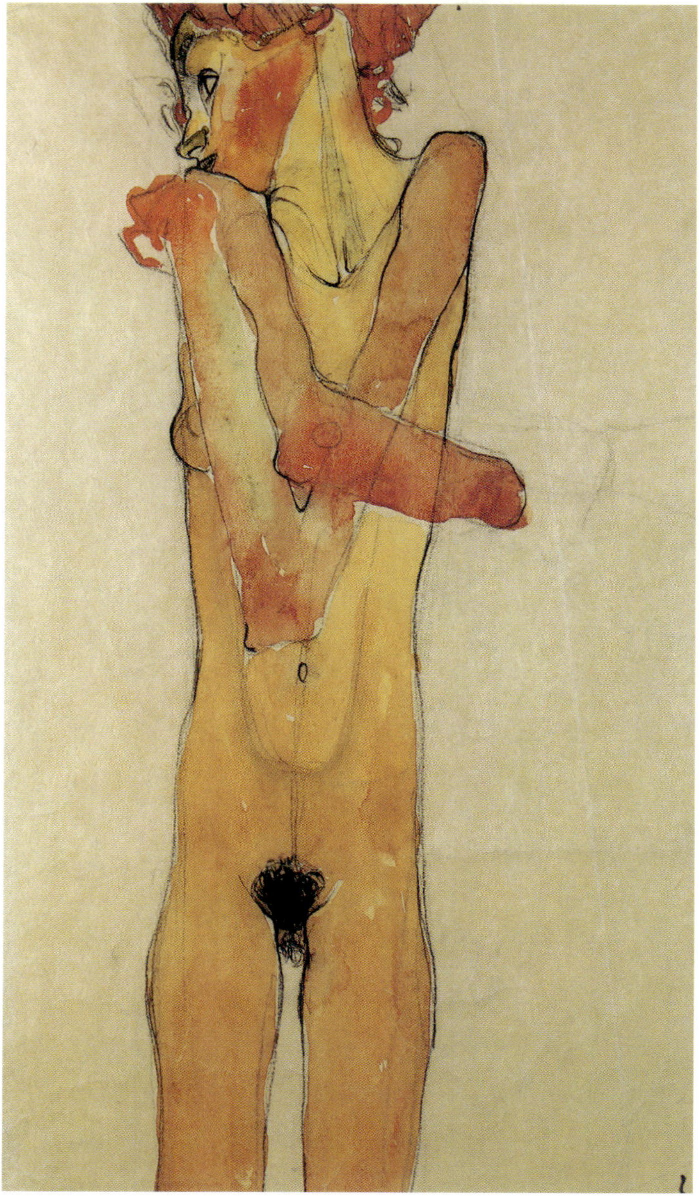

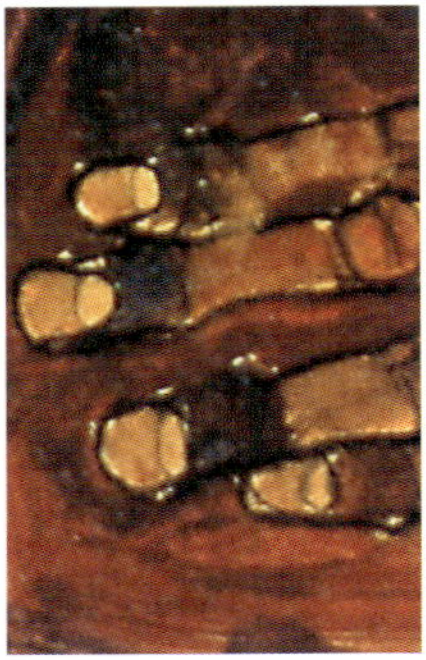

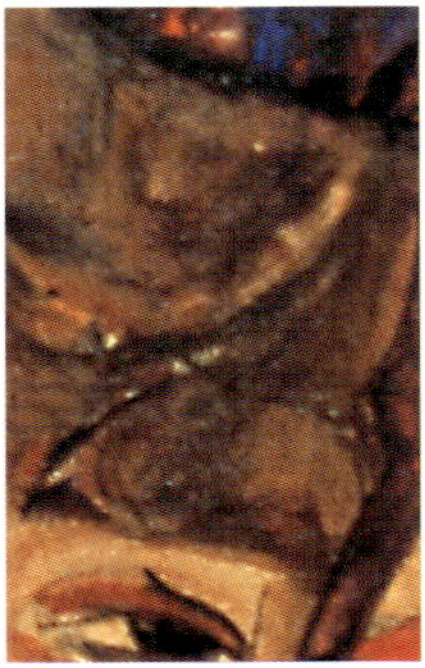

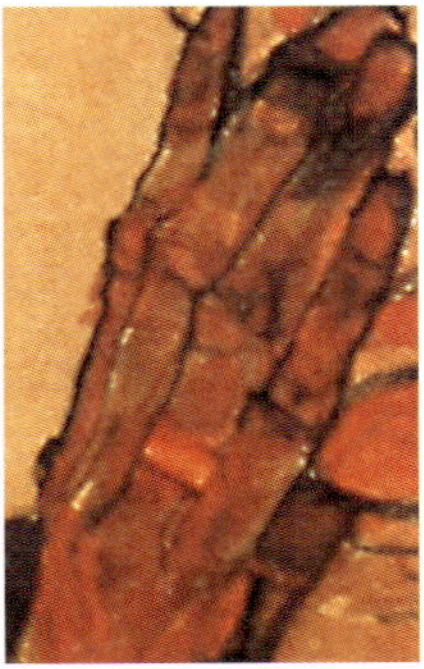

He finally died after a long period of suffering on New Year's Day 1905. The father, who during a fit of insanity burned all his railroad stocks, left his wife and children destitute. An uncle, Leopold Czihaczek, chief inspector of the imperial and royal railway, assumed joint custody of the fifteen-year-old Egon, for whom he planned the traditional family role of railroad worker. During this time, young Schiele wore second-hand clothing handed down from his uncle and stiff white collars made from paper. It seems that Schiele had been very close to his father for he, too, had possessed a certain talent for drawing, had collected butterflies and minerals and was drawn to the natural world.

Self-Portrait Pulling Cheek

1910
Gouache, watercolour and pencil
44.3 x 30.5 cm
Albertina, Vienna

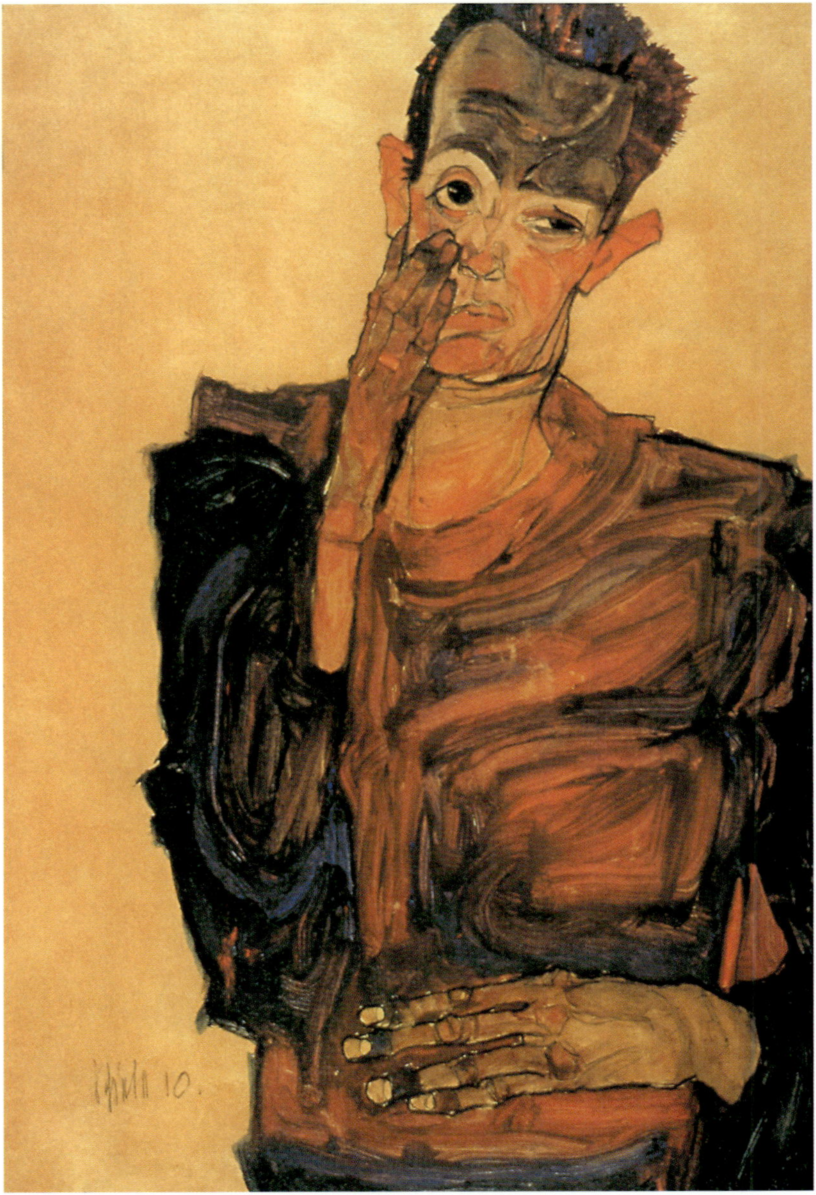

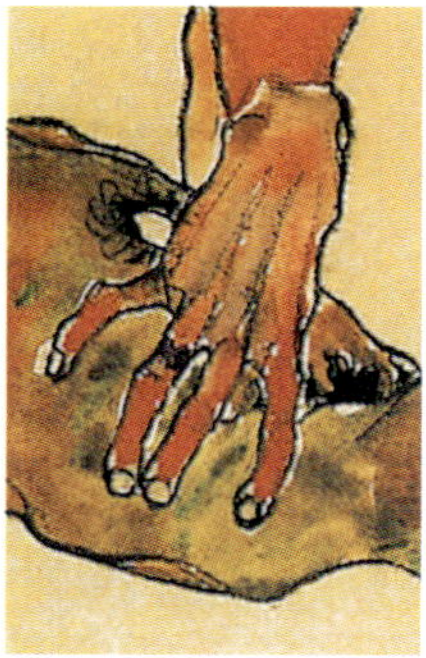

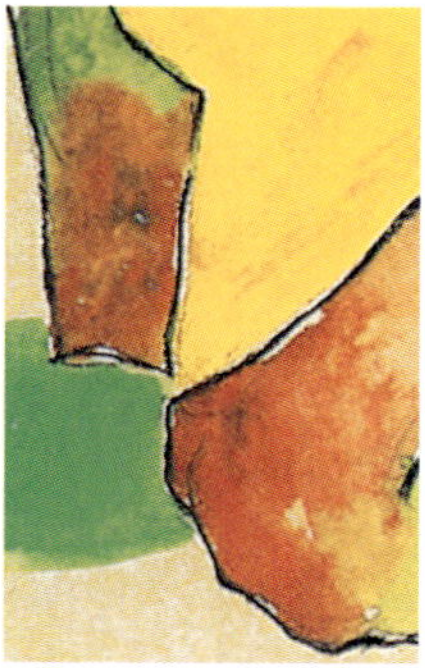

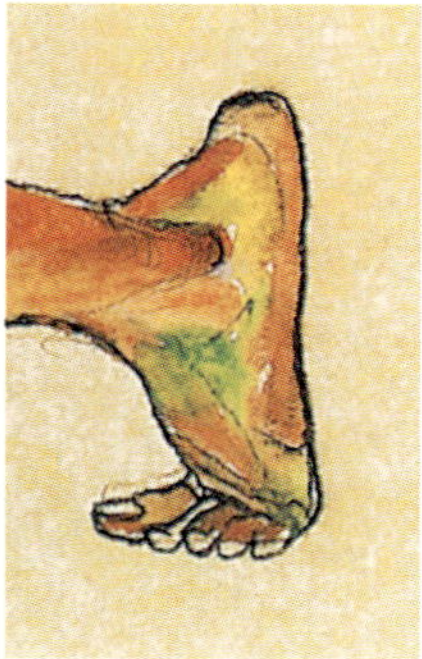

Years later, Schiele wrote to his sister: "I have, in fact, experienced a beautiful spiritual occurrence today, I was awake, yet spellbound by a ghost who presented himself to me in a dream before waking, so long as he spoke with me, I was rigid and speechless." Unable to accept the death of his father, Schiele let him rise again in visions. He reported that his father had been with him and spoken to him at length. In contrast, distance and misunderstanding characterised his relationship with his mother who, living in dire financial straits, expected her son to support her; in return, the older sister would work for the railroad.

Reclining Male Nude with Yellow Pillow

1910
Gouache, watercolour and black pencil on paper
31.1 x 45.4 cm
Private collection

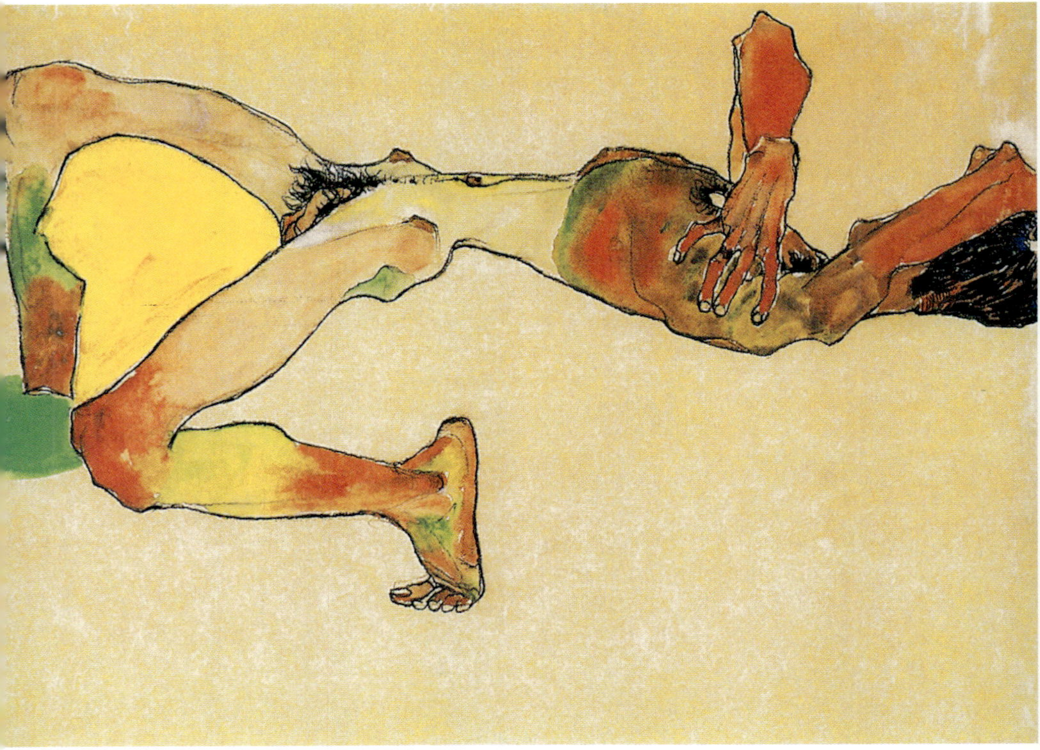

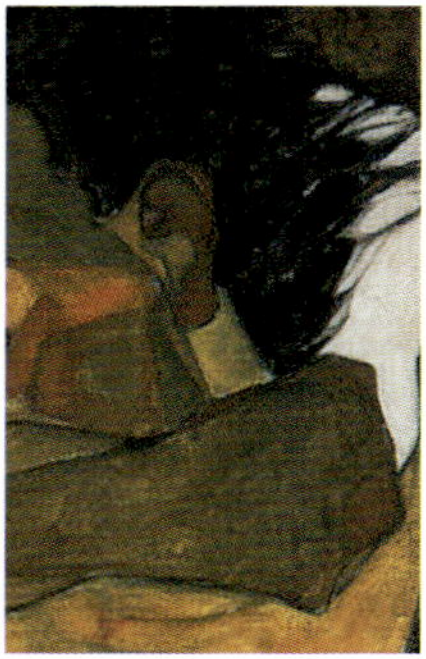

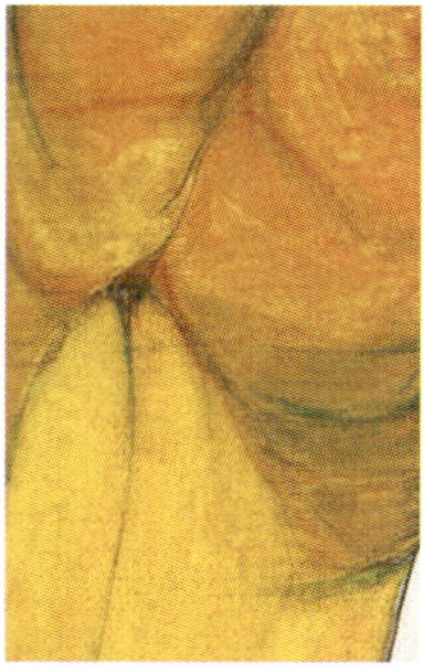

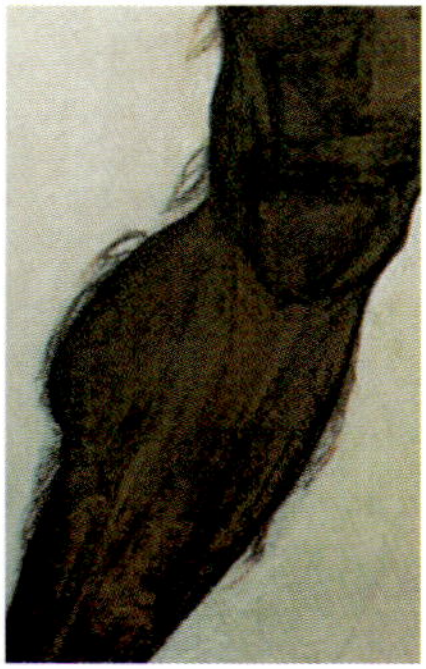

However, Schiele, who had been pampered by women during childhood, claimed to be "an eternal child". By a stroke of fate, the painter Karl Ludwig Strauch (1875-1959), instructed the gifted youth in draftsmanship; the artist Max Kahrer of Klosterneuburg looked after the boy as well. In 1906, at the age of only sixteen, Schiele passed the entrance examination for the general art class at the Academy of Visual Arts in Vienna on his first attempt. Even the strict uncle, in whose household Schiele now took his midday meals, sent a telegram to Schiele's mother: "Passed."

Seated Male Nude (Self-Portrait)

1910
Oil and gouache, 152.5 x 150 cm
Leopold Museum, Vienna

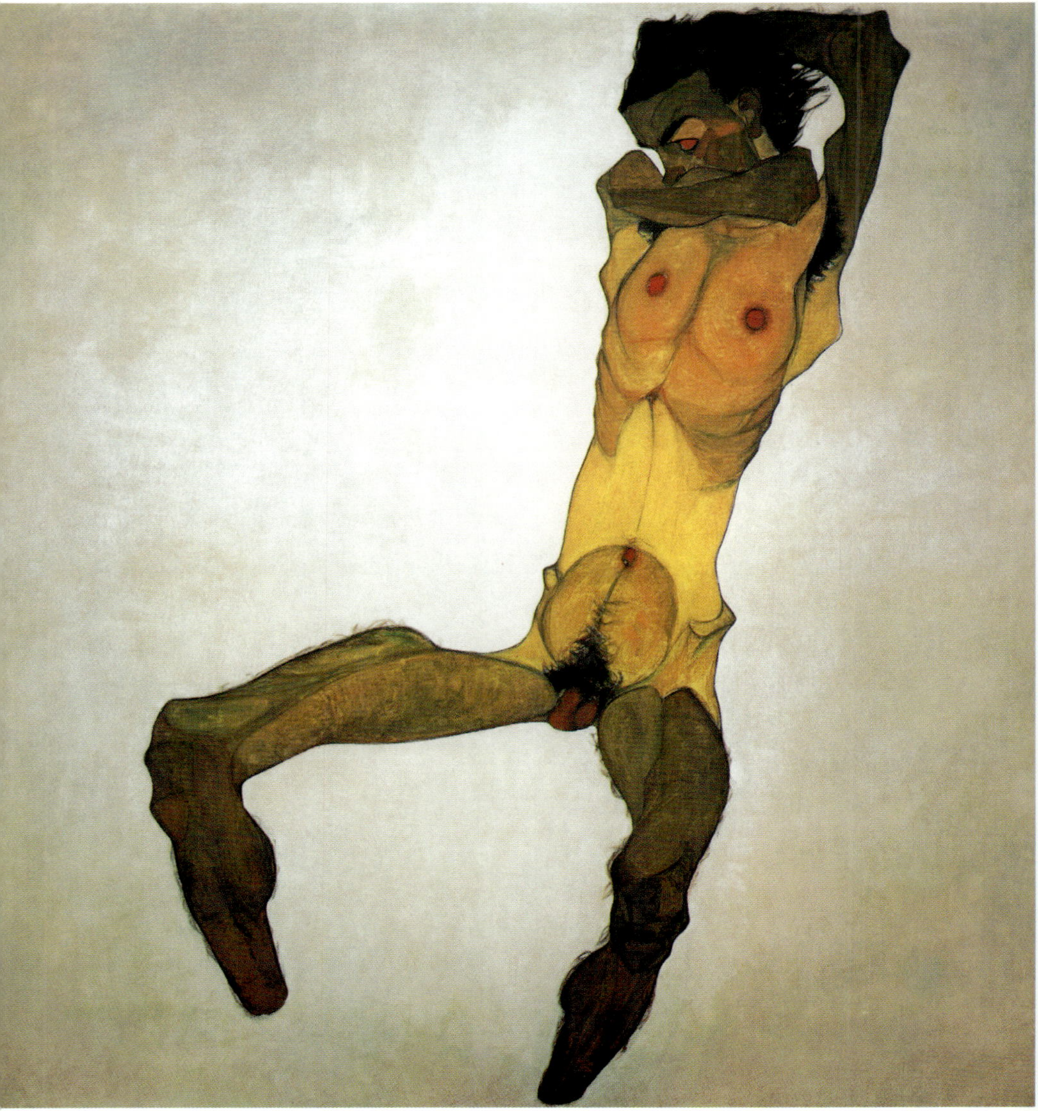

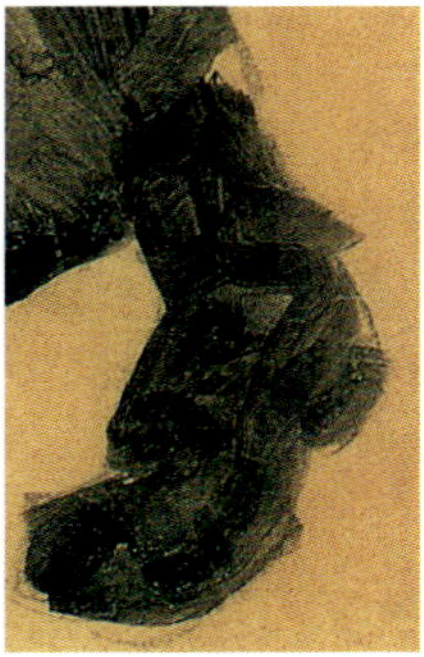

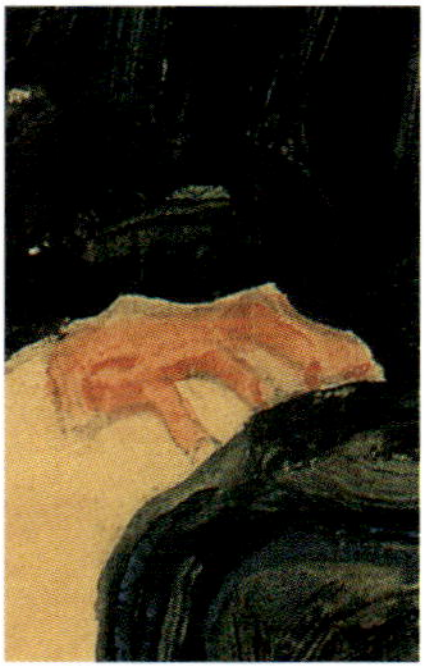

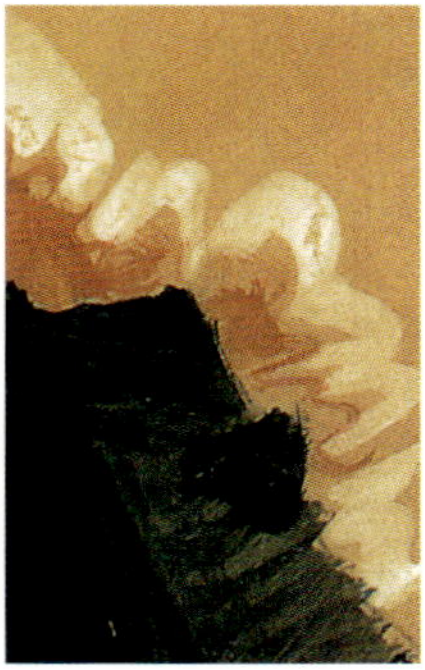

His sister Gertrude (1894-1981), called "Gerti", four years his junior, was a compliant subject for him. In a watercolour, Gerti reclines backwards, still fully clothed with black stockings and shoes, and lifts the black hem of her dress from under which the red orifice of her body gapes. Schiele draws no bed, no chair, only the provocative gesture of his sister's body offering itself (*Reclining Girl in a Dark Blue Dress,* 1910). Incestuous fantasies? At the same time as Sigmund Freud discovered that self-discovery occurs by way of erotic experiences,

Reclining Girl in a Dark Blue Dress

1910
Gouache, watercolour and pencil with white highlights
45 x 31.3 cm
Stefan T. Edlis Collection

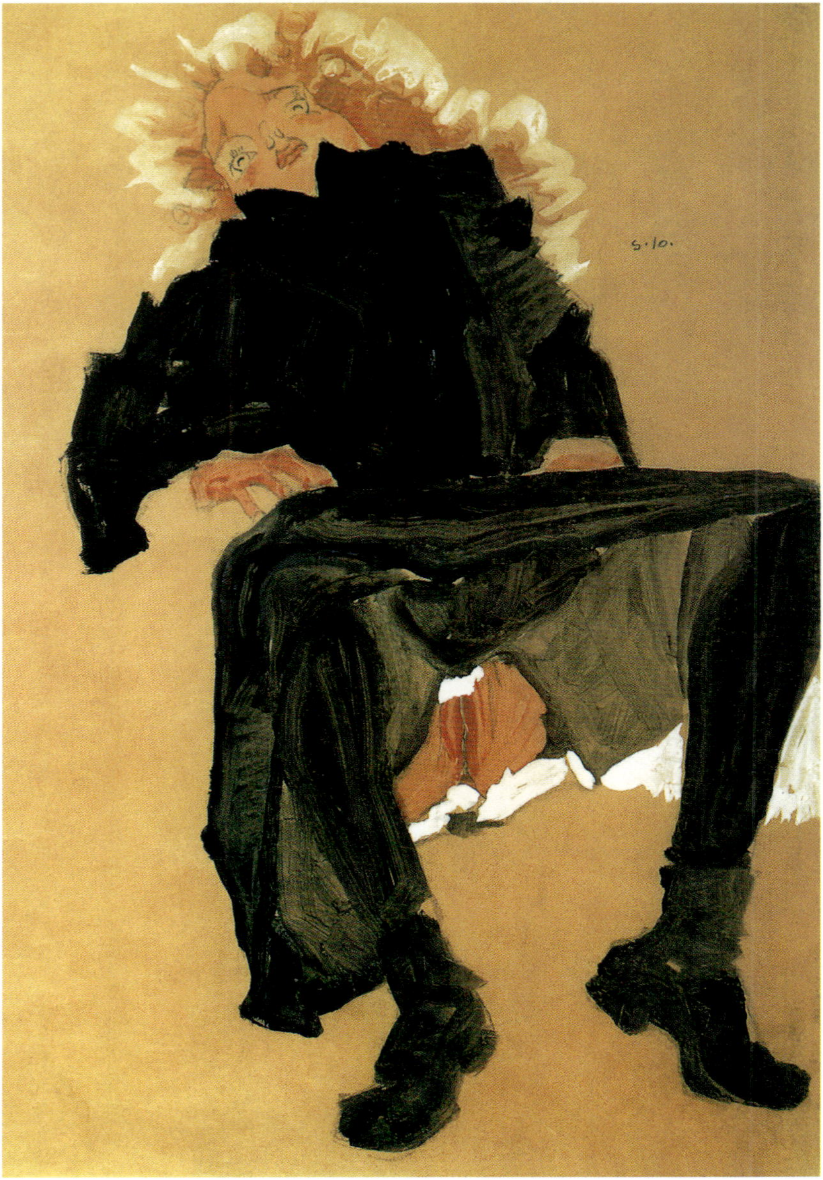
S.10.

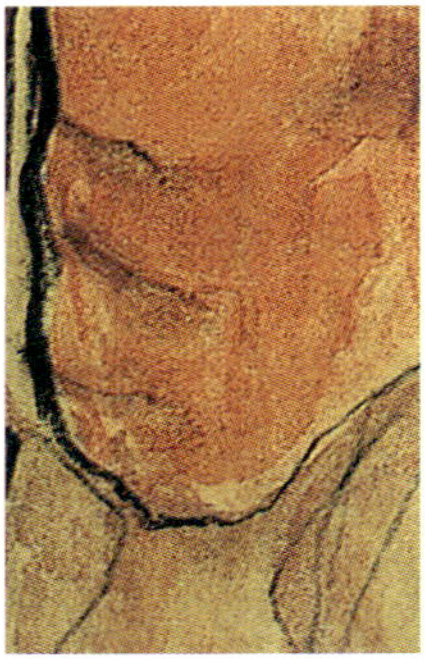

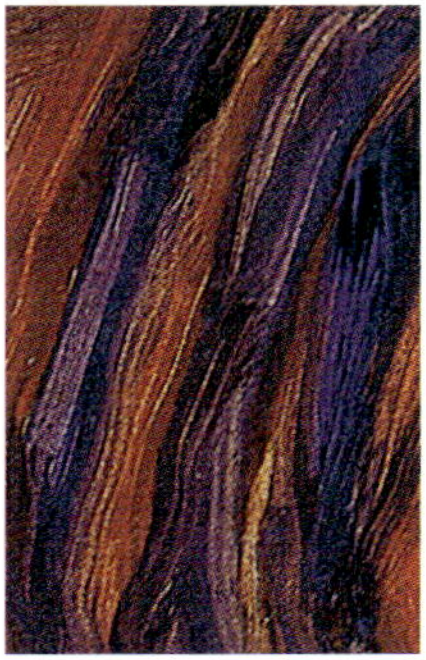

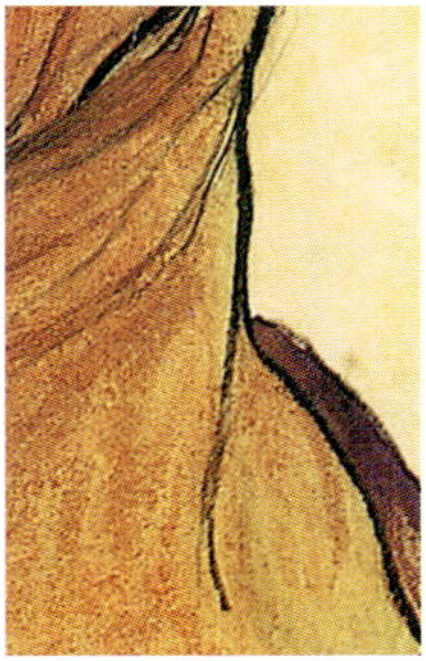

and the urge to look emerges as a spontaneous sexual expression within the child, young Egon recorded confrontations with the opposite sex on paper. He incorporated erotic games of discovery and showed an unabashed interest in the genitalia of his model into his nude studies – the forbidden gaze, searching for the opened female vagina beneath the rustling of the skirt hem and white lace. Gerti with her freckled skin, the green eyes and red hair is the prototype of all the later women and models of Schiele.

Grimacing Man (Self-Portrait)

1910
Charcoal, watercolour and gouache on paper
44 x 27.8 cm
Leopold Museum, Vienna

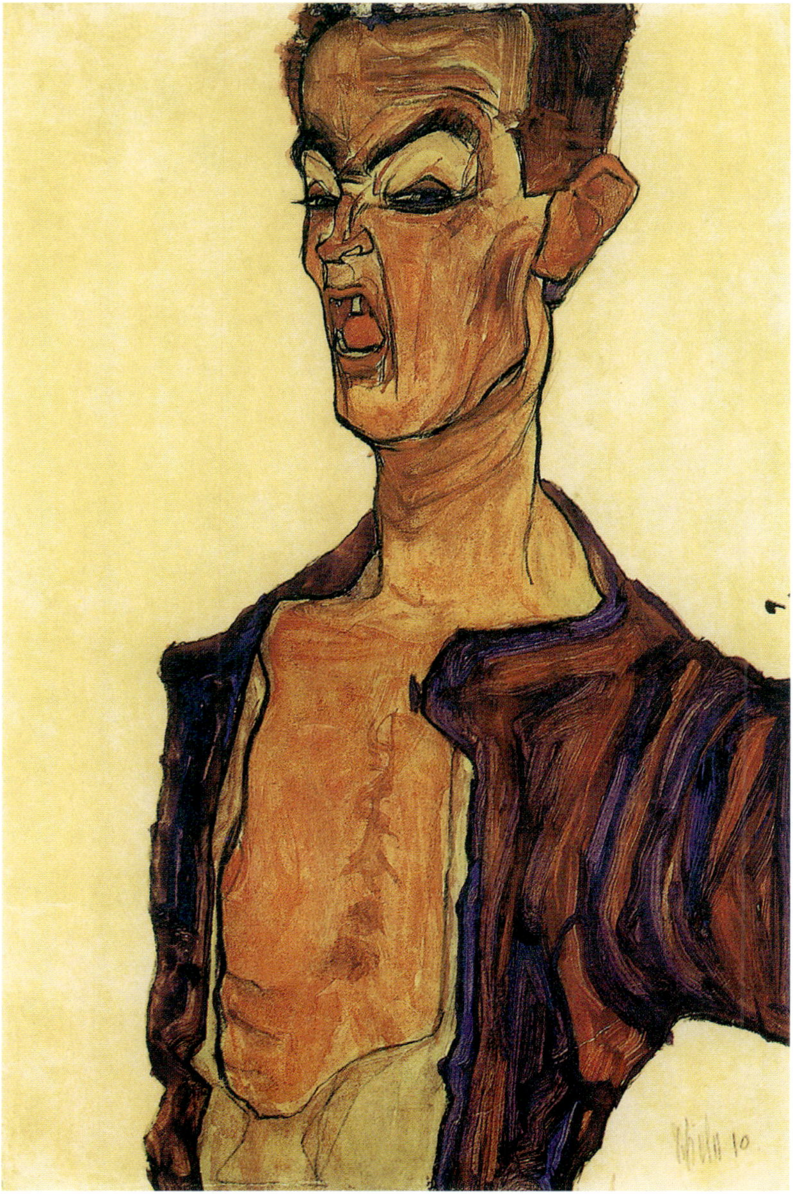

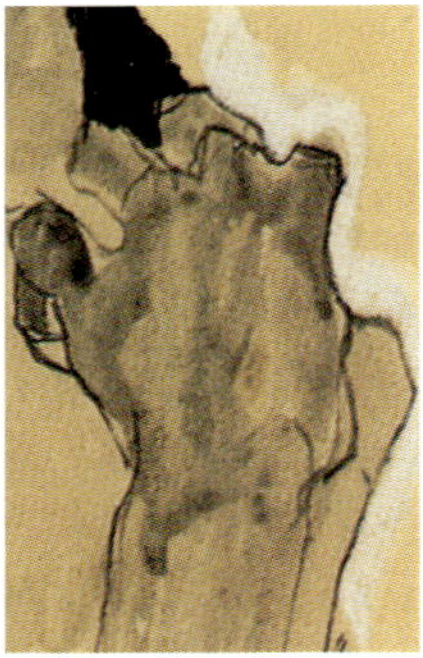
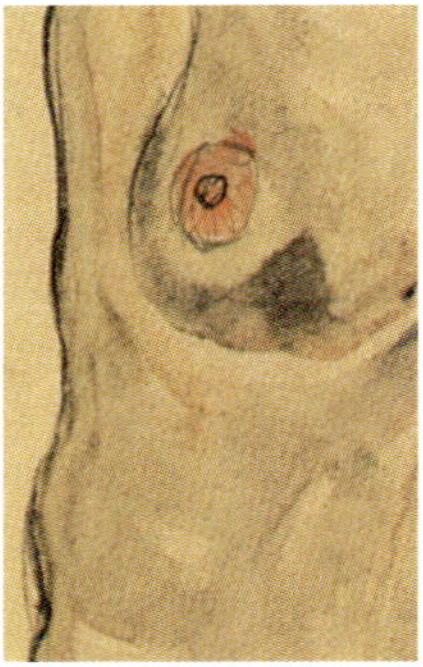
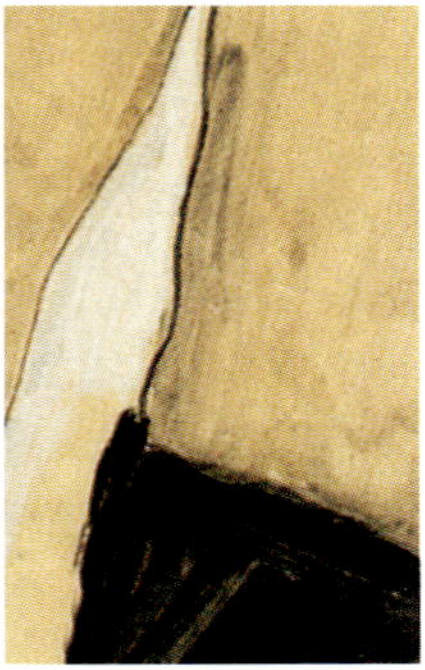

Klimt's Paternity

Vienna was the capital city of the Habsburg monarchy, a state of multiple ethnicities consisting of twelve nations with a population of approximately thirty million. Emperor Franz Josef maintained strict Spanish court etiquette. Yet, on the government's fortieth anniversary, he began a large-scale conversion of the city, with its approximately 850 public and private monumental structures and buildings. During this time, the influx of the rural population selling itself to the big city was increasing.

Black-Haired Nude Girl, Standing

1910
Watercolour and pencil with white highlights
54.3 x 30.7 cm
Albertina, Vienna

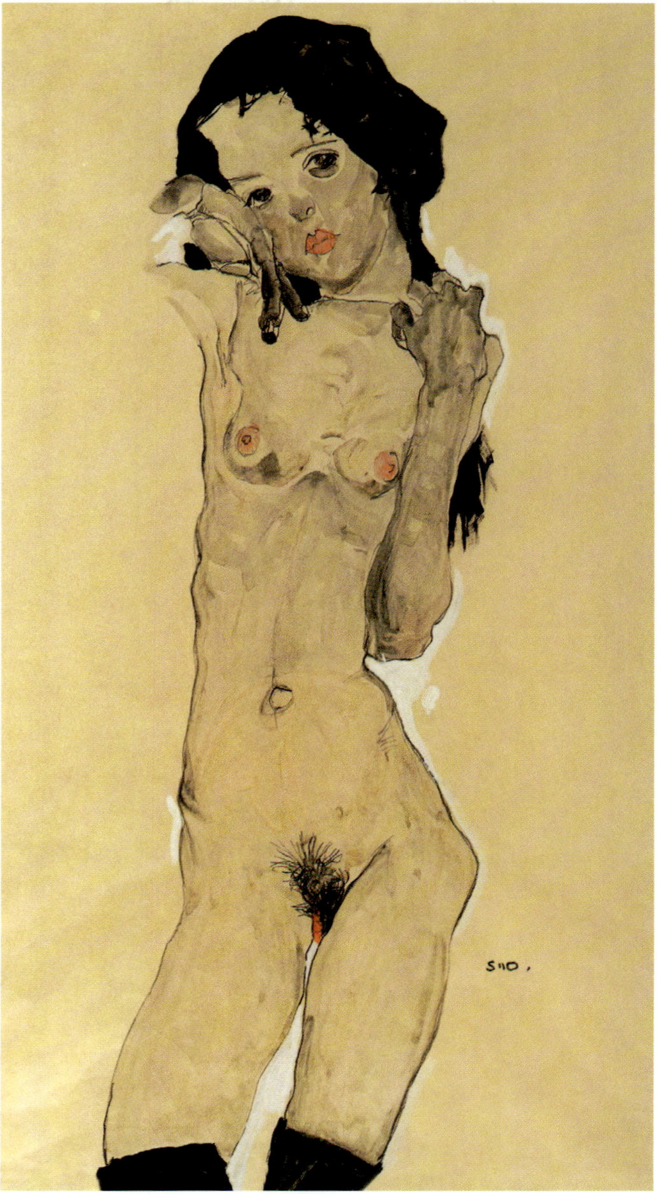
S10.

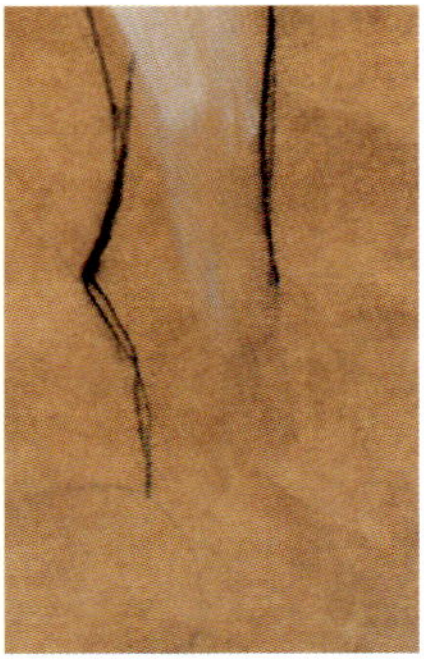

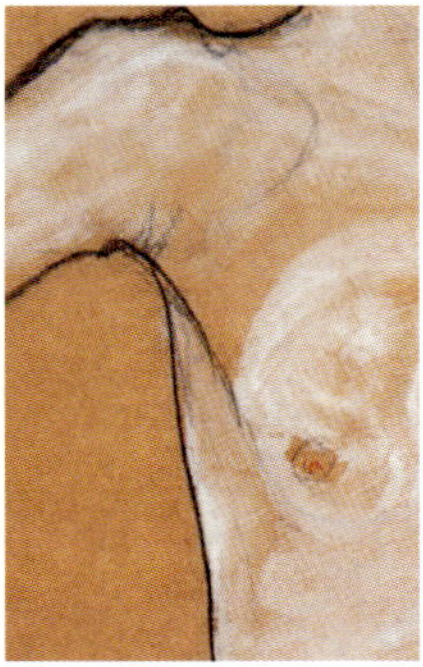

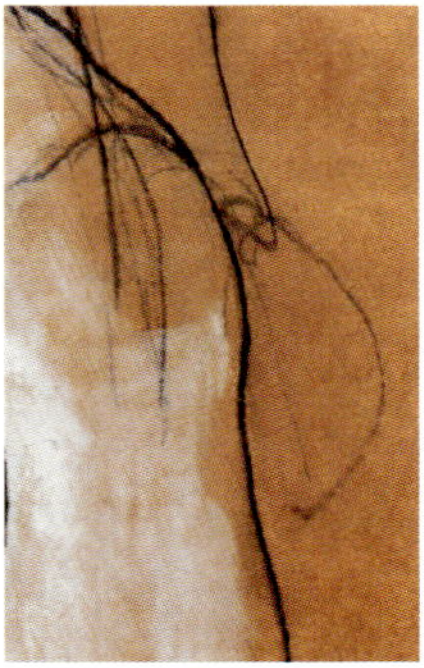

The increasing industrialisation resulted in the emergence of a proletariat in the suburbs, while the newly rich bourgeoisie settled in the exclusive Ring Street. In the writers' cafés, Leo Trotsky, Lenin and, later, Hitler consulted periodicals on display and brooded over the beginning century.

Just how musty the artistic climate in Vienna was is evidenced by the scandal which erupted in 1893 over Engelhard's picture *Young Girl under a Cherry Tree*. The painting was repudiated on the grounds of "respect for the genteel female audience,

Seated Nude Girl

1910
Gouache and black pencil with white highlights
44.8 x 29.9 cm
Albertina, Vienna

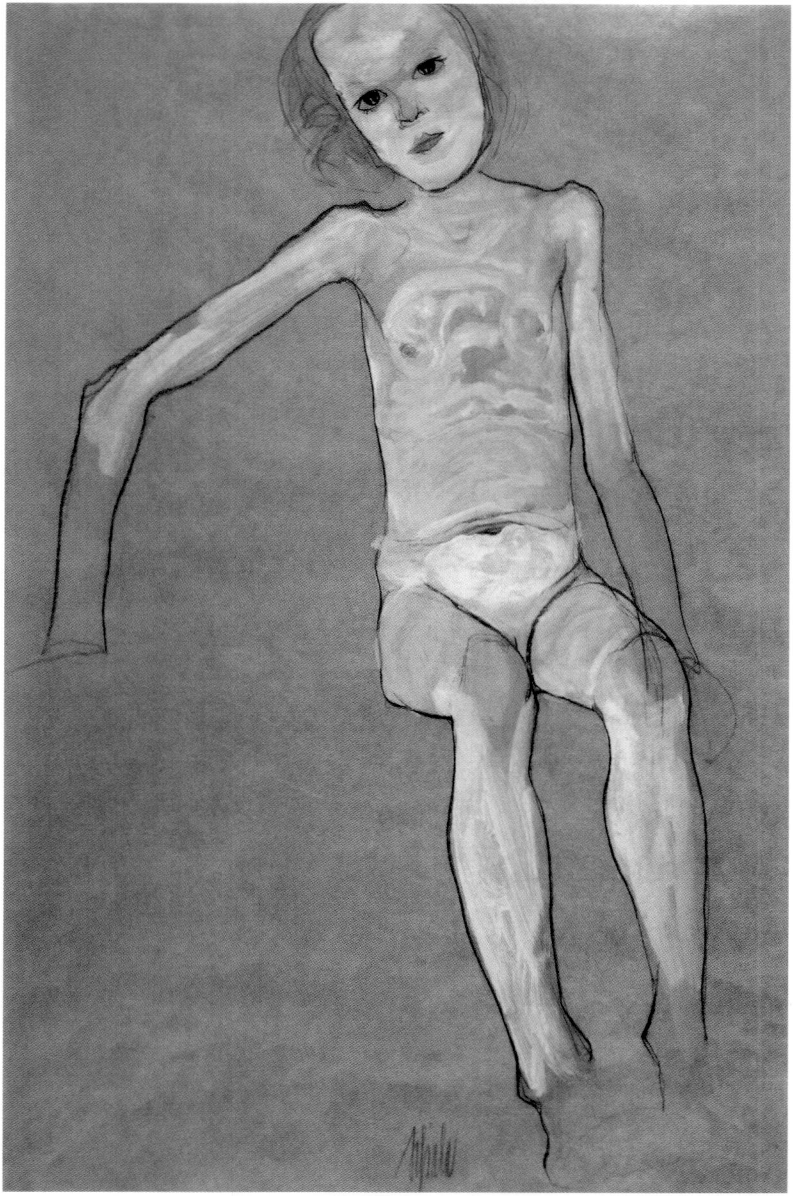

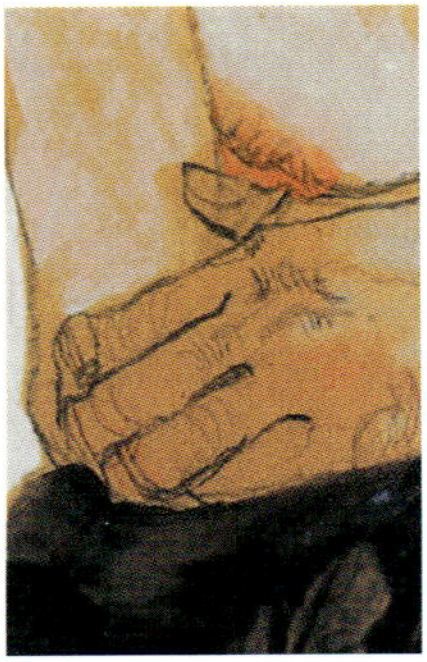
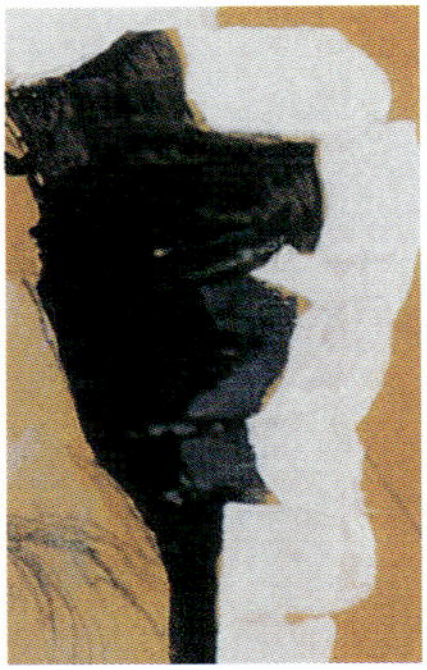
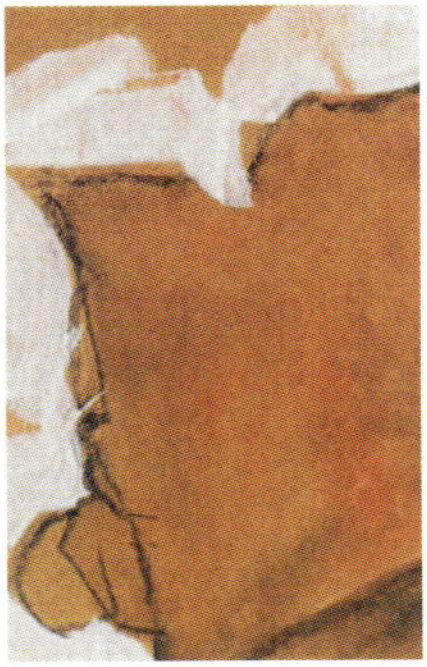

which one does not wish to embarrass so painfully vis-à-vis such an open-hearted naturalistic study". What hypocrisy, when official exhibitions of nude studies, the obligation of every artist, had long been an institution.

In 1897 Klimt, together with his Viennese fellow artists, founded the Vienna Secession, a splinter group separate from the officially accepted conduct for artists with the motto: "To the times its art, to the art its freedom."

The Scornful Woman (Gertrude Schiele)

1910
Gouache, watercolour and charcoal with white highlights
45 x 31.4 cm
Private collection

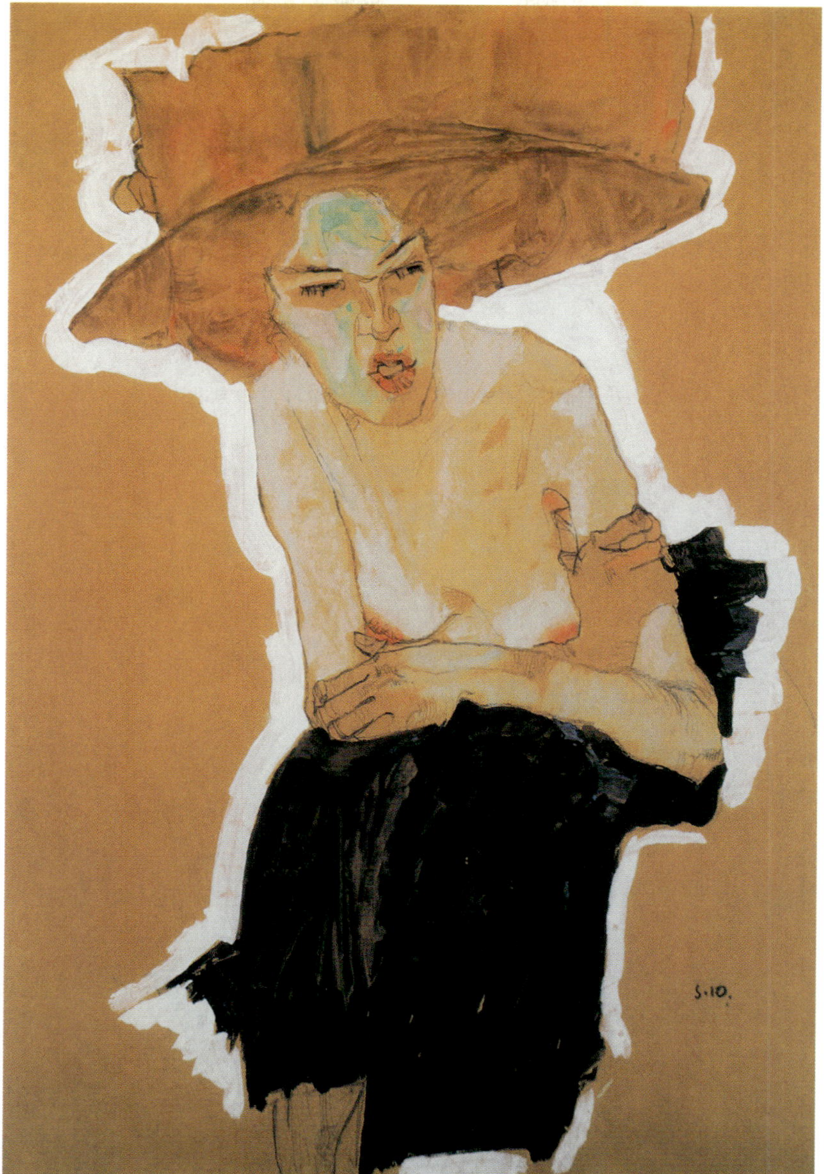
S.10.

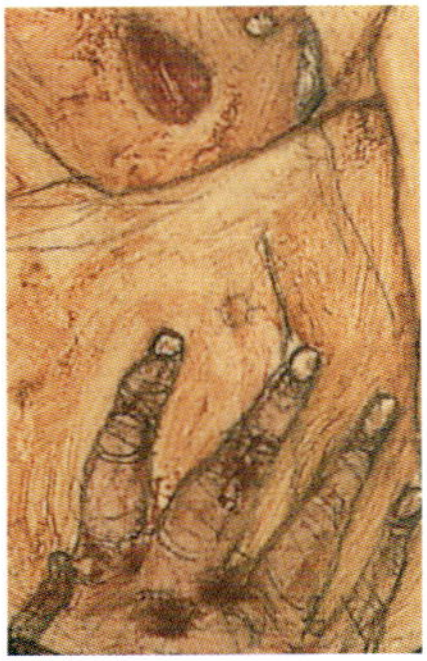

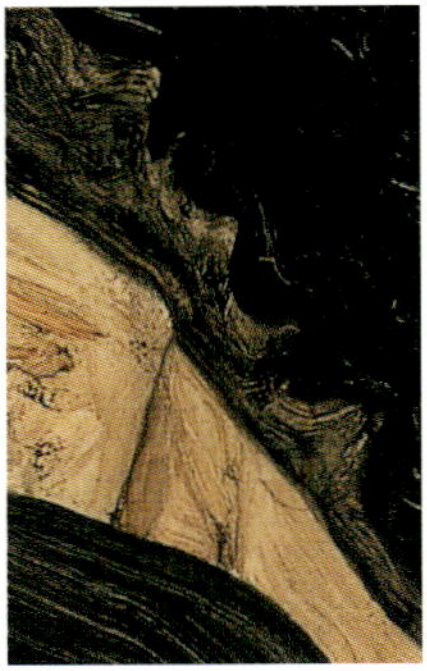

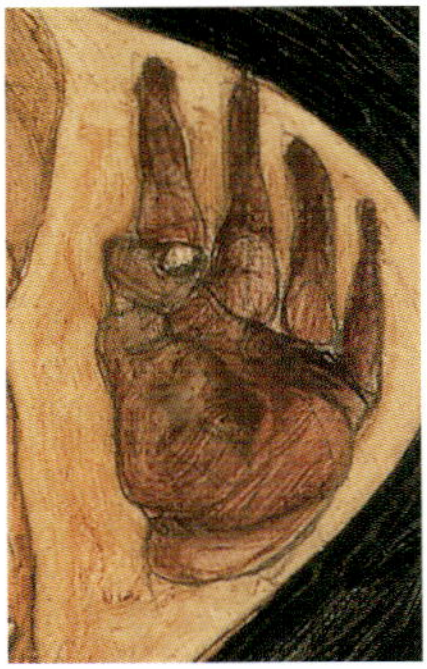

In 1898, the first exhibition took place in a building belonging to the horticultural society. It was distinguished from the usual exhibitions which usually included several thousand works by offering an elite selection of 100 to 200 works of art. The proceeds, generated by the attendance of approximately 100,000 visitors, financed a new gallery designed by the architect Olbrich. Exhibitions by Rodin, Kollwitz, Hodler, Manet, Monet, Renoir, Cézanne and Van Gogh opened the doors to the most up-to-date international art world.

The Dead Mother I

1910
Pencil and oil on wood, 32.4 x 25.8 cm
Leopold Museum, Vienna

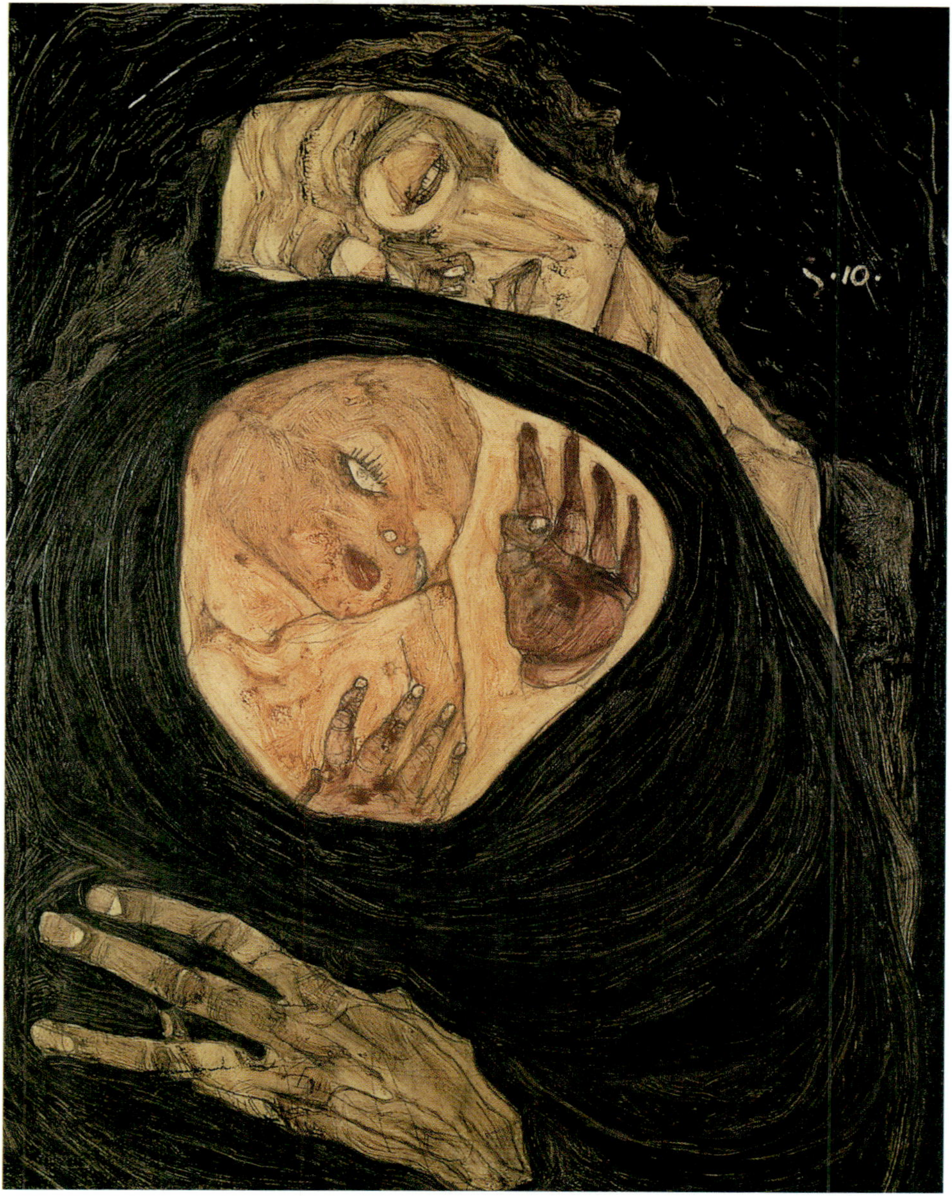
S.10.

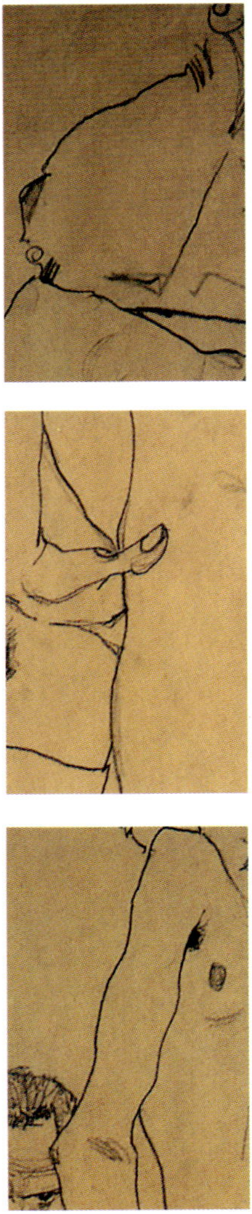

Visual artists worked beside renowned writers and musicians such as Rilke, Schnitzler, Alternberg, Schönberg and Alban Berg for the periodical *Ver Sacrum.* Here, they developed the idea of the 'complete' work of art which encompassed all artistic areas. Simultaneously, the Secession required the abolition of the distinction between higher and lower art, art for the rich and art for the poor and declared art common property. Yet, this demand of the art nouveau generation remained a privilege of the upper class striving for the ideal that "art is a lifestyle", which encompassed architectural style, interior design, clothing and jewellery.

Schiele Drawing a Nude Model
in front of a Mirror

1910
Pencil, 55.2 x 35.3 cm
Albertina, Vienna

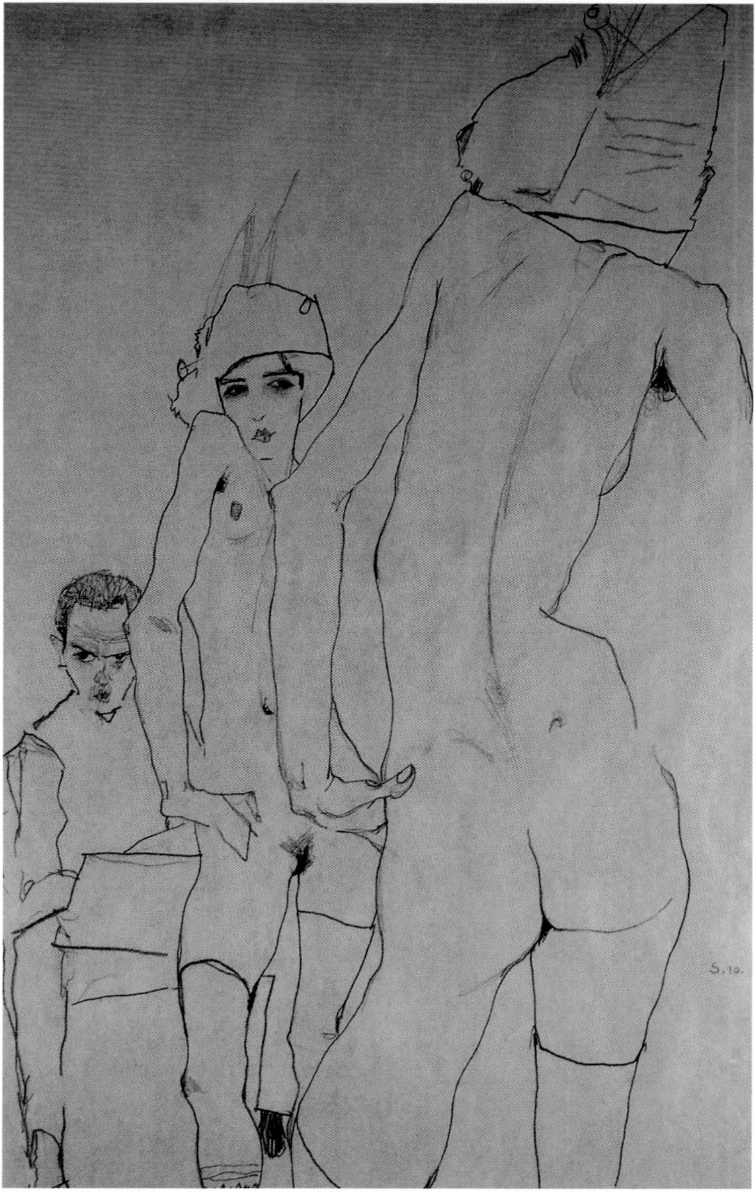

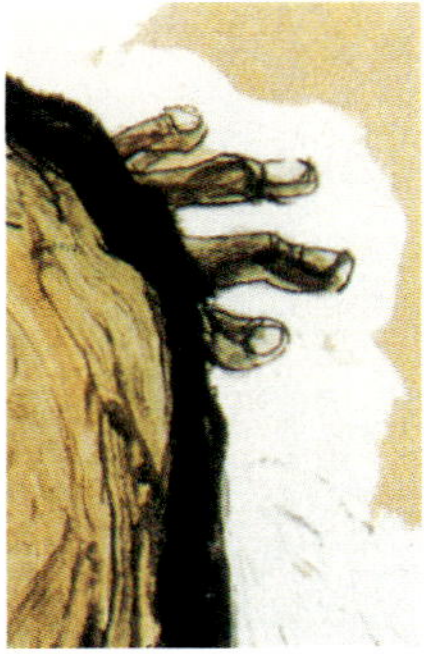

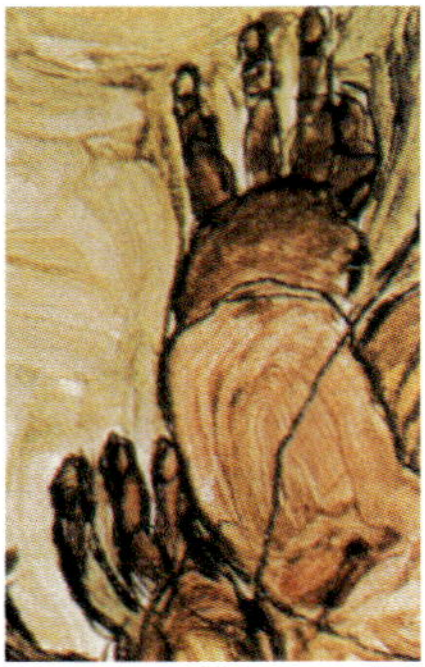

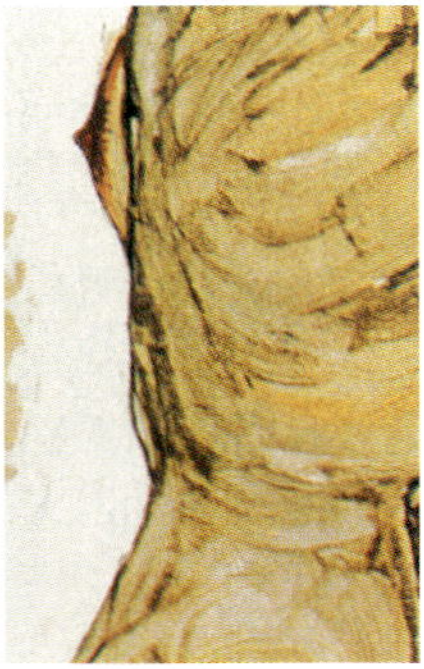

Schiele's artistic roots were in the "Jugendstil" of the Viennese Secession movement. Like a whole generation, he came under the influence of Vienna's most charismatic and celebrated artist, Gustav Klimt (1862-1918). In Vienna's creative effervescence, the two major figures of Austrian expressionism, Schiele and Kokoschka, would fully expand their talents under the tutelage of Klimt.

Mother and Child

1910
Gouache, watercolour and pencil
55.6 x 36.5 cm
Wien Museum, Vienna

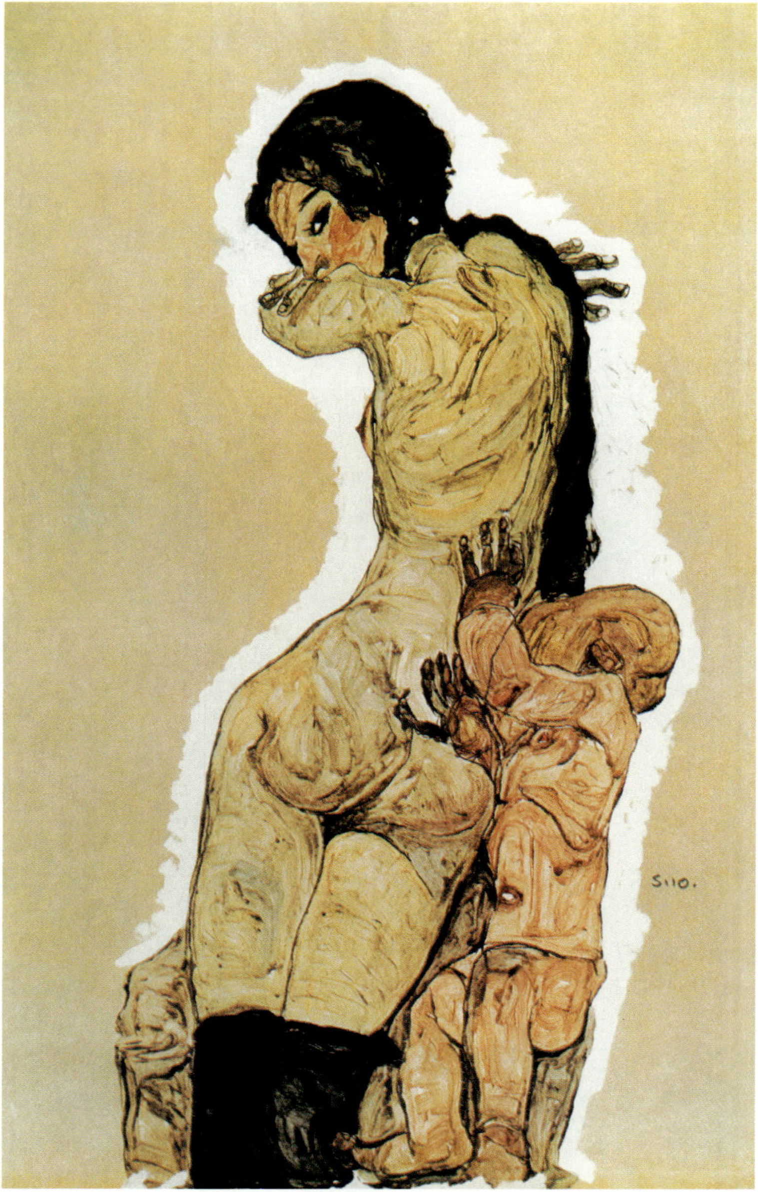
S10.

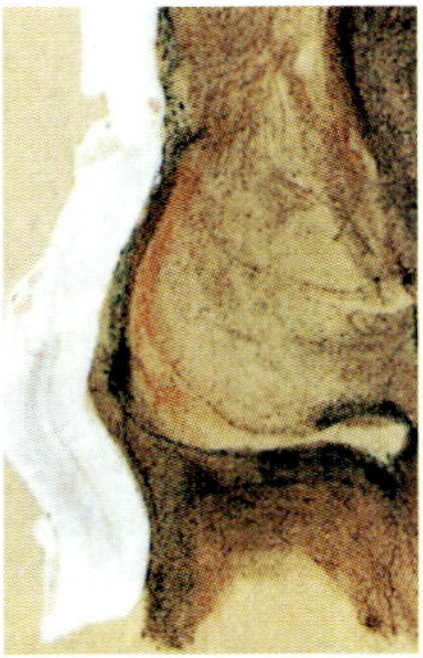

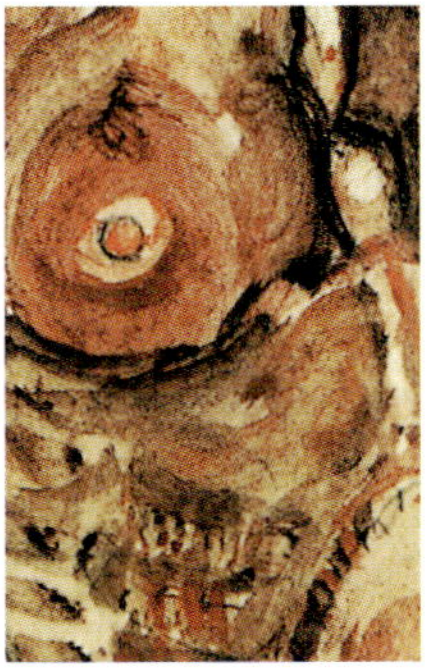

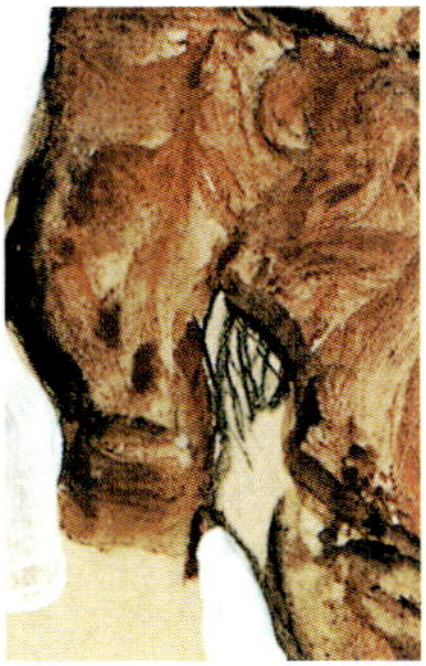

In 1907, Schiele made the acquaintance of Gustav Klimt who became his father figure and generously supported the talent of the young genius for the rest of his life. They exchanged drawings with one another and Klimt even modelled for Schiele. In his career, Klimt profited from the large volume of commissioned work, such as the 34.14 metre long *Beethovenfries* created for the faculty. Nevertheless, he ran into misunderstanding from his contemporaries about the central motif of a nude couple embracing.

Nude Self-Portrait

1910
Gouache, watercolour and black pencil with white highlights, 44.9 x 31.3 cm
Leopold Museum, Vienna

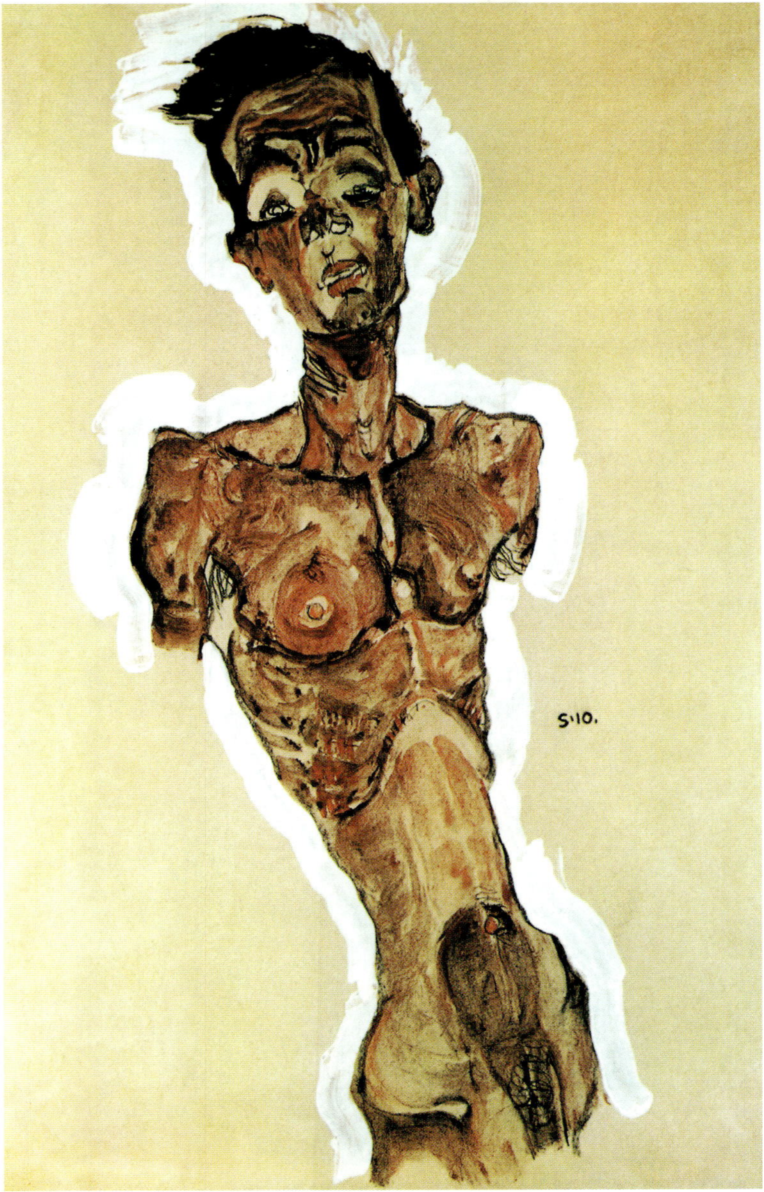
S10.

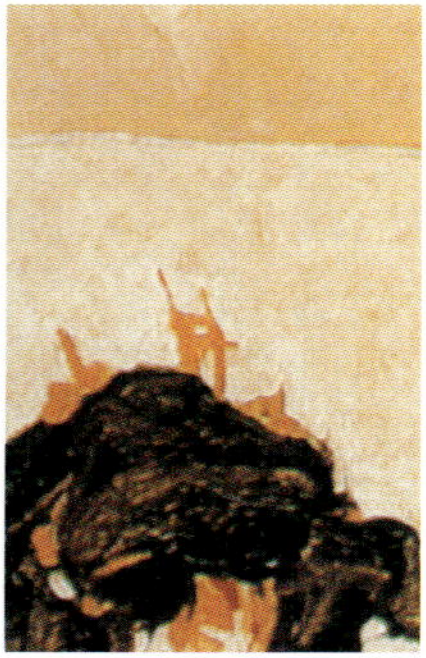

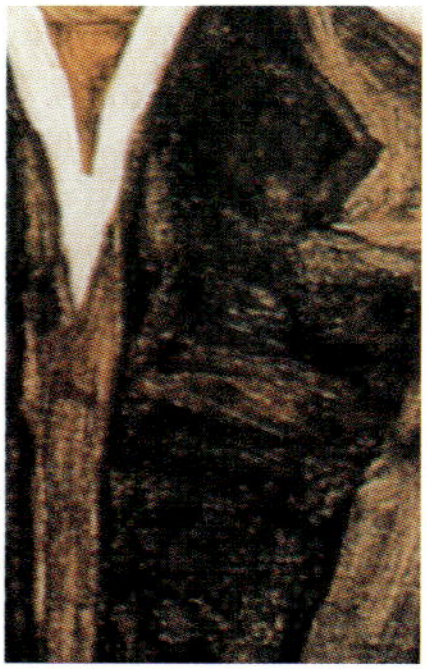

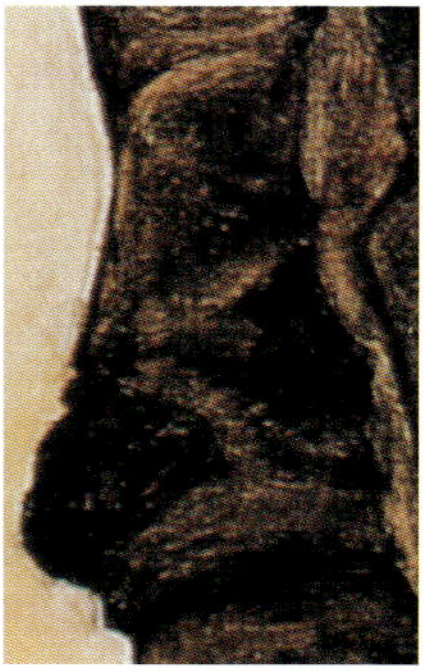

Criticism of Klimt became more vehement when the periodical *Ver Sacrum* published his drawings and was confiscated by a public prosecutor because "the depiction of the nude grossly violated modesty and, therefore, offended the public". Klimt answered that he wanted nothing to do with stubborn people. What was decisive for him was who was it to please? For Klimt, who was supported by private patronage, this meant his clientele of Viennese middle-class patrons.

Portrait of Eduard Kosmack

1910
Oil on canvas, 100 x 100 cm
Österreichische Galerie Belvedere, Vienna

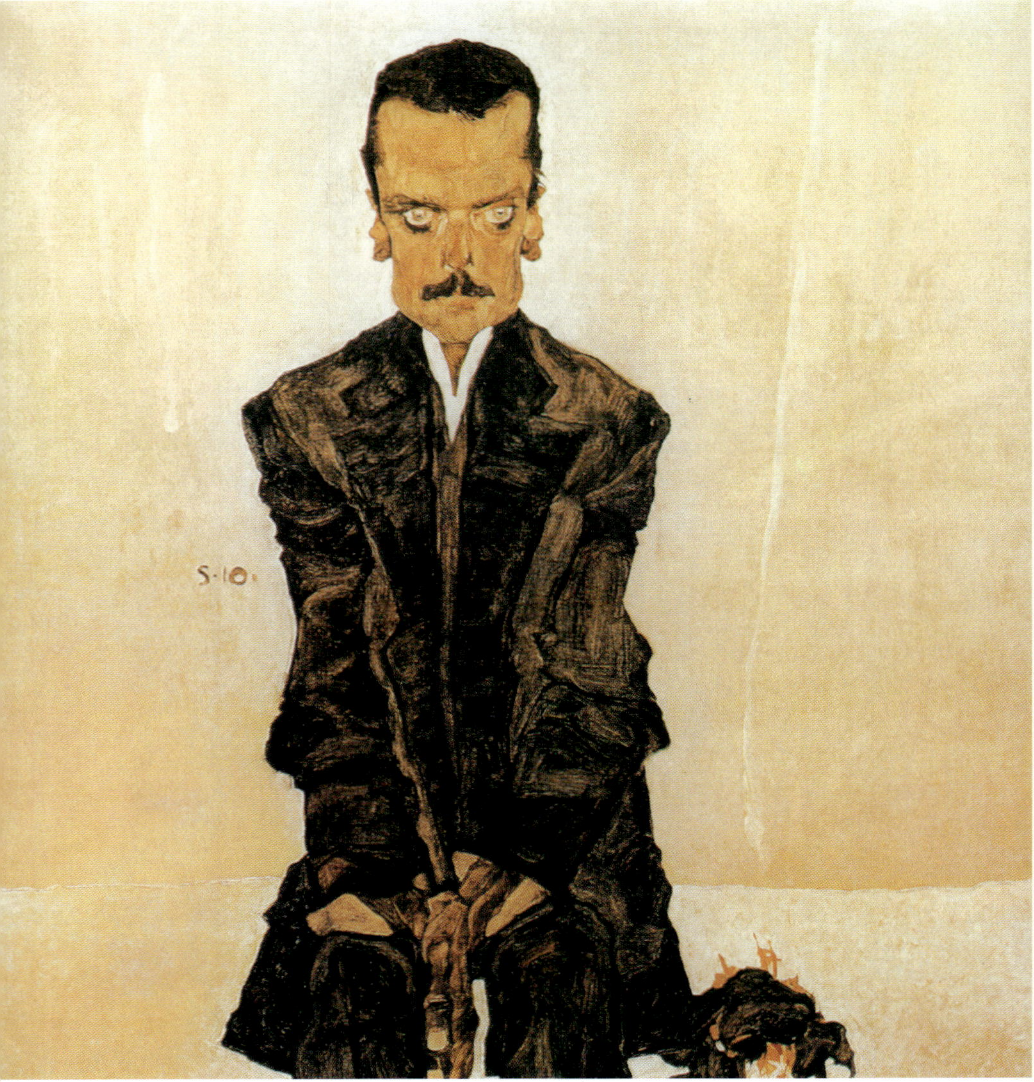
S.10.

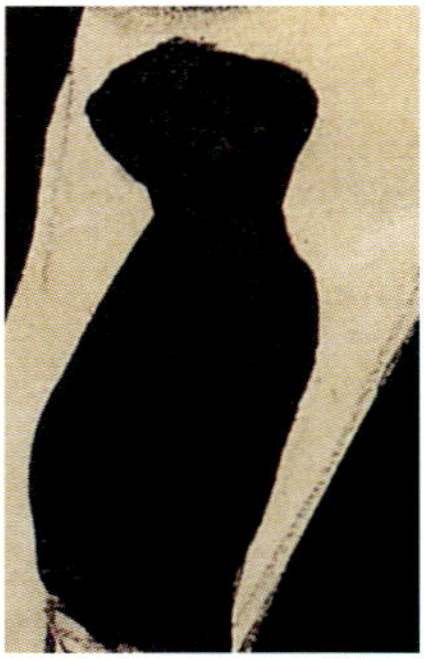

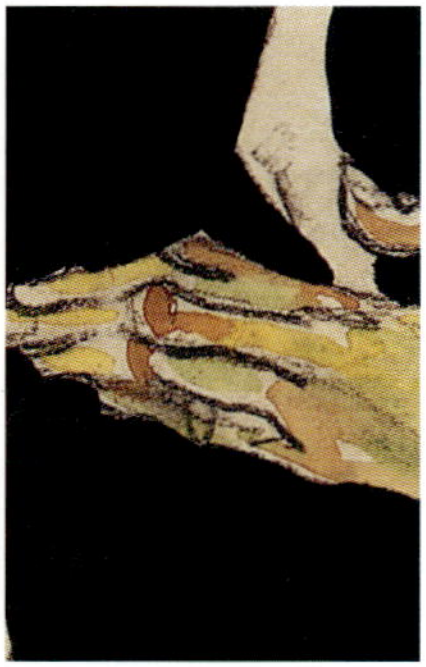

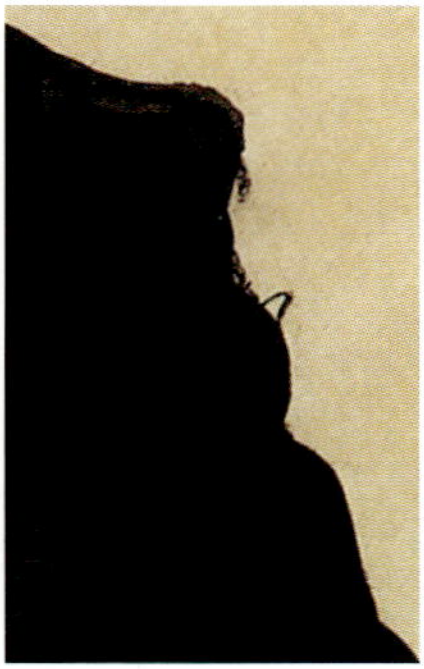

A crucial turning point in Viennese artistic life was the *Kunstschau* of 1908. This exhibition was mounted by Klimt and his colleagues to survey the best of contemporary Austrian art, including a strong representation of the decorative arts and the work of promising students. It launched the career of the young Kokoschka. The following year's *Kunstschau*, in 1909, introduced the public to the work of Schiele, then still a nineteen-year-old student, but already convinced of his own genius.

The Painter Max Oppenheimer

1910
Black pencil, ink and watercolour on paper
45 x 29.9 cm
Albertina, Vienna

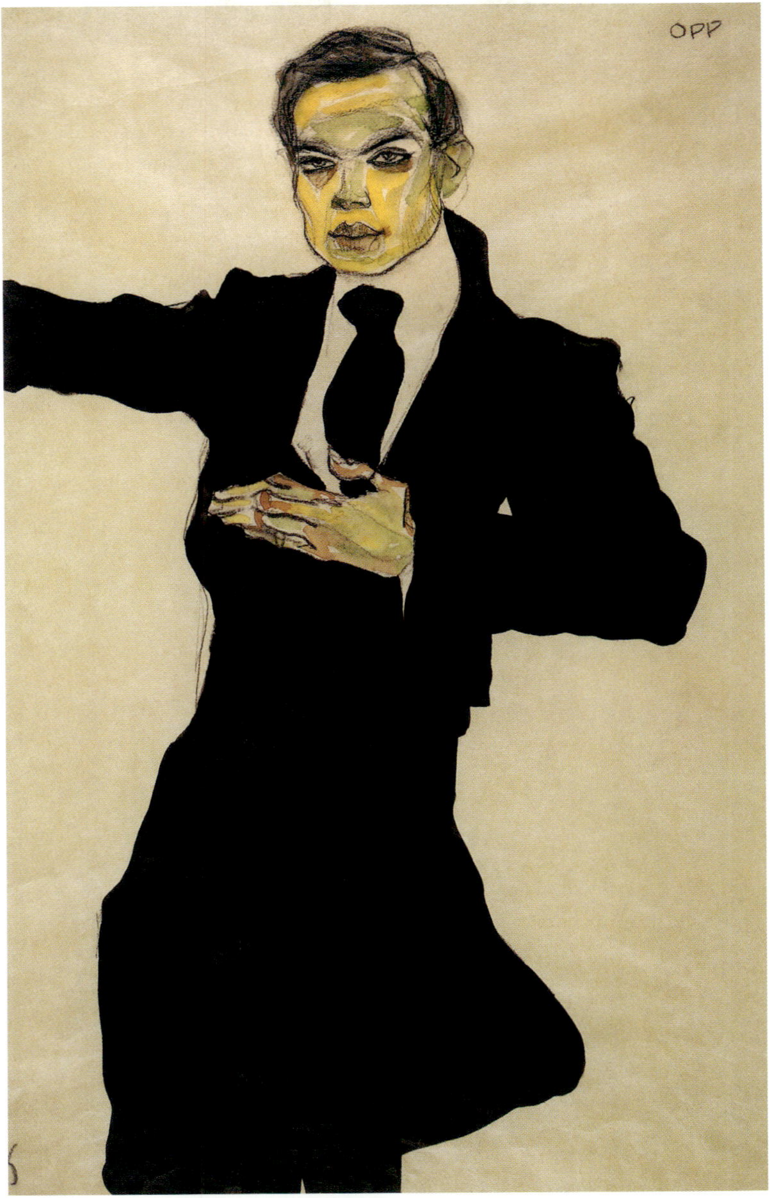
OPP

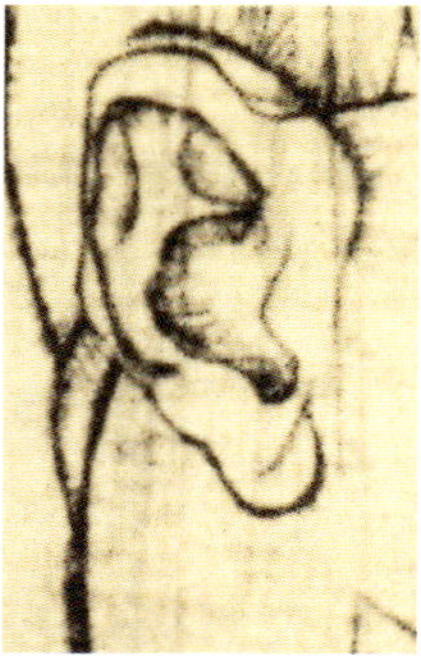
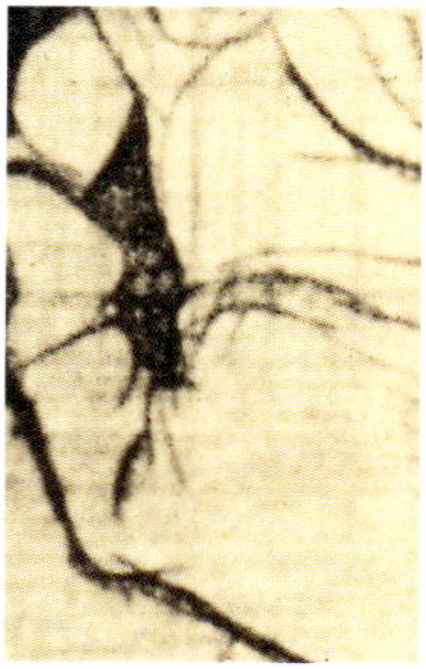
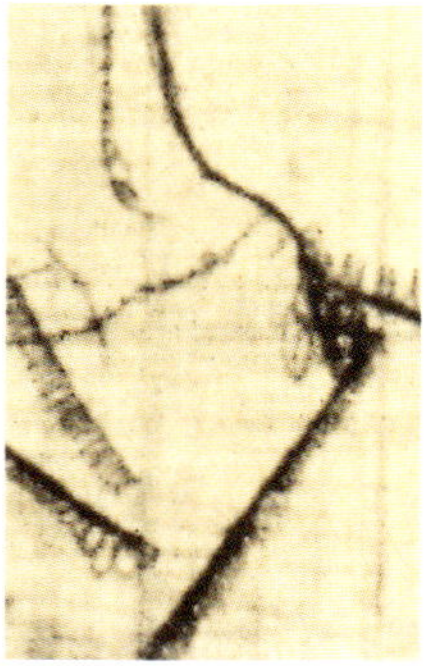

Of the two young artists, Schiele was most affected by Klimt's work. He even called himself, precociously, the "Silver Klimt." Schiele's exhibits included a portrait of his fourteen-year-old sister in the public guise of a demure, fashionable young woman. The new direction in which this younger artist was taking art – away from "Jugendstil" and towards Expressionism – becomes clear if we compare Klimt's most celebrated work, *The Kiss*, with a painting,

Portrait of Arthur Roessler

1910
Pencil, 35 x 50 cm
Private collection

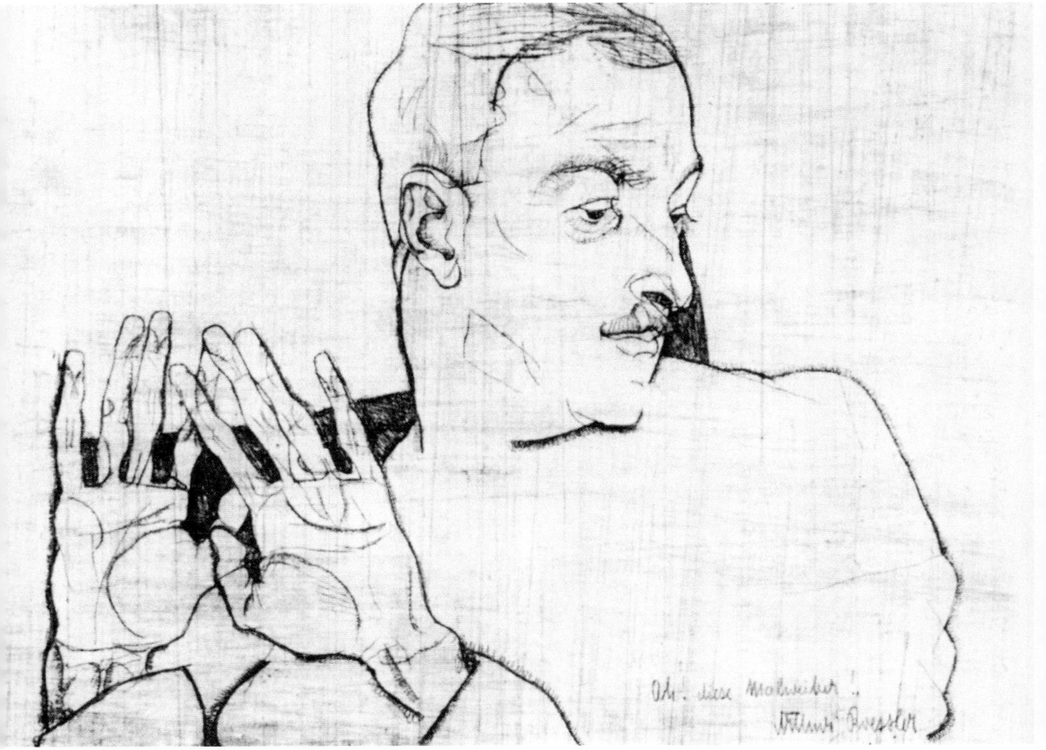

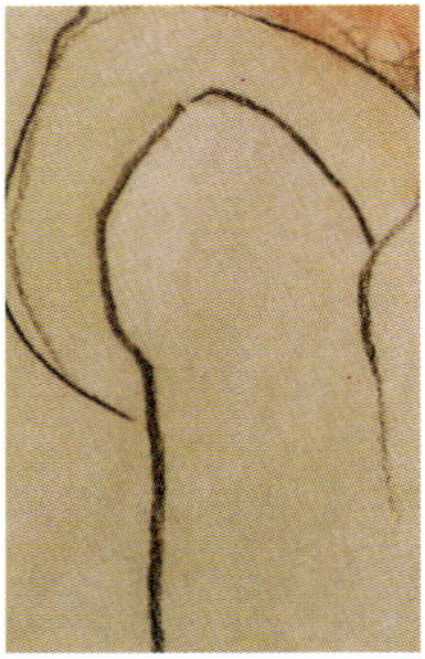

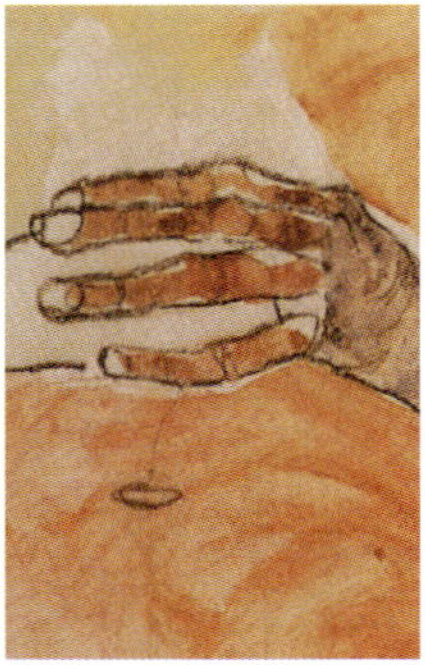

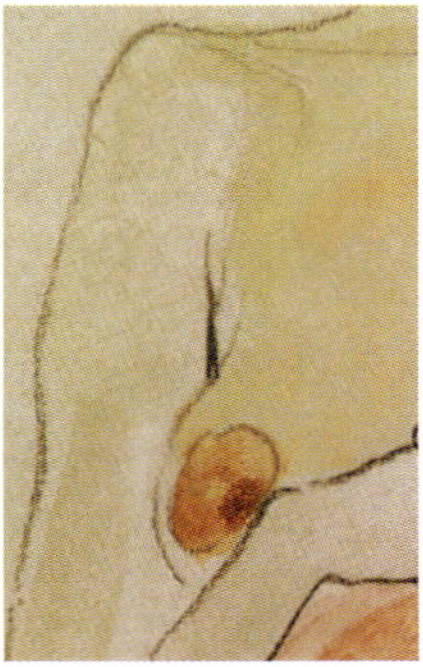

produced a few years later, by his one-time protégé. Klimt's painting was exhibited for the first time at the 1908 *Kunstschau* in a special room, the centrepiece of the whole show, reverently devoted to sixteen of his most recent works. *The Kiss* had its sources in two luxuriant mural schemes that he had already completed: the *Beethoven Frieze* of 1902 and the mosaics he designed in 1905-9 to adorn the dining room of Josef Hoffman's Palais Stoclet in Brussels. It is an opulent icon to sensuality, but just decorous enough that it was bought by the government. In a magical, ethereal dreamscape,

Red Nude, Pregnant

1910
Watercolour and charcoal, 44.5 x 31 cm
Private collection

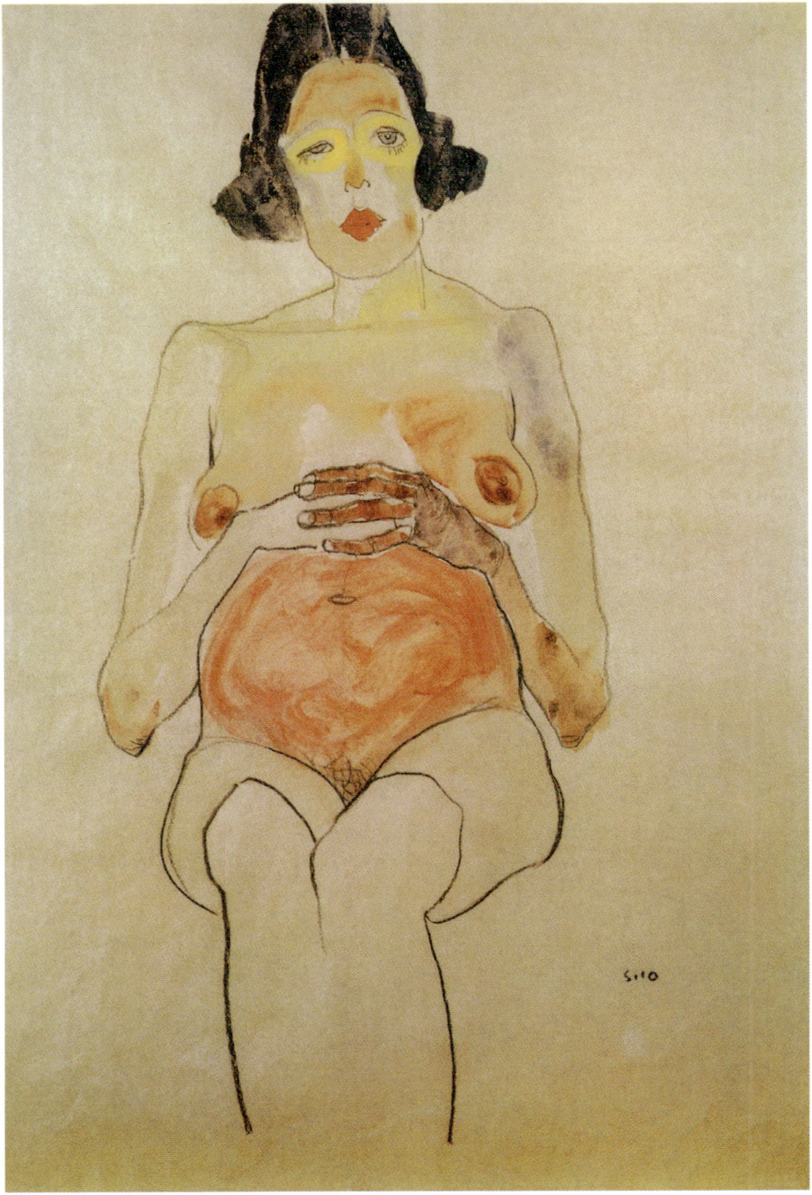
S10

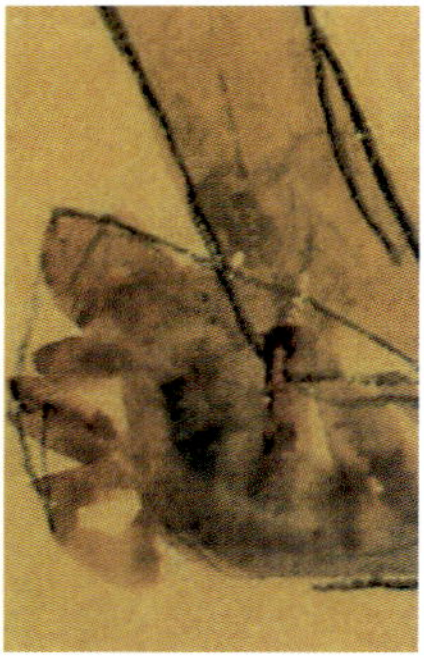

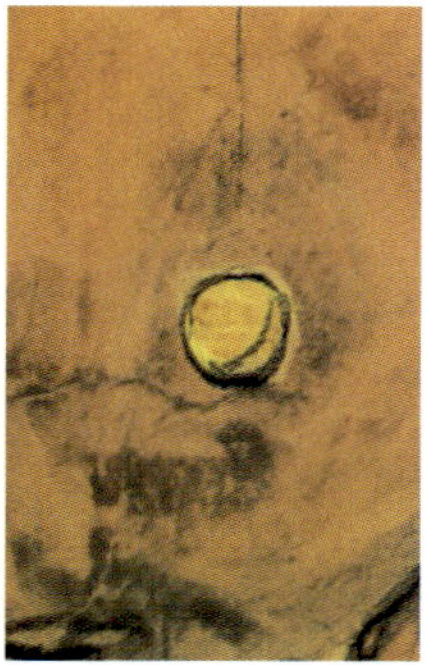

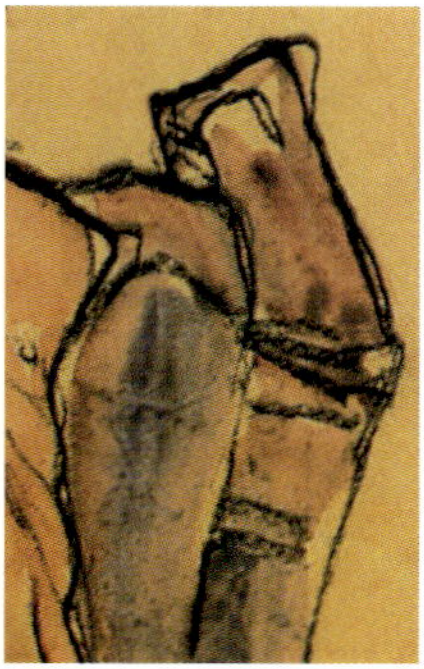

a man embraces and supports a woman who swoons at the touch of his kiss to her cheek. All glitters with silver, gold and tiny flower-blossoms. The biomorphic shape of a halo-like aura surrounding the couple evokes simultaneously the religiosity of an altarpiece and the fertile blossoming of sexual passion. Klimt himself was characteristically blunt about his painting's eroticism. He explained to friends (including Schiele) that in the neck of the man, he meant to evoke not only his potency, but also the back of the penis.

Newborn Baby

1910
Watercolour and charcoal, 46 x 32 cm
Private collection

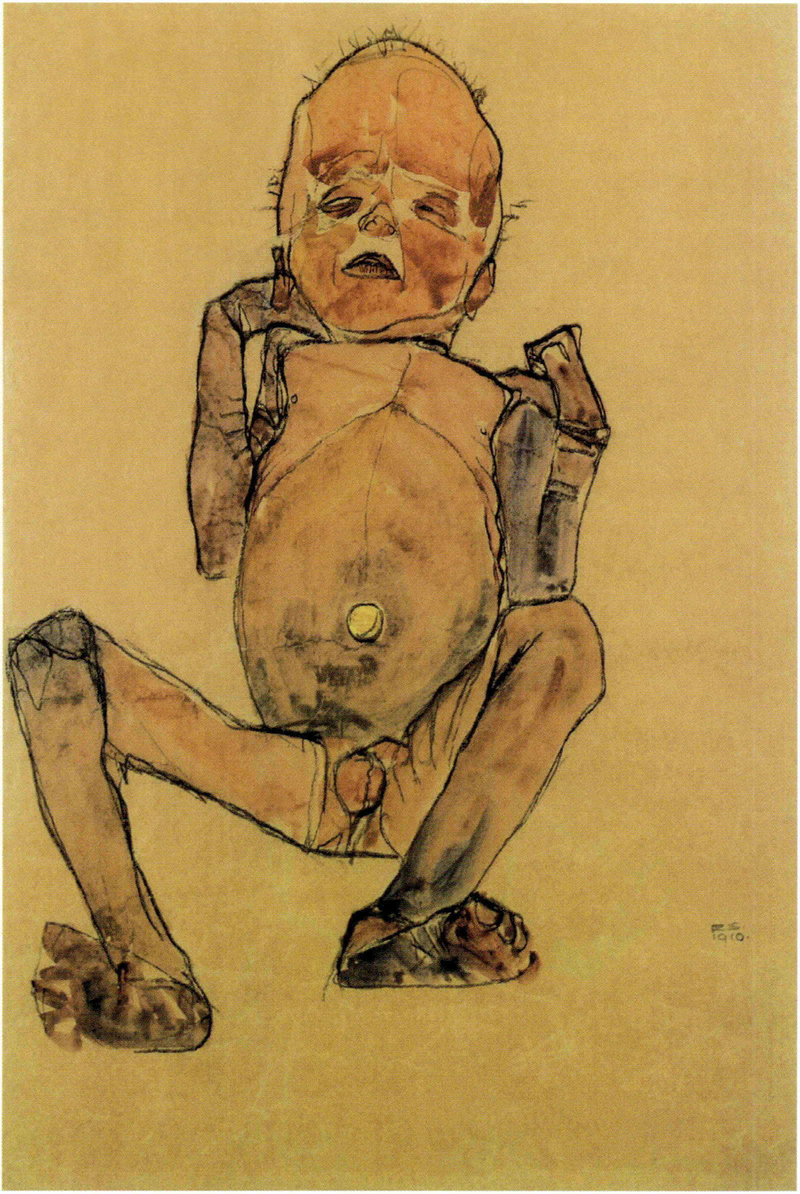

E.S.
1910.

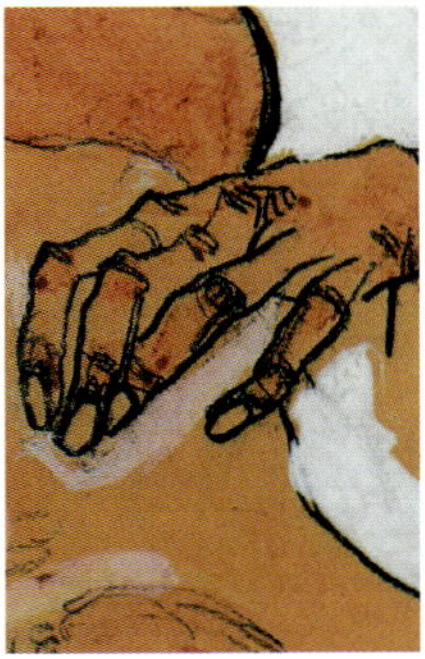

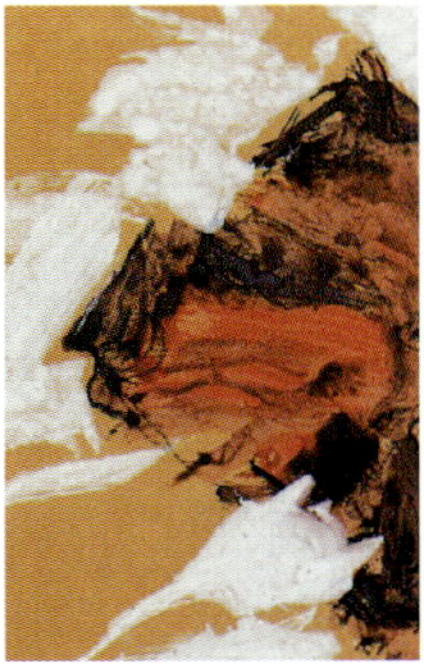

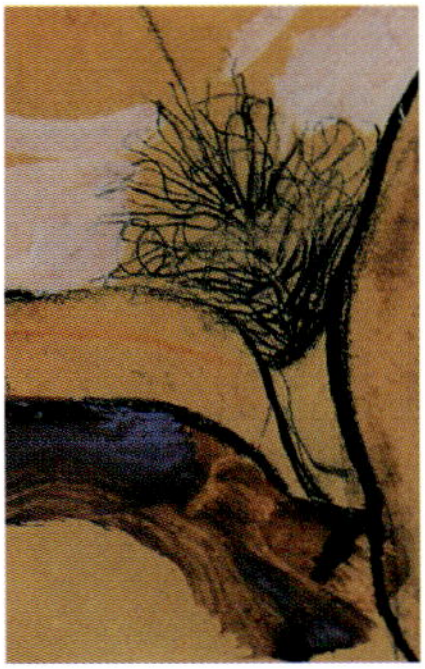

Schiele knew Klimt's painting very well. He made several drawings related to it, some more irreverent than others (one had Klimt's couple at a somewhat further stage of foreplay). But these were small, private works. It was in 1912 that he took on its vision of the loving embrace, overturned it, and presented it in a bold gesture of defiance to the wider public. Schiele converted the blissful, self-absorbed lovers into furtive fumblers in the dark, anxious and painfully self-aware. Schiele's *Cardinal and Nun* is also sometimes known by the ironic title he gave it, *Liebeskosung;*

Female Nude

1910
Gouache, watercolour and pencil with white highlights, 44.3 x 30.6 cm
Albertina, Vienna

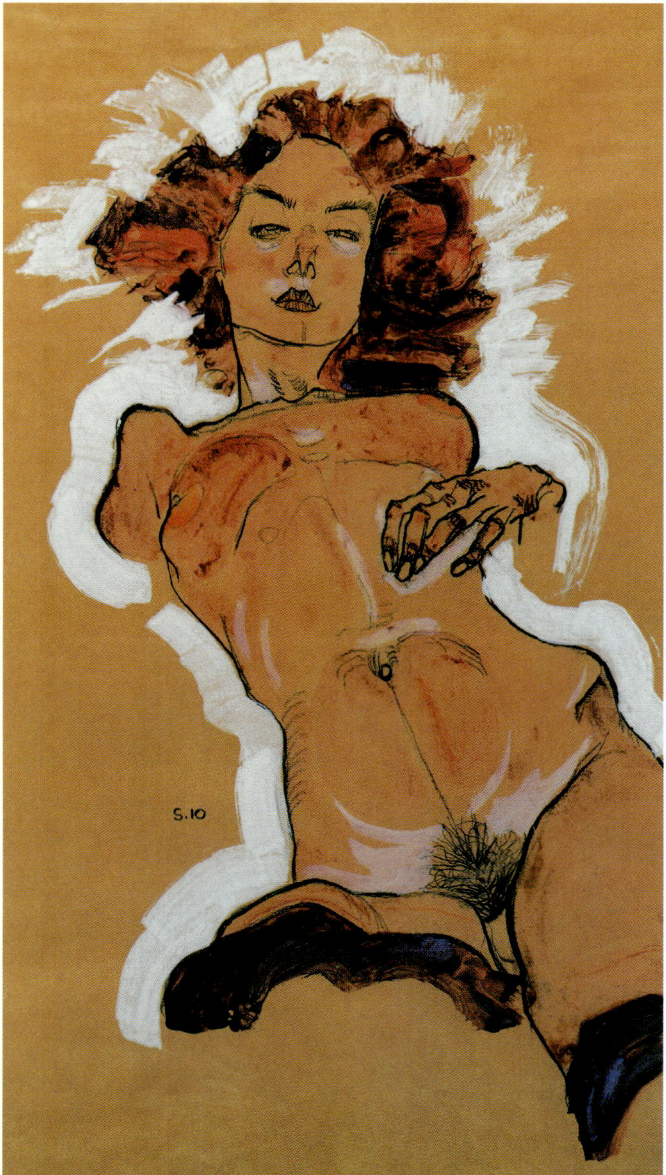
S.10

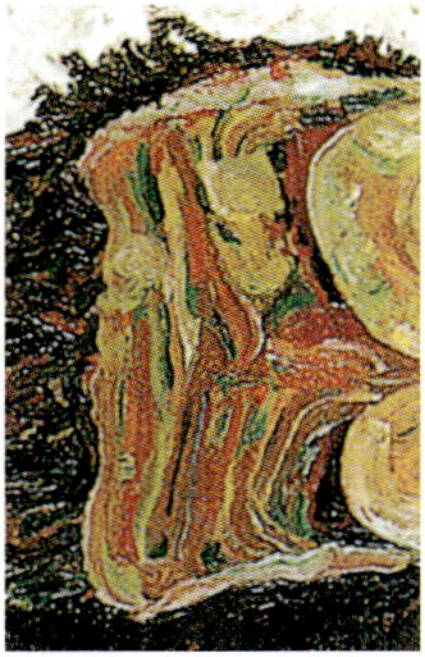

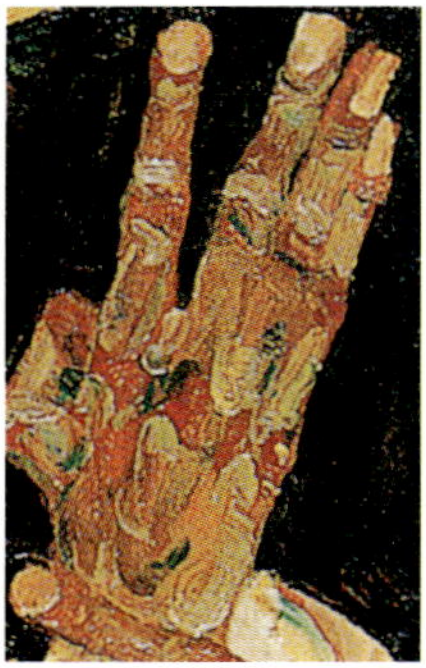

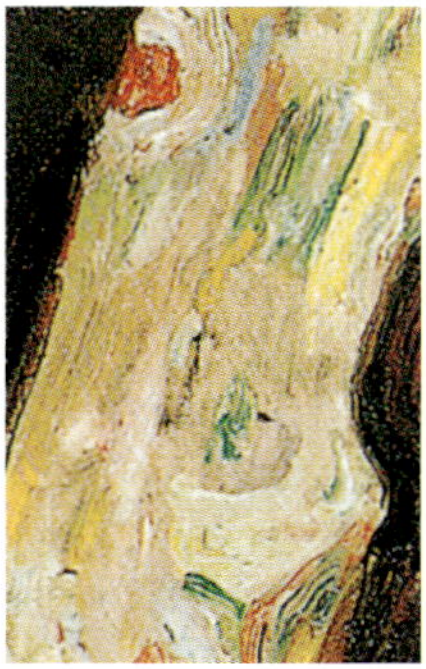

meaning a loving "caress" or "embrace." He painted it on release from his spell in prison, after some of his drawings had been confiscated and he had been accused of a range of offences against public morality. This sheds light on the underlying pleasure and pain ridden theme of the painting: neither prescriptive moral laws nor attempts at emotional repression (what the guidance books for the youth of the day called "*Selbstbeherrschung*," or "self-control") can contain the power of the erotic urge.

The Poet (Self-Portrait)

1911
Oil on canvas, 80.1 x 79.7 cm
Leopold Museum, Vienna

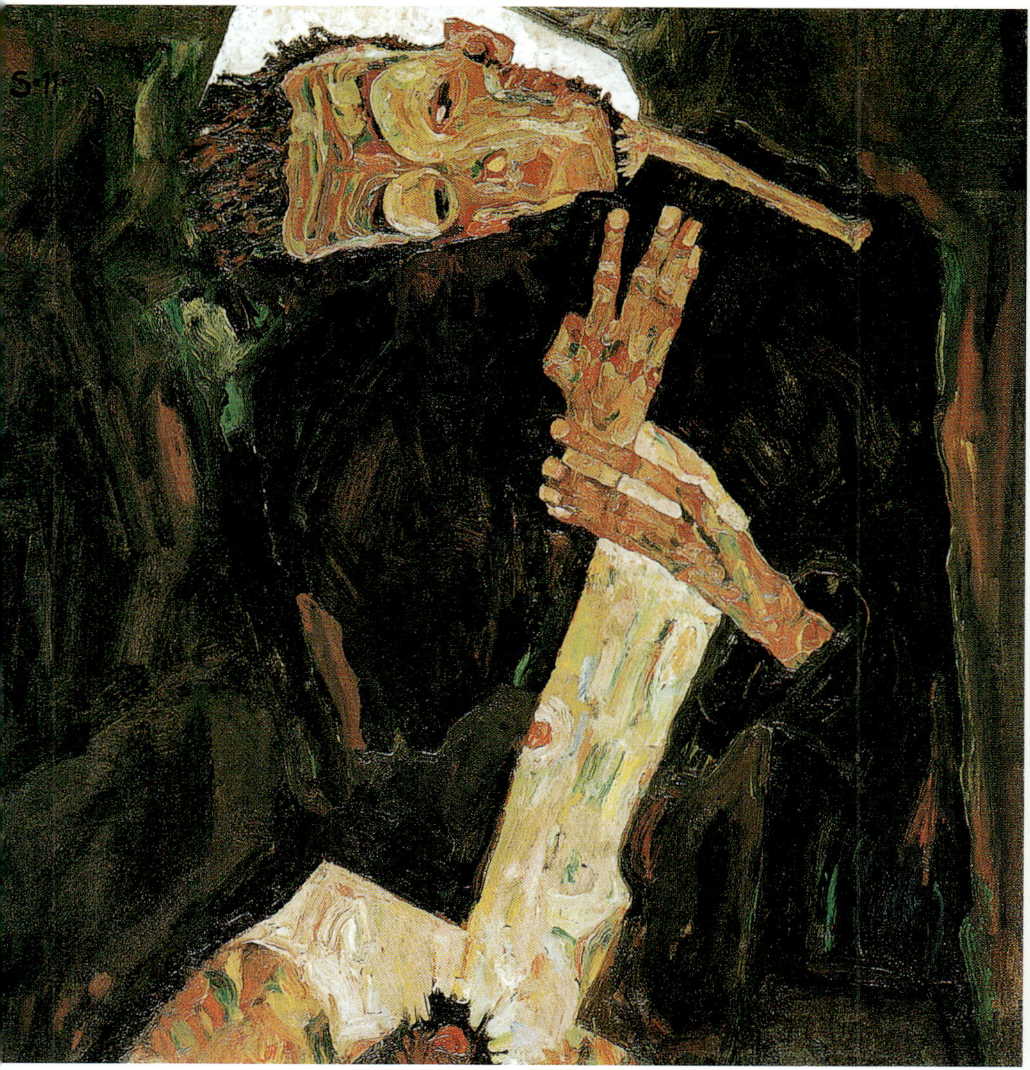

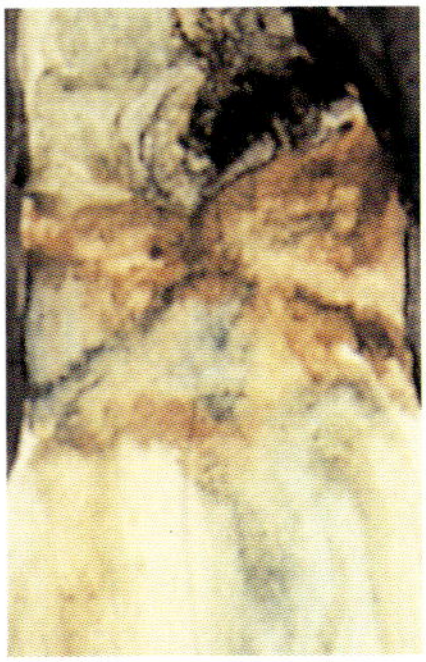

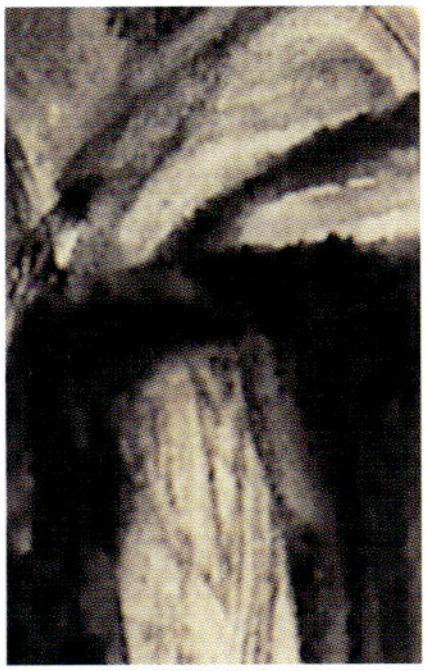

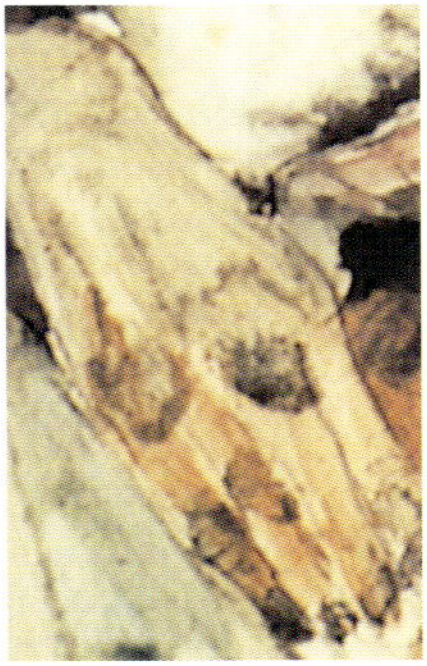

Comparing the two great paintings is instructive of the differences between the sophisticated decadence that Klimt worked to enfold his subjects in, and the raw, conflicting psychosexual instincts that Schiele worked to reveal. Schiele converted Klimt's differentiated decoration of the masculine and feminine drapery (stereotypically, one geometric, the other biomorphic) into a stark play-off between the cardinal's red and the nun's black. The luxuriant "halo" of hair, literally blossoming around the head of Klimt's woman, contrasts with the starkness of the nun's habit.

Self-Portrait with Black Cloak Masturbating

1911
Gouache, watercolour and pencil, 48 x 32.1 cm
Albertina, Vienna

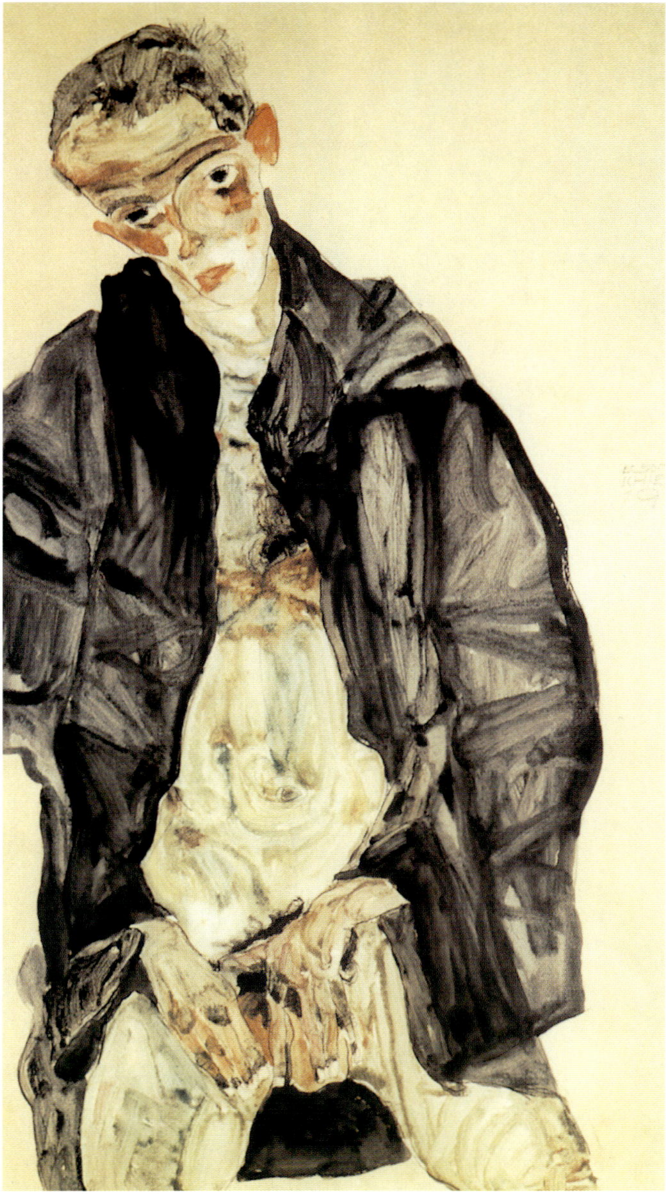

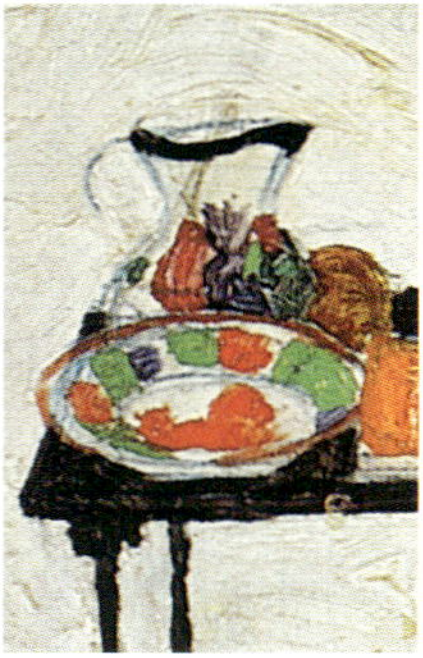

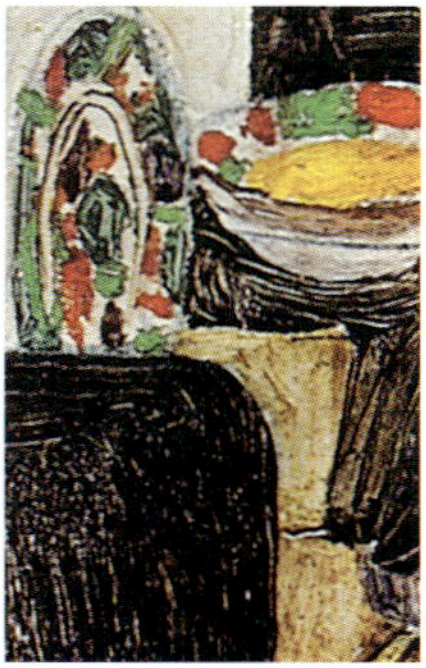

Her pliancy in the arms of her lover becomes, in Schiele's vision, a petrified stiffness as the nun presses herself rigidly against the cardinal's body in an ambivalent gesture that suggests both resistance and submission. While Klimt's figures float on a verdant carpet in a starred cosmos, Schiele's cling to one another against a dark abyss. The most adroit, and doubly iconoclastic, aspect of Schiele's image of the guilt-laden couple, however, is their posture. Working from the blueprint of the kneeling position of Klimt's woman, Schiele has his ecclesiastical lovers locked in the position of prayer as they embrace.

The Artist's Room in Neulengbach

1911
Oil on wood, 40 x 31.7 cm
Wien Museum, Vienna

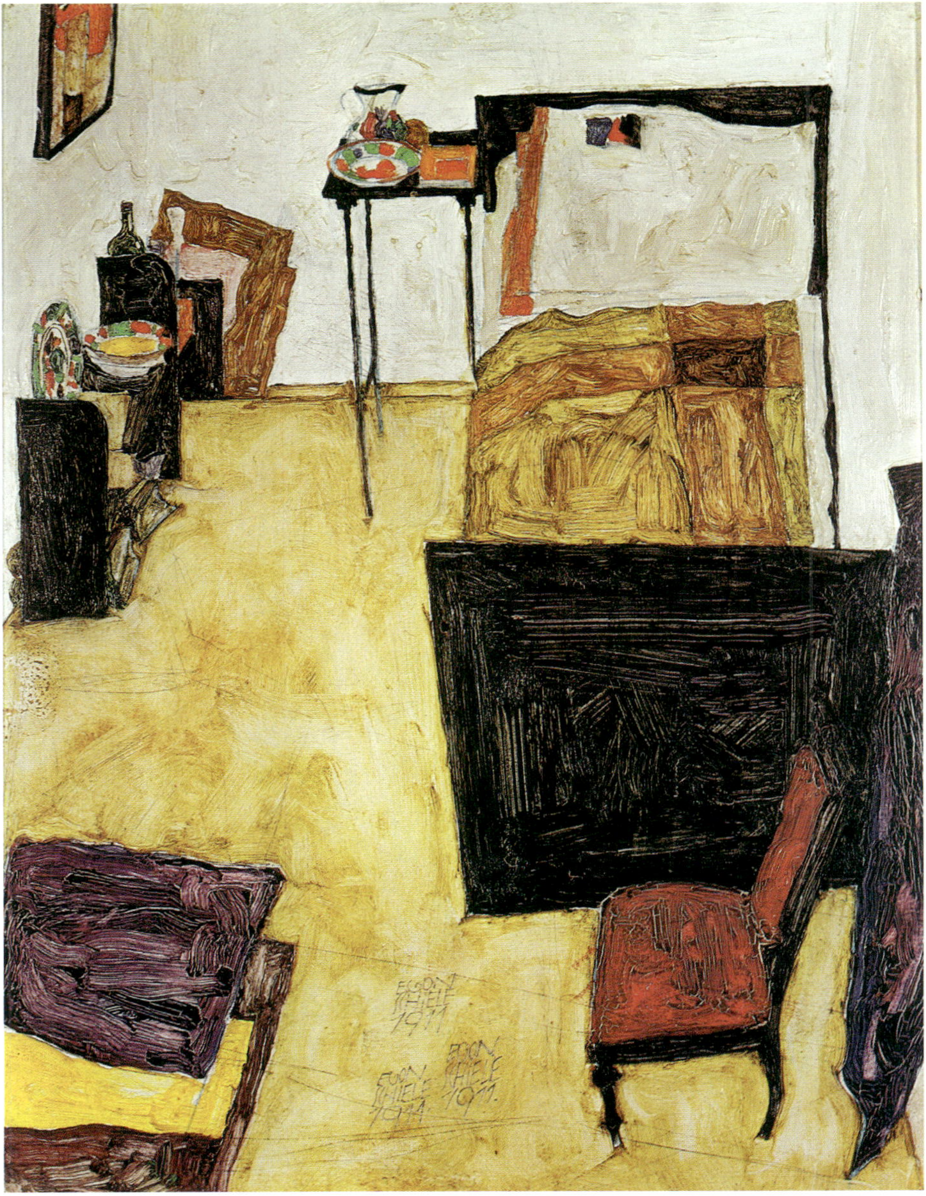
EGON SCHIELE 1911
EGON SCHIELE 1911
EGON SCHIELE 1911

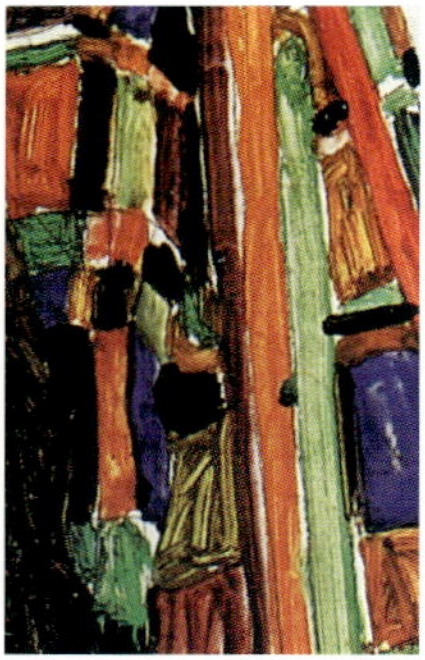

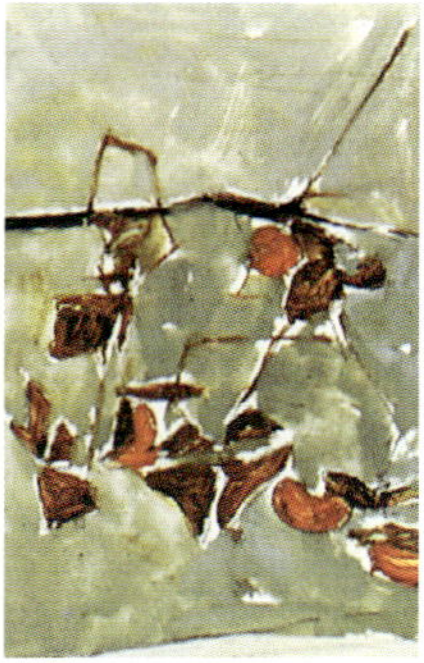

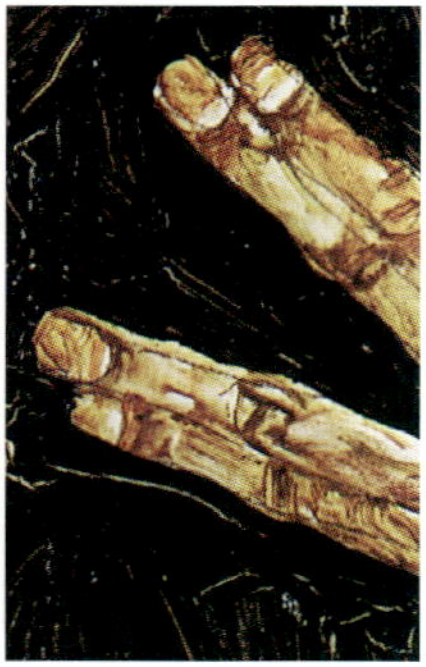

Thus, veneration of the loved one is the theme common to both paintings, but while Klimt makes the sexual act sacred, Schiele makes the sacred act sexual.

Expressionist Liberation

At the core of his creation, Schiele sets the difference with his master: his muses are not those of Klimt. Schiele found his models on the streets: young girls of the proletariat and prostitutes; he preferred the child-woman androgynous types. The thin, gaunt bodies of his models characterised lower-class status, while the full-bosomed,

Self-Portrait with Black Vase
and Spread Fingers

1911
Oil on canvas, 27.5 x 34 cm
Wien Museum, Vienna

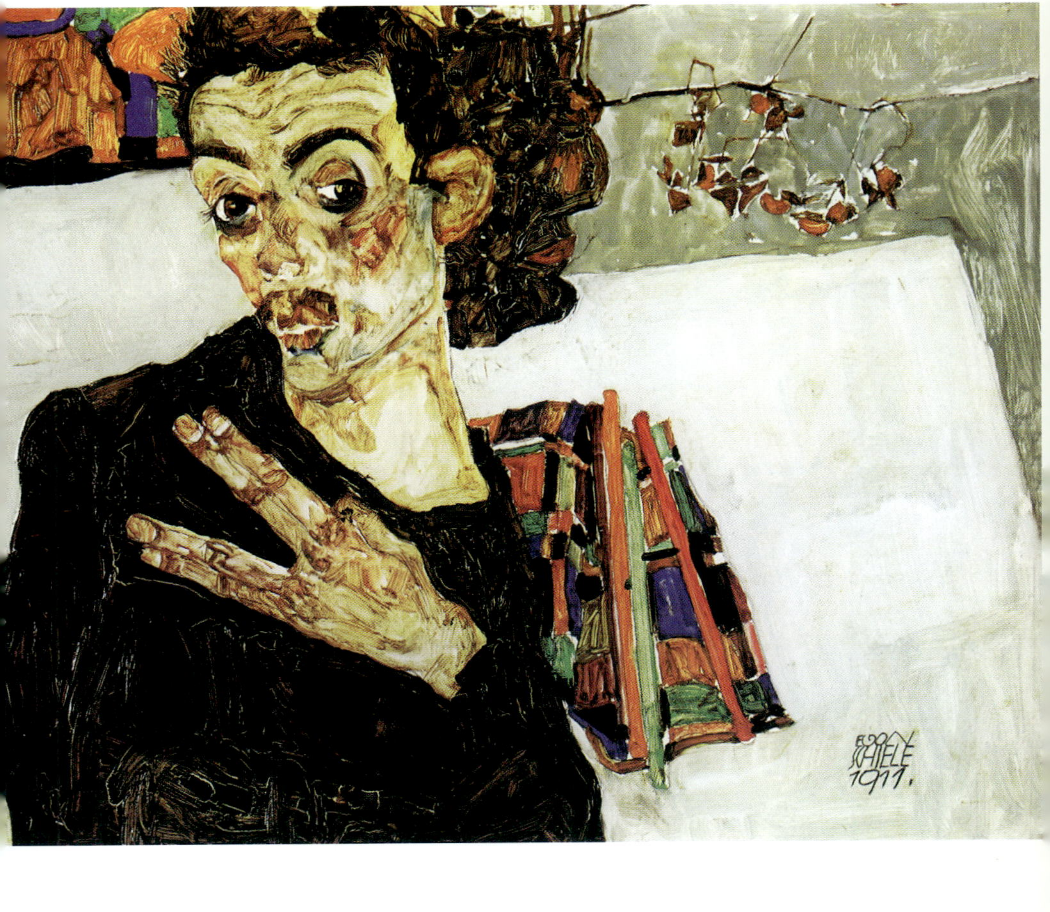
EGON
SCHIELE
1911.

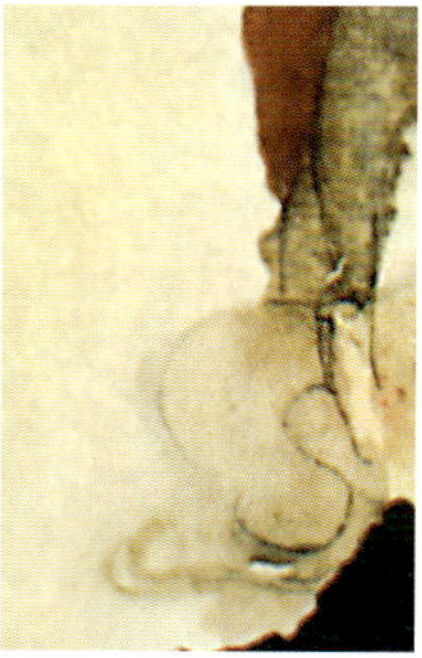

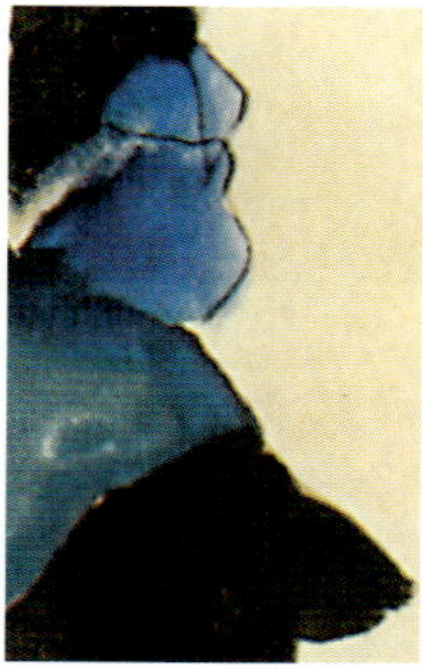

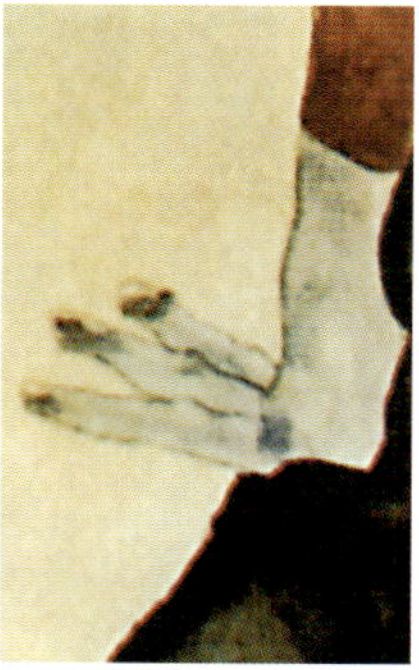

luscious ladies of the bourgeoisie expressed their class through well-fed corpulence. Yet, the attitude of the legendary Empress Sissi is symptomatic of a time in which the conventional image of woman began to change. She indeed bore the desired offspring; however, she rebelled against the maternal role which was expected of her. The ideal of a youthful figure nearly caused her to become anorexic. At the same time, she shocked Viennese court society not only with her unconventional riding excursions, but also in that she wore her clothing without the prescribed stockings.

Two Little Girls

1911
Gouache, watercolour and pencil, 40 x 36 cm
Albertina, Vienna

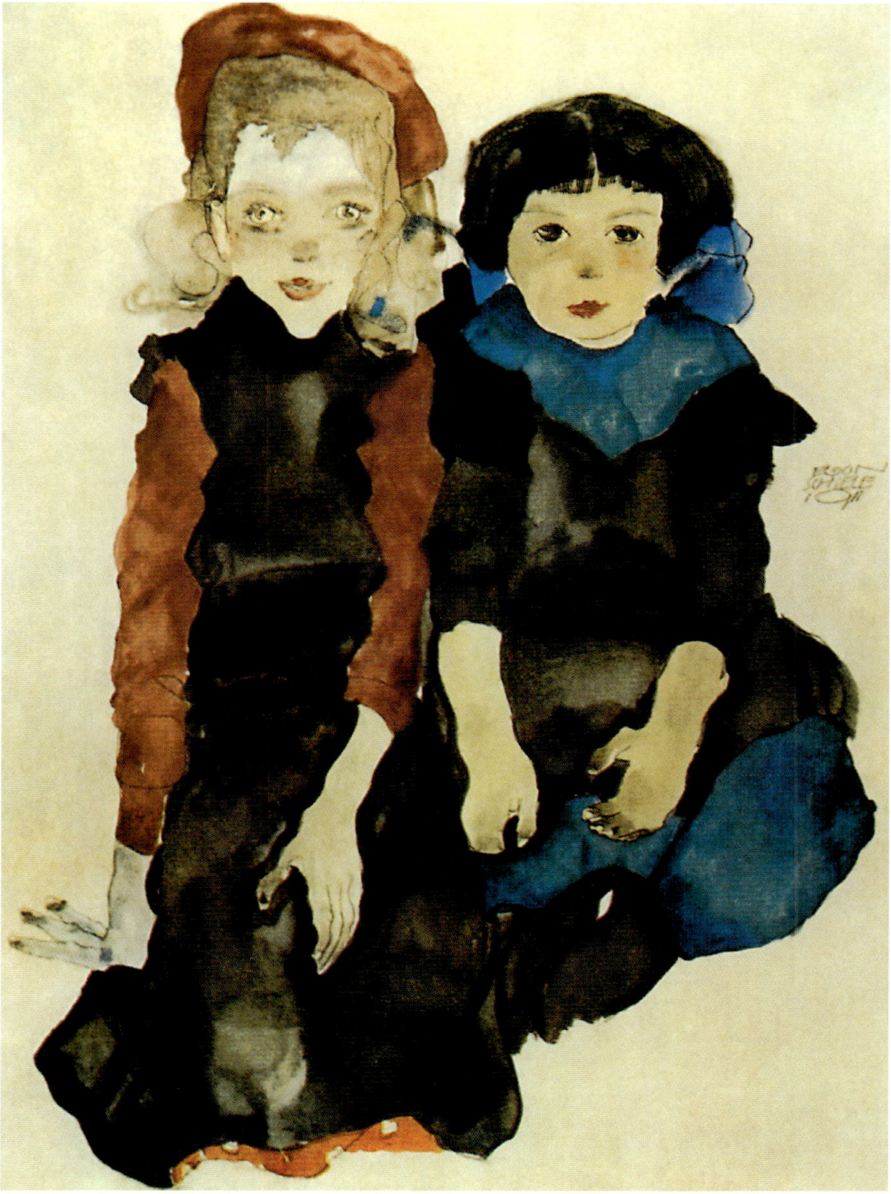

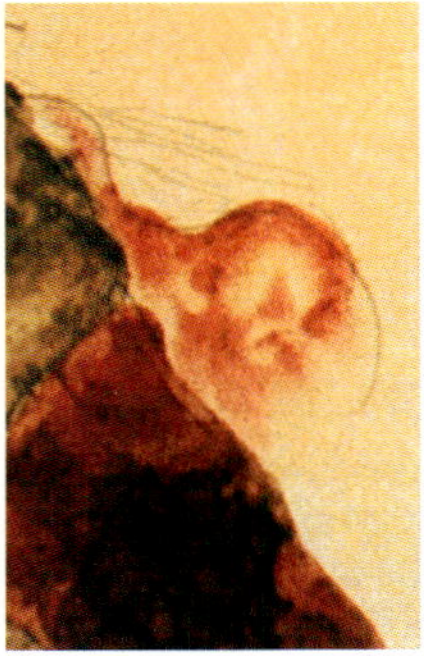

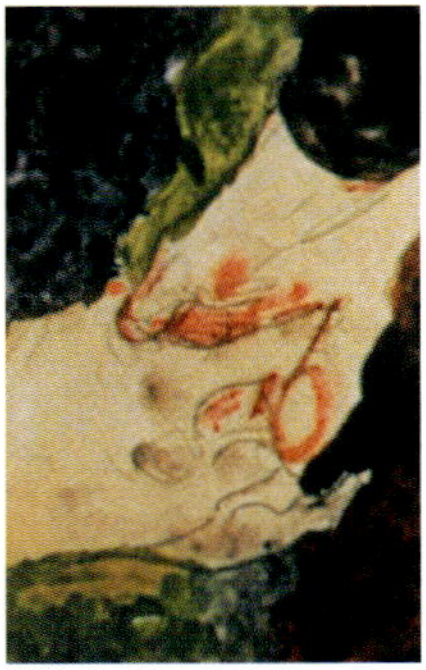

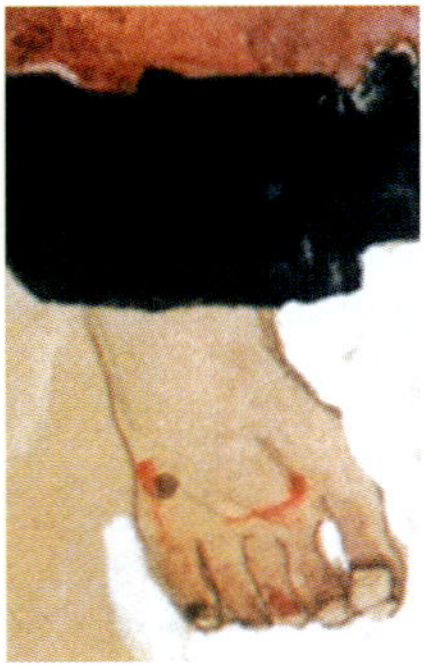

Around the time of the *fin de siècle,* Schiele portrayed young working class girls. The number of prostitutes in Vienna ranged among the highest per capita of any European city. Working class women were where upper-class gentlemen found the defenceless objects of their desire, which they did not find in their own wives. The young, gaunt bodies in Schiele's nude drawings almost stir pity; red blotches cover their thin skin and skeleton-like hands. Their bodies are tense; however, the red genitalia are full and voracious. Like little animals, they lie in wait for the lustful gaze of the beholder.

Group of Three Young Girls

1911
Gouache, watercolour and pencil with white highlights, 44.4 x 30.8 cm
Albertina, Vienna

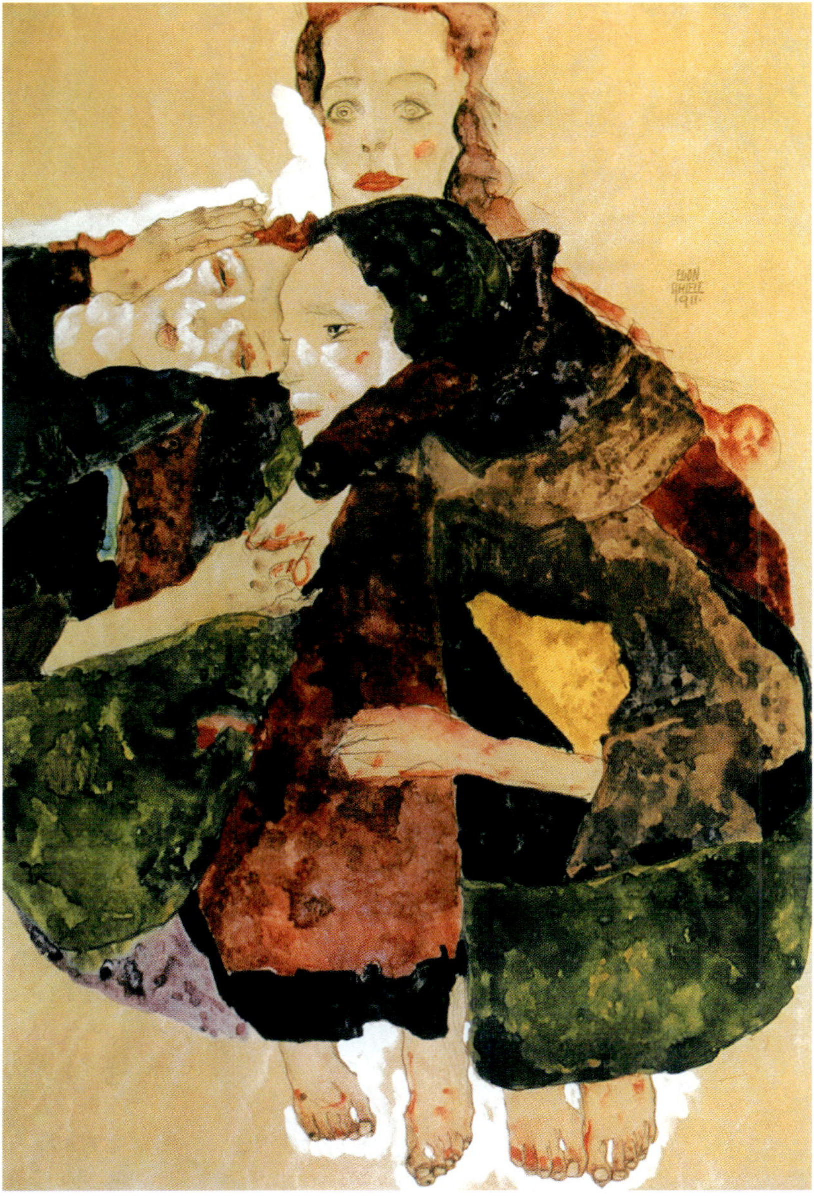

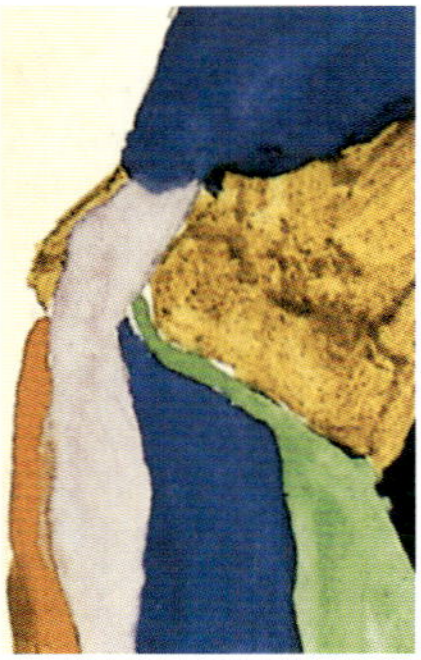

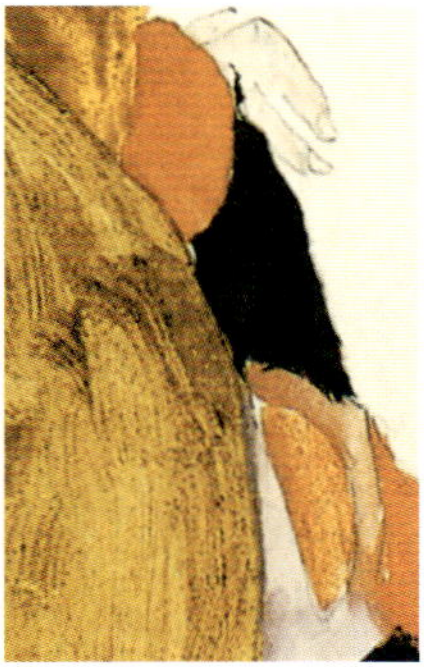

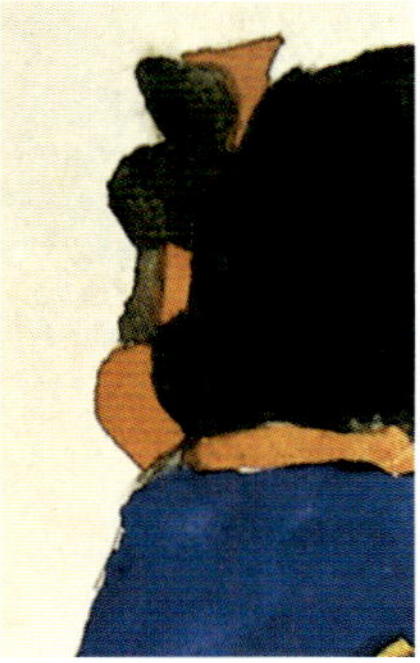

Despite their young age, Schiele's models are aware of their own erotic radiance and, skilfully, know how to pose. The masturbating gesture of the hand on the vagina accompanies the provocative gaze of the model. Contrary to the hygienic taboos of the upper class, for example; not to linger overly long while washing the lower body and not to allow oneself to be viewed in the nude, Schiele's drawings testify to a simple body consciousness and a matter-of-fact attitude. For the lower levels of society, love for sale pertained to earning one's daily bread.

The Dancer Moa

1911
Pencil, watercolour and gouache on paper
47.8 x 31.5 cm
Leopold Museum, Vienna

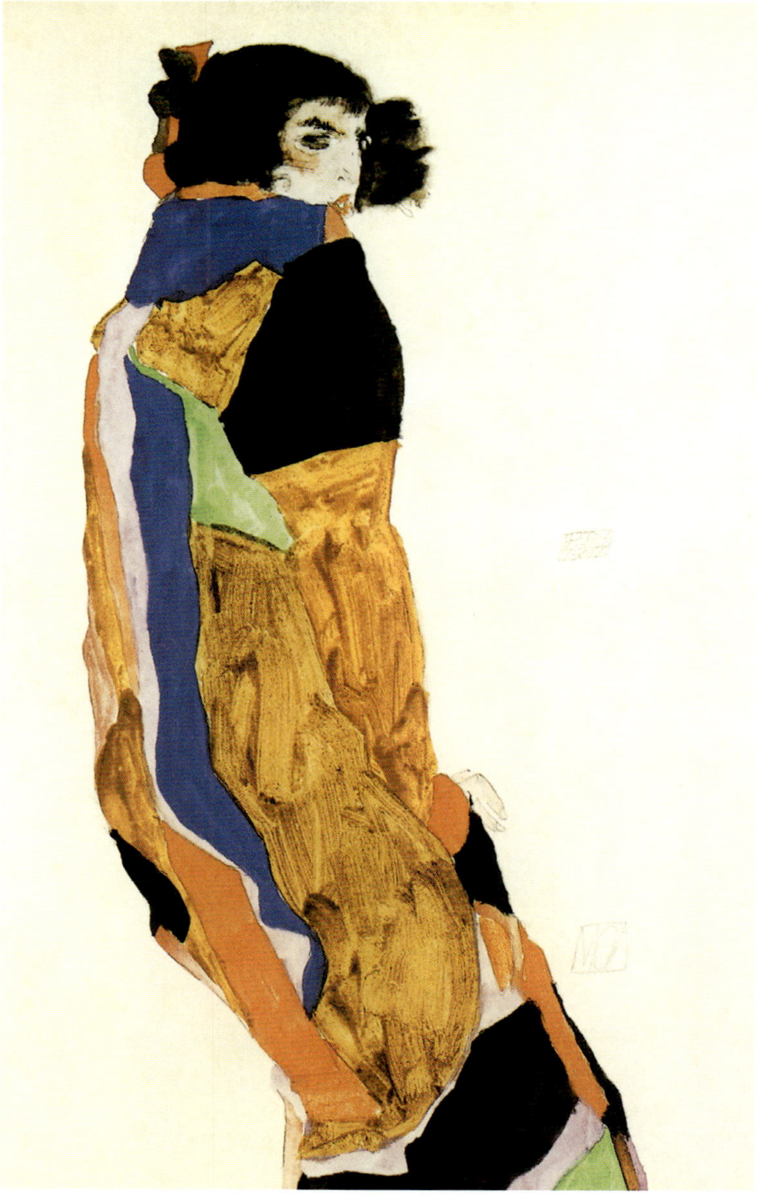

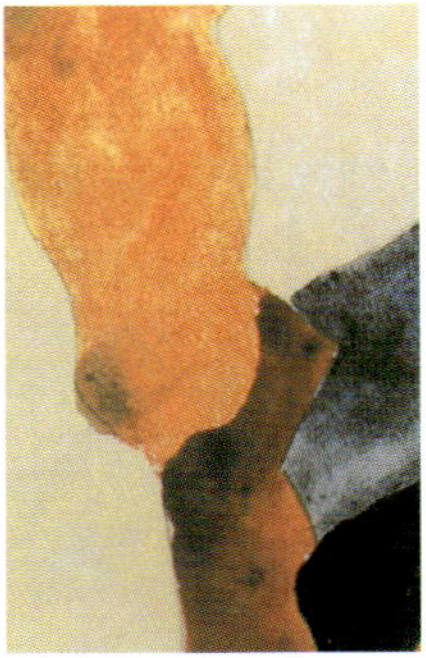

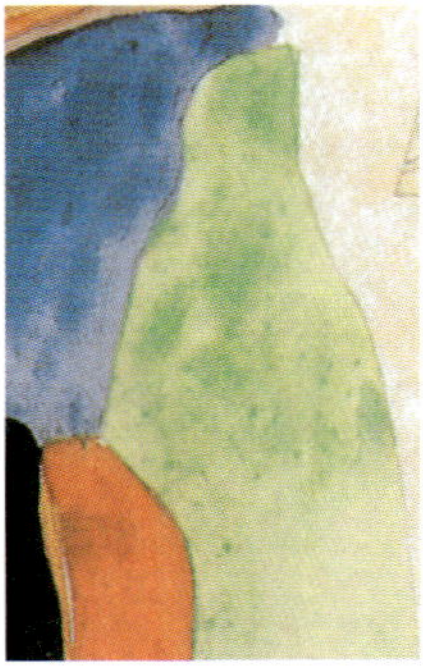

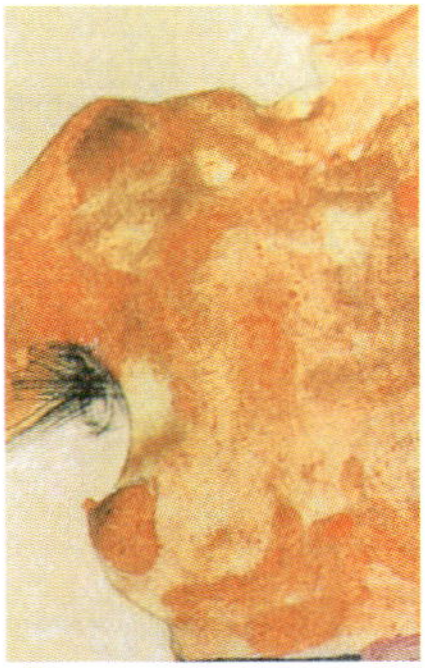

Outraged, the Viennese public lashed out at Schiele, stating that he painted the ultimate vice and utmost depravation, while he confronted both male and female spectators with their own, hypocritical sexuality. In a letter he wrote: "Doing an awful lot of advertising with my prohibited drawings", and went on to cite five notable newspapers which referred to him. Were his nude drawings but a sales strategy that helped drawing attention to himself?

Moa

1911
Gouache, watercolour and pencil, 48 x 31 cm
Private collection

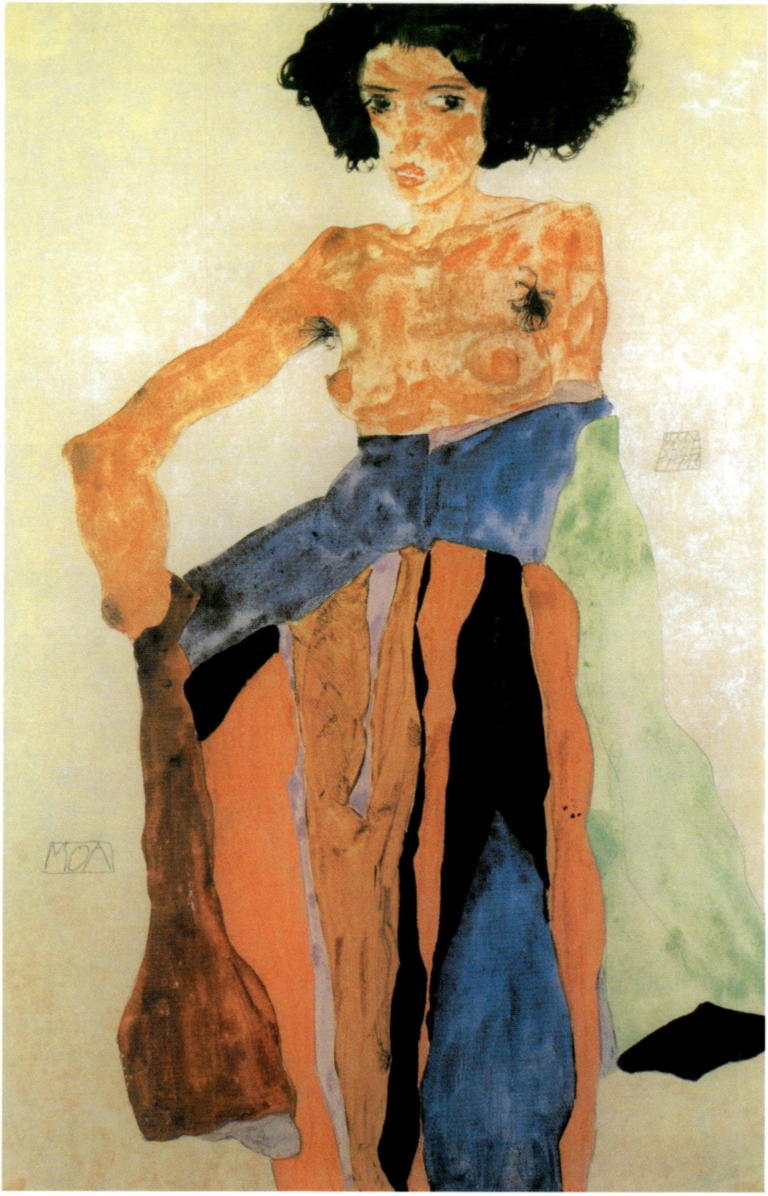
MOA

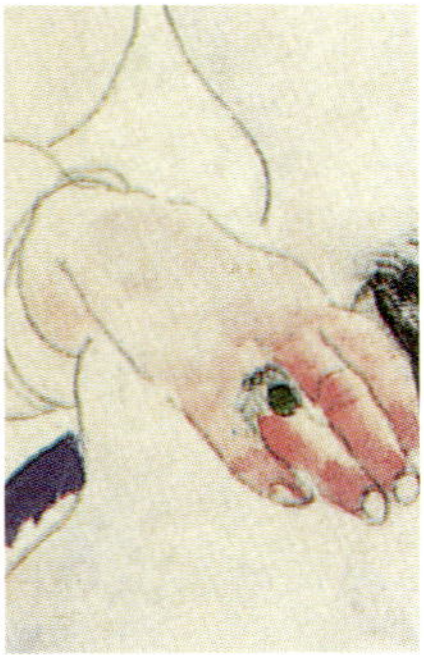

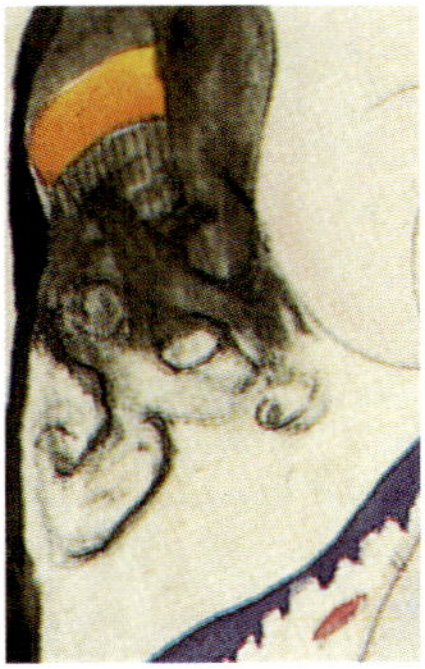

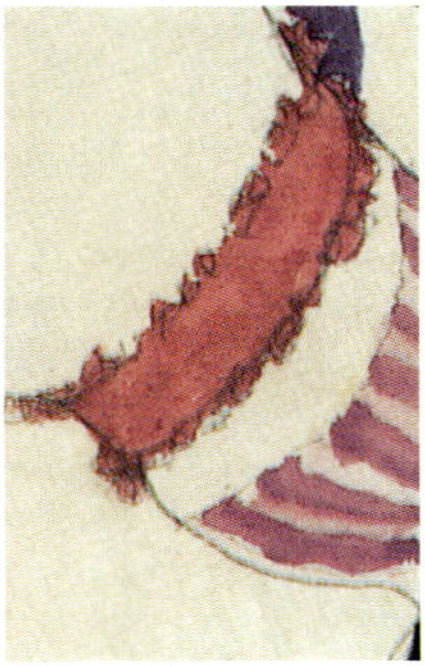

The nature of Schiele's subject shock, but even more so does the way they are depicted. Klimt's picture of woman is based on the analogy of the female body as a personification of nature. Curled tresses become stylised plant formations and the wave-like silhouette melts into a consecrated atmosphere. Schiele, however, broke with the beautiful cult of organic "Jugendstil" ornamental art. Schiele effectively annihilates the buffer of distance created by conventional notions of decorum or traditional concepts of "the nude."

One Contemplated in Dreams

1911
Watercolour and pencil, 48 x 32 cm
The Metropolitan Museum of Art, New York

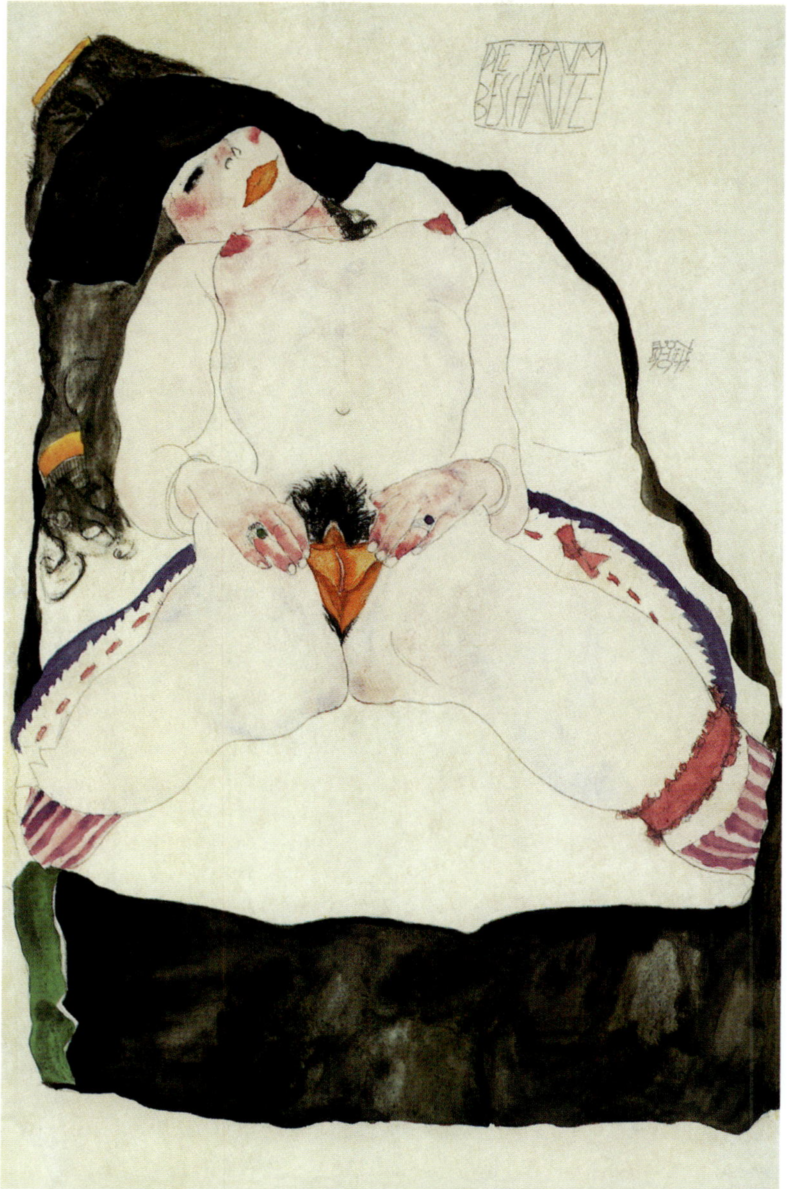
DIE TRAUM
BESCHAUTE

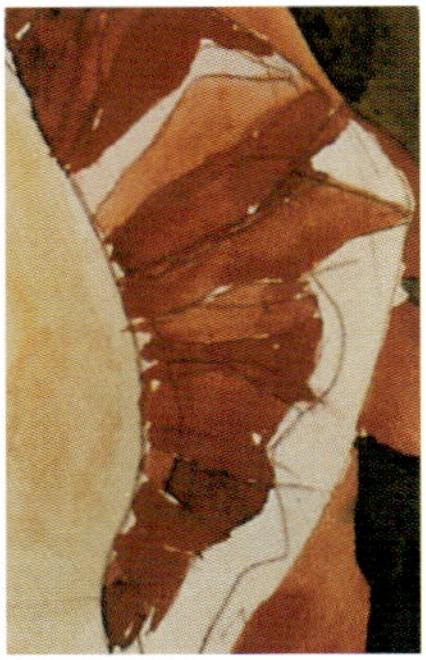

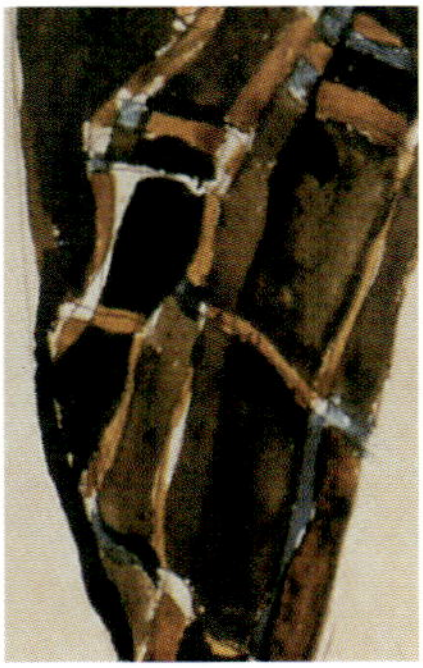

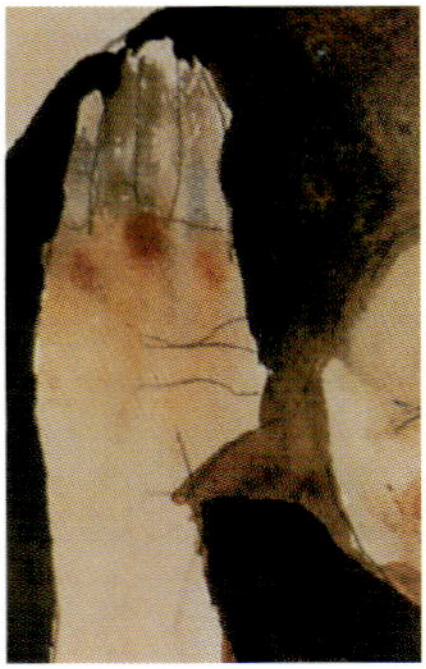

It is here, where Klimt offended the authorities in various episodes, namely in violating modesty, that Schiele found his main objective. He bared his models of every decorative accessory and concentrated solely on their bodies. Yet, in contrast to the academic nude drawings, which mainly limited themselves to a neutral portrayal of anatomy, Schiele showed erotically aroused bodies. He knew of the erogenous function that charms the eye and sets erotic signals with red painted lips, fleshy labia and dark moon circles under the eyes. The *One Contemplated in Dreams* (*Die Traumbeschaute*, 1911) opens her vulva.

Two Girls (Lovers)

1911
Gouache, watercolour and pencil, 48.3 x 30.5 cm
Private collection

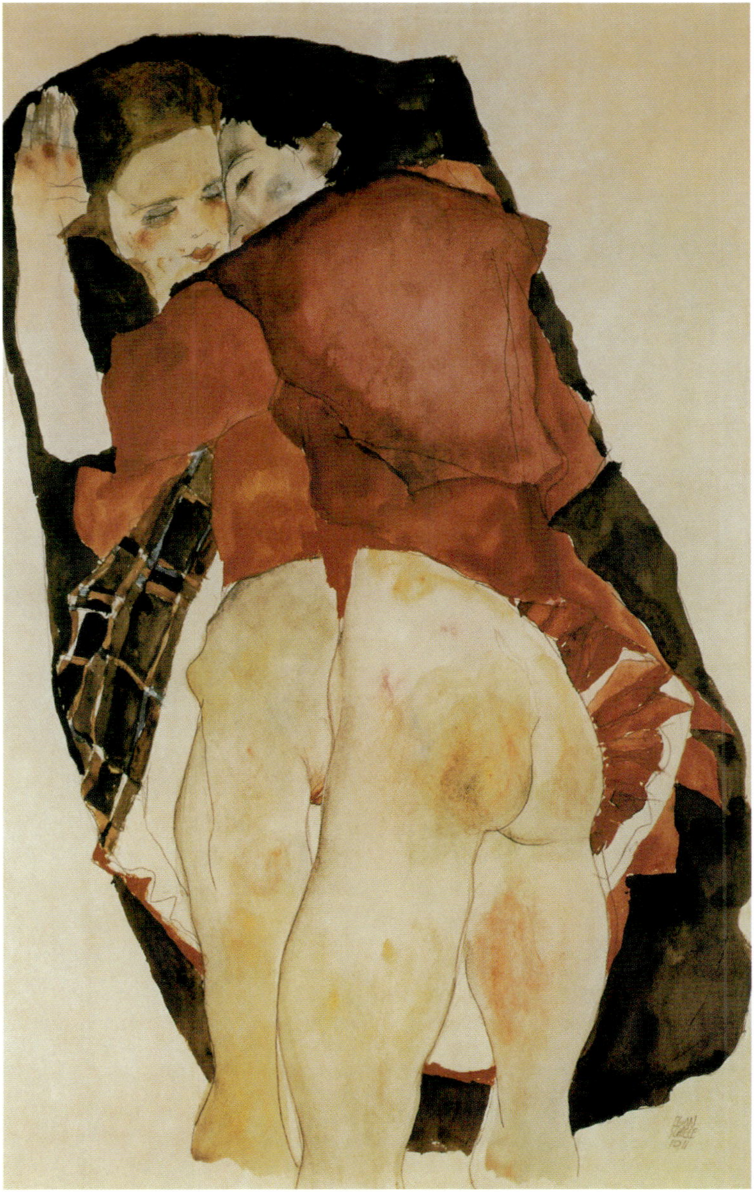

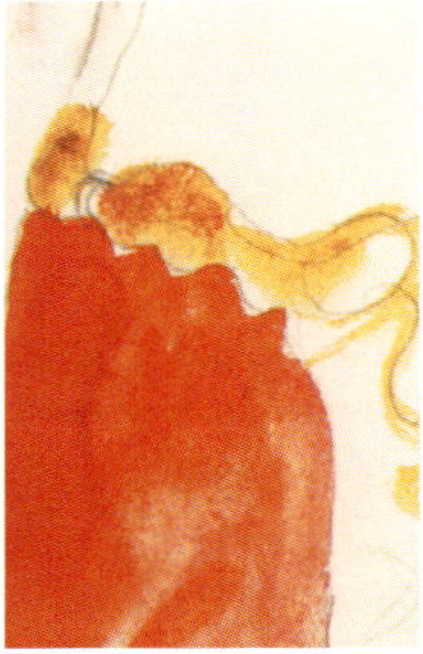

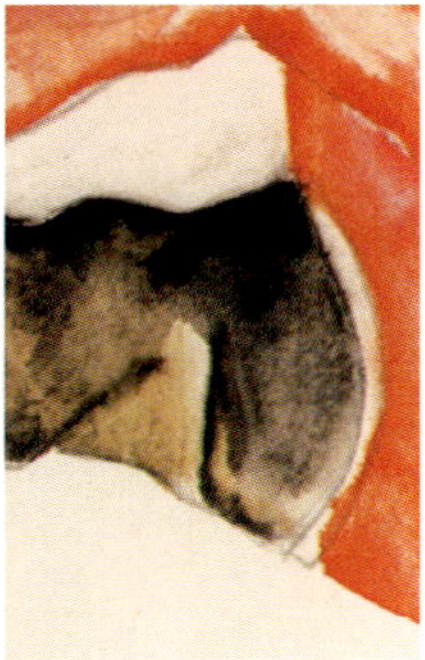

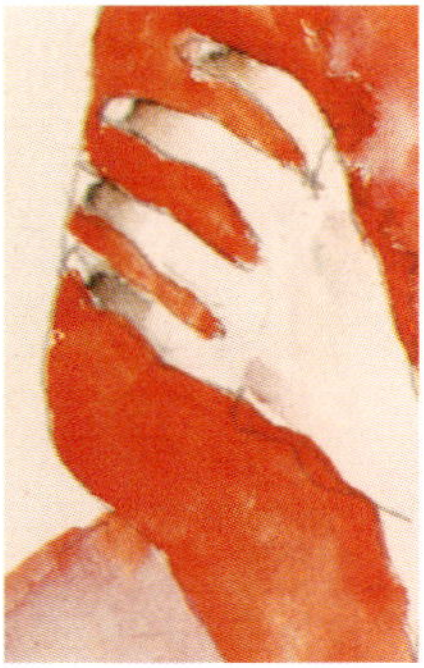

Moreover, drawings served Klimt as preliminary studies for his paintings. In contrast, Schiele signs his watercolour sketches as finalised works of art. It is precisely the sketch-like, unfinished product that characterised Schiele, who unfolded the art process even in his oil paintings. In contrast to the ornamental surface decoration of art nouveau painting, his sharp line executions and jagged aggressive style suggest the artist's subjective guiding hand. With a few lines, Schiele sketched the outlines of the body on paper. A thigh is reduced to two lines. The stroke is dynamic, grows fainter,

Seated Little Girl

1911
Watercolour and pencil, 46.5 x 31.8 cm
Bayerische Staatsgemäldesammlungen, Munich

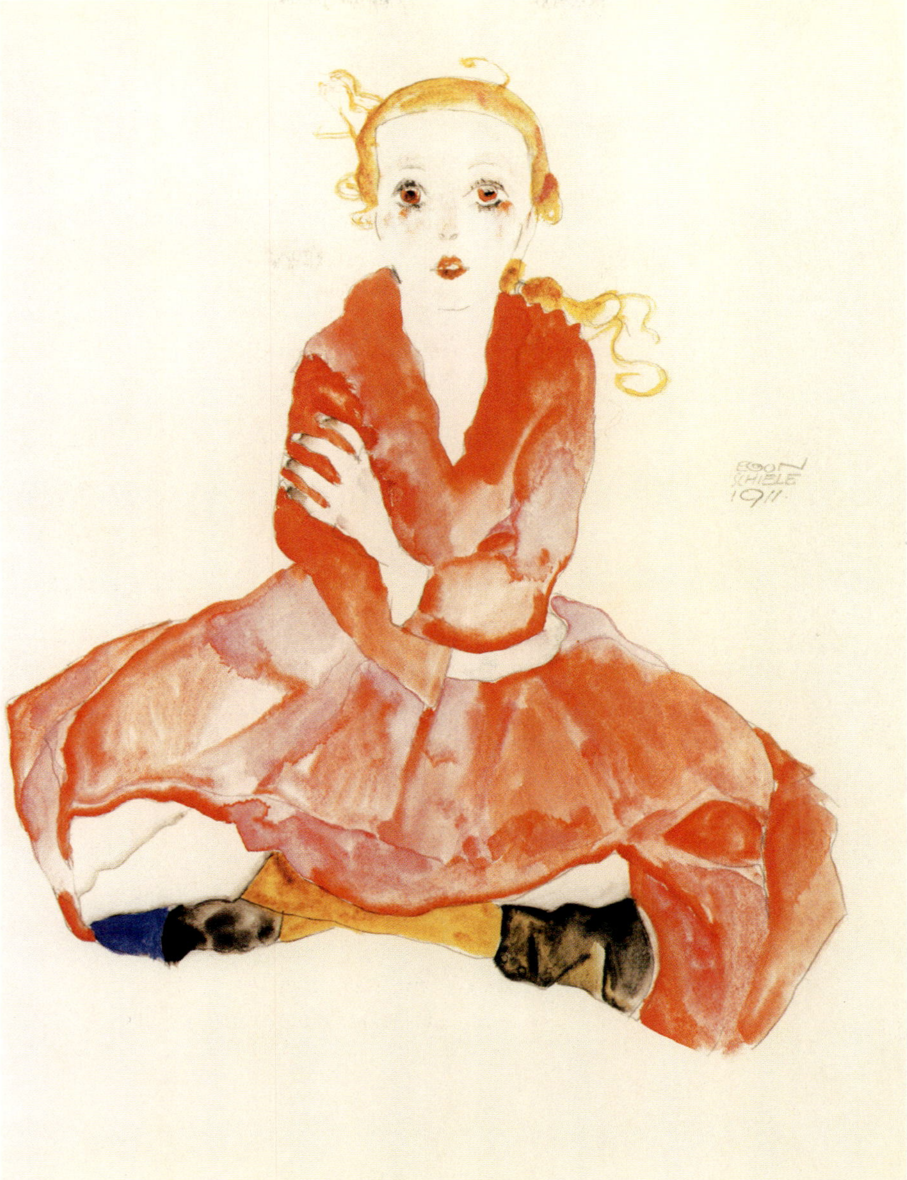
EGON
SCHIELE
1911.

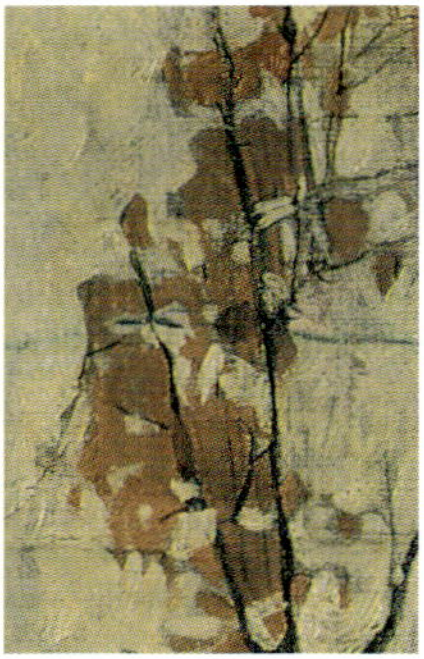

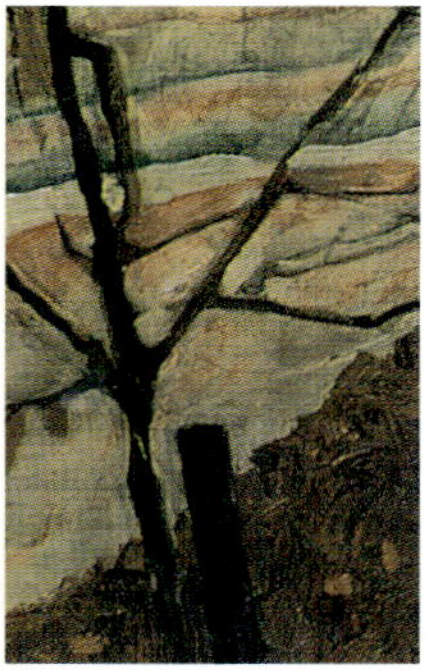

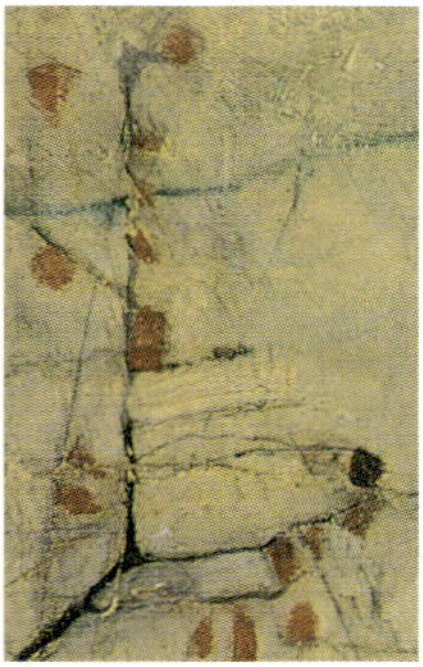

following the structural ductility of a fast thrown-in movement. Jagged, with hard angles he loves the bone structure. Schiele's strokes are like calligraphy, which captures the body's expression in just a few lines. In contrast to the reluctant, bony aspect of the shoulders and pelvis is the round diffraction of the chest. Orange nipples and vulva become wounds. The physiognomy of his models, however, remains anonymously phantom-like; the button eyes could sooner belong to a doll, which could be any woman. The body posture is directed at the gaze of the viewer, before whom she exhibits her genitals.

Autumn Trees

1911
Oil on canvas, 79.5 x 80 cm
Private collection

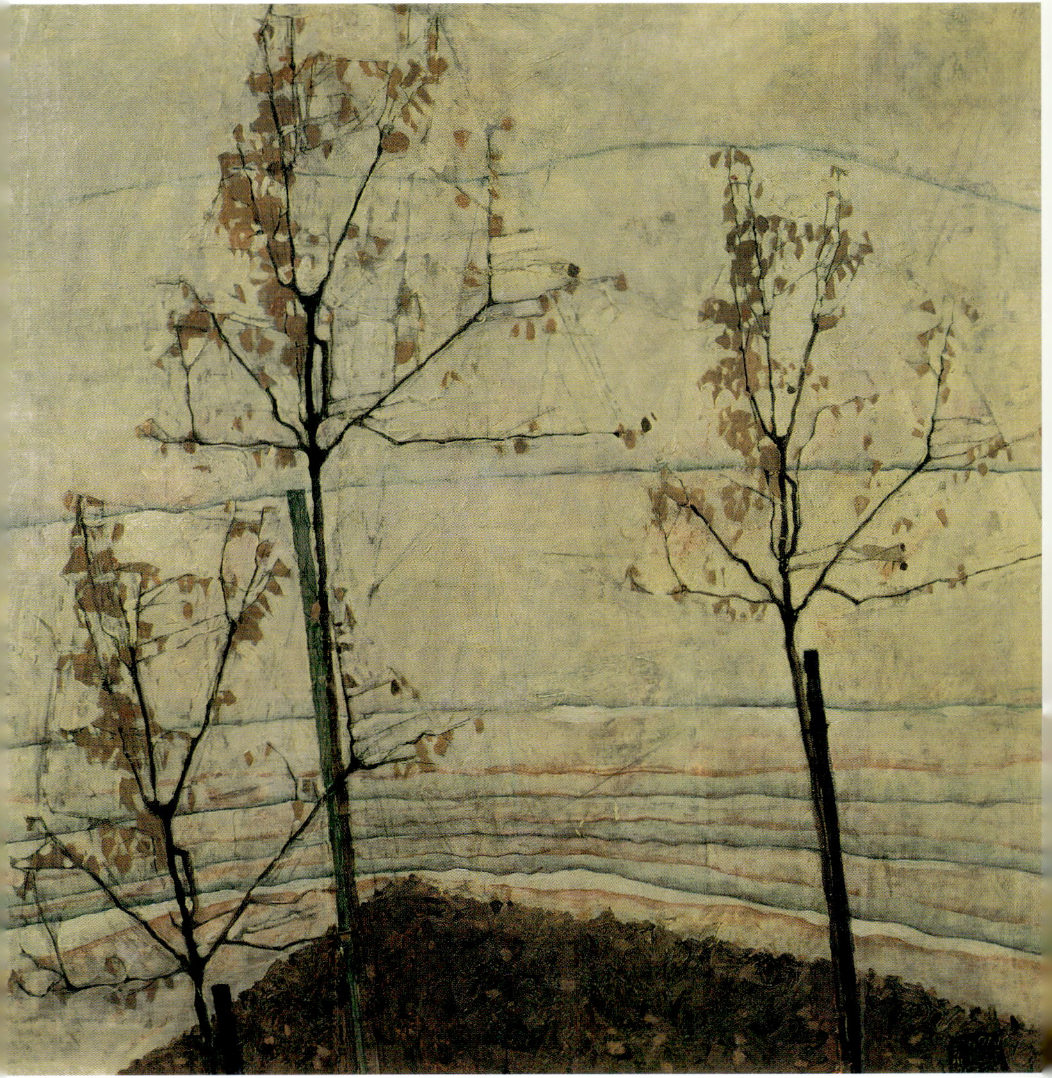

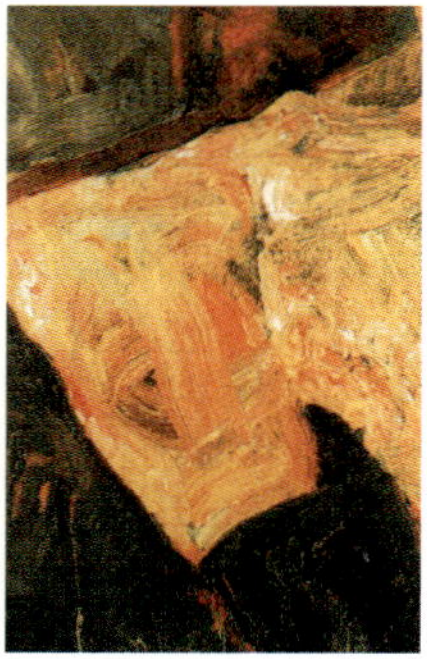

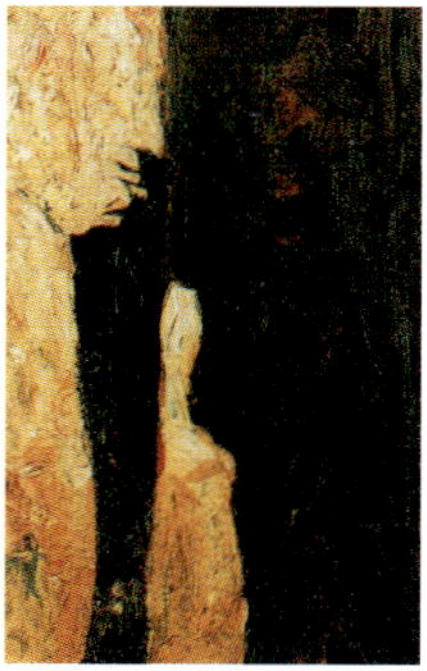

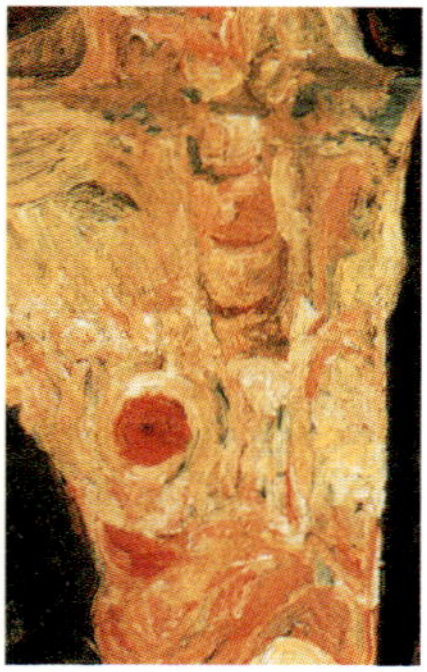

Female Nude is a work on paper from 1910. The sure fluidity of Schiele's line, in thick black crayon, is amplified by the opaque white 'halo' around the figure. Schiele used this technique in several works of the period. It has the effect of enhancing the presence of the figure by underlining its isolation in space. The woman reclines, her half-closed eyes suggesting drowsiness, intoxication or even death. Schiele's figures often seem stripped of more than just their clothes (some critics likened his nudes to skinned rabbits) and here,

Prophets (Double Self-Portrait)

1911
Oil on canvas, 110.3 x 45.3 cm
Staatsgalerie, Stuttgart

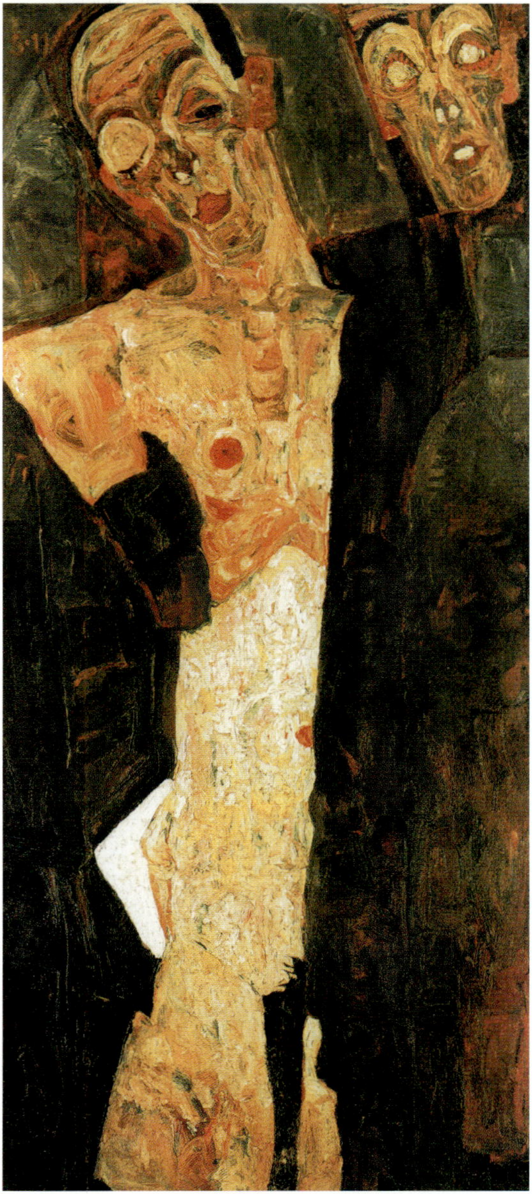

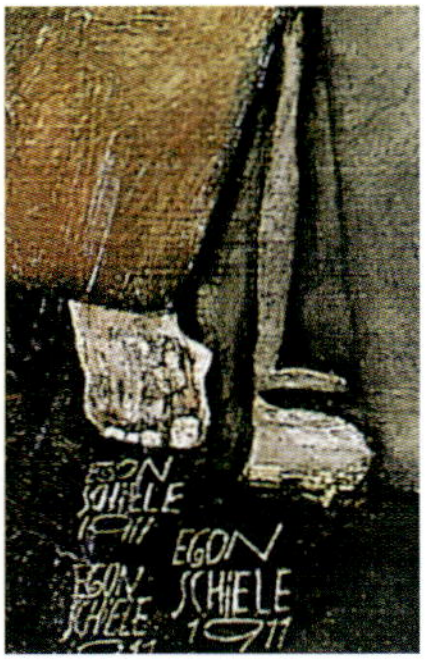

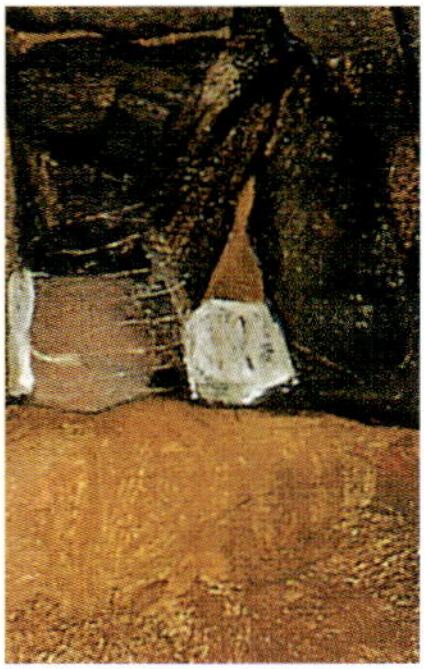

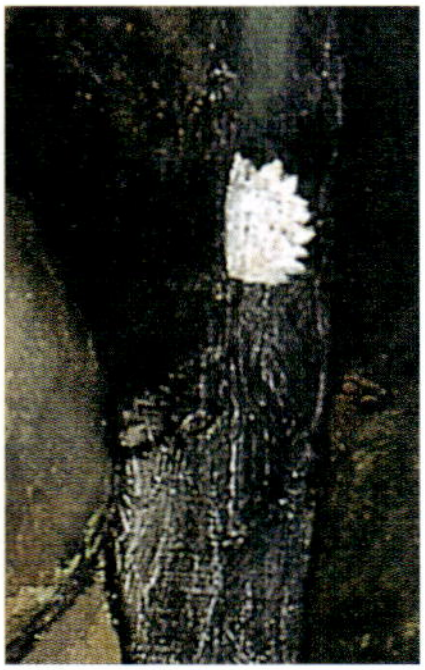

the eye-sockets and nose cavity of the skull beneath the woman's skin are finely traced, reminding us of her underlying mortal structure. This work also demonstrates Schiele's assured confidence in the power of his line to convey the whole in paraphrase; both of the girl's legs 'end' where her stockings begin, and her arms are lacking altogether and yet none of the tangibility of the form is lost. Schiele's work often treads a fine line between the beautiful and the grotesque. Here, the sensuous curves of the woman's belly and hips are invaded by a gnarled hand.

Procession

1911
Oil on canvas, 100 x 100.5 cm
Serge Sabarsky Collection, New York

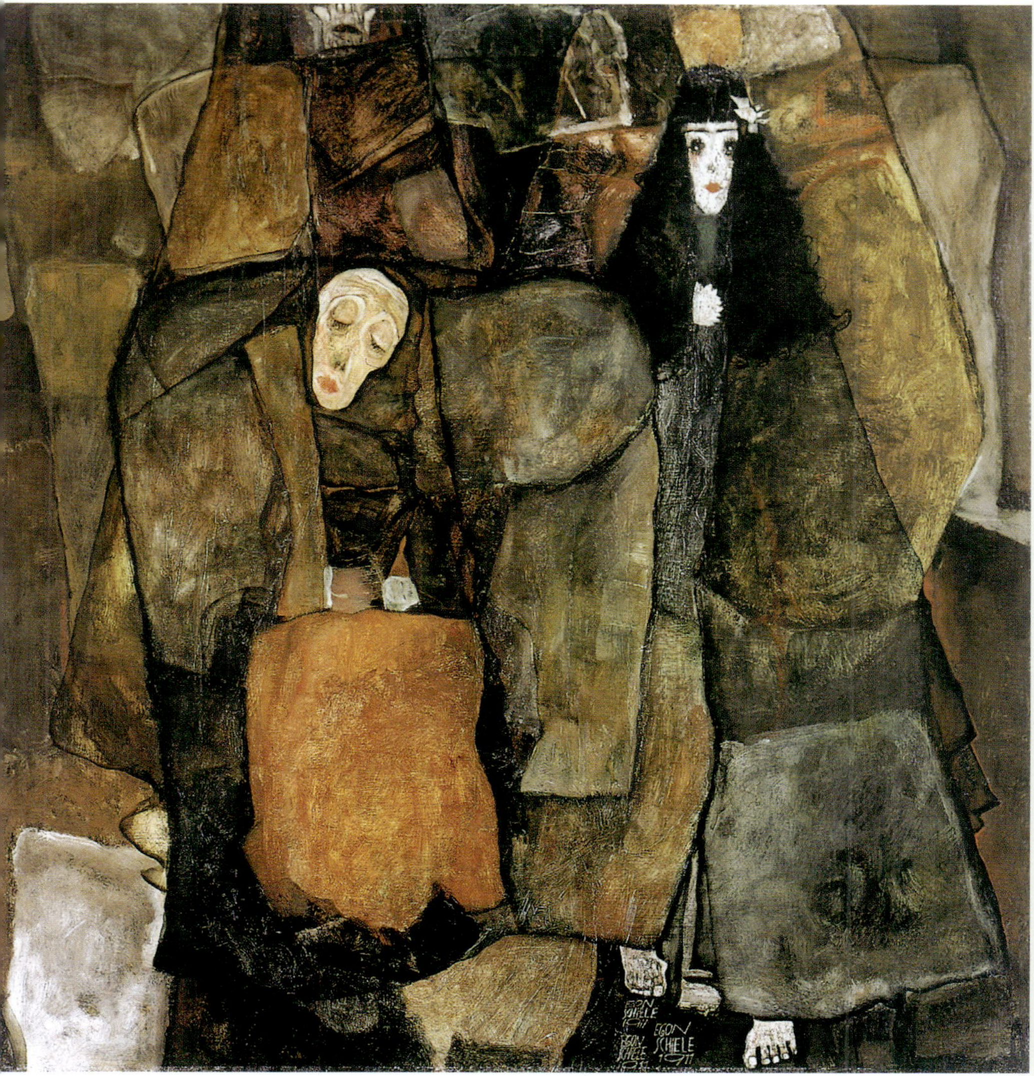
EGON SCHIELE 1911

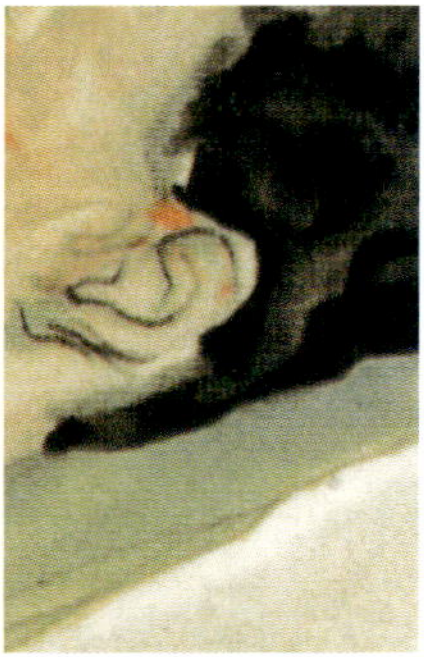

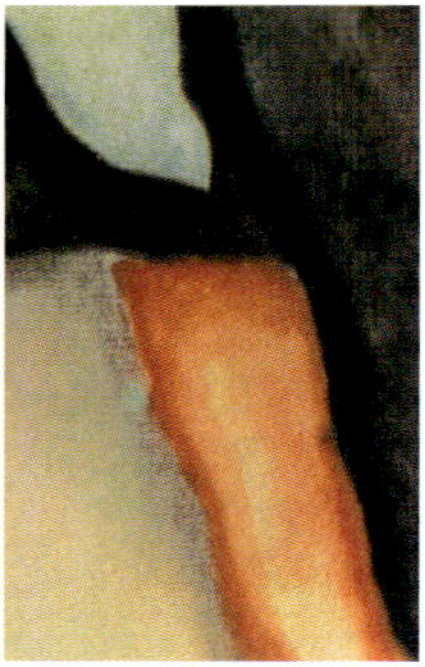

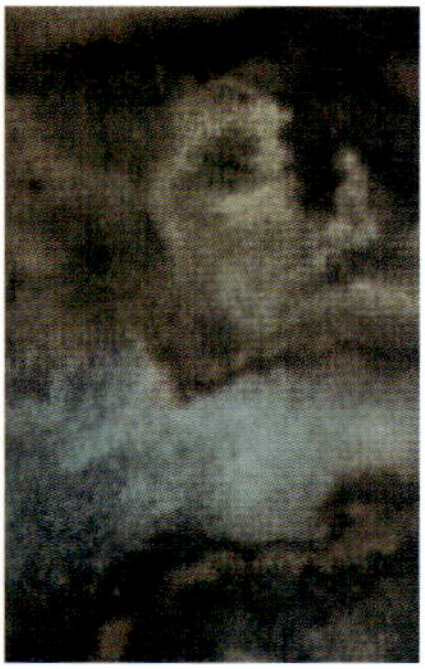

In fact, hands in Schiele's work are almost always exaggeratedly long and bony, and the lack of arm connecting the hand to the woman's body is entirely in keeping with the skilful economy of Schiele's drawing. Nonetheless, the slight ambiguity that these kinds of ruptures introduce (whose hand is this?) is compelling.

If usually the contour line captures the physical presence and becomes a sculpture-like containment within space, Schiele dispensed with every spatiotemporal specification. The fluid lines and the sketched curves dramatically remodel the perspective of the subject.

The Artist's Mother, Sleeping

1911
Watercolour and pencil, 45 x 31.6 cm
Albertina, Vienna

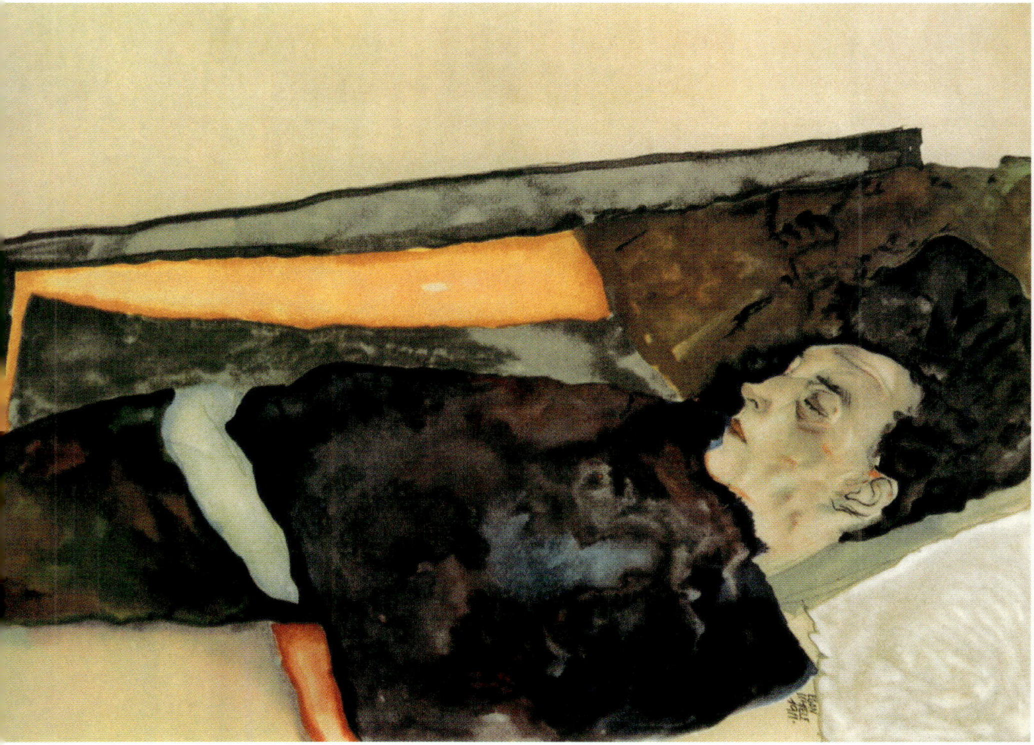

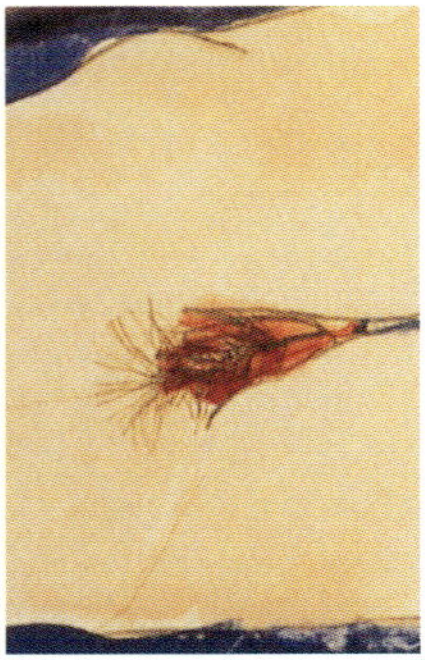

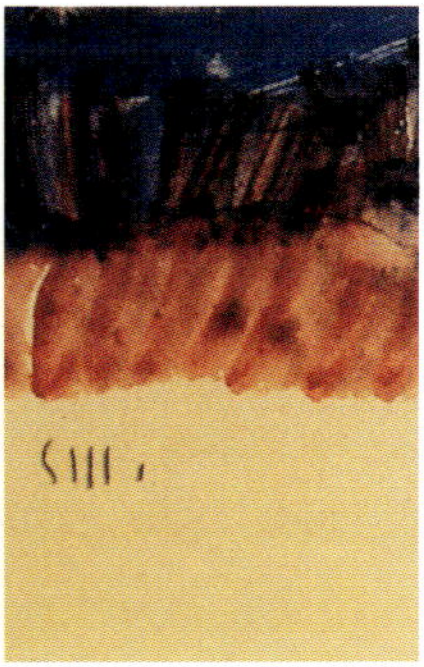

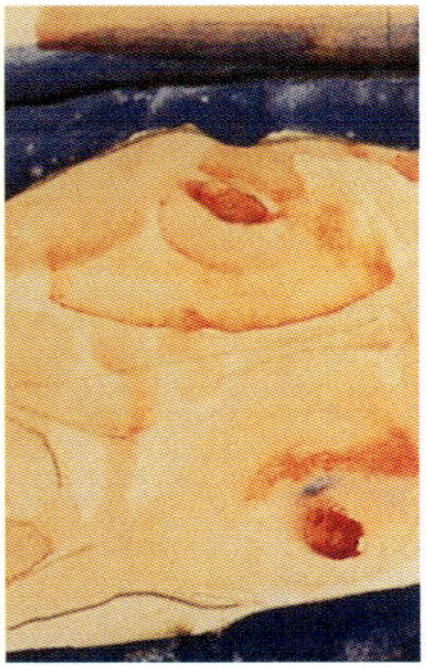

Schiele ignored light and shadow effects which model the body, dispensed with shadow strokes and divests the character of all spatial containment. In his atelier, he often worked on a ladder from where he captured his models from a bird's eye view perspective in an extreme visual angle of under and oversight. This calls to mind one of his verses: "An intimate bird sits in a leafy tree, he is dull coloured, hardly moves and does not sing; his eyes reflect a thousand greens." He isolated the creatures in his view, set them in a world without time or place. Bodies form space.

Reclining Nude with Black Stockings

1911
Watercolour and pencil, 22.9 x 43.5 cm
Private collection

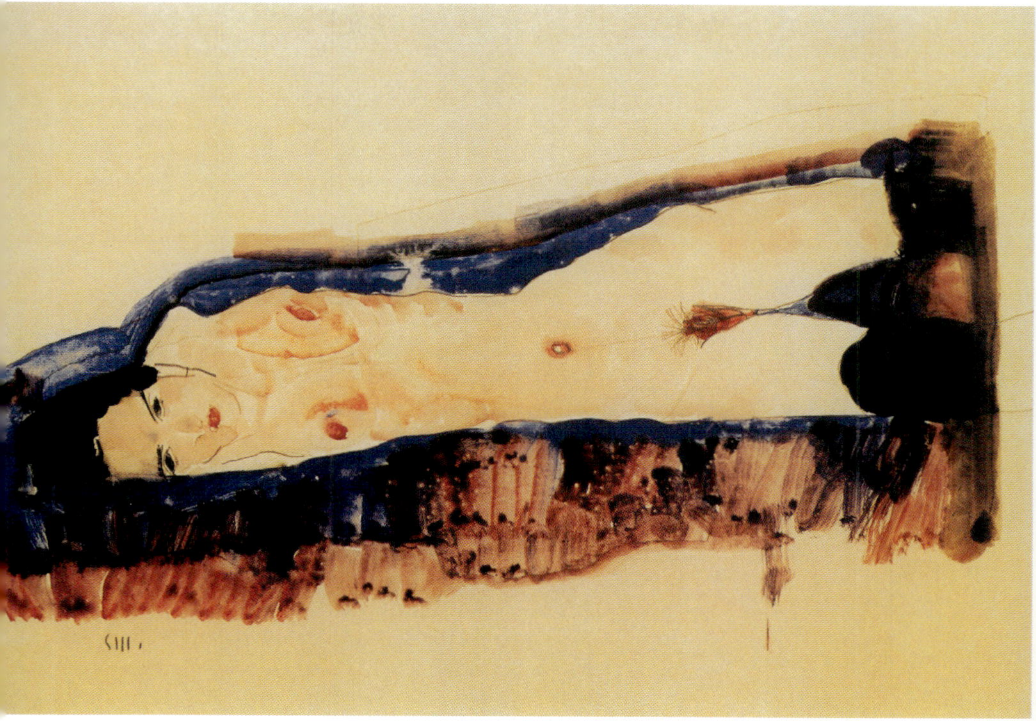

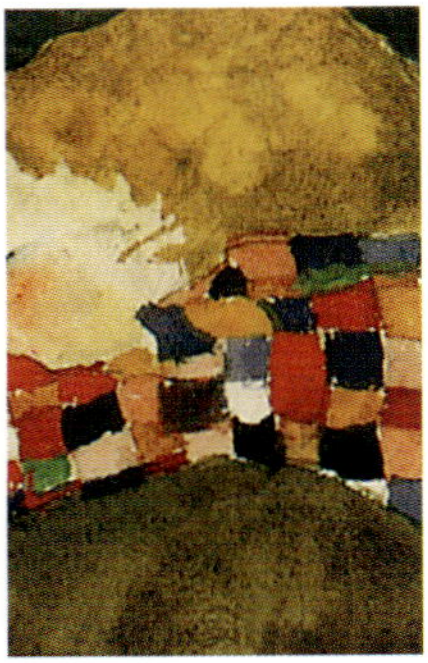

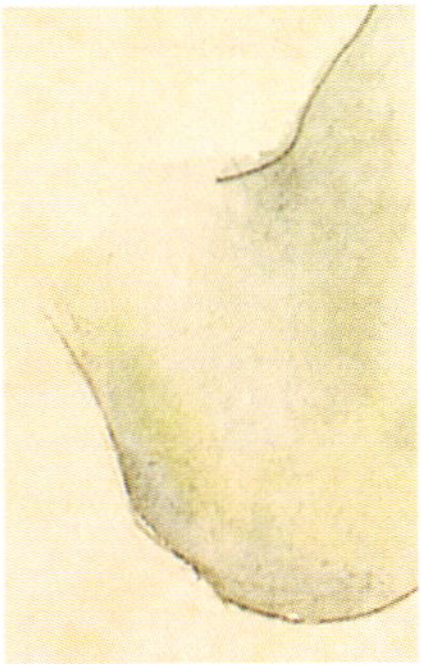

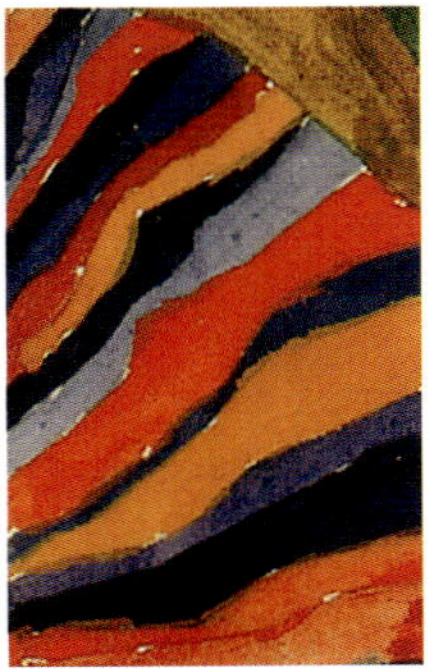

An example of the spatial lack of orientation of his subjects is the commissioned artwork for Friederike Maria Beer (1914), the fashion conscious daughter of a cabaret proprietor who actively followed Viennese art events. On Schiele's suggestion, she allowed her full body likeness to be painted on the ceiling. It shows her in a colourful patterned dress in a rigid pose, her body strangely floating, free of all gravitational pull, her raised arms with the indefinable hand gesture call to mind Schiele's self-portraits once again.

Reclining Semi-Nude

1911
Pencil, watercolour and gouache on paper
47.9 x 31.4 cm
Private collection

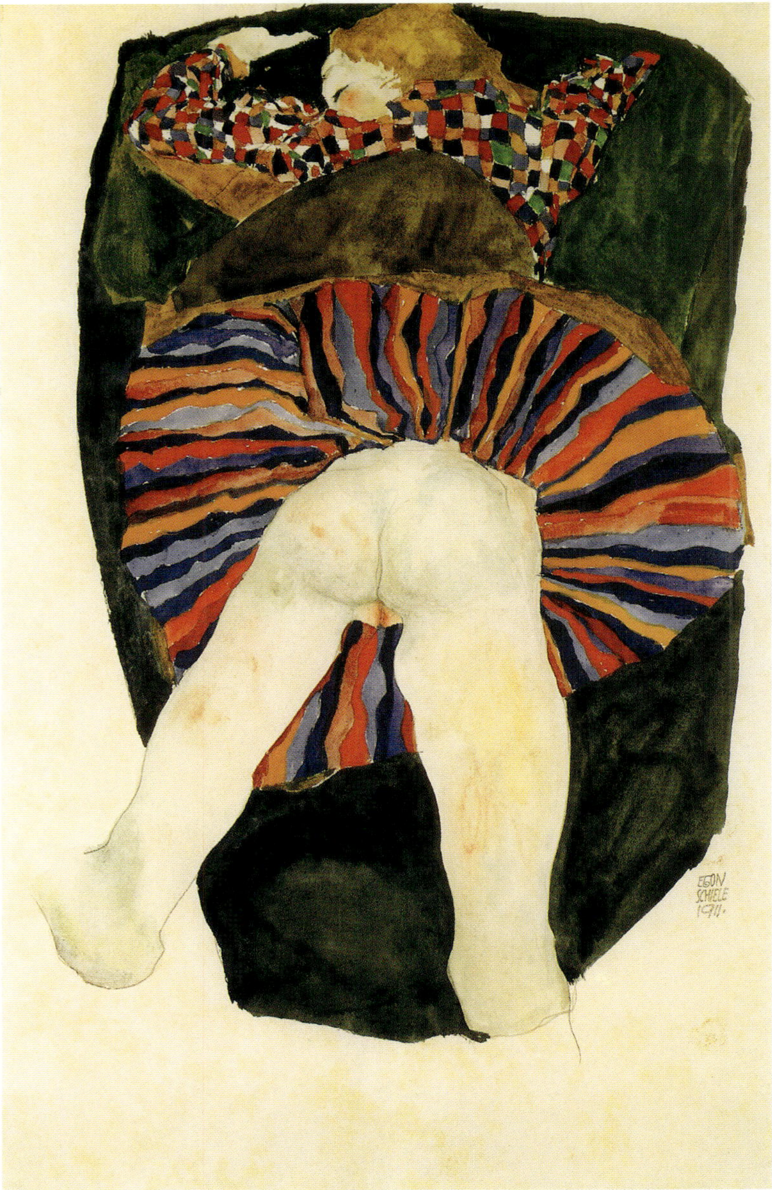
EGON
SCHIELE
1911.

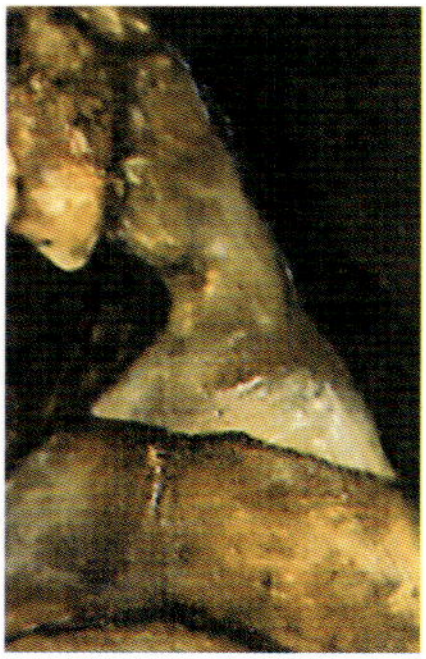

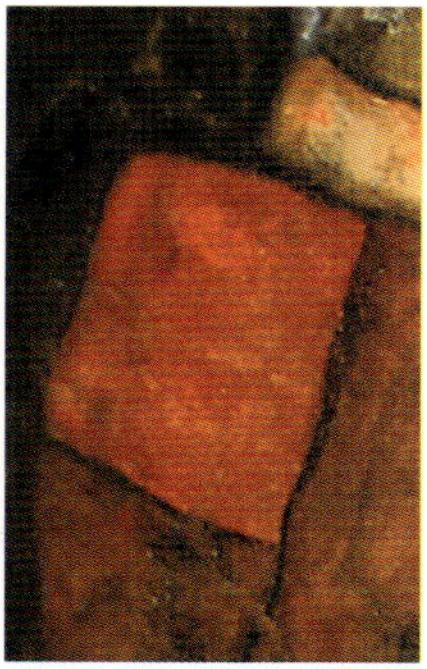

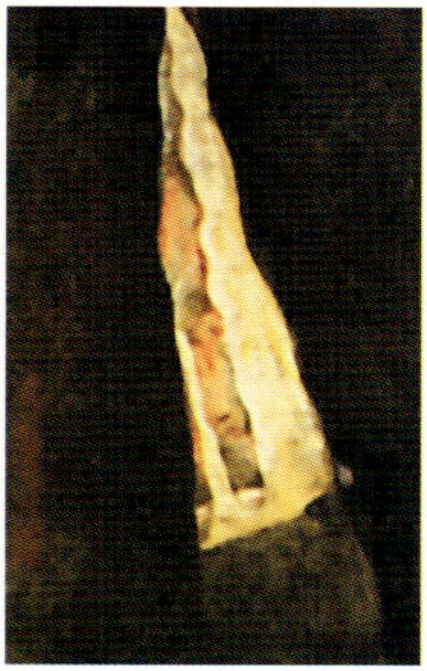

Like a person regarding himself in a mirror, only seeing his face and body, like a lover who, within the body of his love, forgets the world around him, Schiele created his self-portraits before a mirror too, as well as some of his female nude drawings. *Schiele, Drawing a Nude Model in front of a Mirror* illustrates this (1910). The scene is illuminating, the duplication of frontal and rear views of the nude woman are revealed in the reflection, however, there, where the mirror is, stands the viewer. He functions as the mirror in which the model regards herself, reassuring herself of her body, and in whose gaze it moves.

Pregnant Woman and Death
(Mother and Death)

1911
Oil on canvas, 100.3 x 100 cm
Národní Galerie, Prague

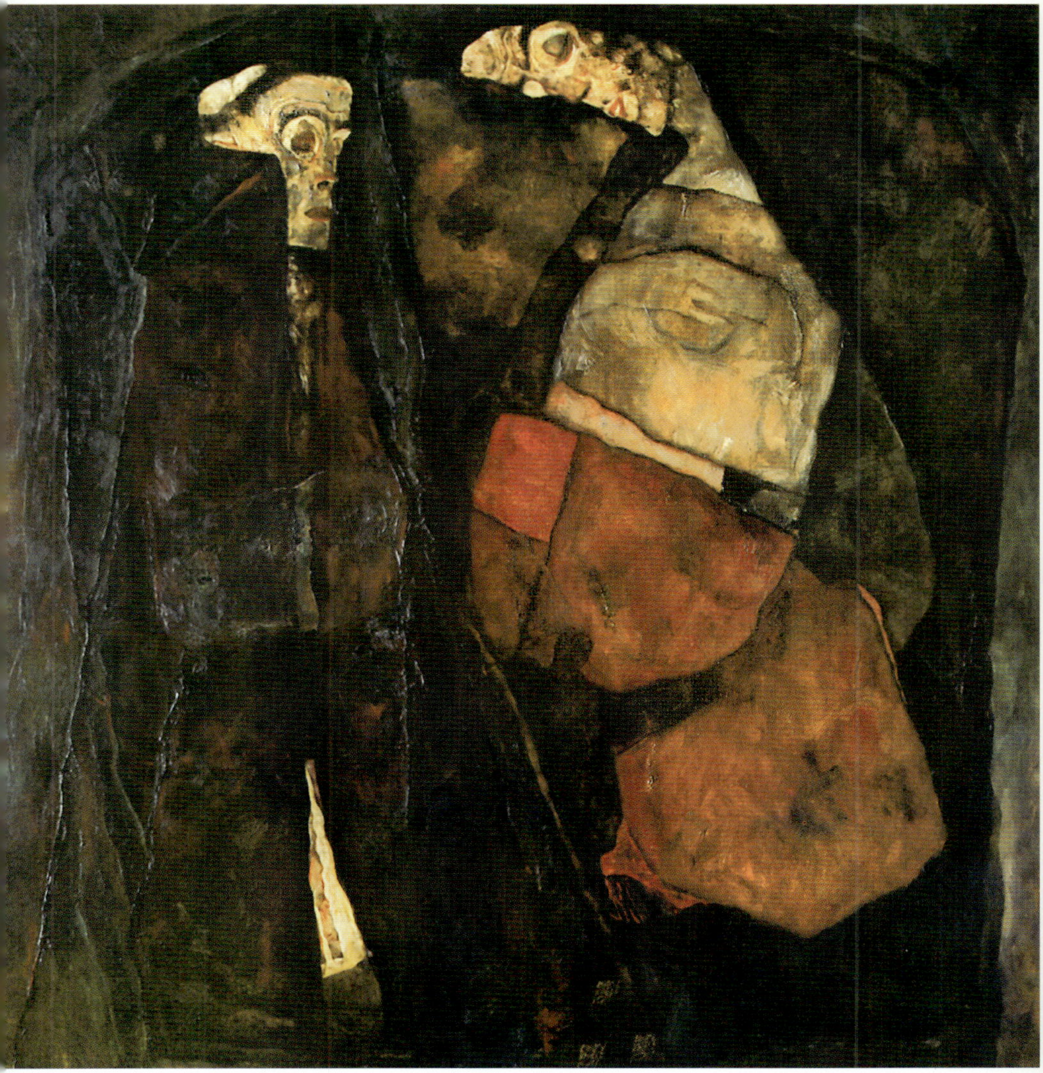

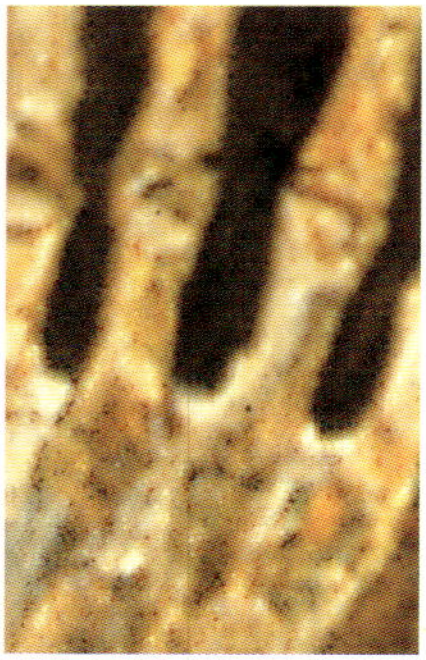
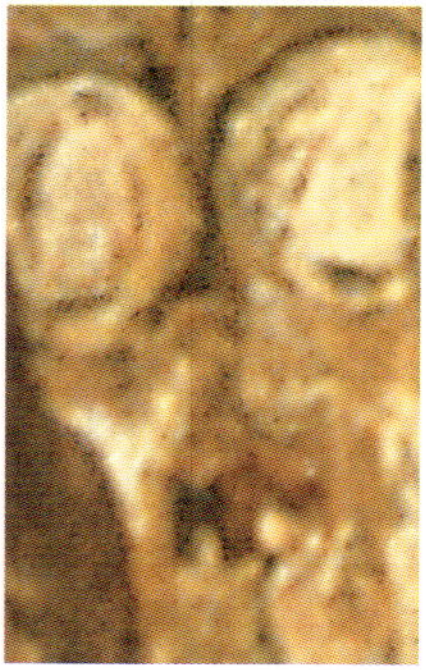
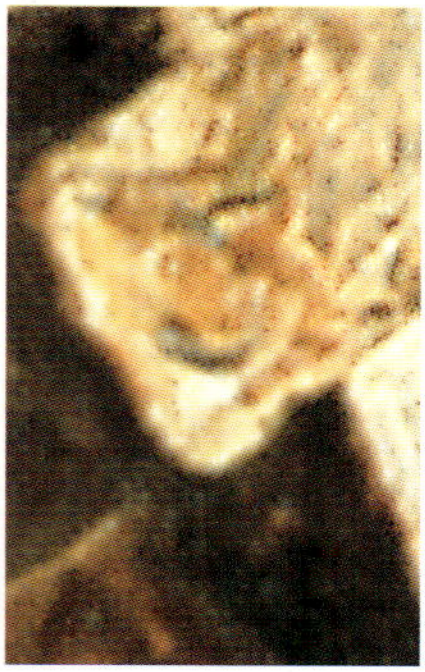

The intimacy between painter and model is countered in relationship to viewer and drawing.

First Exhibitions and Schiele's Radicalism

In 1908, Schiele took part in a public exhibition in the imperial hall of the Klosterneuburg Monastery for the first time. He exhibited small-scale landscapes which he had painted from summer through to the autumn. *Sunflower I*, from the same year, illustrates to a certain extent a link beetween his landscapes and his human subjects.

The Self-Seer II (Death and the Man)

1911
Oil on canvas, 80 x 80 cm
Private collection, Vienna

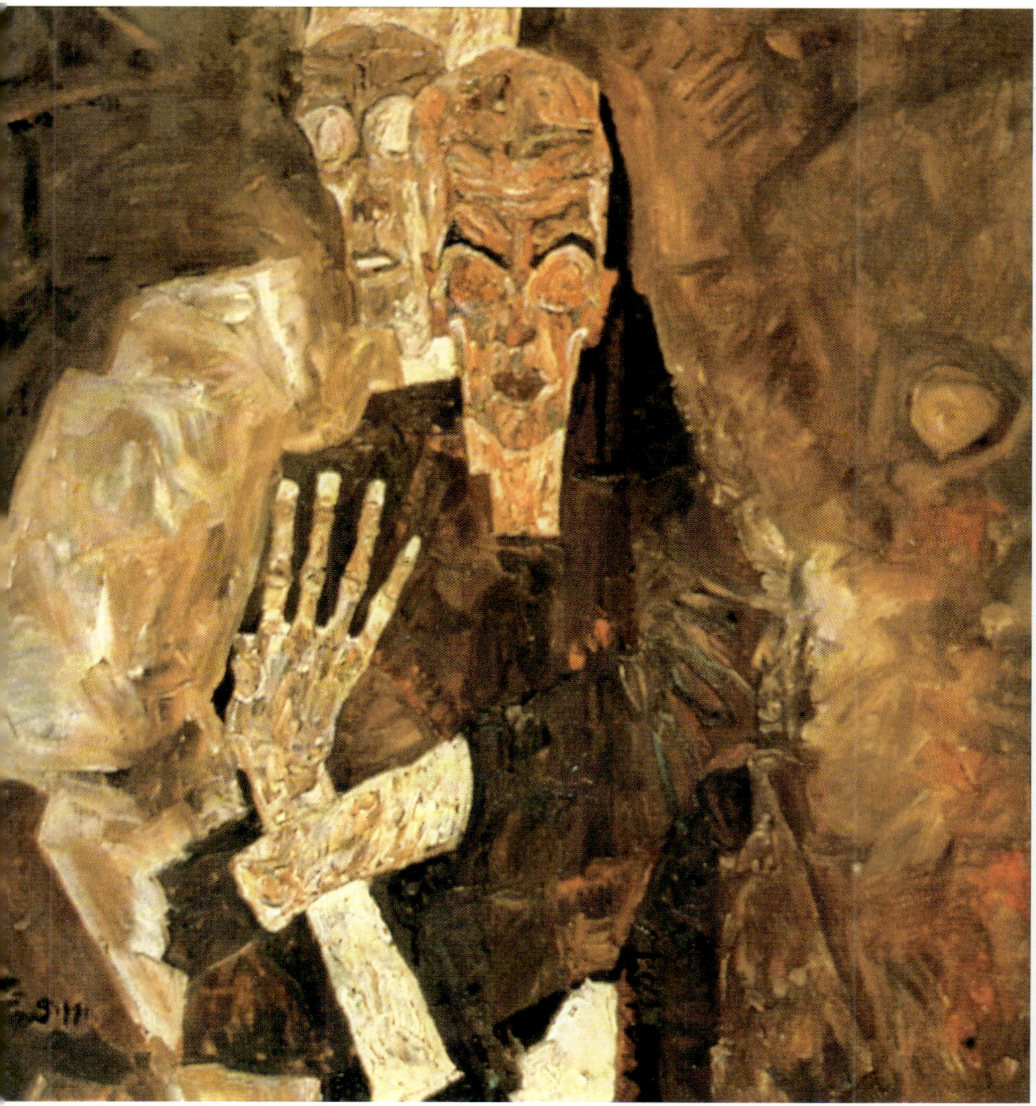

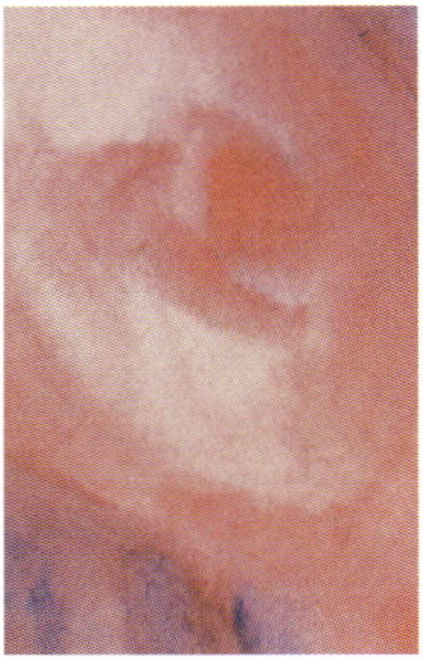

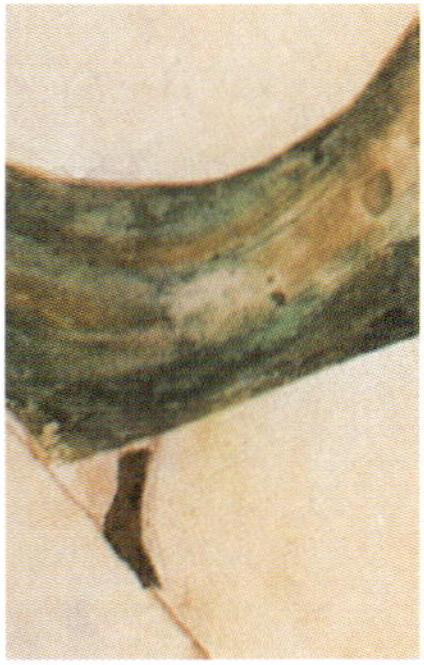

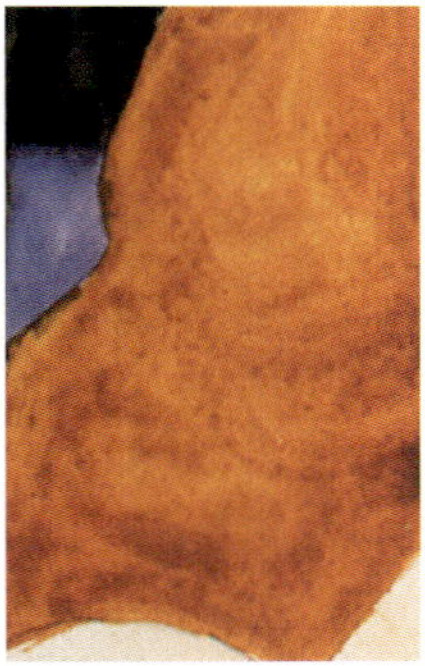

Schiele was never primarily interested in the actual replication of appearance and this is particularly noticeable in his successive portrayals of sunflowers. Schiele would have been very familiar with this theme which had, of course, already been much explored by Van Gogh and this is the first known image in this particular series. It is certainly derivative of the Secession's decorative tradition but adds something personal and distinctive. The entire top plane of the canvas is taken up by the bloom and, despite its ripeness and bounteous colour, the sunflower is also on the verge of death.

Three Girls

1911
Watercolour and pencil, 48 x 31.5 cm
Private collection

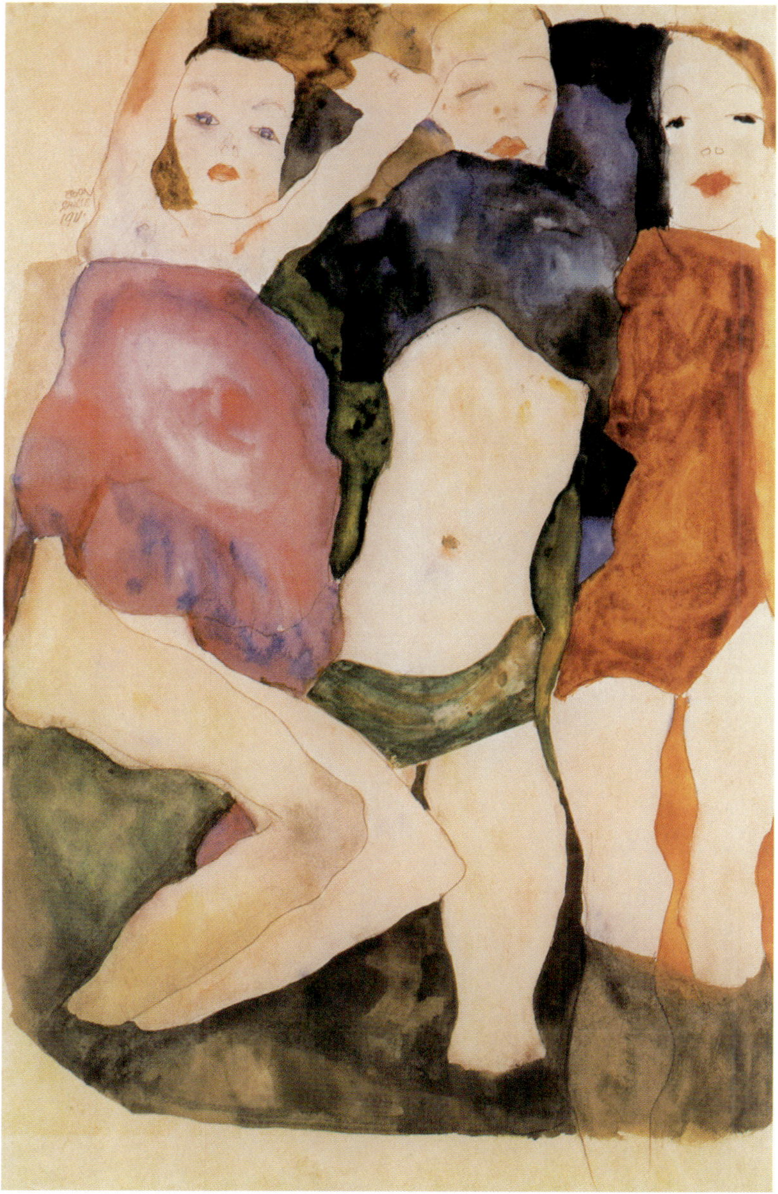

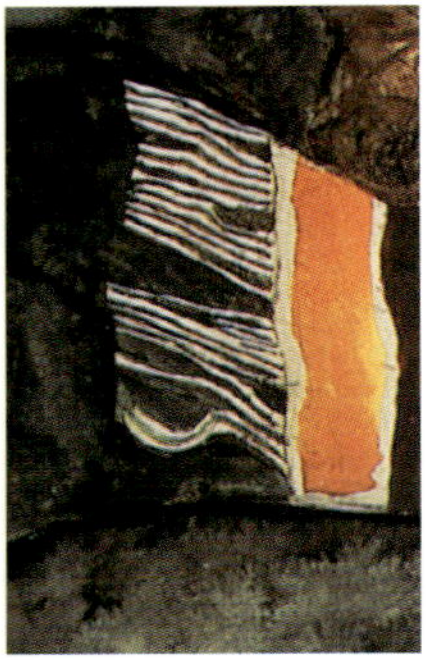

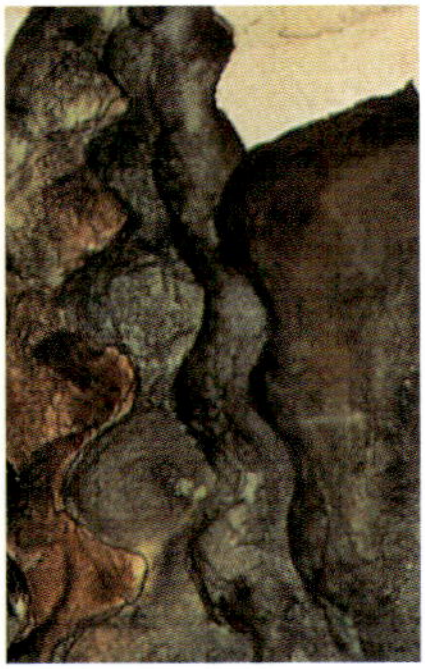

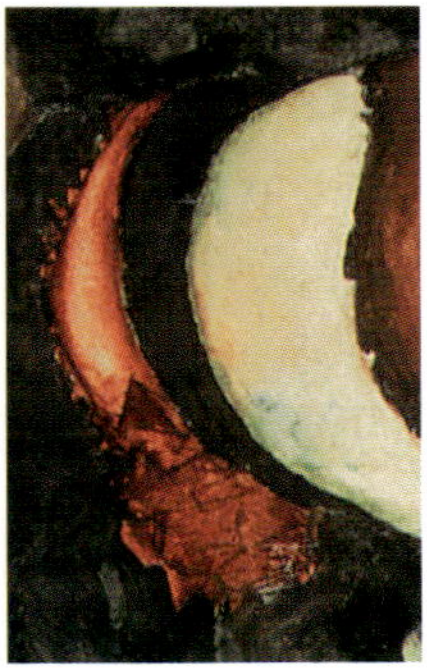

While the flower and the presence of the seeds, therefore, suggest youth and energy the implication is that life follows death which, in its turn, follows life all over again. The patterning of the line is rather obvious since the leaves suggest a horizontal plane while the stalk provides the vertical. This makes it a rather juvenile work, and one not fully achieved spatially, but already the themes that would become prevalent in his remaining oeuvre are much in evidence with a focus on cycles of life and death and distorted, unexpected proportions in the subject itself.

Two Girls on a Fringed Blanket

1911
Gouache, watercolour, ink and pencil
56 x 36.6 cm
Private collection

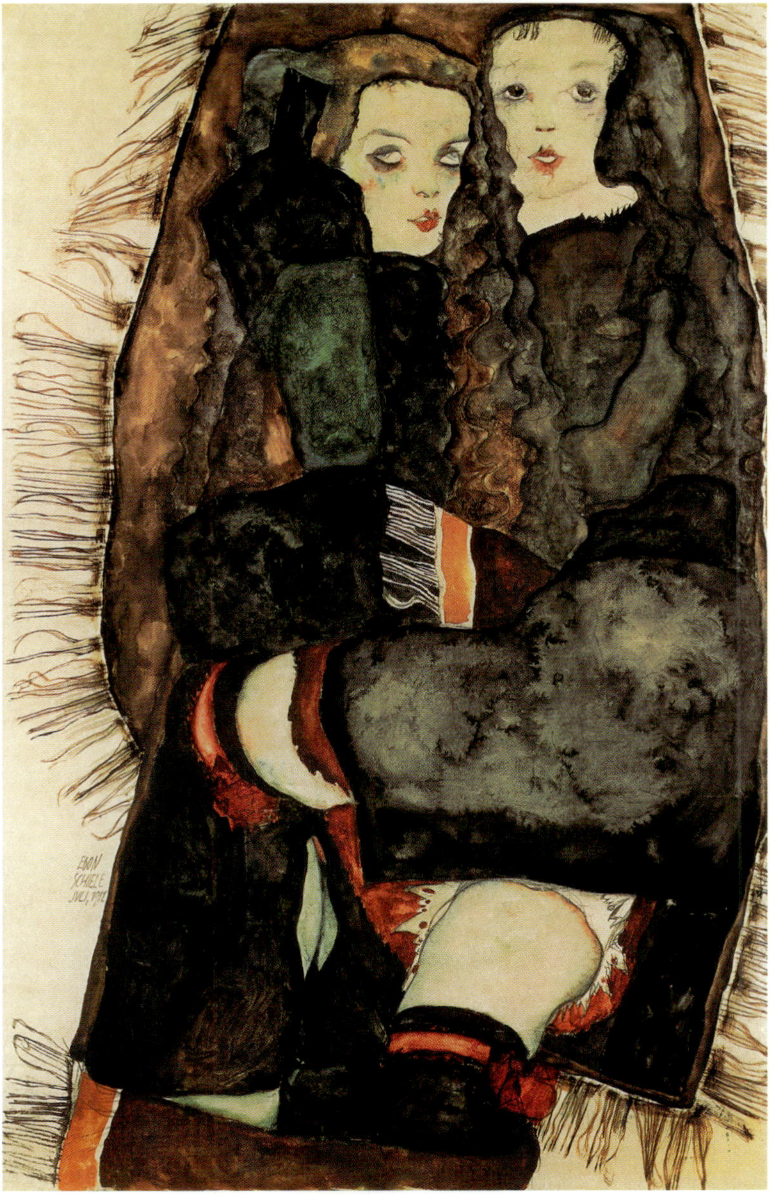
SCHIELE
JULI, 1912

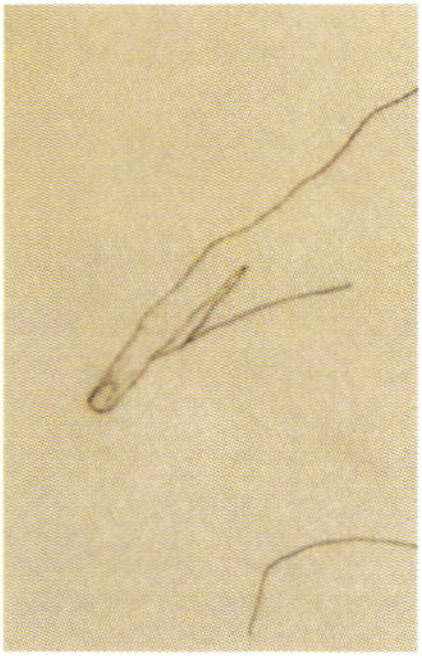

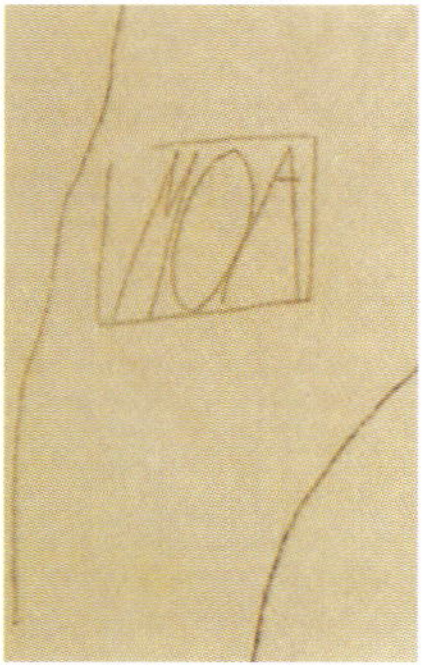

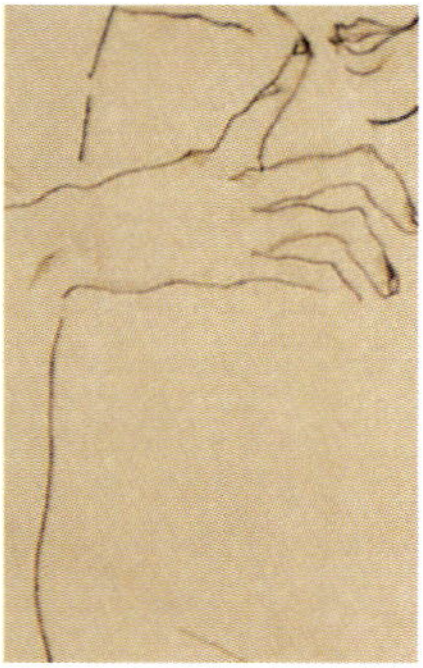

In his still lifes, as his landscapes, it is striking that even when un-peopled, the natural or man-made world of objects is invested with a psychological aspect. The image of the old town of Krumau recurs constantly in his work. It very frequently plays a dual role both as a crumbling ruin and a place teeming with young, vibrant life. His paintings of trees have been referred to as "portraits" and are most often autumnal, with all the melancholic connotations that brings.

Portrait of a Woman (The Dancer Moa)

1912
Pencil, 48.2 x 31.9 cm
Albertina, Vienna

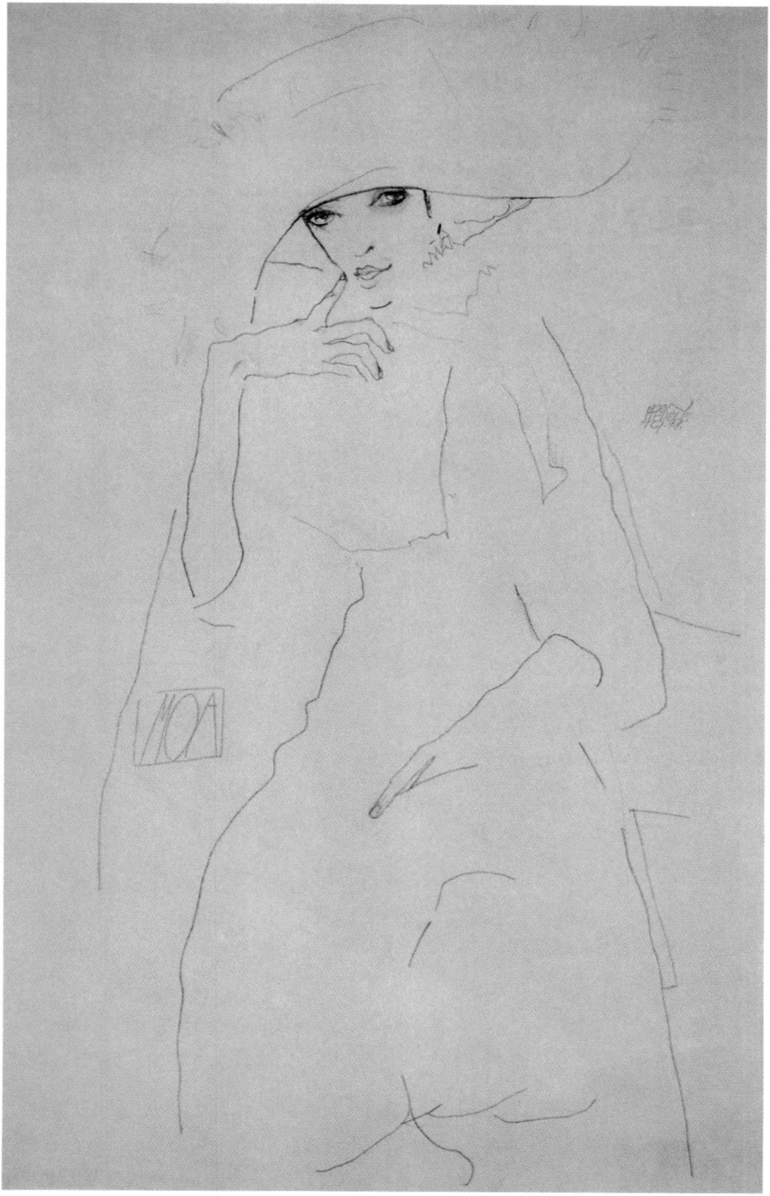
MOA

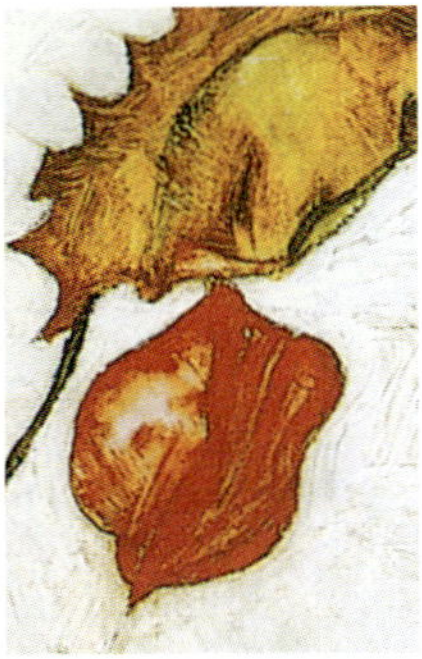

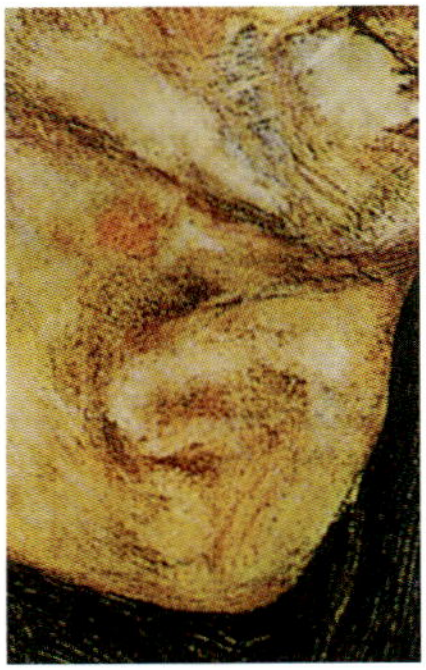

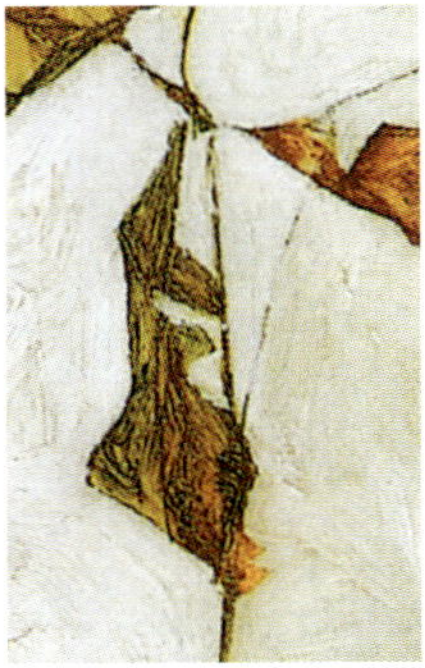

It was only in 1909 that Schiele's artistic creativity reached a great turning point. He left the academy and the reactionary professor Christian Griepenkerl, and established together with Anton Peschka, Albert Paris von Gütersloh, Anton Faistauer, Sebastian Isepp, Franz Wiegele and others from the "New Art Group" (Neukunstgruppe). The theme of the new artists was 'opposition'. Schiele's retreat from the subjective experience of the individual was a counter-reaction to Viennese historicism and its prince of painters,

Self-Portrait with Chinese Lantern Plant

1912
Oil and gouache on wood, 32.2 x 39.8 cm
Leopold Museum, Vienna

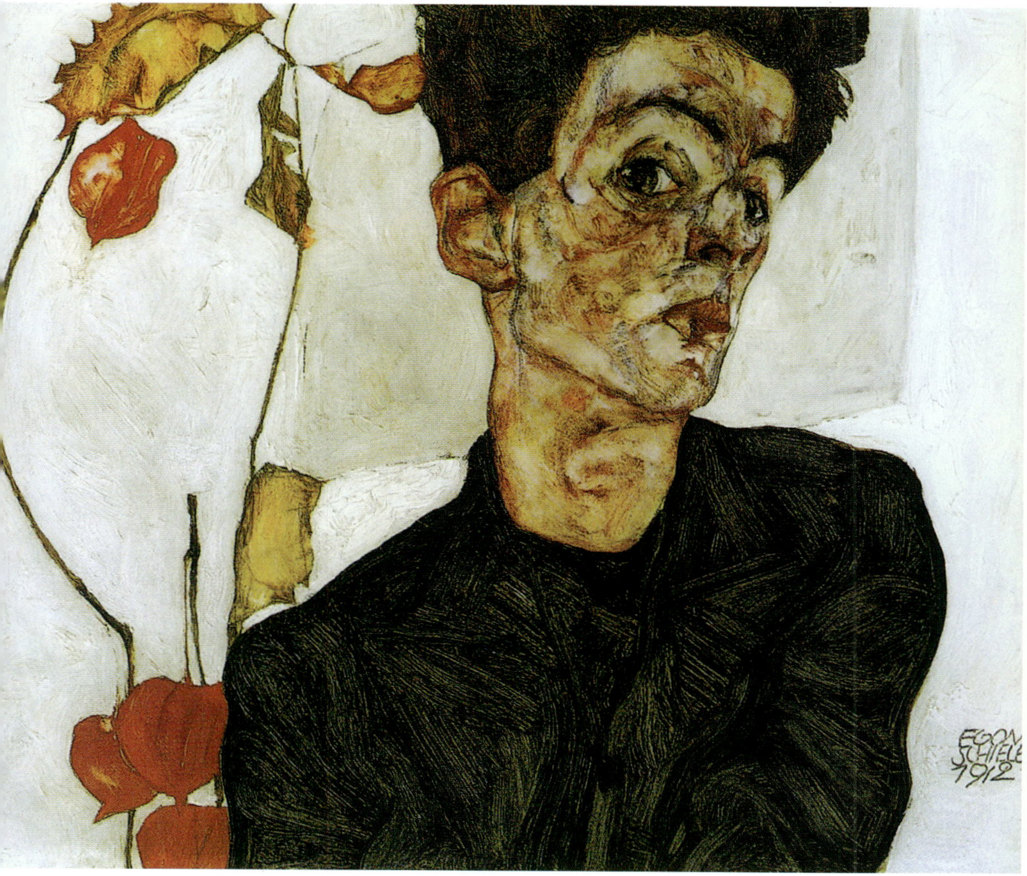
EGON
SCHIELE
1912

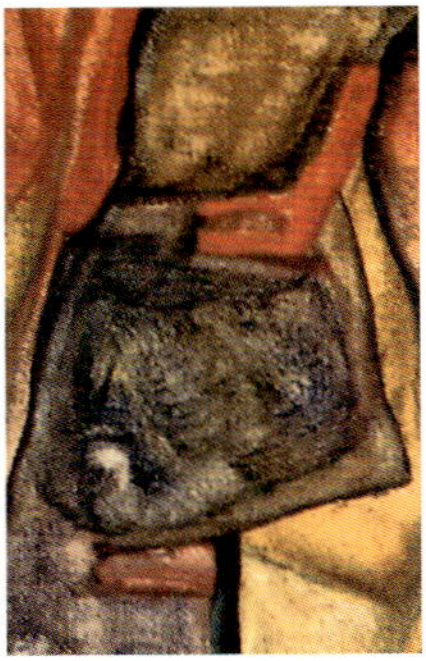

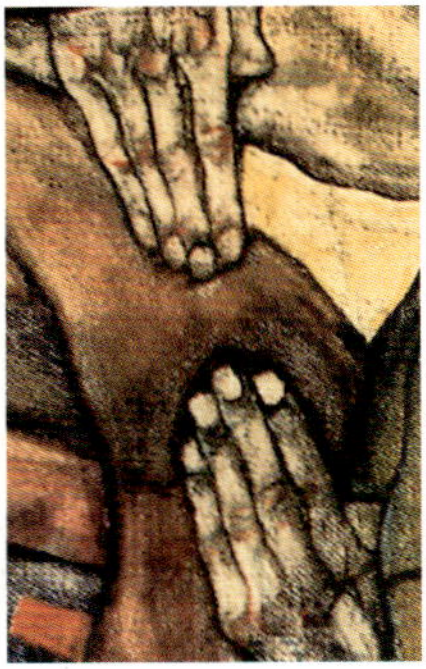

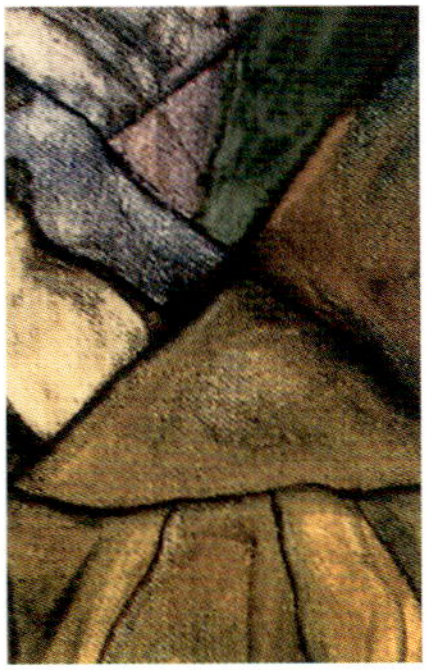

Hans Makart, who was celebrated by the government. Schiele distanced himself from their allegoric similes. He turned Catholicism's conventional values upside down and placed them in the service of sexuality. His strategy: he wanted to shock. In the painting provocatively titled *The Red Communion Wafer*, Schiele reclines on his back in an orange shirt with his abdomen bared, his spread legs suggesting the feminine gesture of submission, while before him, gazing at the viewer, a nude strawberry-blonde holds his enormous phallus.

Death Pangs (Agony)

1912
Oil on canvas, 70 x 80 cm
Bayerische Staatsgemäldesammlungen, Munich

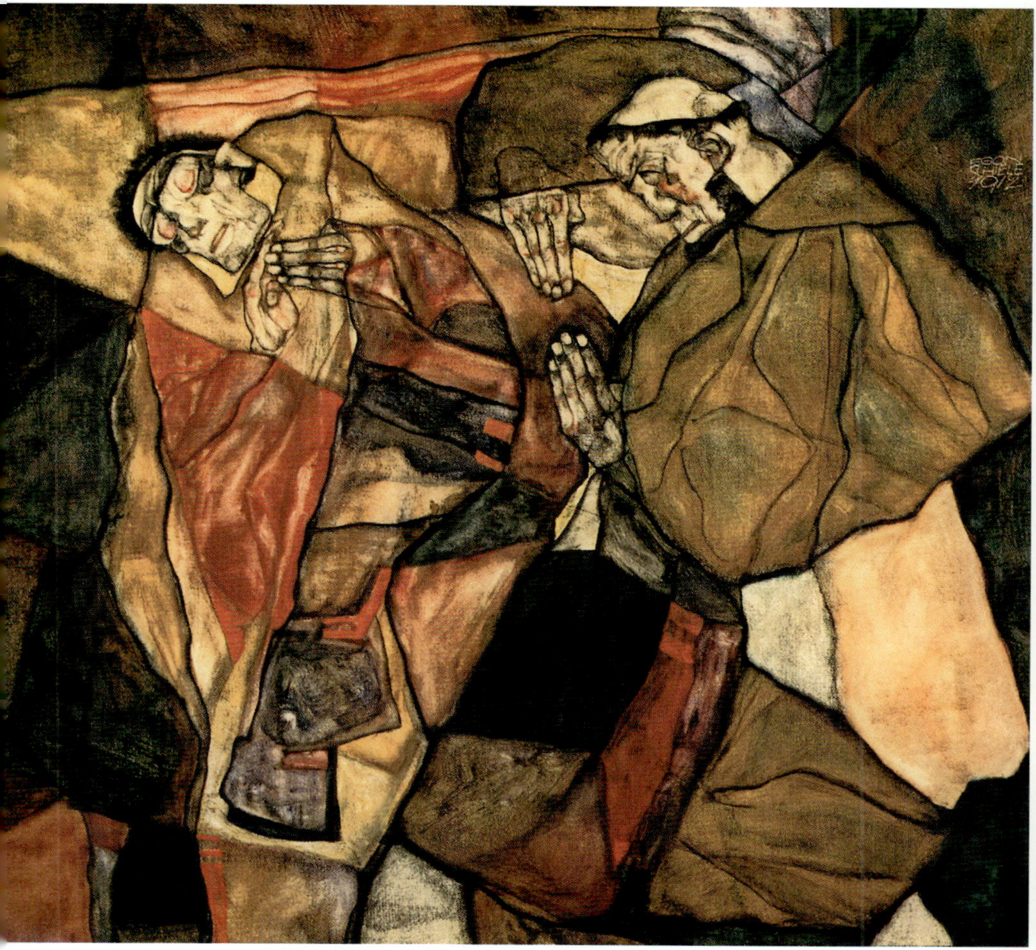
EGON SCHIELE 1912

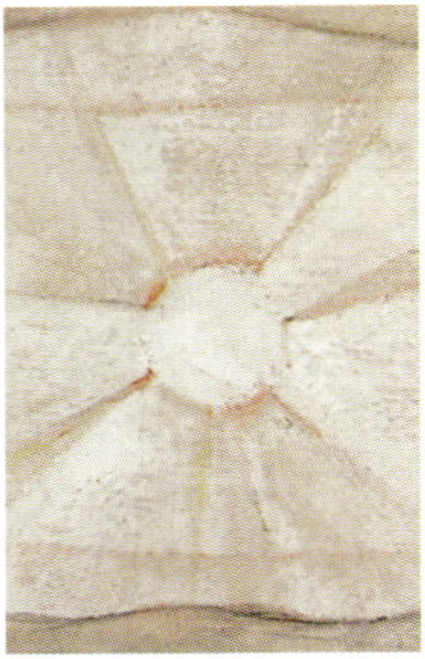

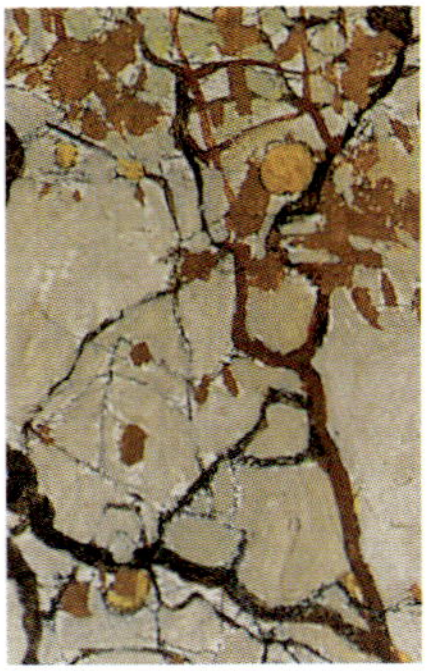

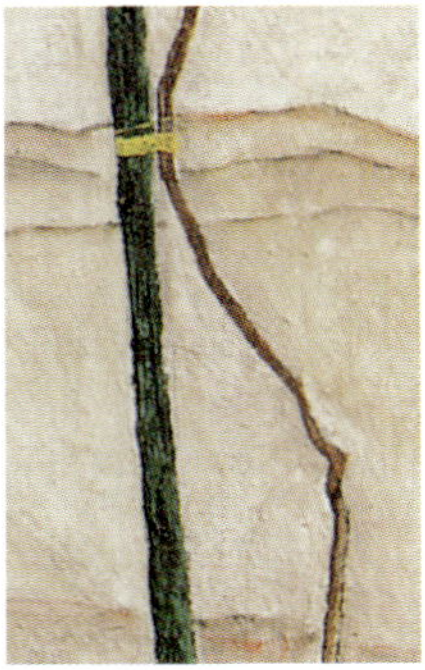

In other paintings, as previously mentioned, monks make love to nuns and expectant women who were often unwelcome and repudiated by strict Viennese society. "The nun prays chafed and nude before Christ's Agony on the Cross" (Georg Trakl, Munich, 1974). Furthermore, Schiele painted homosexual couples, transgressing taboos and provoked the fantasies of his contemporary viewers. In turn, Schiele found acknowledgement at the international art show in Vienna where he was represented by four paintings next to the expressionist works of Vincent van Gogh, Edvard Munch and Oskar Kokoschka.

Autumn Sun I (Rising Sun)

1912
Oil on canvas, 80.2 x 80.5 cm
Private collection

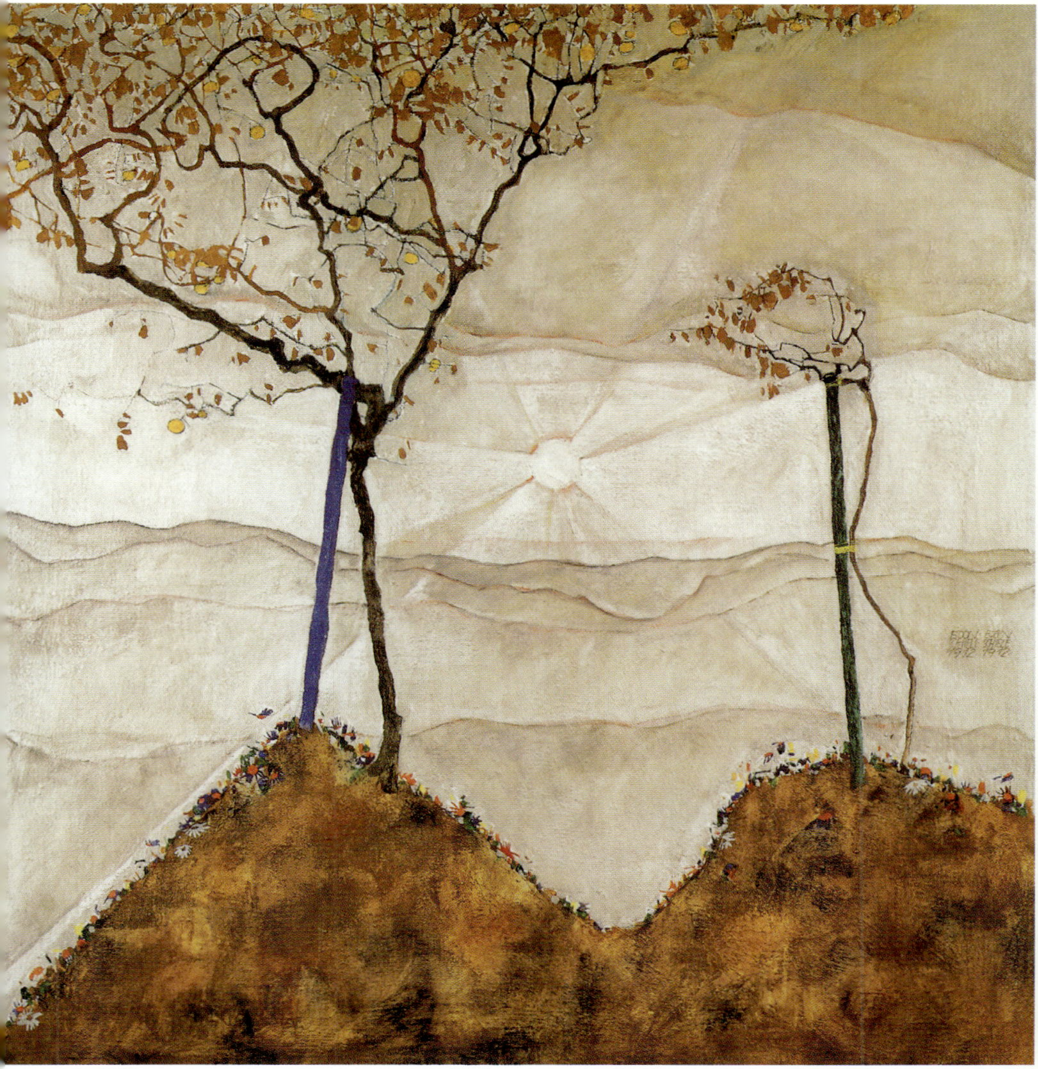

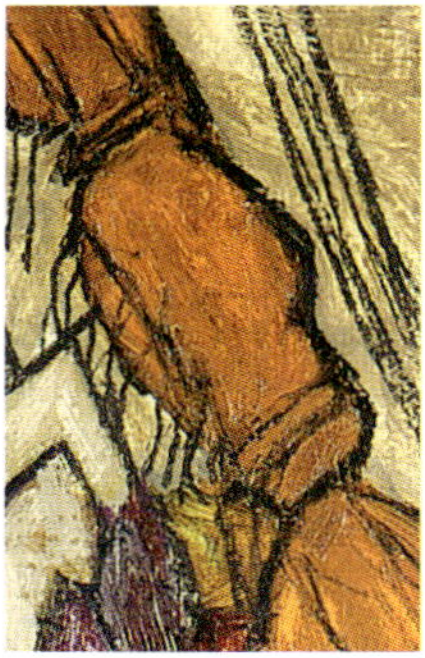

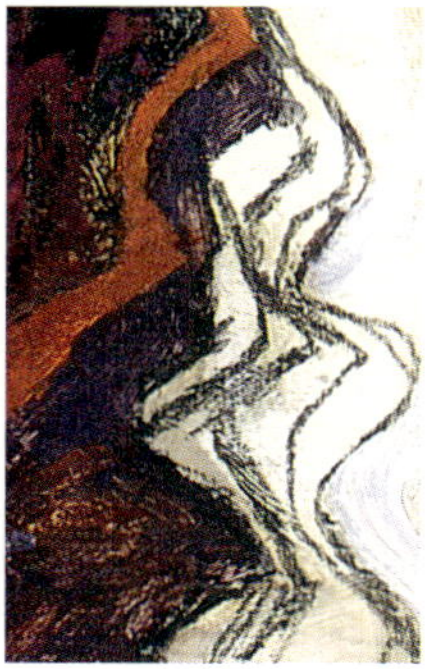

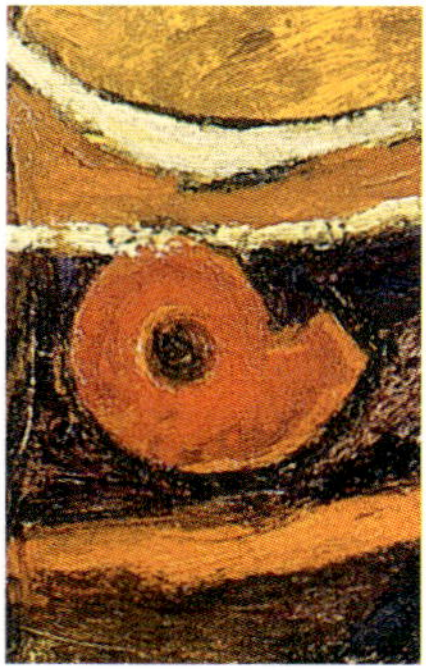

He made the acquaintance of Josef Hoffman, the director of the Vienna workshop. In December of 1909, the first exhibition of the "New Art Group" took place at Pisko's fine art dealership.

The same year, thus relatively early, Schiele had made the acquaintance of decisive personalities of the Viennese art scene, whose portraits he painted and who were to remain loyal to him for his entire life and beyond. Schiele made the acquaintance of Arthur Roessler, writer and art critic, who became one of his most decisive friends and promoters.

Trieste Fishing Boat

1912
Oil and pencil on canvas, 75 x 75 cm
Private collection

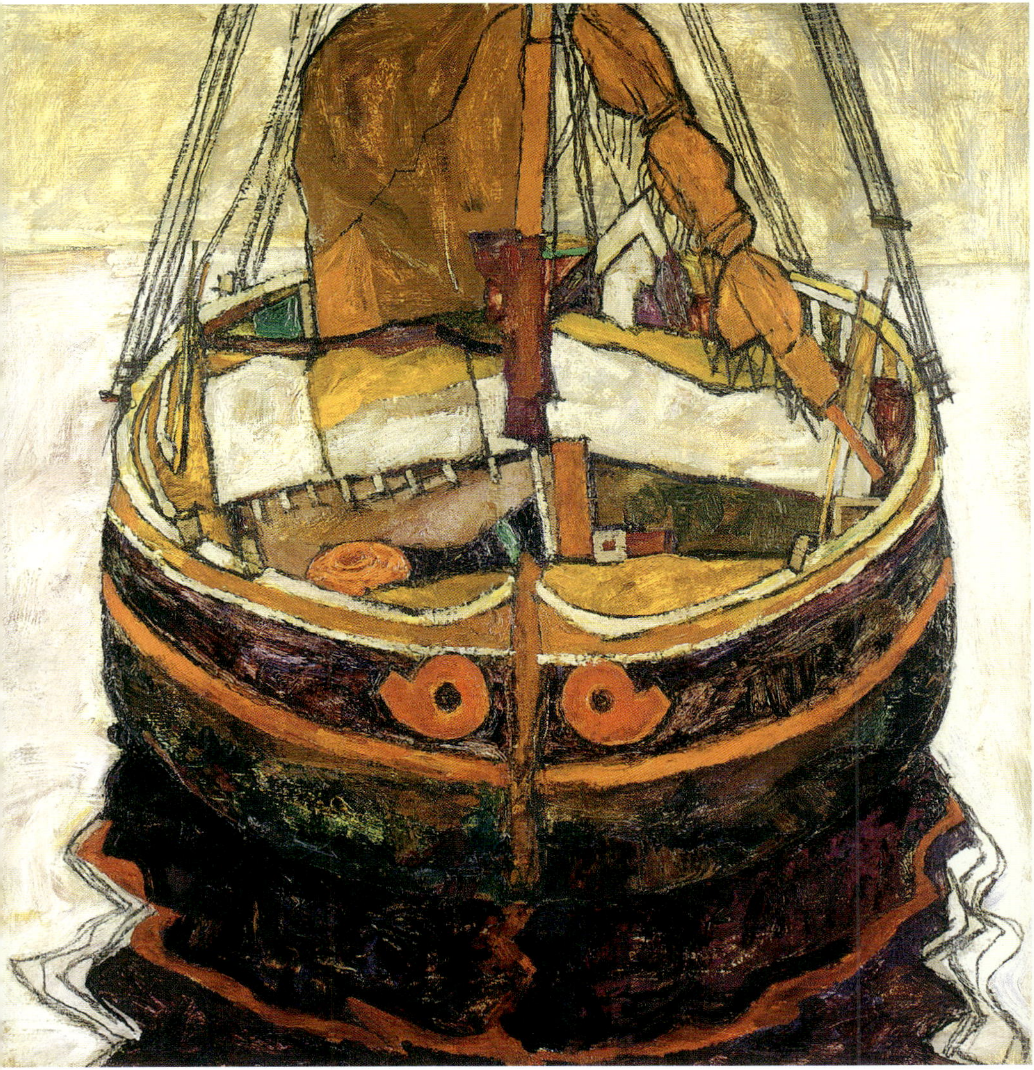

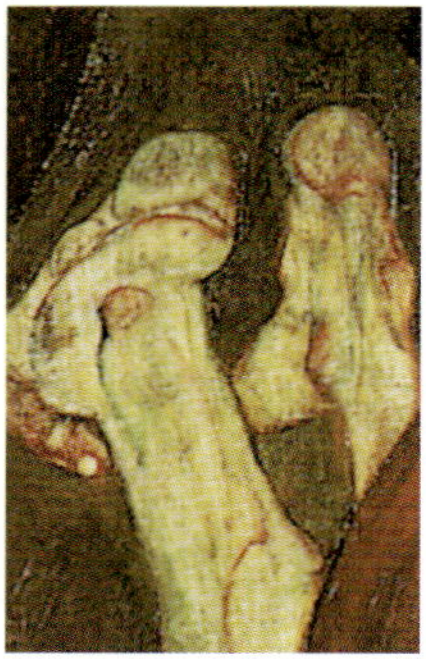

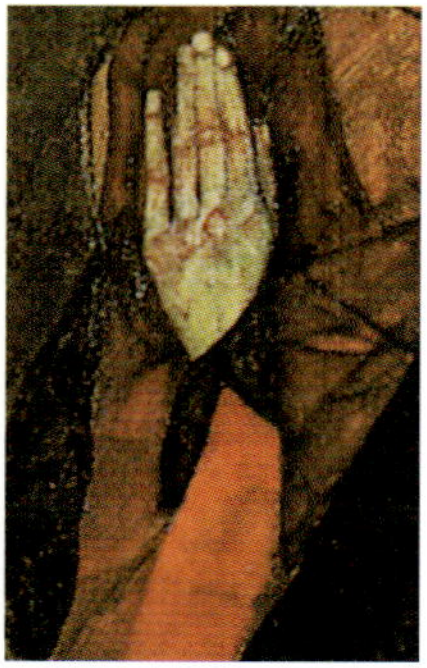

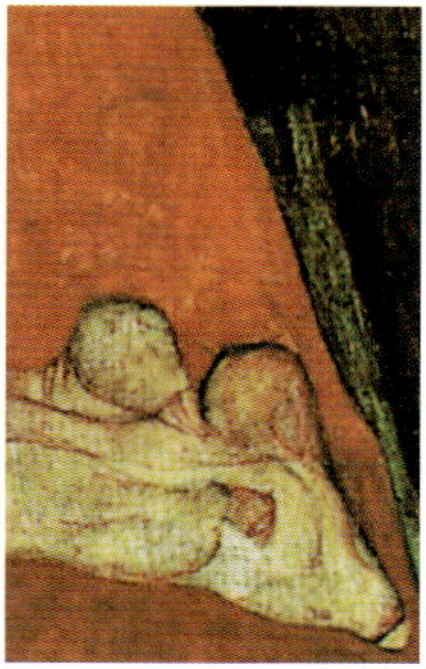

Further figures who influenced his career were Eduard Kosmack: the publisher of the magazines *The Architect* and *The Interior*, Carl Reininghausen (1857-1929), who was one of the most important Viennese collectors, and the railroad official and Schiele collector Heinrich Benesch (1862-1947), who later dedicated a book to Schiele.

Nevertheless, the year 1910 promised to be challenging for the young artist. Perhaps because Schiele opposed the plans of his uncle who tried to persuade his ward to enter military service,

Cardinal and Nun (Caress)

1912
Oil on canvas, 69.8 x 80.1 cm
Leopold Museum, Vienna

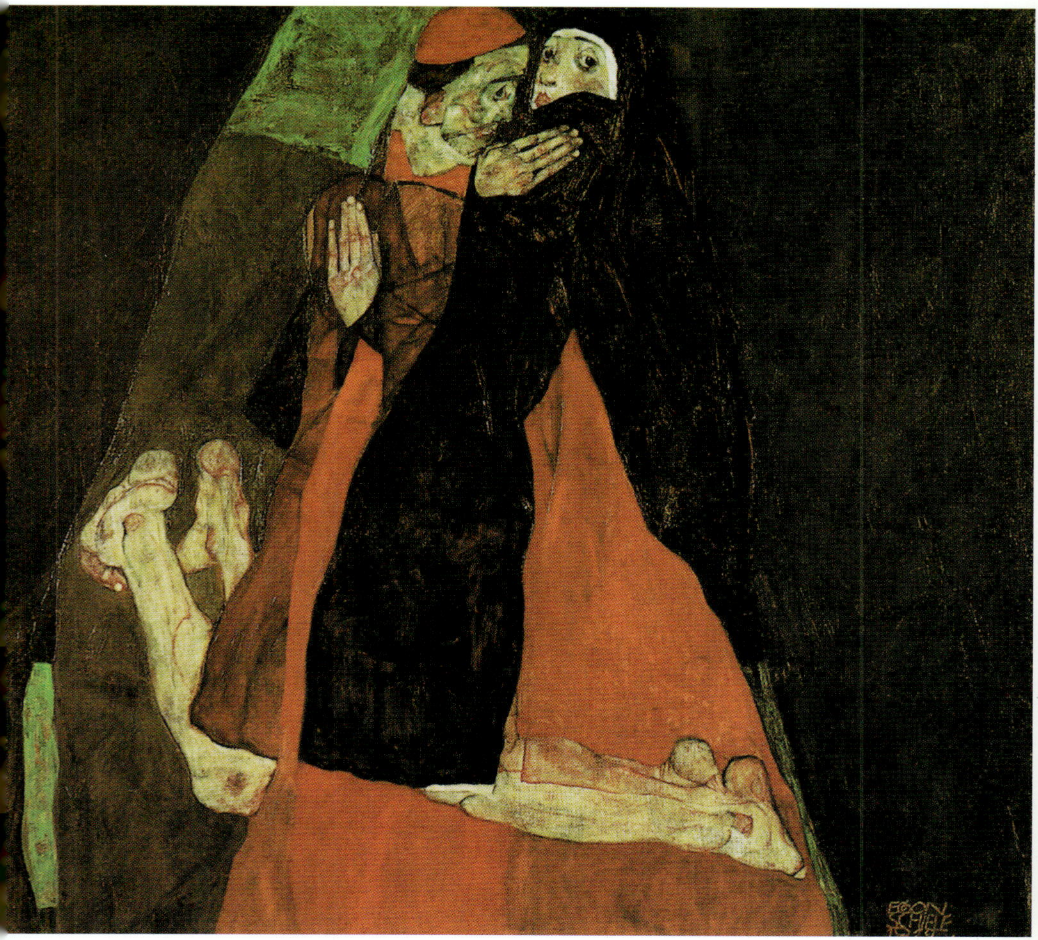
EGON
SCHIELE

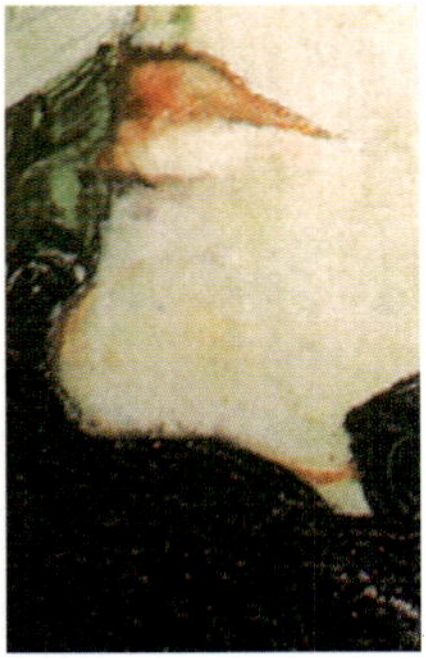
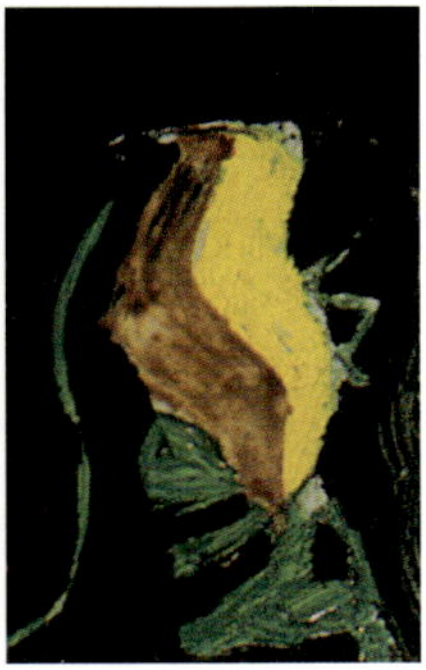
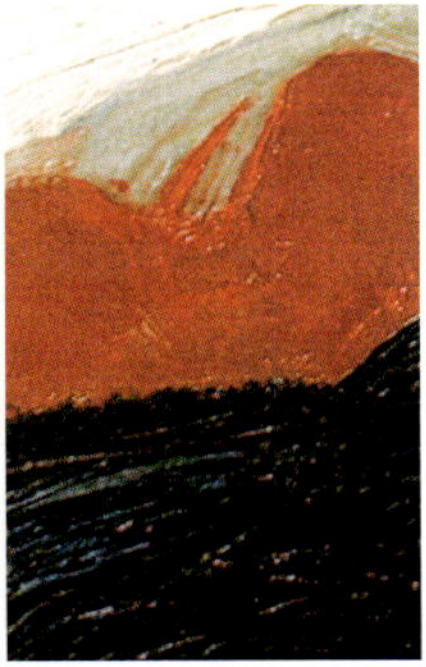

Czihaczek withdrew his guardianship. During the same period, the incident with the mysterious lover occurred, of which, with the exception of an exchange of letters with the gynaecologist Erwin von Graff who assured Schiele that he had admitted her to his clinic and was attending to her, nothing is known. Schiele dealt with this incident in several paintings: *Birth of the Genius* and *The Dead Mother I* (1910). *The Dead Mother I* is a small painting in highly varnished oil on wood. The size, wooden block support, and mother-and-child subject prompt associations with the tradition of icon painting.

Portrait of Ida Roessler

1912
Oil on wood, 31.6 x 39.4 cm
Wien Museum, Vienna

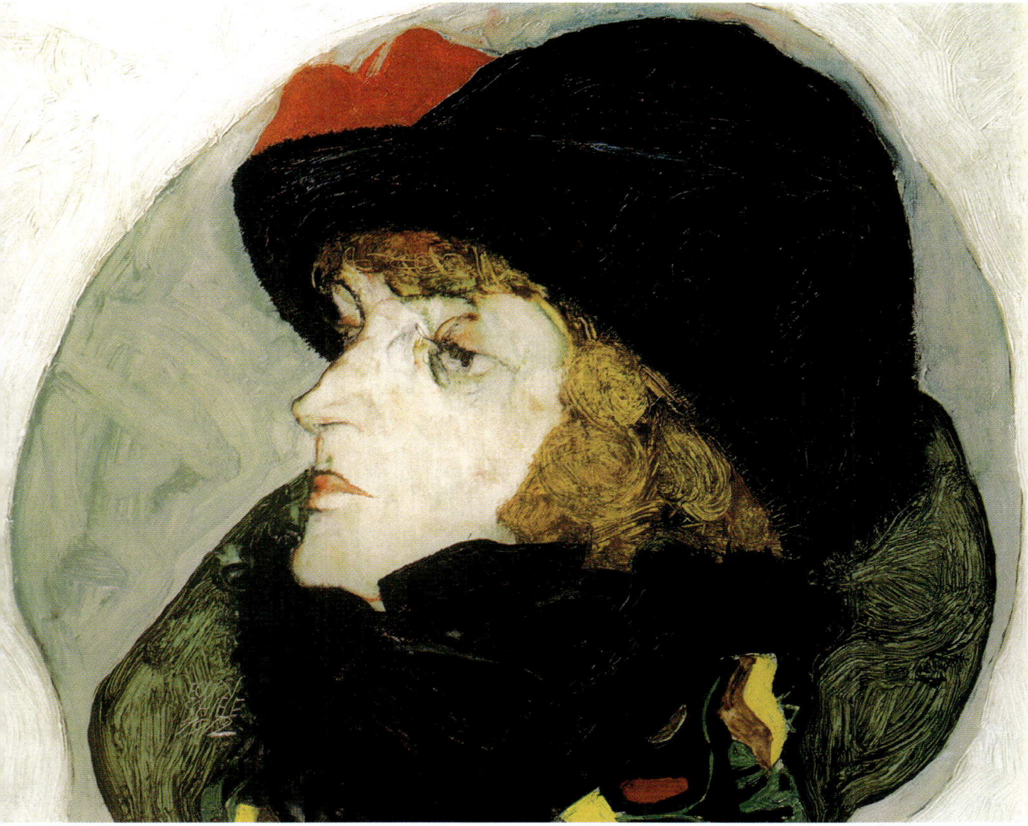

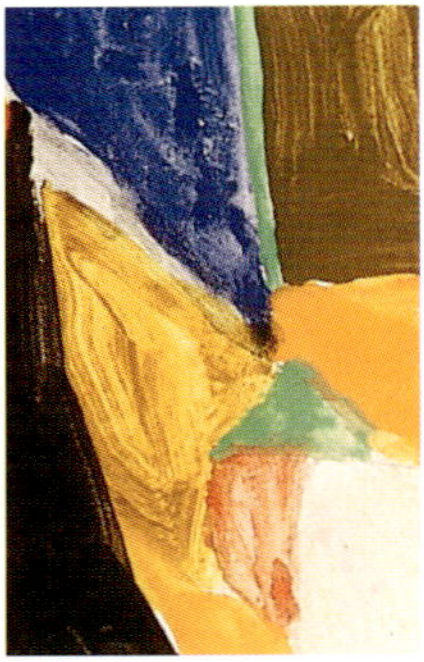

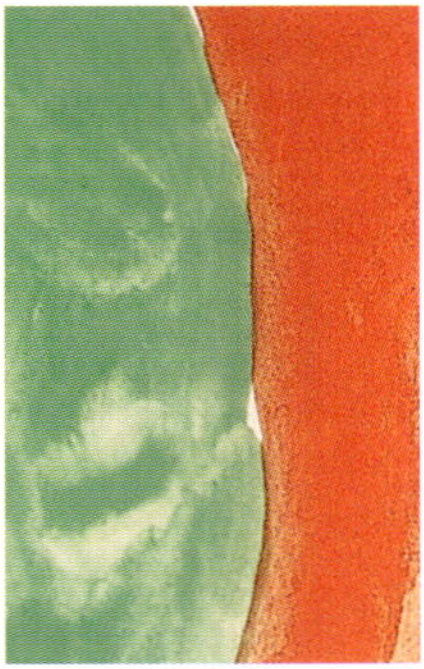

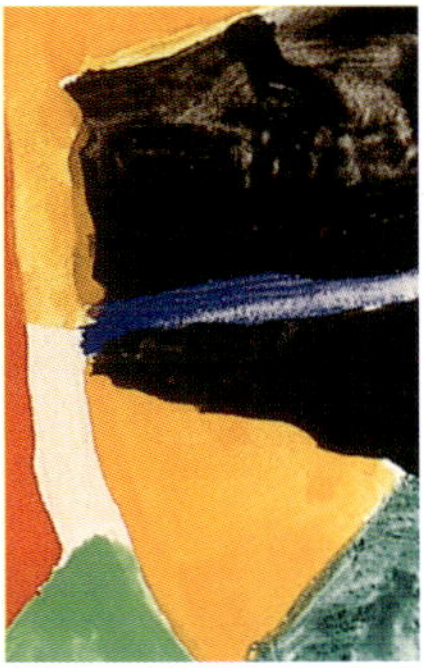

Beyond these comparisons, however, it is a highly original composition around a subject given a harrowing immediacy in the Expressionist vision. Shrouded in black, an unborn child, at the brink of birth, is locked in the loving, protecting, yet imprisoning body of its mother. The wan face of the mother, mournful in her own death, contrasts with the warm, living tones of the infant's flesh, pulsating with blood. The child's hands already suggest nascent vitality and individuality.

Portrait of a Woman (Valerie Neuzil)

1912
Gouache and pencil on paper, 24.8 x 24.8 cm
Albertina, Vienna

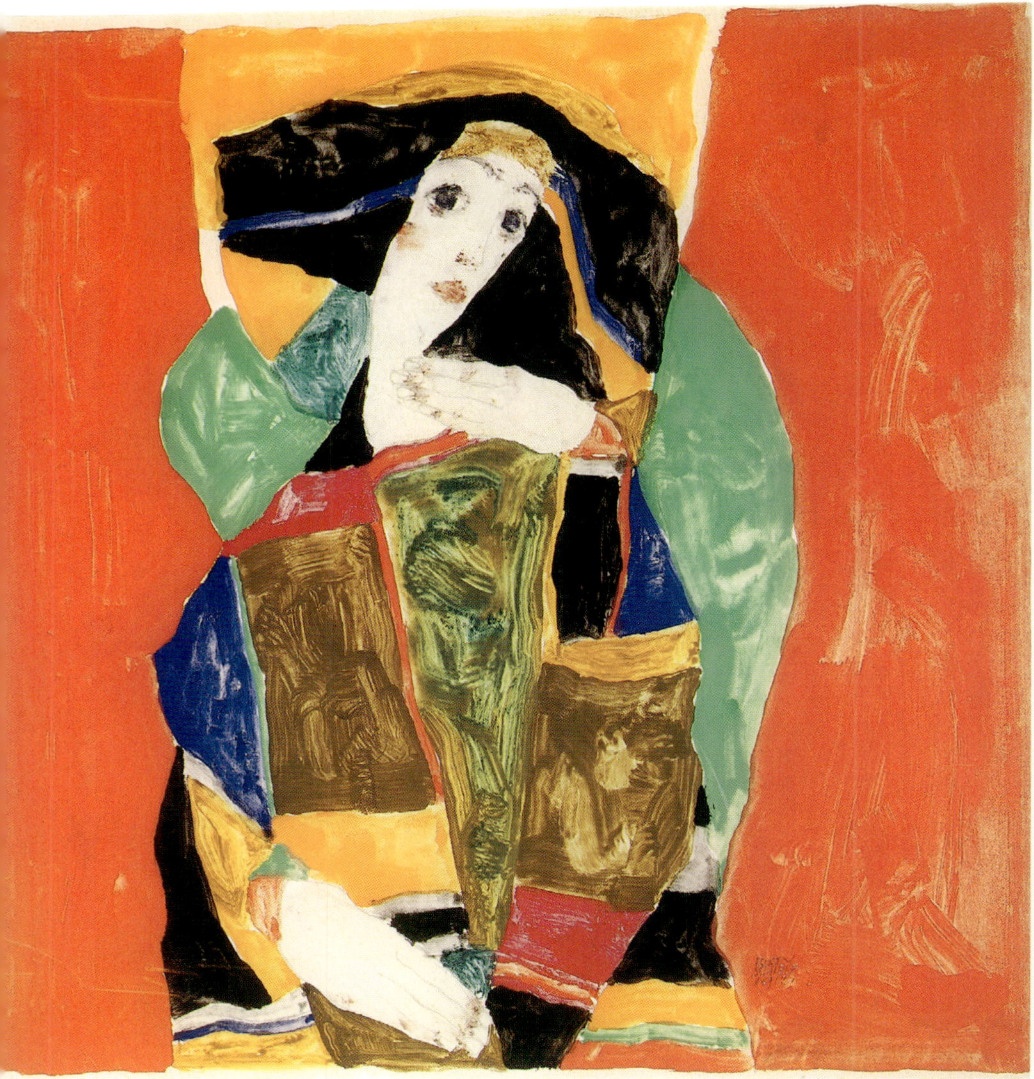

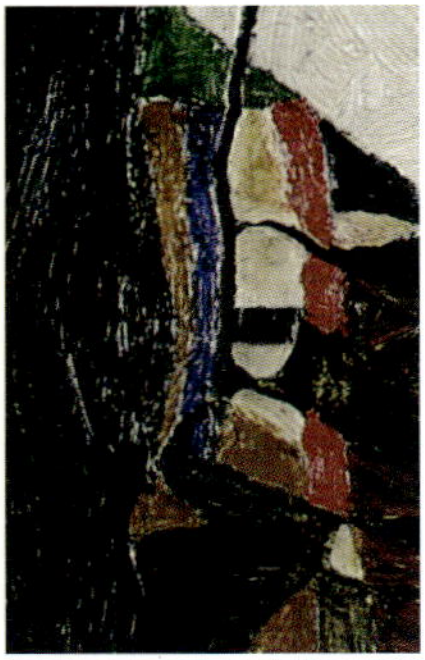

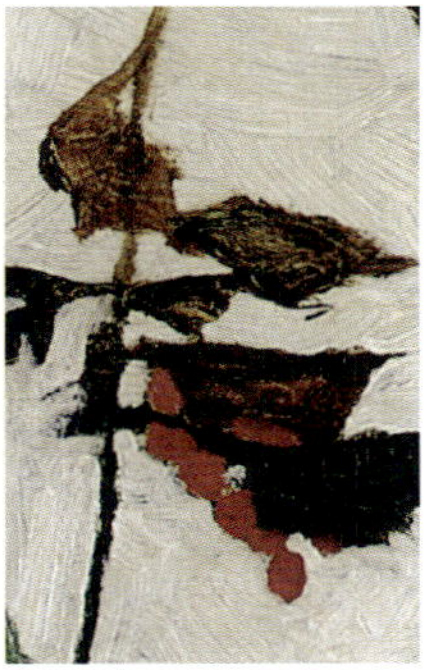

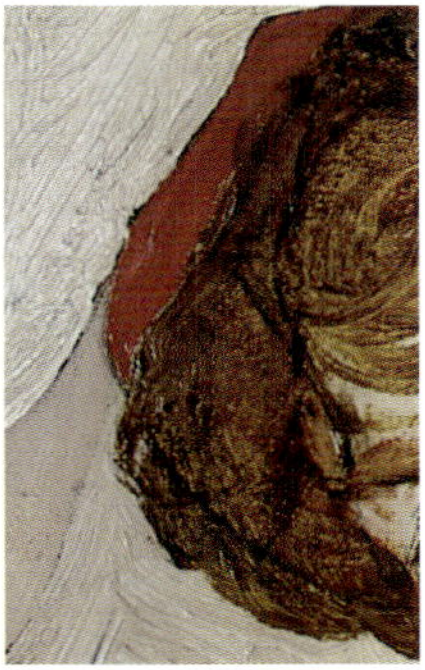

During this time, love and death studies went hand-in-hand. On the one hand, the sexual act is associated with the danger of pregnancy and the possibility of dying in childbirth. The life-giving body may be destroyed by death. On the other hand, syphilis lurked in every kiss. Is it possible to explain the subliminal, morbid trait in Schiele's world? The role of woman was limited solely to her biological function of childbearing in the cult book of that time by the author Otto Weininger,

Portrait of Valerie Neuzil ("Wally")

1912
Oil on wood, 32 x 40 cm
Leopold Museum, Vienna

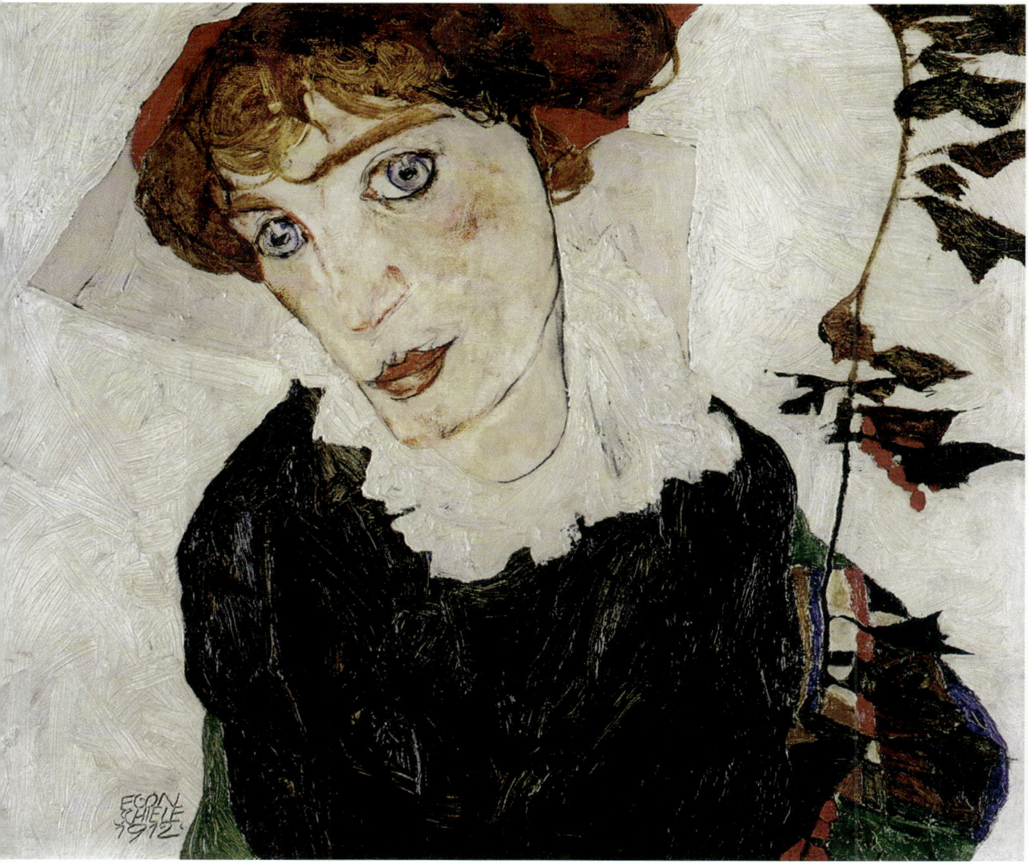
EGON
SCHIELE
1912

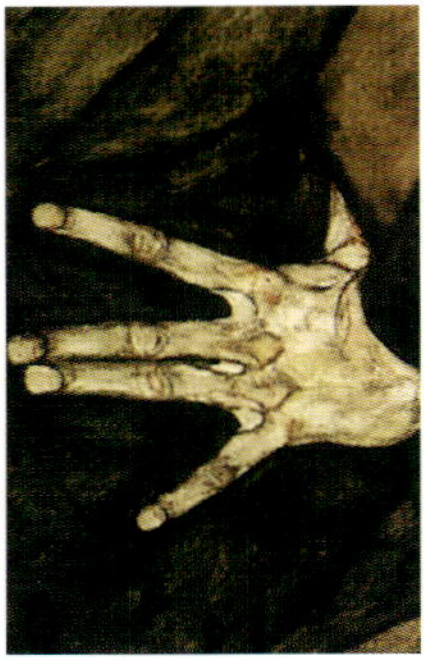

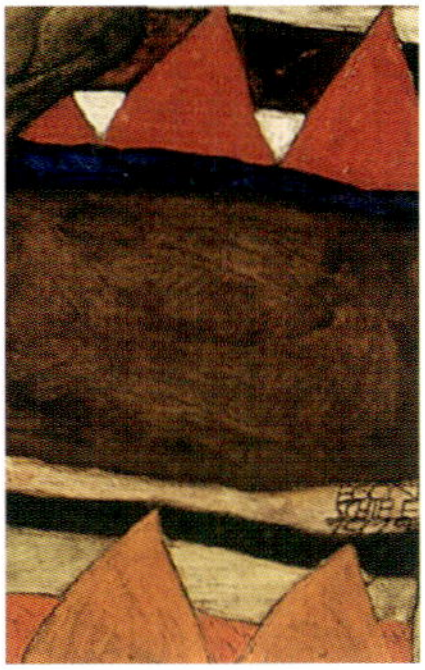

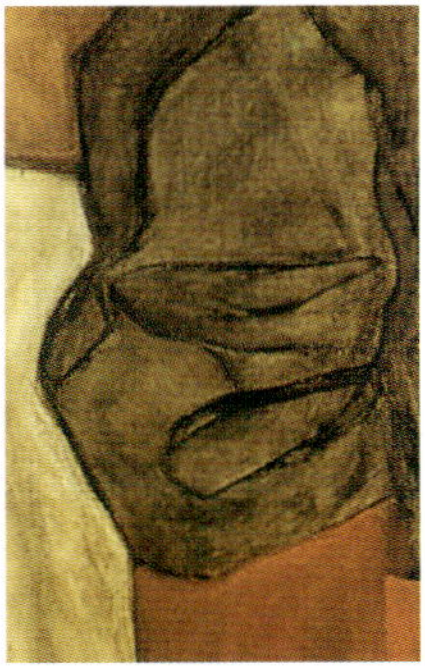

Sex and Character, who commented that men of significance should only get involved with prostitutes. Whereas Freud discovered: "Their upbringing denies women the ability to deal on an intellectual level with sexual problems. Which is where they have the greatest need for knowledge, yet society reacts with condemnation of this desire for knowledge as unfeminine and as a sign of a sinful predisposition." Freud attributed the alleged intellectual inferiority of women to sexual repression, which resulted in inhibition of thought.

Portrait of Erich Lederer

1912-1913
Oil on canvas, 139 x 55 cm
Kunstmuseum, Basel

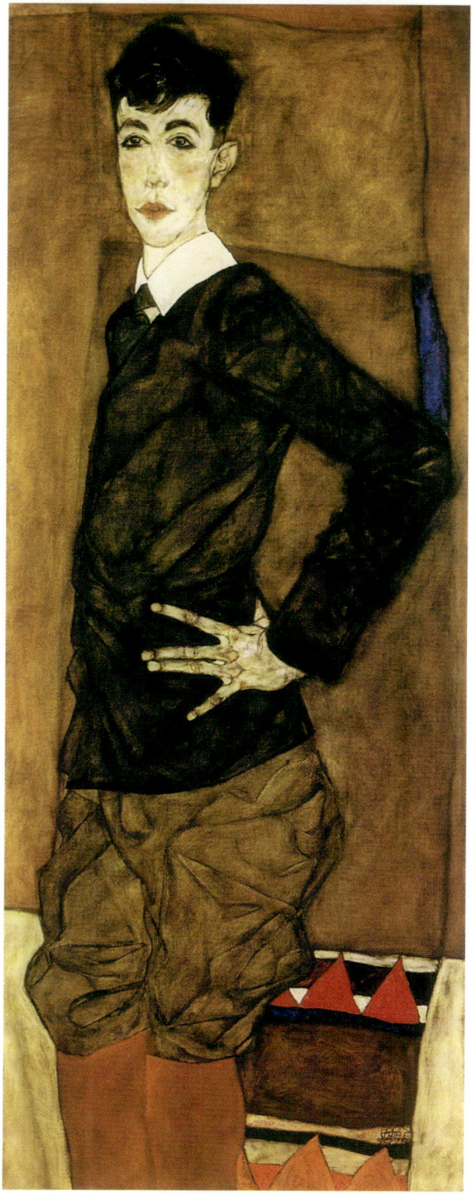

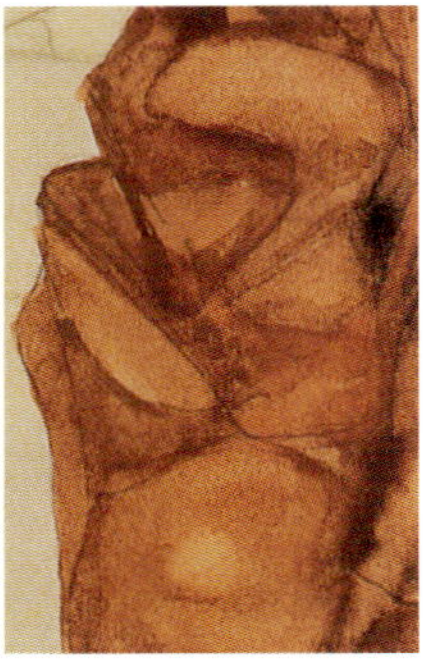

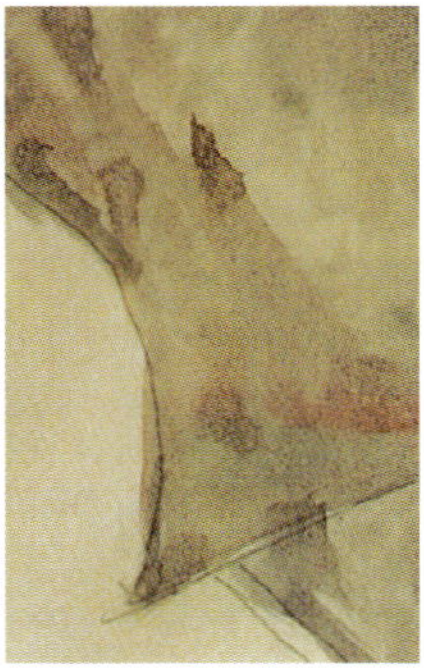

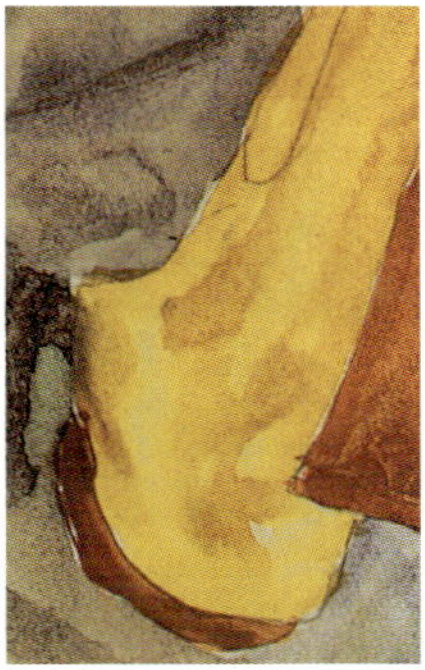

Accompanied by his friend, the painter and mime Erwin Osen, Schiele fled to Krumau where they spent the summer with a dancer named Moa, the lover of Osen. Many of Schiele's drawings at this time were of this young woman. In *The Dancer Moa* (1911), Osen's girlfriend is made to look almost like a figure from a work by Klimt with her wildly patterned dress cutting a swathe of hedonistic colour across a plain white background. Klimt's ornamental vision, however, has been subverted by glaring colours and a sense of movement.

Hindering the Artist is a Crime, it is Murdering Life in Bud!

1912
Watercolour and pencil, 48.6 x 31.8 cm
Albertina, Vienna

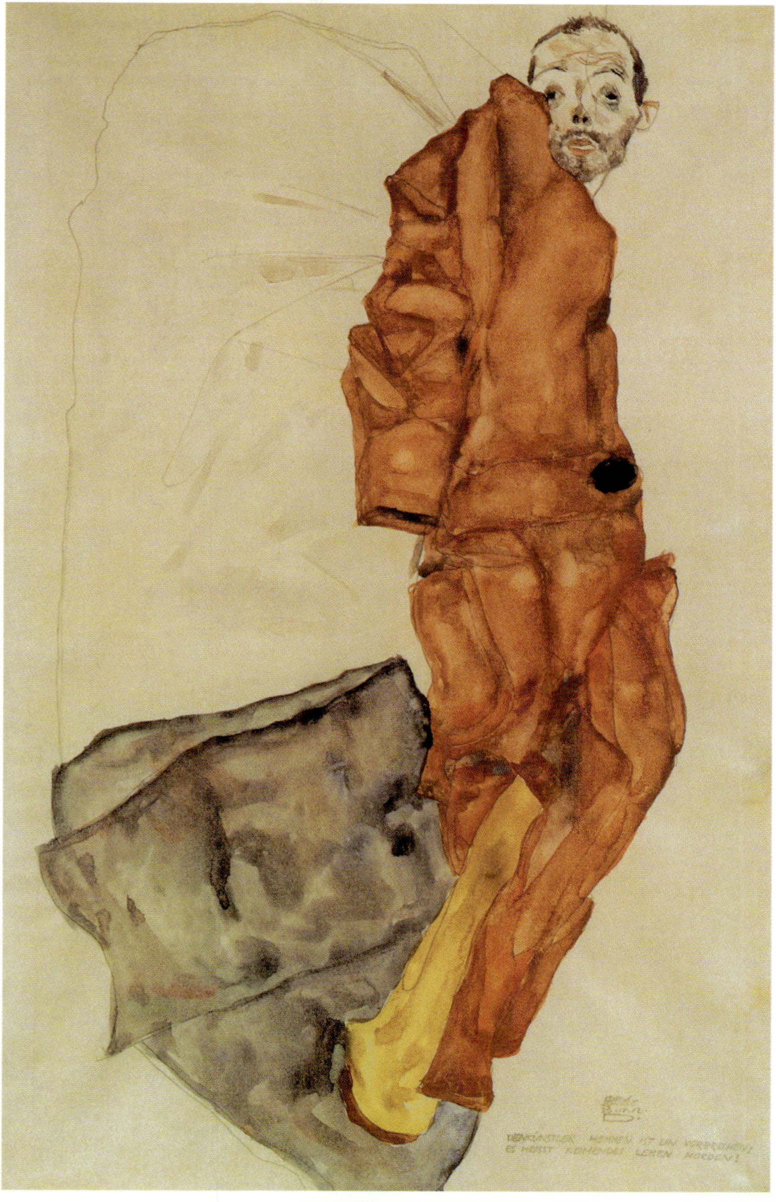

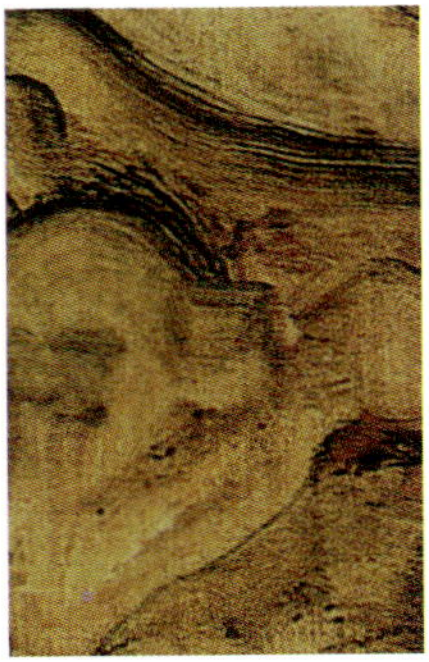

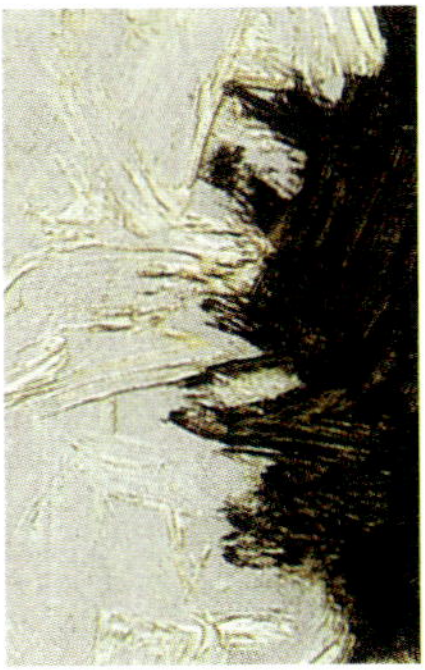

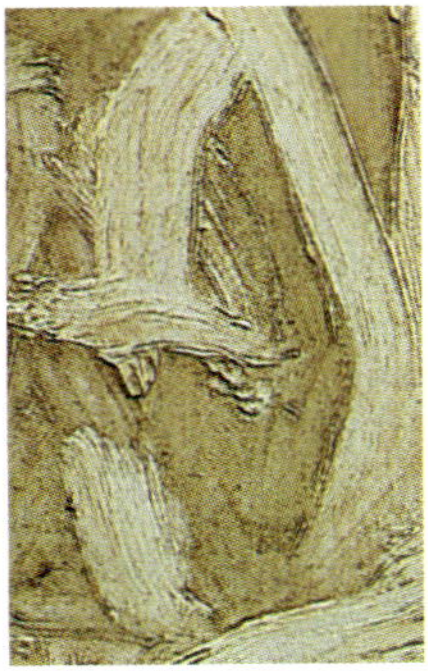

With her dark hair and eyes, she is clearly a bohemian creature and a sensual one. The dress is more of a wrap than an item of clothing and there is a sense that it might be unrolled at any moment to reveal her nakedness underneath. Even the title makes it clear that she is an exotic beast of the night, defining her as her profession. The word MOA is inscribed in capital letters on the blank part of the canvas suggesting a boldness and strength of character uncontainable in the visual image itself.

Self-Portrait with Lowered Head
Study for The Hermits

1912
Oil on wood, 42.2 x 33.7 cm
Leopold Museum, Vienna

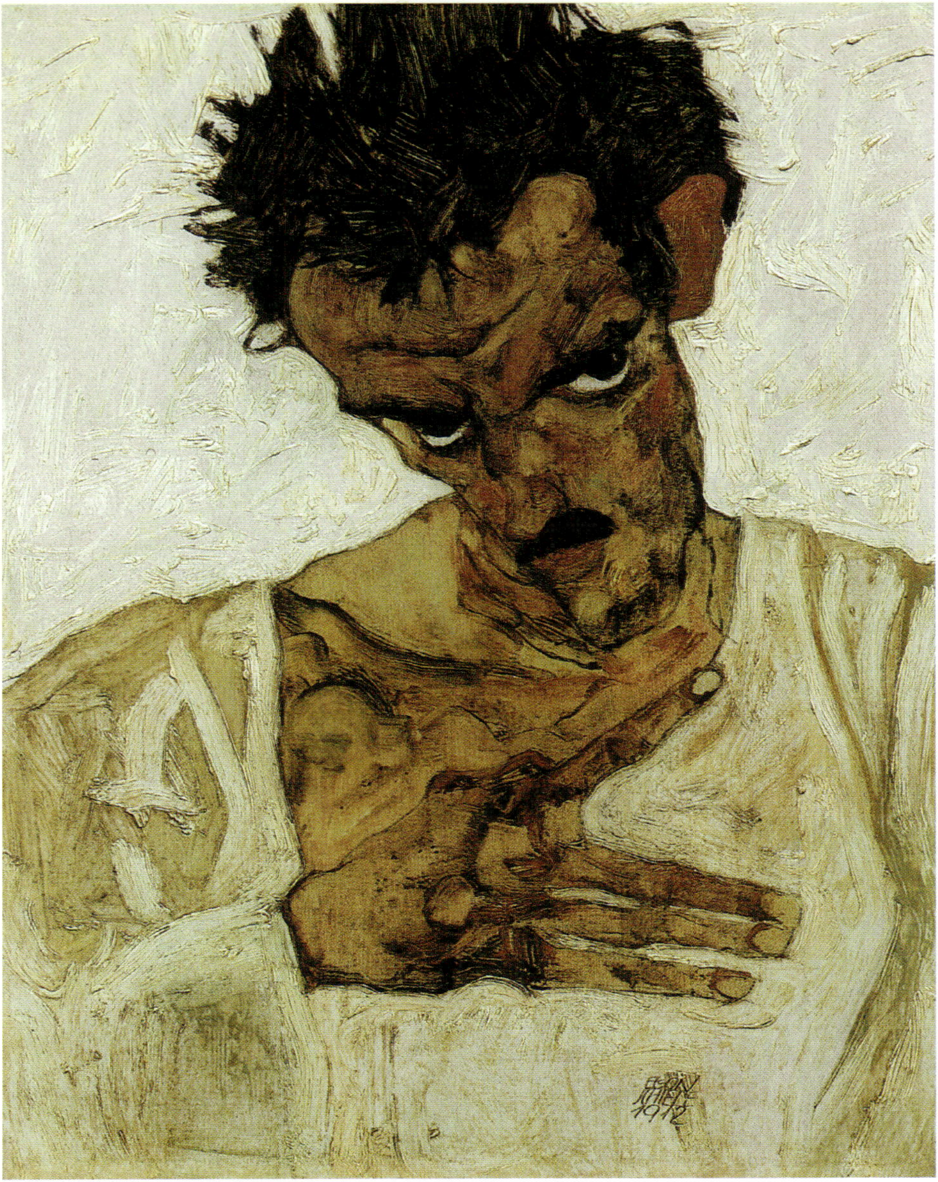
1912

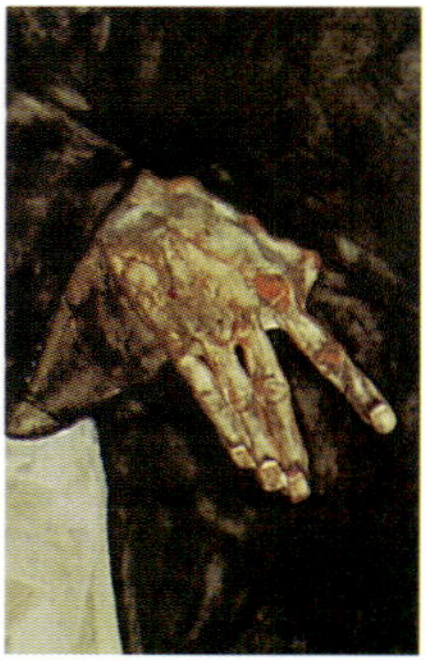

In Krumau, Schiele also made the acquaintance of the young baccalaureate Willy Lidl, who vowed deep love for him.

Back in Vienna, Schiele shared his atelier with Max Oppenheimer (1885-1954). Day in, day out, he lived from hand to mouth. For several years of his life his finances were precarious, he was often in debt and sometimes he was forced to use cheap materials, painting on brown wrapping paper or cardboard instead of artists' paper or canvas.

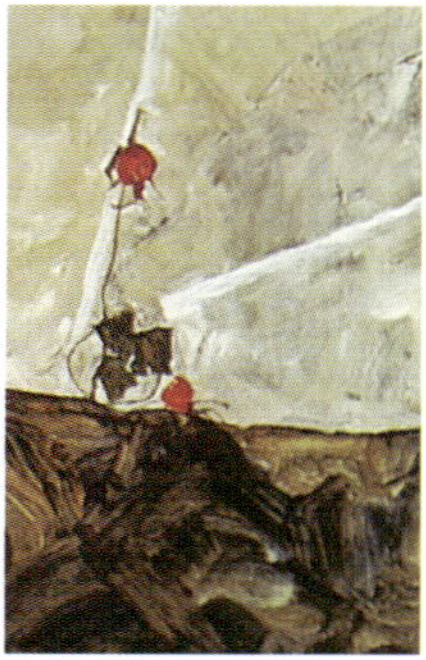

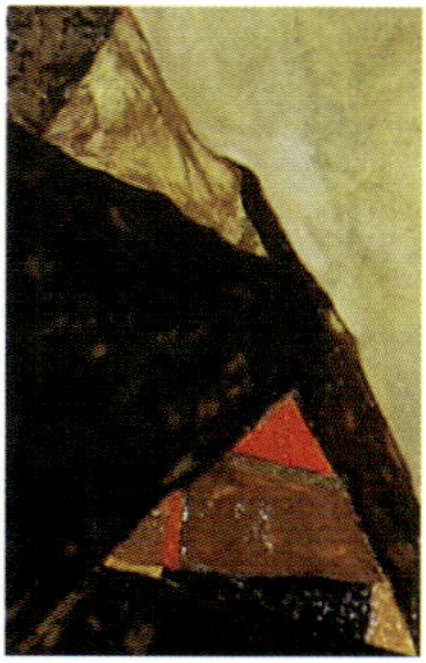

The Hermits

1912
Oil on canvas, 181 x 181 cm
Leopold Museum, Vienna

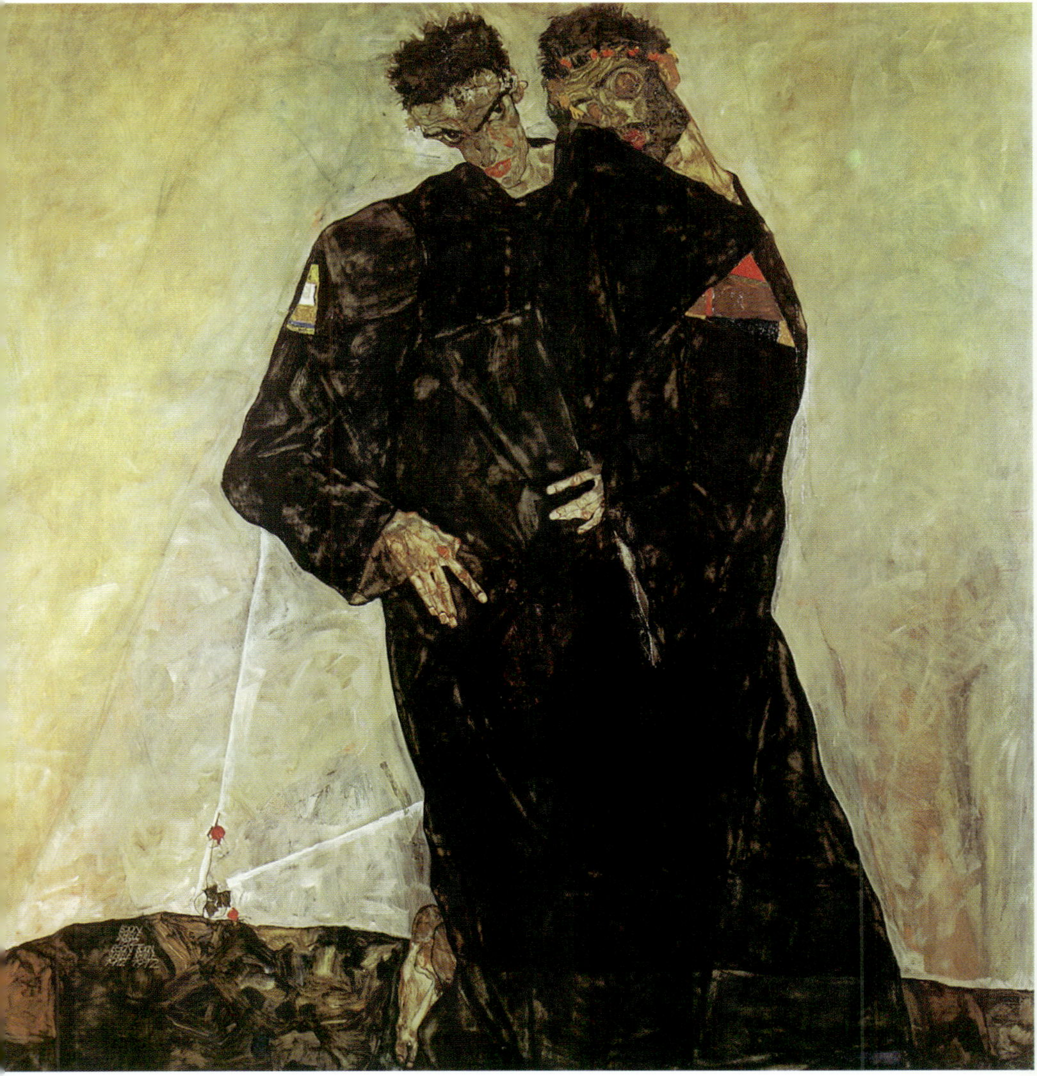

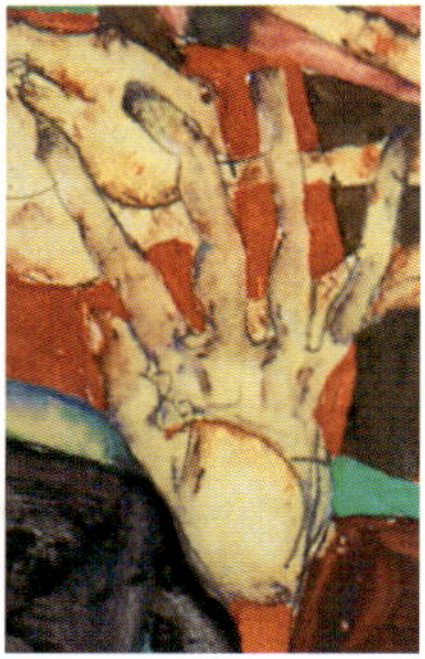

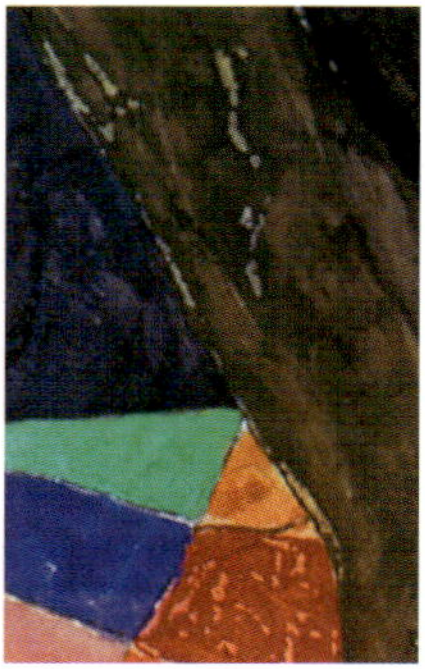

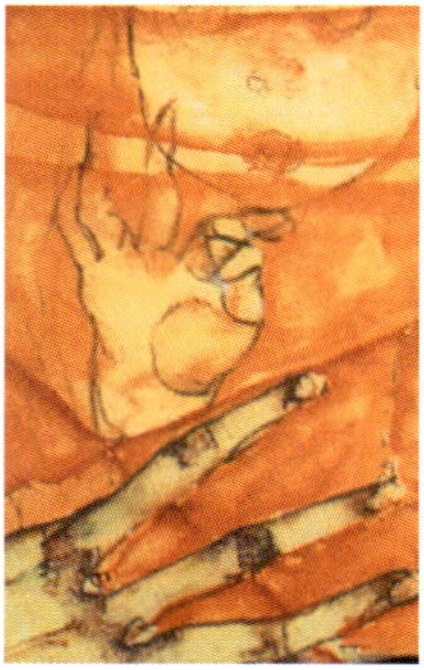

However, if young Schiele lamented his financial woes, he quickly managed to get on his feet again and find support from friends and patrons. In 1910, Vienna workshops, established in 1903, printed three of Schiele's picture cards; at the same time one of his paintings was shown at the international hunters' exhibition in the context of the Klimt group. A further exhibition at the Klosterneuburg monastery exhibited the *Portrait of Eduard Kosmack* and that of a boy, Rainerbub, son of the Viennese orthopedist and surgeon Max Rainer (1910).

Holy Family

1913
Gouache and pencil on parchment-like paper
47 x 36.5 cm
Private collection

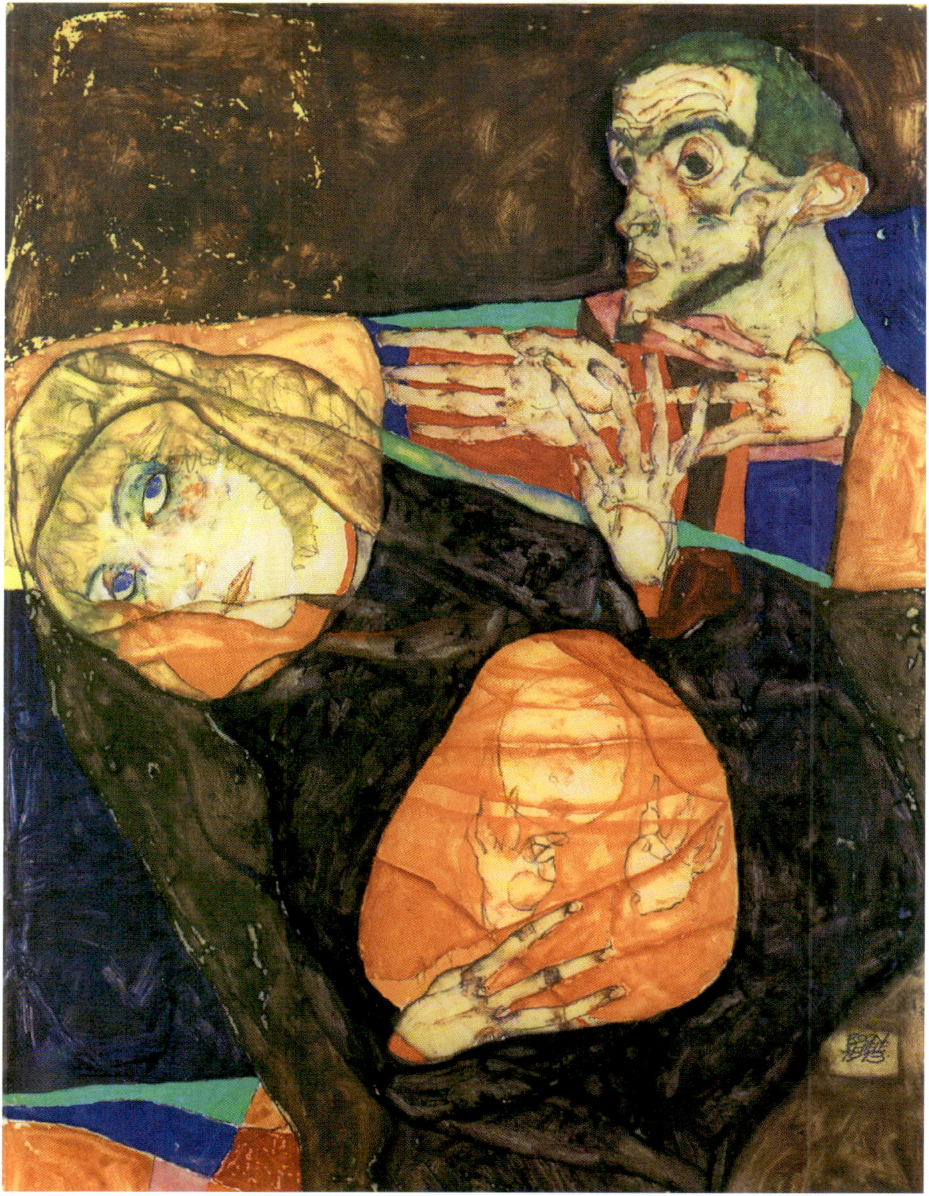

As early as 1911, the first monograph on Schiele, penned by the artist and poet Albert Paris von Gütersloh, was published. In the same year, Arthur Roessler reviewed Schiele's works in the monthly periodical *Bildende Künstler*. In Vienna, Schiele took part in the collective exhibition at the Miethke Gallery.

Once again, Schiele wanted to get away. "Vienna is full of shadows, the city is black. I want to be alone [in] to the Bohemian Woods, that I need not hear anything about myself," he wrote in his diary.

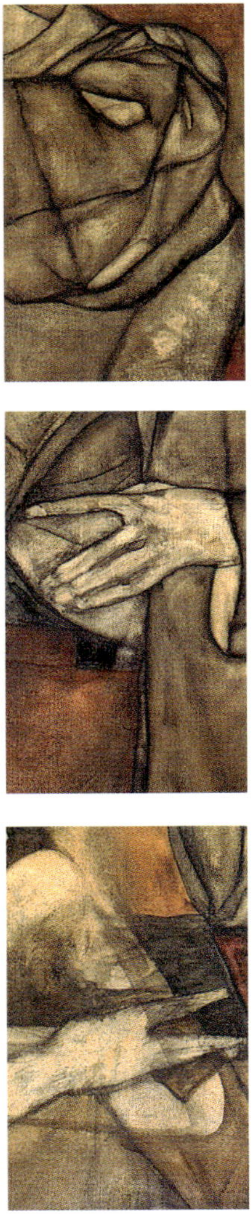

Self-Portrait with Model (Fragment)

1913
Oil on canvas, 70.2 x 241 cm
Private collection, New York

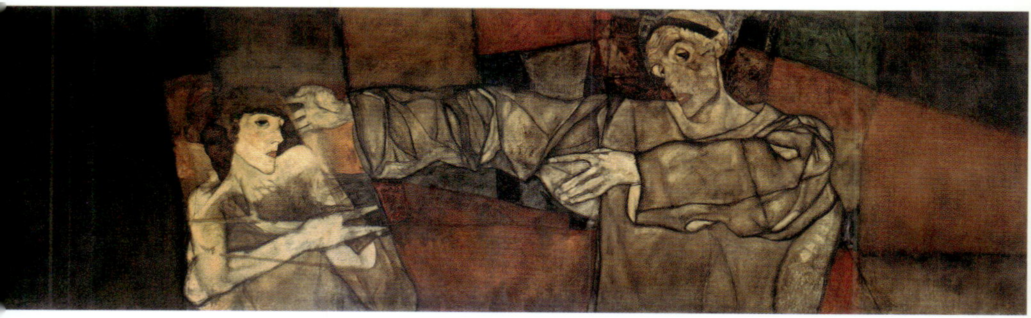

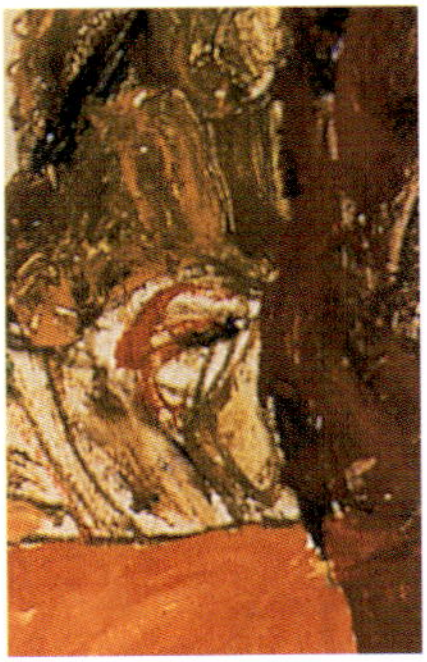

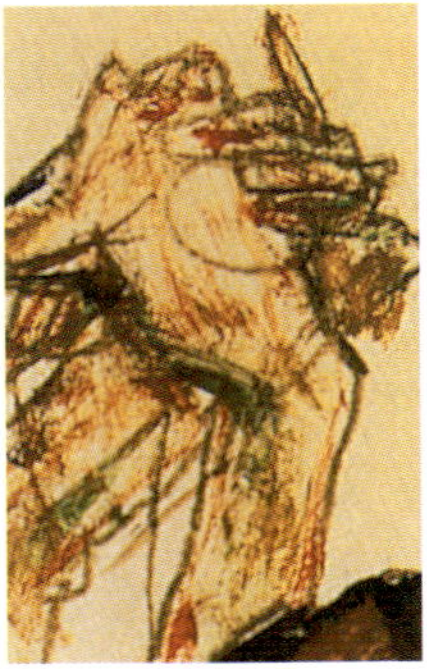

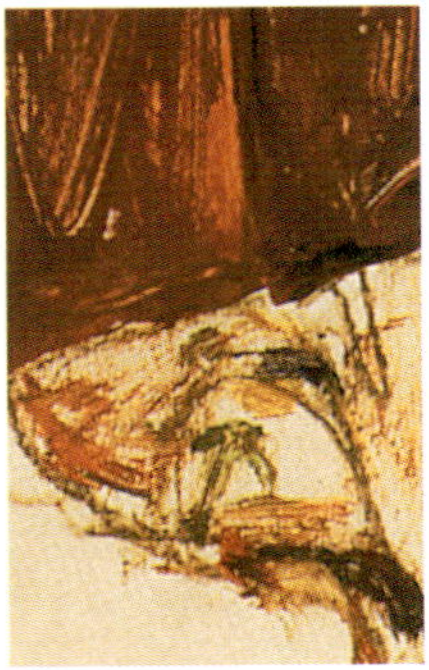

Wally (Valerie Neuzil), former model and lover of Klimt who supposedly gave herself to Schiele, accompanied him. They moved to his mother's home town in Krumau on the Moldau. The devoted Lidl had procured an atelier with a garden. A very productive working phase began for Schiele. Besides a few landscapes, he mainly worked on nude studies of himself and Wally, his "twittering lark". Like the diary drawings, numerous studies depict the erotic cohabitation of two bodies.

Truth Revealed

1913
Gouache, watercolour and pencil
48.3 x 32.1 cm
Private collection

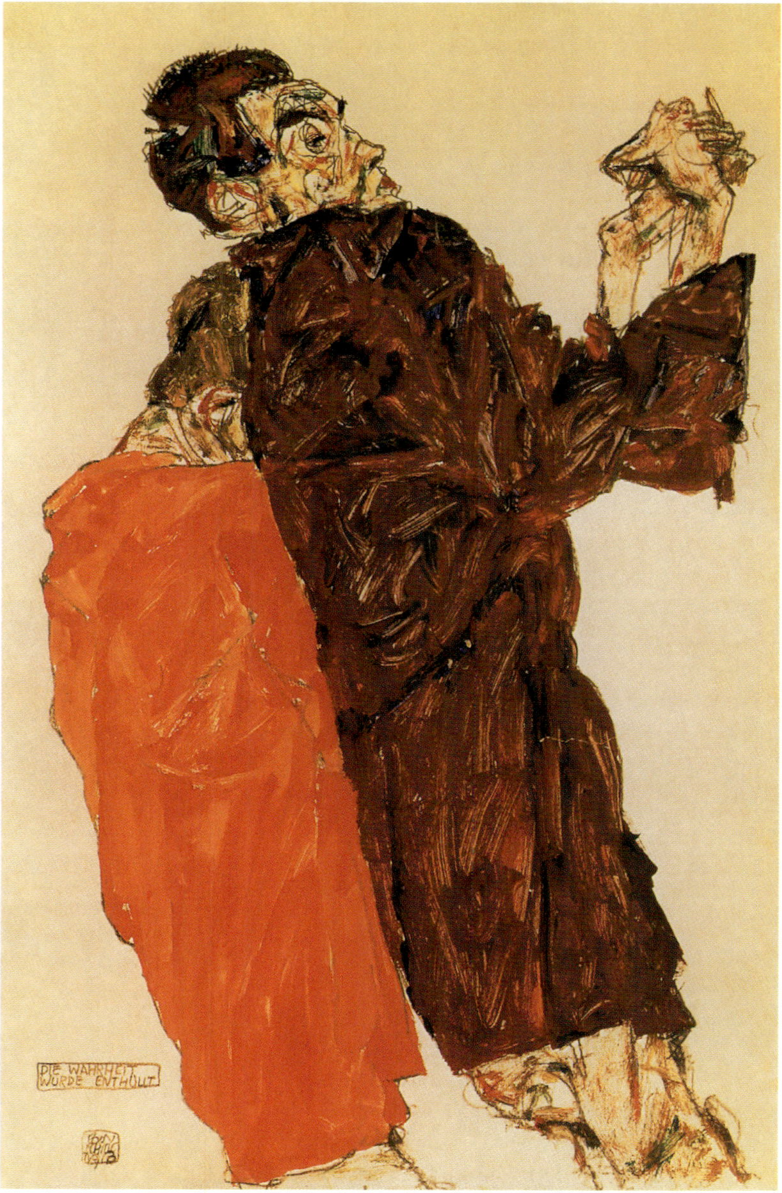
DIE WAHRHEIT
WURDE ENTHÜLLT

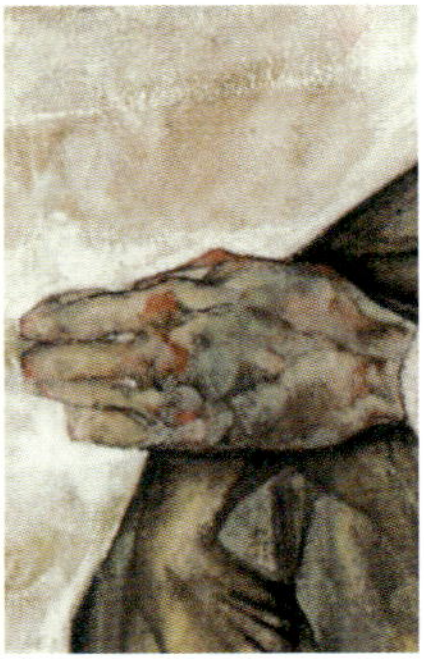

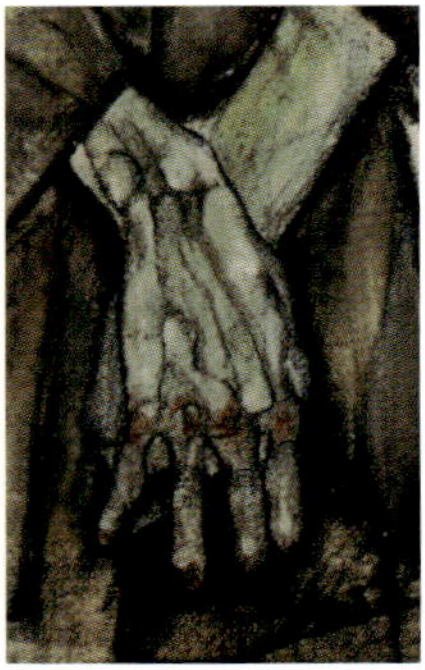

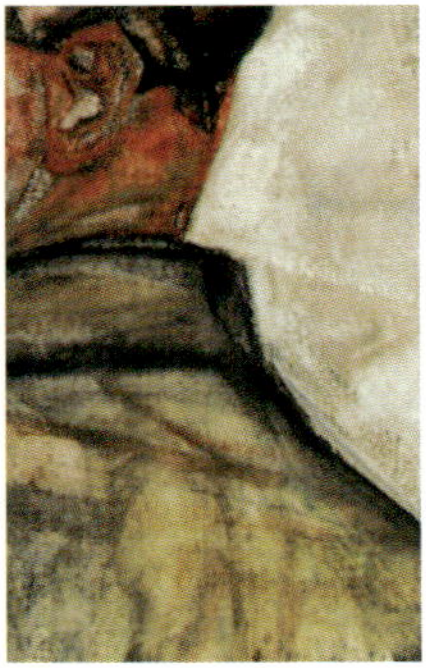

Self-Portrait: Facing Death in the Nude

There are approximately 100 self-portraits including several nude studies of Schiele. Study of the male nude was obligatory at the academy, psychological self-portraits, however, apart from Richard Gerstl in 1908, were the exception. The self-portrait as nude study positions the artist not only as a person of sight, but also as a physical being. Schiele did not act as a voyeur in baring his models; rather, he brought himself into play.

Double Portrait (Chief Inspector Heinrich Benesch and His Son Otto)

1913
Oil on canvas, 121 x 131 cm
Wolfgang-Gurlitt-Museum, Linz

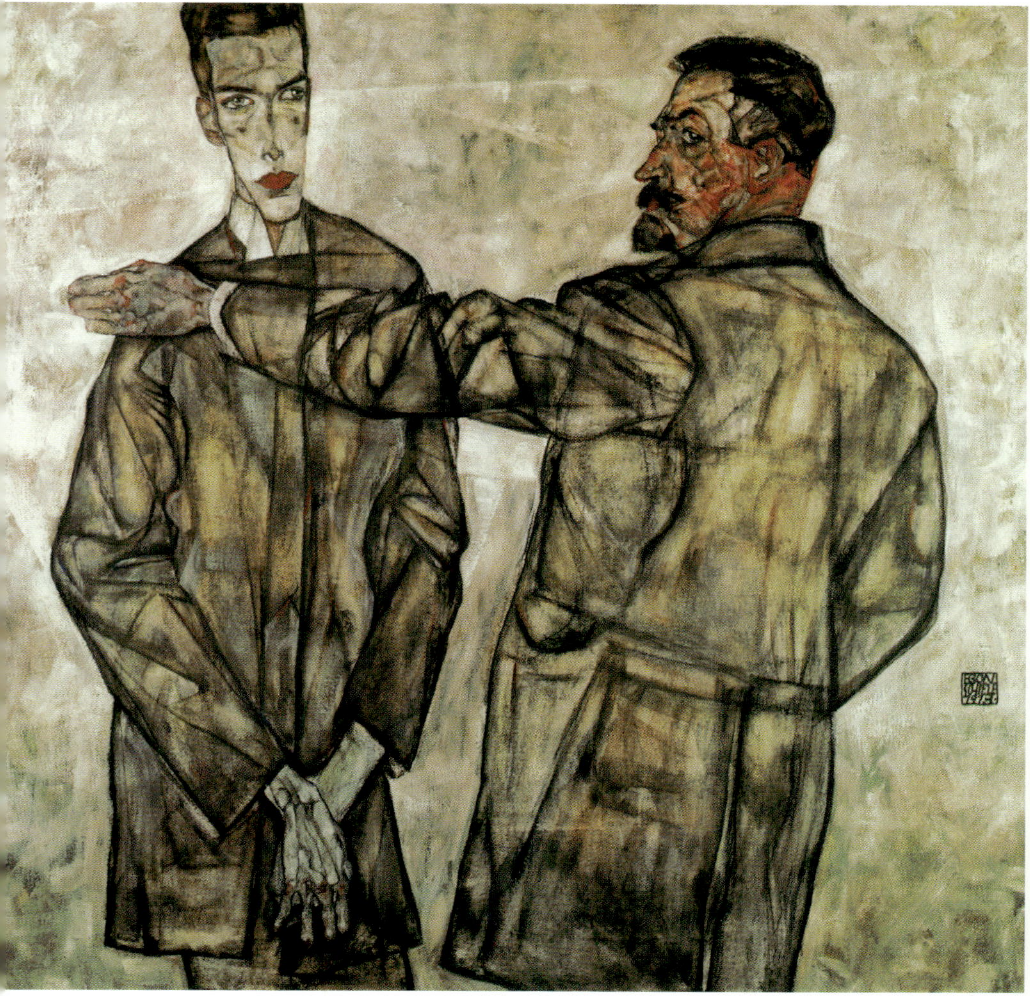

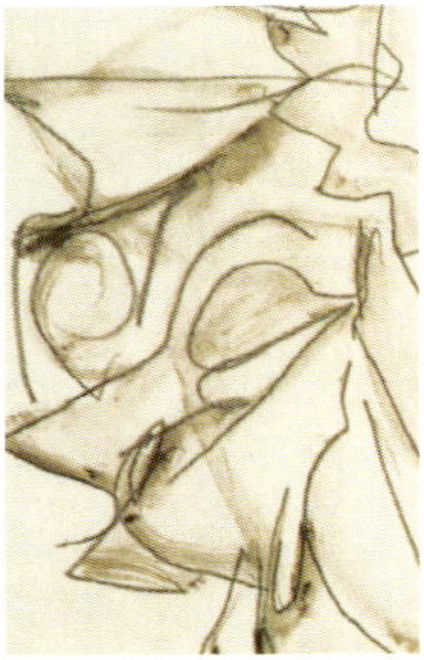

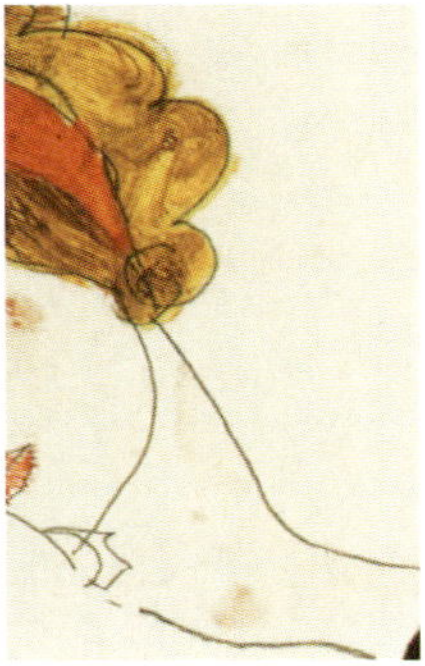

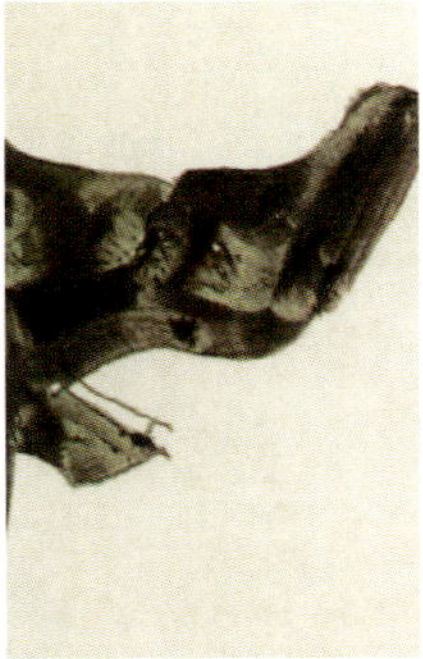

The nude study depicting a rigid member in the act of masturbation went a step further and shows he was a man fascinated by his own sexuality. This reversal in passivity accompanies the setting of a new goal: to be looked at. The urge to look is indeed autoerotic from the beginning; it surely has an object but finds it in its own body. In turn, showing the genitals is well known as an apotropaic action. Accordingly, Freud interprets "the showing of the penis and all its surrogates" as the following statement: "I am not afraid of you, I defy you."

Woman with Black Stockings
(Valerie Neuzil)

1913
Gouache, watercolour and pencil, 32.2 x 48 cm
Private collection

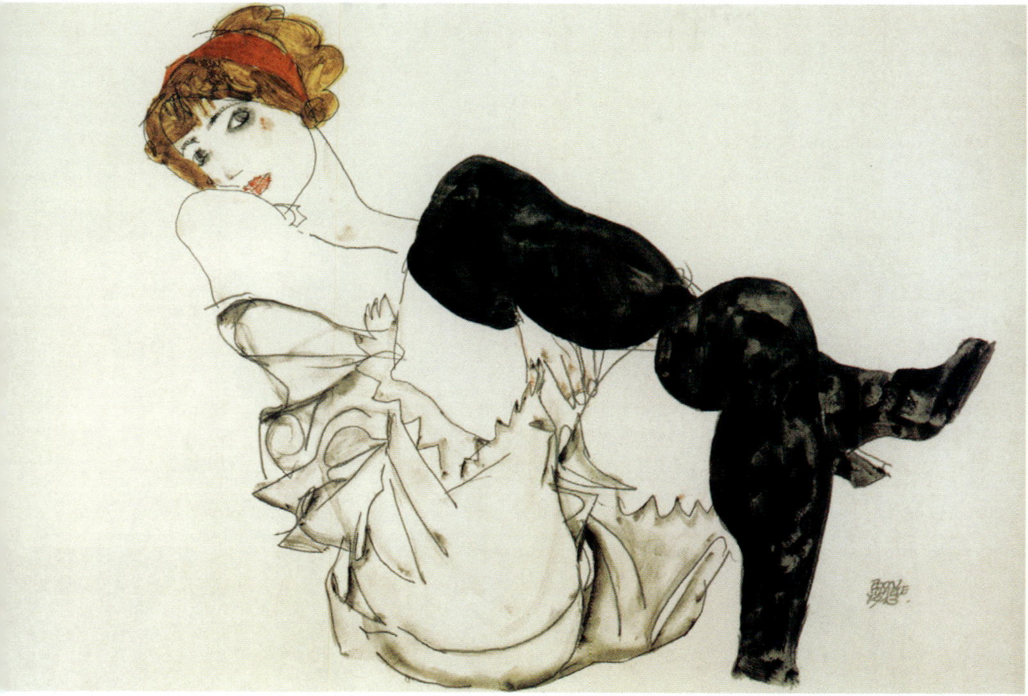

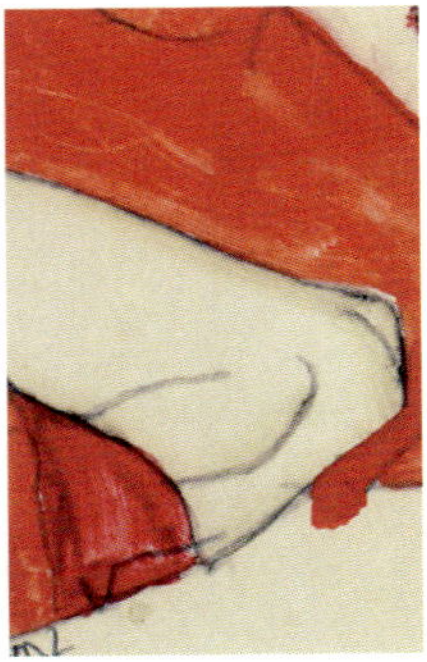

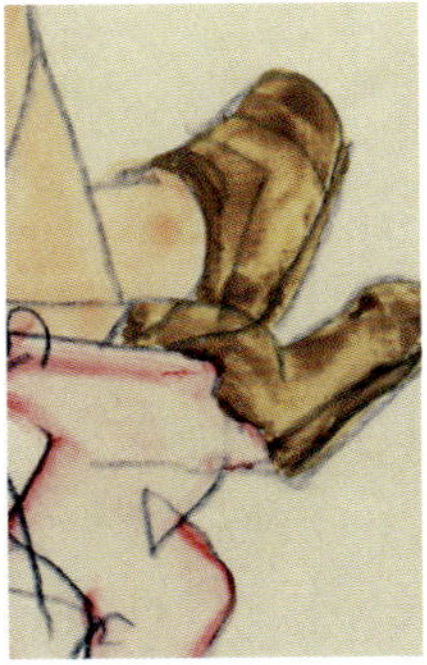

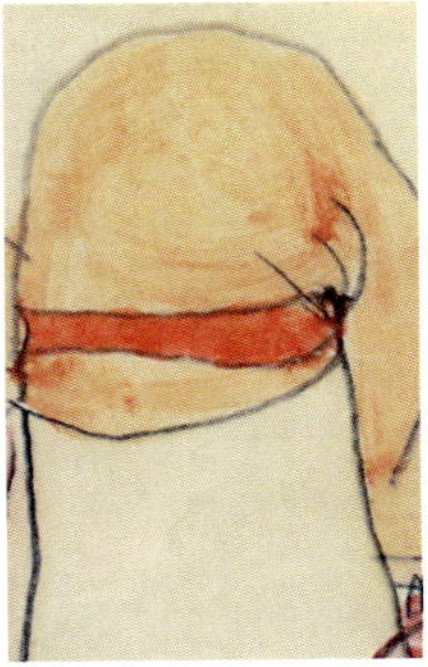

The discrepancy between Schiele's external appearance and his repulsively ugly self-portraits is astonishing. Gütersloh described Schiele as "exceptionally handsome", of well-maintained appearance, "someone who never had even a day-old beard", an elegant young man, whose good manners contrasted strangely with his reputedly unpalatable manner of painting. Schiele, on the other hand, painted himself with a long high forehead, wide opened eyes deep in their sockets and a tortured expression, an emaciated body,

Wally in Red Blouse with Raised Knees

1913
Gouache, watercolour and pencil, 31.8 x 48 cm
Private collection

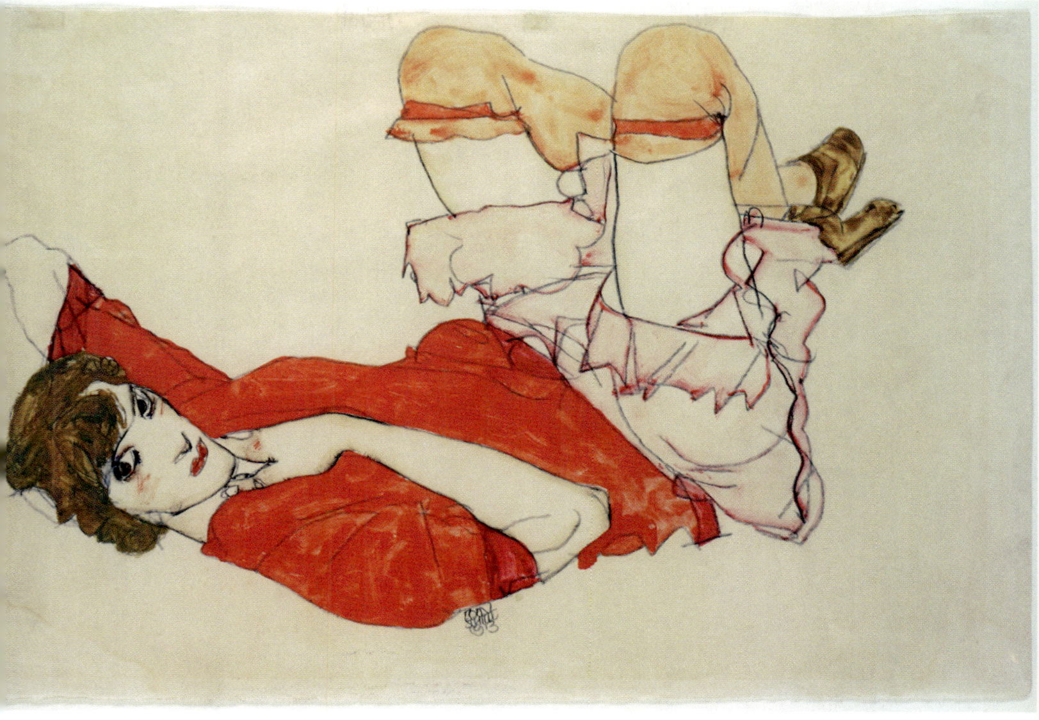

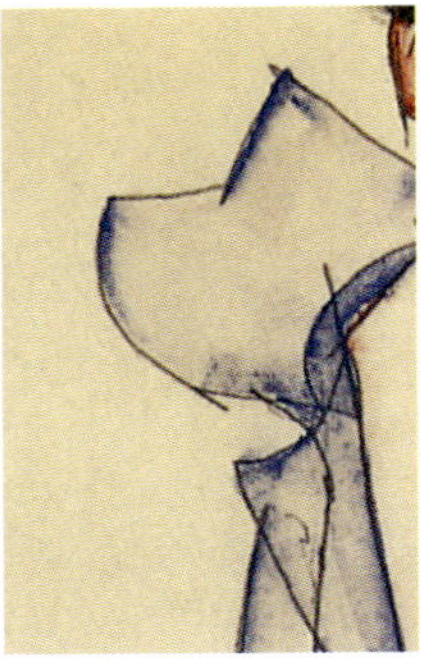

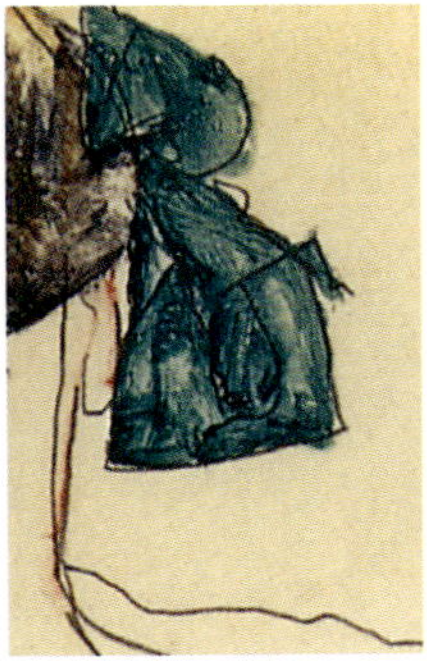

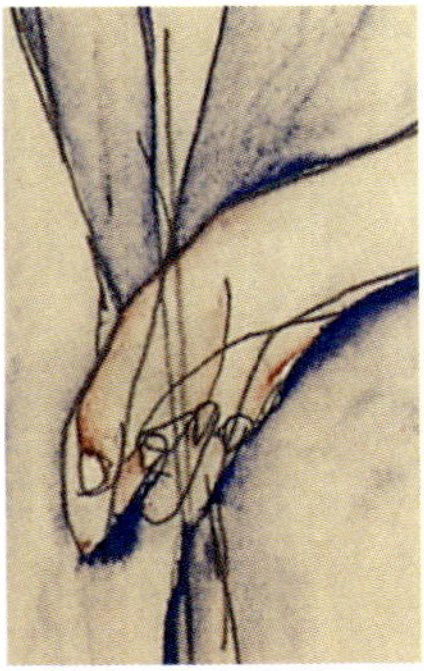

which he sometimes mutilated up to its trunk, with spider-like limbs. The bony hands tell of death at work. His body reflects the sallow colours of decay. In many places, he painted himself with a skull-like face. Schiele admitted in a verse: "everything is living dead". Just as Kokoschka maintained, Schiele soliloquised with death, his counterpart, "and surrounded by the flattery of decay, he lowers his infected lids" (Georg Trakl, Munich, 1974).

Standing Girl in Blue Dress and Green Stockings, Back View

1913
Watercolour and pencil, 47 x 31 cm
Private collection

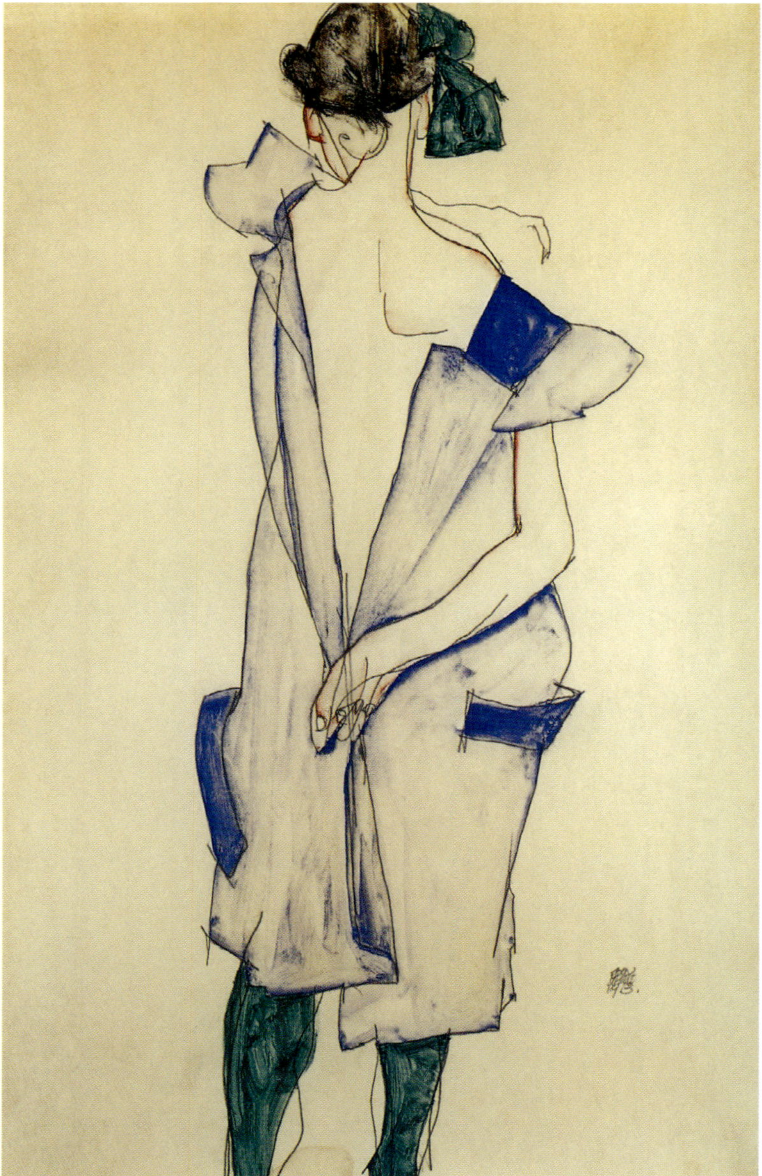

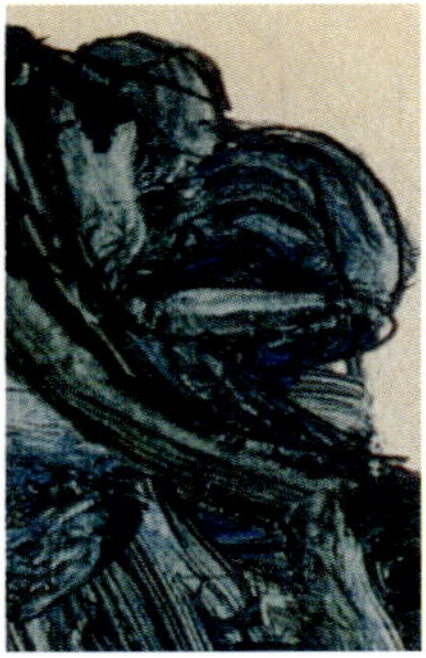

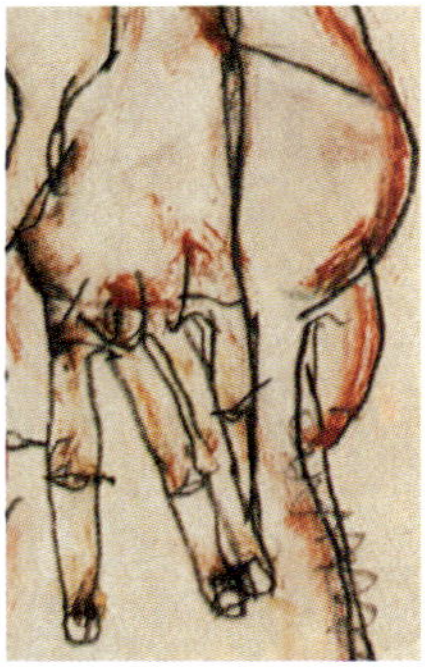

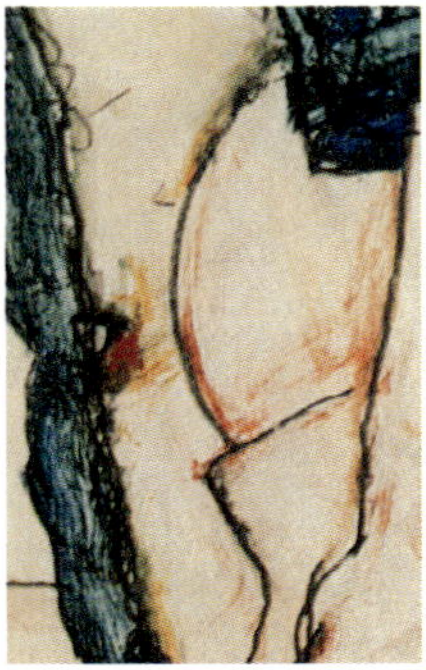

In a work like his 1911 gouache *Self-Portrait*, there is something of the qualities that Dürer's definitive biographer, Erwin Panofsky, saw in the great German master's own rare and uncompromising nude self-portrait. Around the time that Dürer made this private work, in about 1503, he was recovering from a feverish illness that may have been the plague. Panofsky's memorable phrase was: "The convalescent painter looks at his emaciated body and still haggard face with the same mixture of fatigue,

Preacher

1913
Gouache, watercolour and pencil, 47 x 30.8 cm
Leopold Museum, Vienna

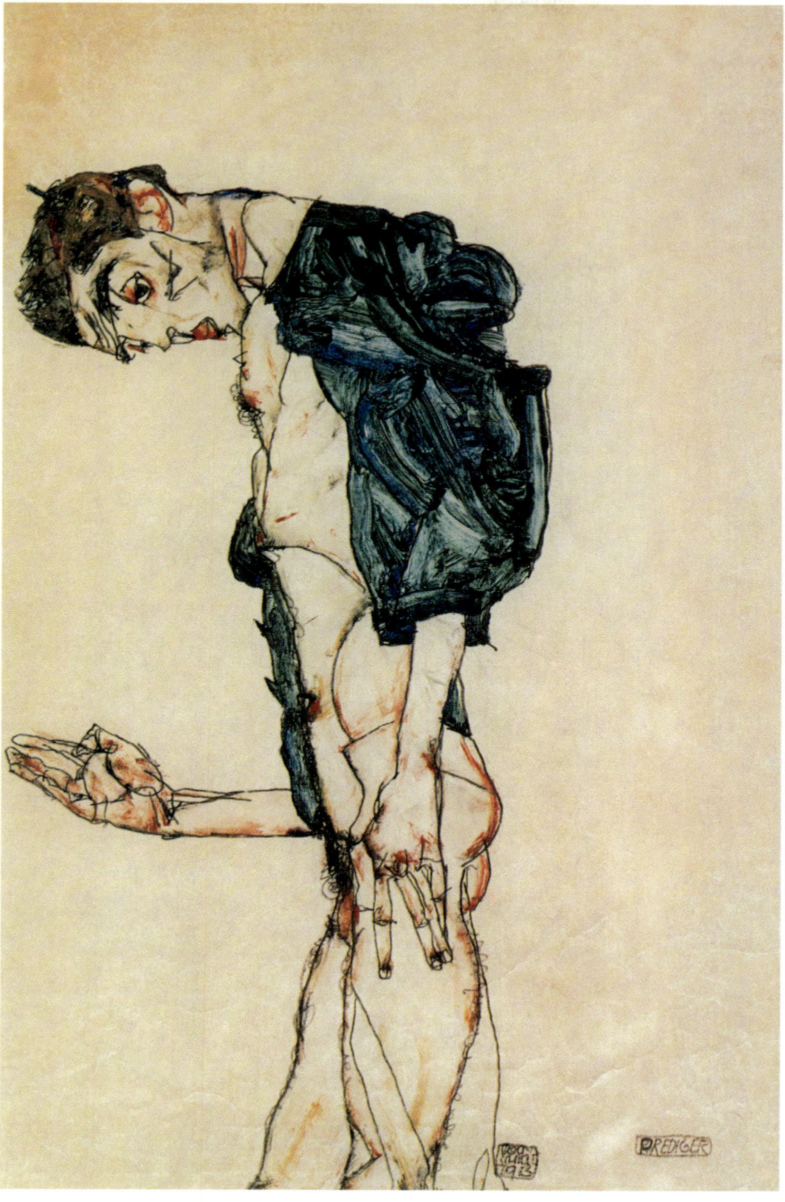
PREDIGER

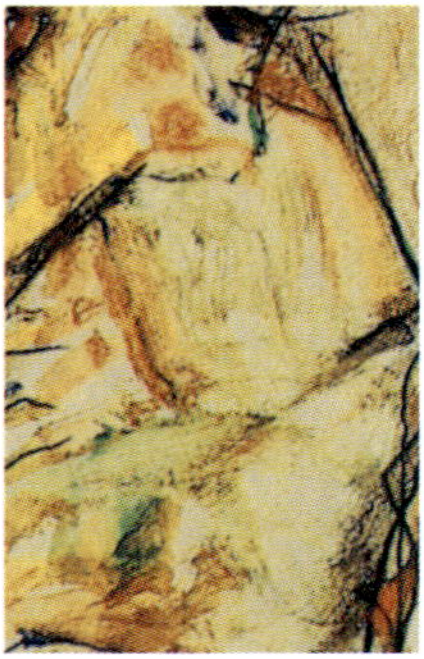

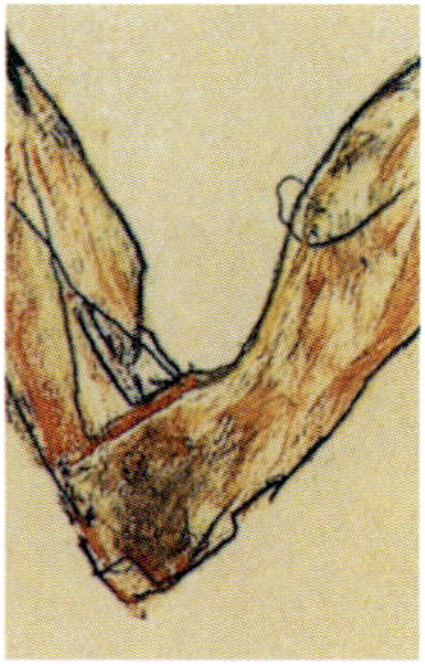

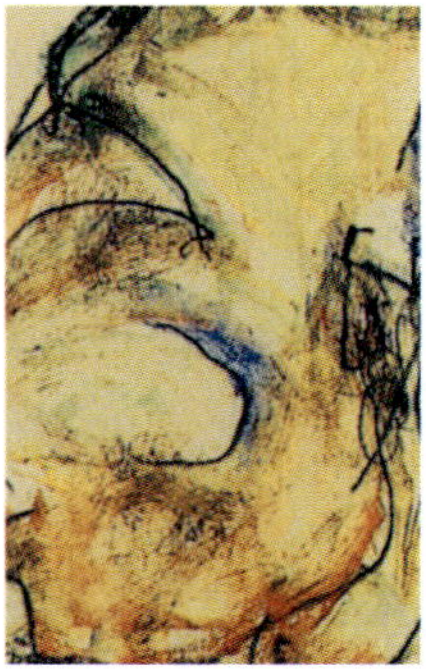

apprehension and dispassionate curiosity with which a farmer might take stock of his crops after a bad storm."

At the same time, Schiele perceived himself as a man of pain: "That I am true I only say, because I ... sacrifice myself and must live a martyr-like existence." If contemporary art banished religious themes from its field of vision, the artist now reincarnated these himself.

The Dancer

1913
Pencil, watercolour and gouache on paper
48 x 32 cm
Leopold Museum, Vienna

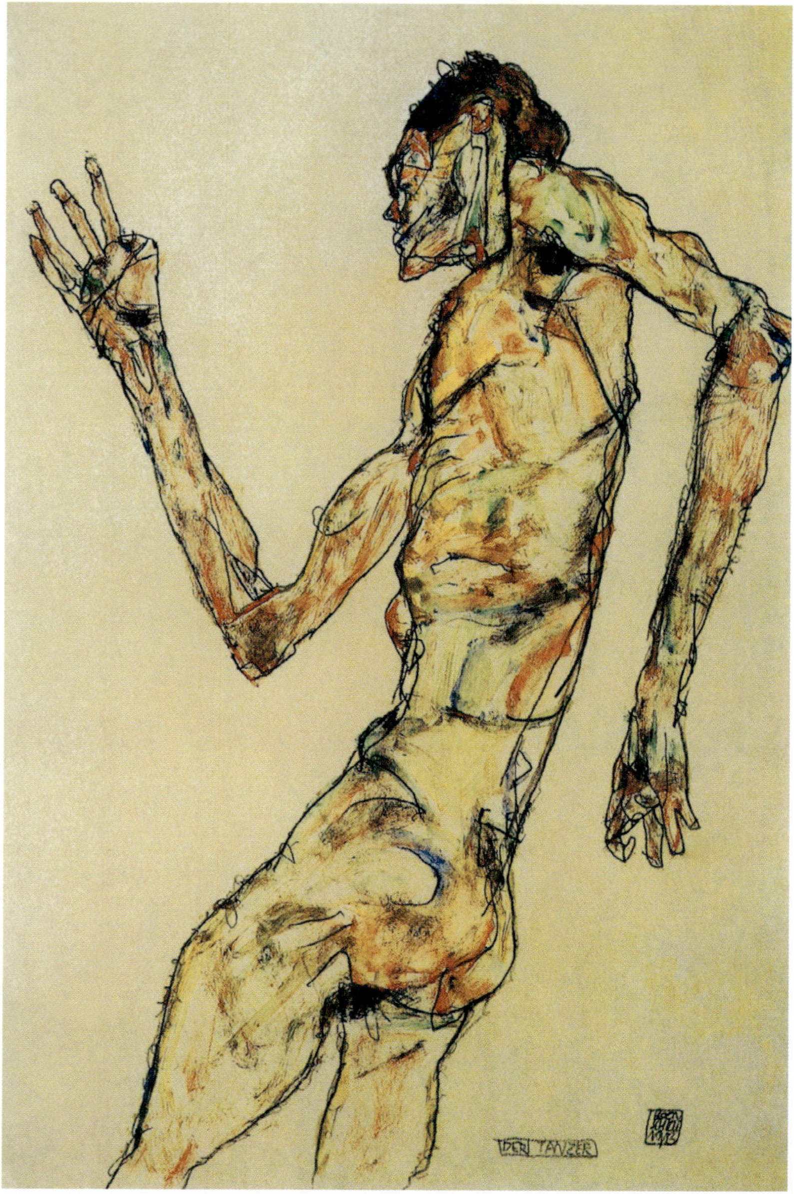
DER TANZER

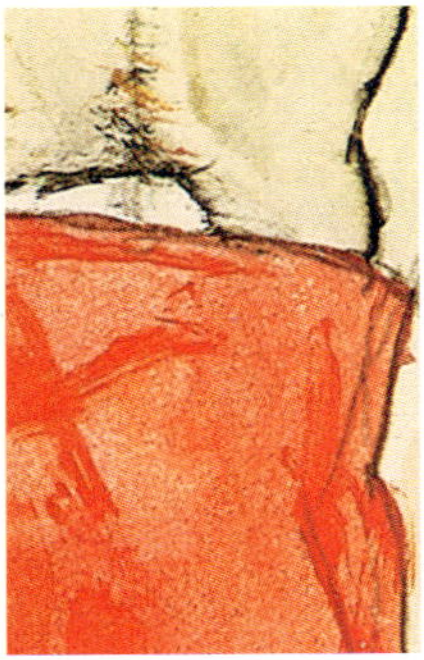

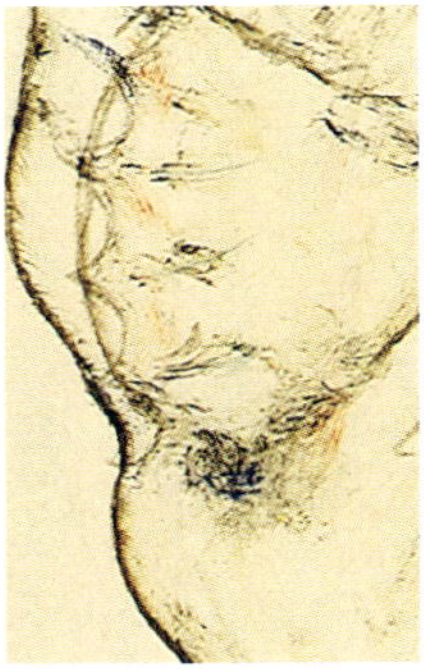

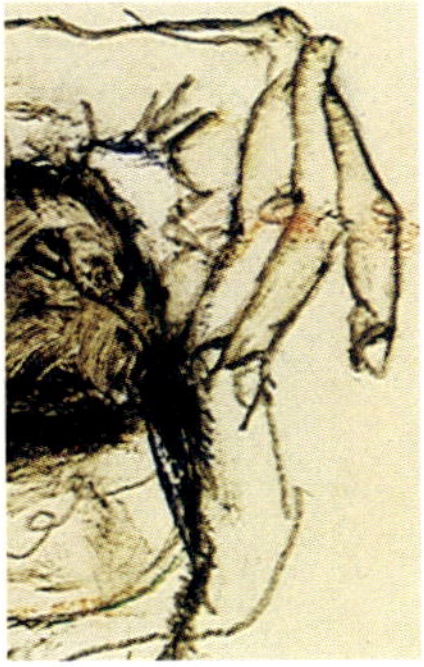

In a letter to Roessler the Christ-likeness becomes clearer still: "I sacrificed for others, for those on whom I took pity, those who were far away or did not see me, the seer." His fate as an outsider led to the ideal of the artist as world redeemer. Later, in 1915, the Viennese Galerie Arnot displayed an exclusive exhibition of sixteen paintings, watercolours and drawings by Schiele, among them, Schiele's *Self-Portrait as St. Sebastian* (1915).

Male Nude with Red Loincloth

1914
Gouache, watercolour and black pencil
48 x 32 cm
Albertina, Vienna

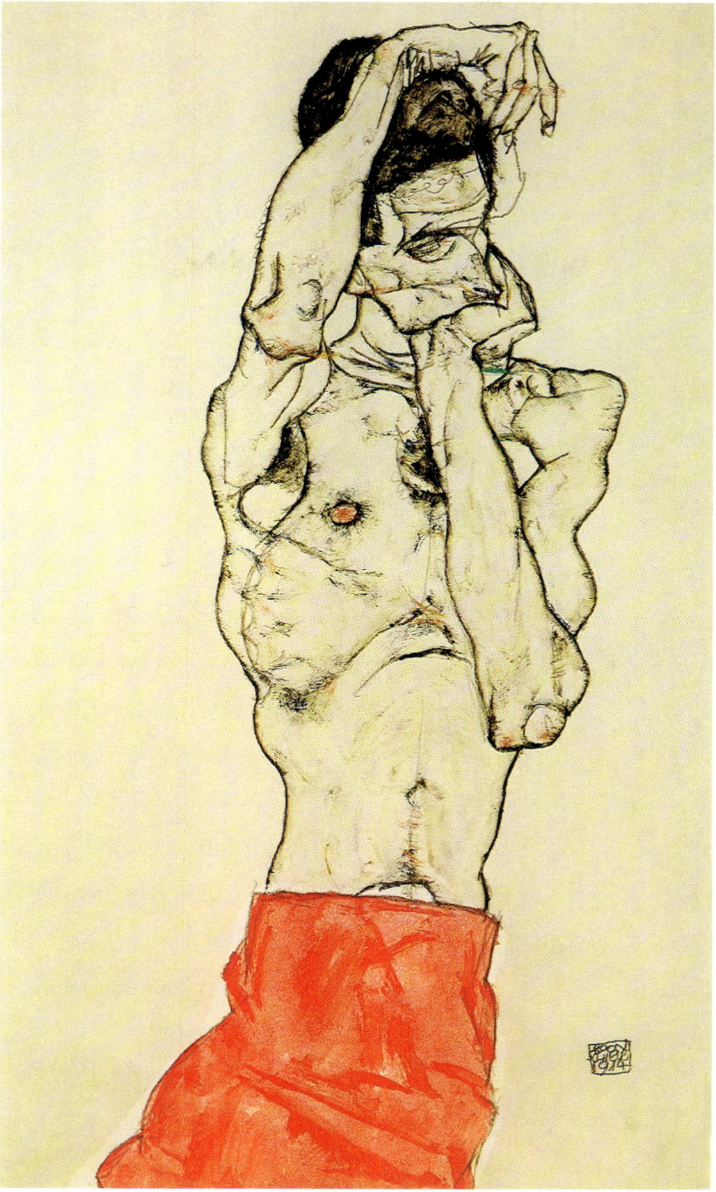

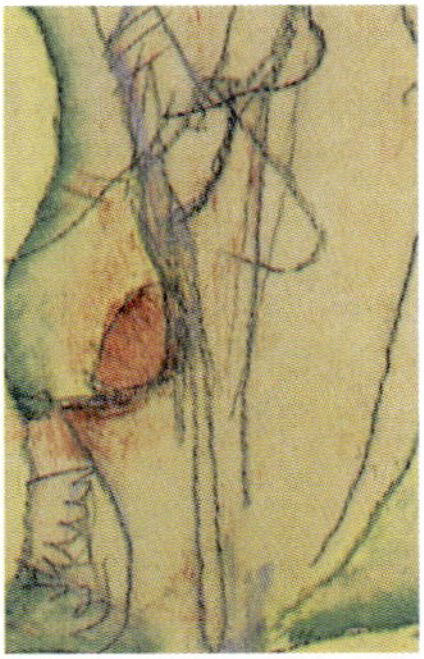

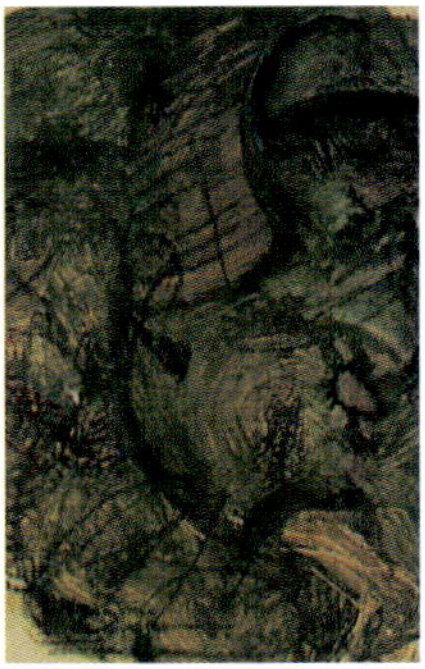

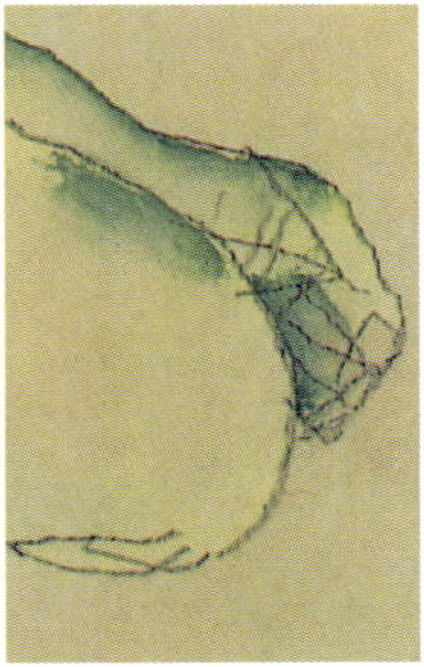

With this religiously engaged role model, he stands in the tradition of Oskar Kokoschka, Rainer Maria Rilke and Georg Trakl, who saw themselves as martyrs tormented by society. The adversarial – and ultimately elitist – notion of the "enlightened" artist pitted against the uncomprehending majority, sheds light on the heroic or pathos-laden identification of the artistic self with holy figures of martyrdom, which can be found in the work of several Expressionists.

Seated Nude

1914
Gouache and pencil, 46.4 x 31.1 cm
Private collection

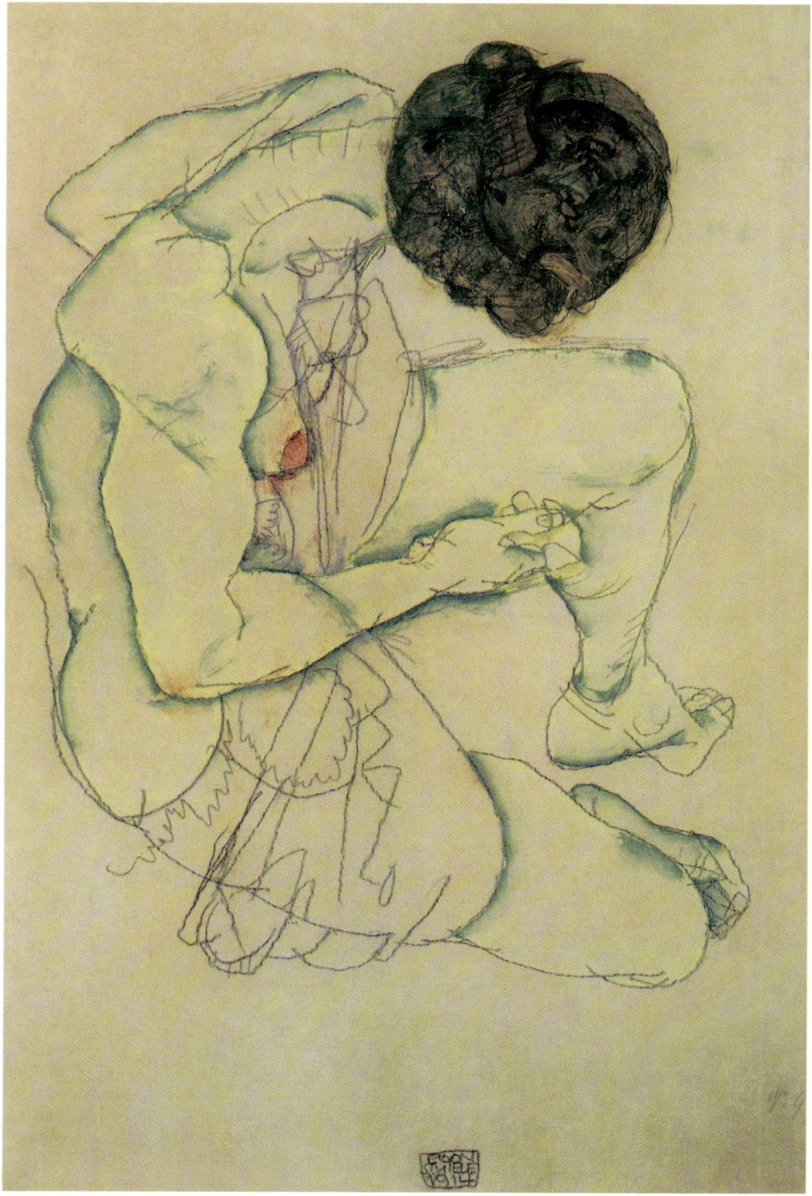

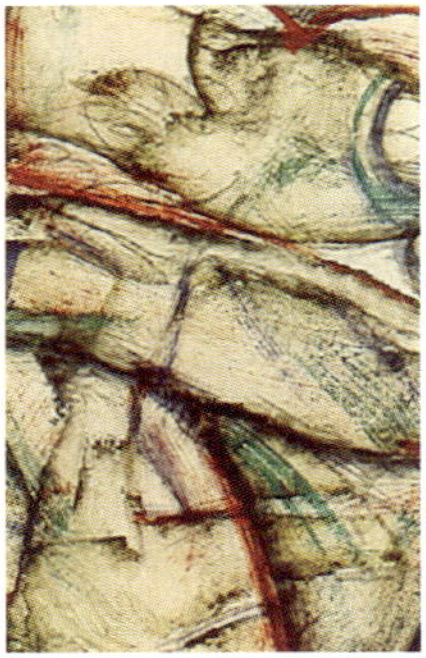

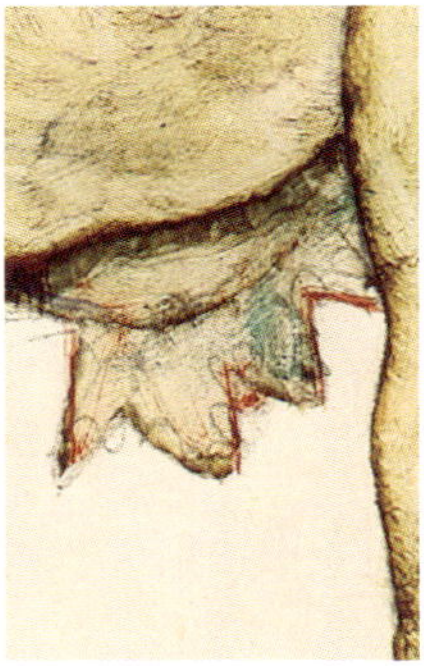

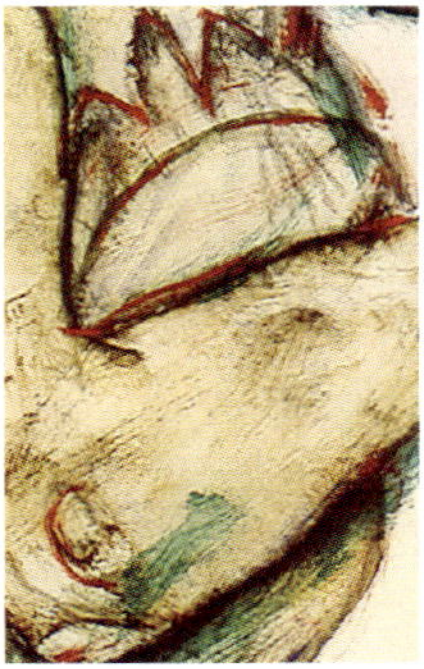

In the programme of the New Artists Schiele explains: "Fellow men feel their results, today in exhibitions. The exhibition is indispensable today ... the great experience in the existence of the artist's individuality." For him, however, this no longer concerned illustration; rather it was a representation of his soul's inner life. The nude study is a revealing study. Thereby, the work in its expressive self-staging becomes a study of his life.

Seated Woman with Left Hand in Hair

1914
Gouache and black pencil, 48.5 x 31.4 cm
Albertina, Vienna

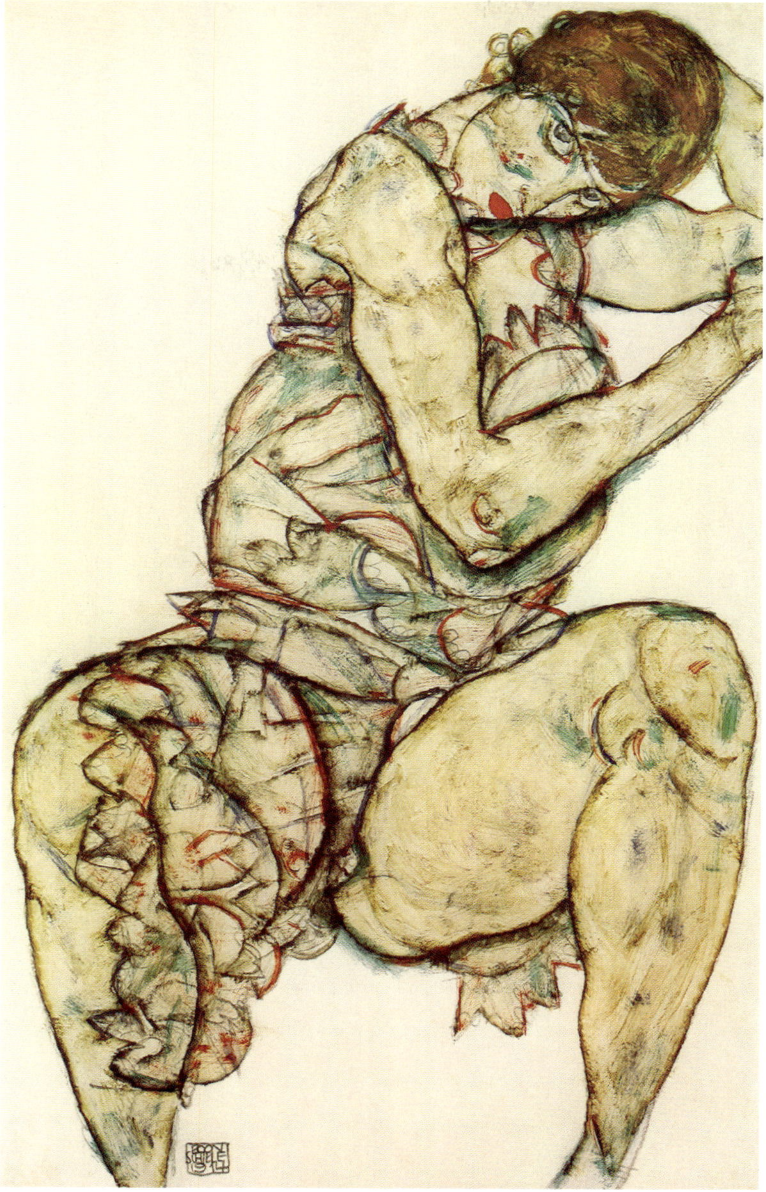

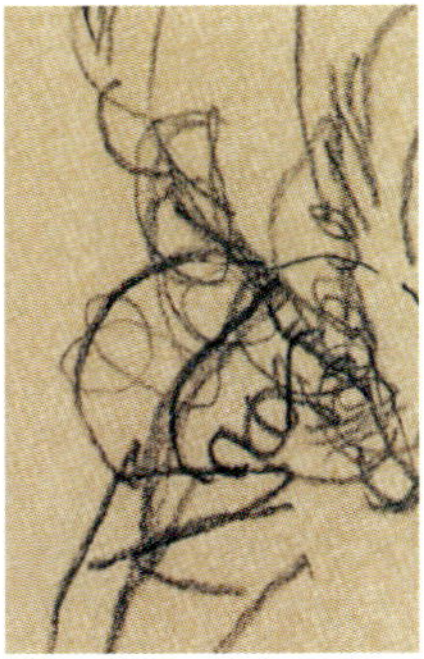

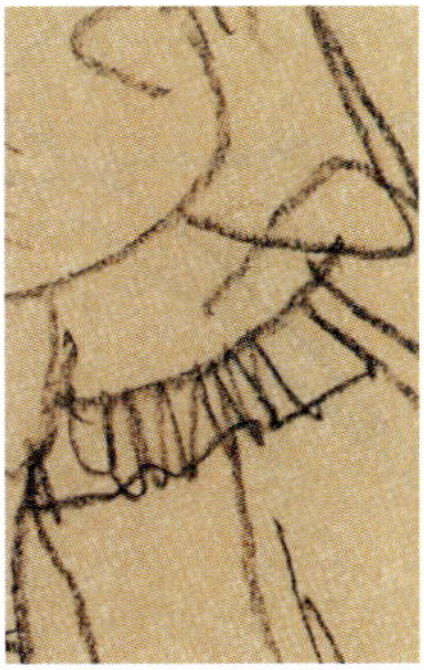

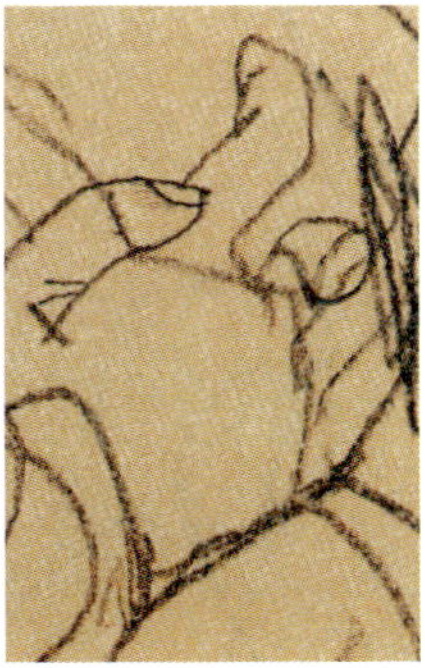

His self-portrait entitled *The Poet* (1911) is generally considered to be one of Schiele's early masterpieces and a fine example of Expressionist portraiture. The title reminds us of Schiele's notion that all artistic forms are inter-related. Here he states that the artist is a condemned creature who, by virtue of his true vision of the world, sees more and is, therefore, condemned to suffer more.

Seated Girl

1914
Pencil, 43 x 30 cm
Staatliche Graphische Sammlung, Munich

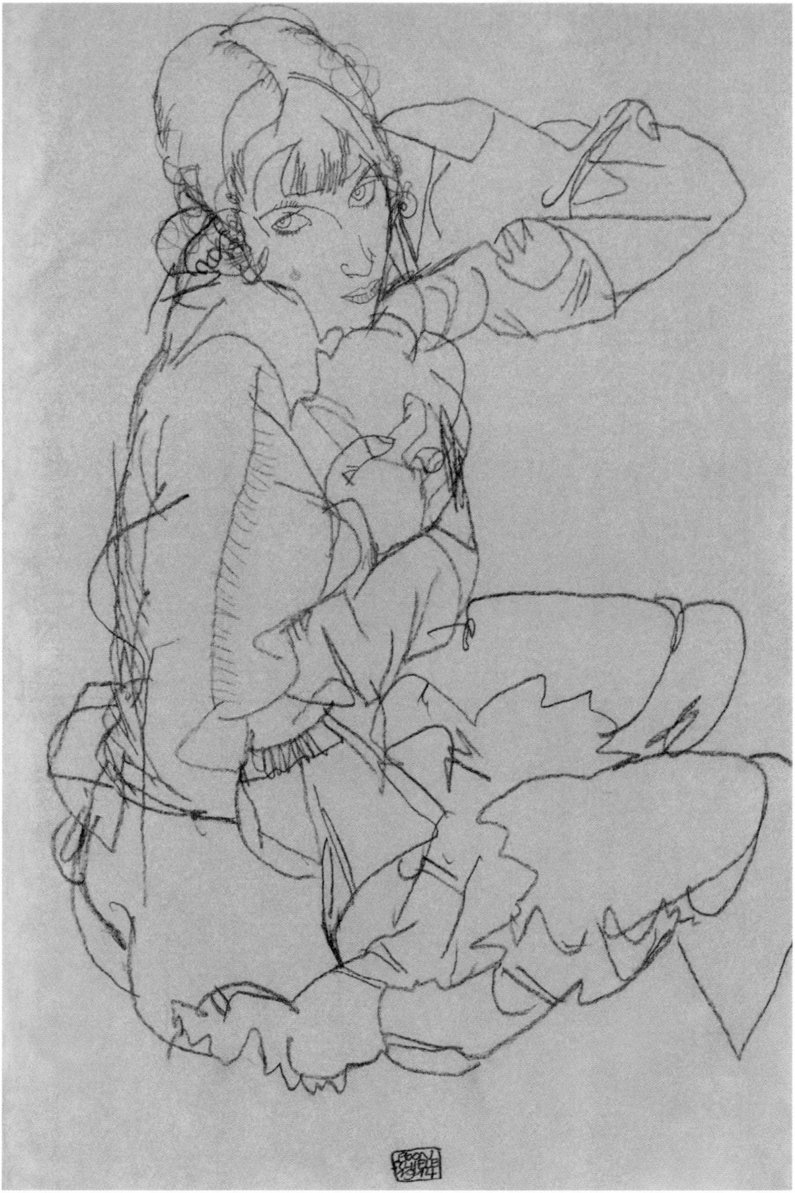

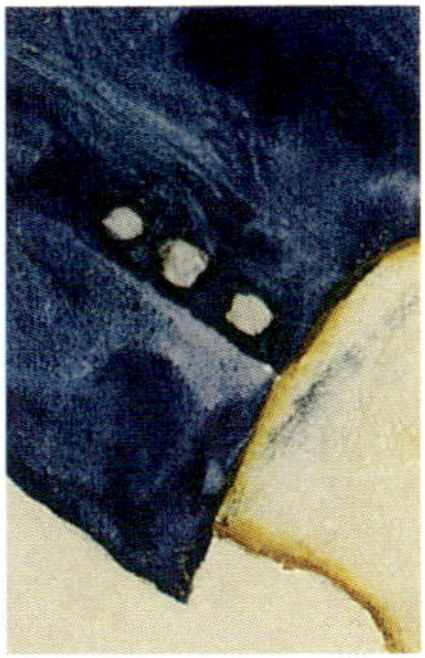

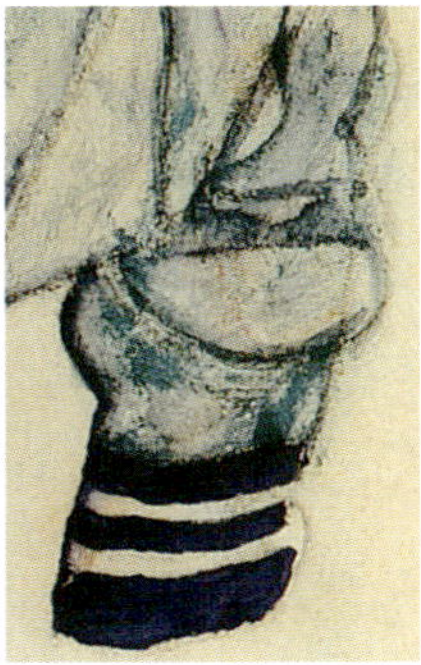

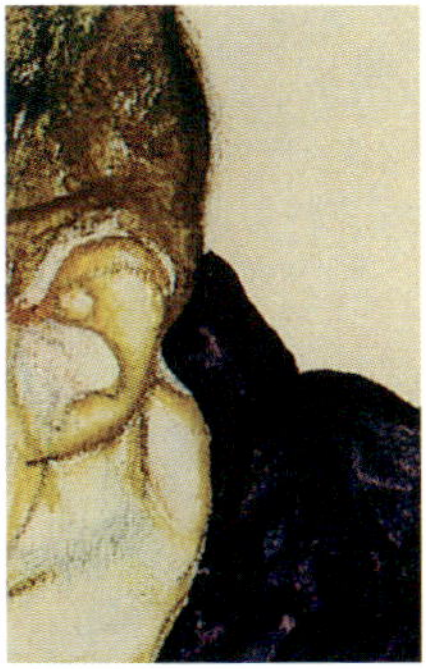

An unusual feature of this painting is that the genitalia appear to be almost hermaphrodite-like, with feminine detail being pierced rather violently by a red-tipped phallic image. This, too, suggests that all artists are as one, whether female or male. It also hints at sexual ambiguities and cross-gender issues which were both fashionable and still slightly outrageous at this period.

Boy in Sailor Suit

1914

Gouache, watercolour, coloured pencil and pencil on paper, 47.8 x 31.2 cm

Private collection

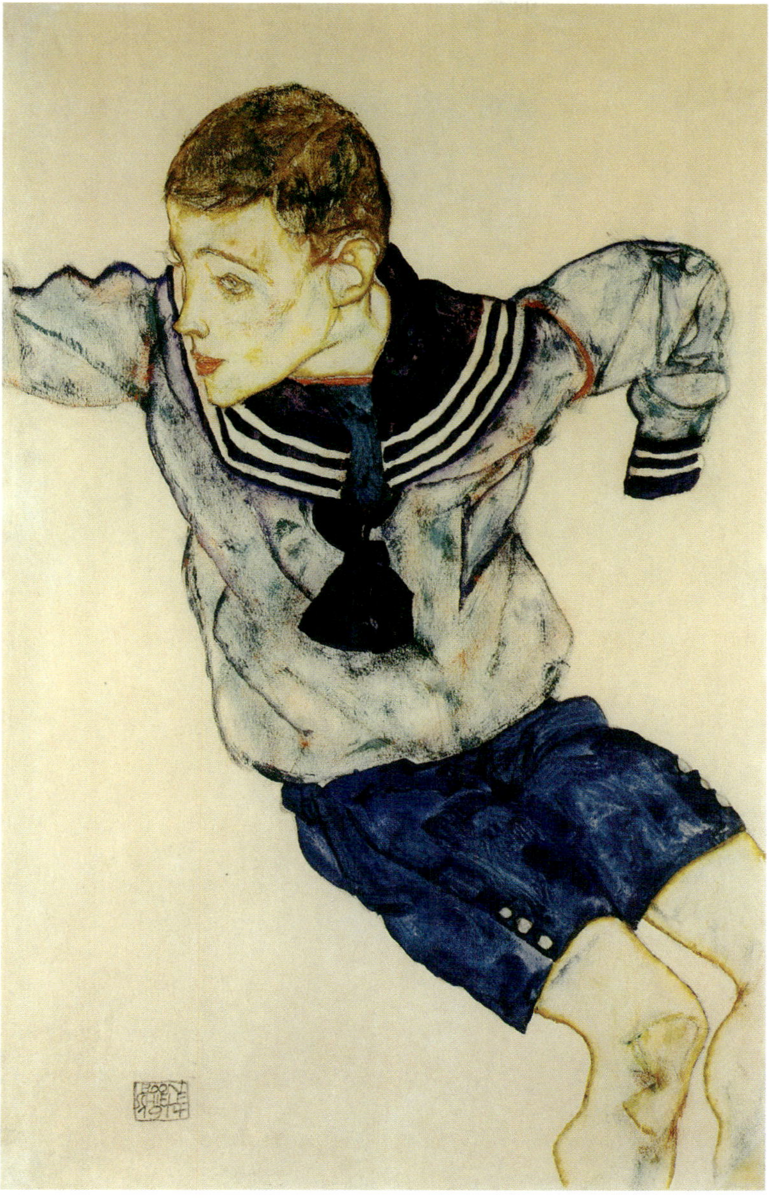
EGON
SCHIELE
1914

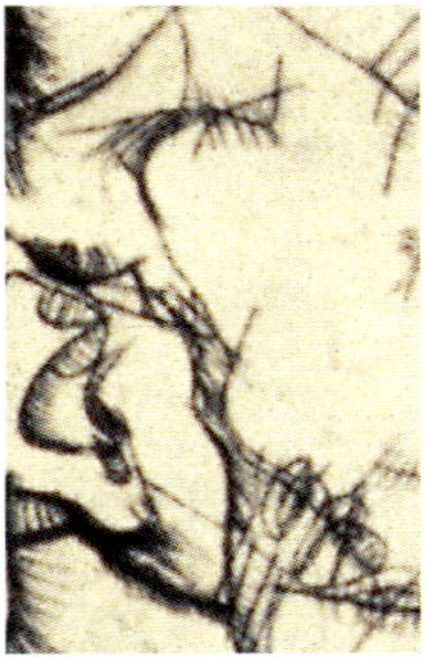

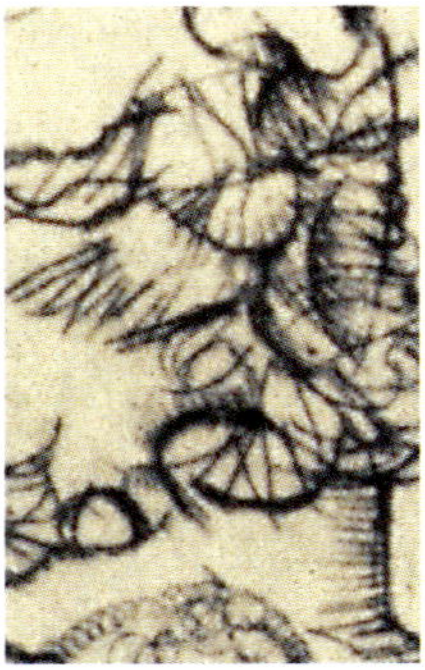

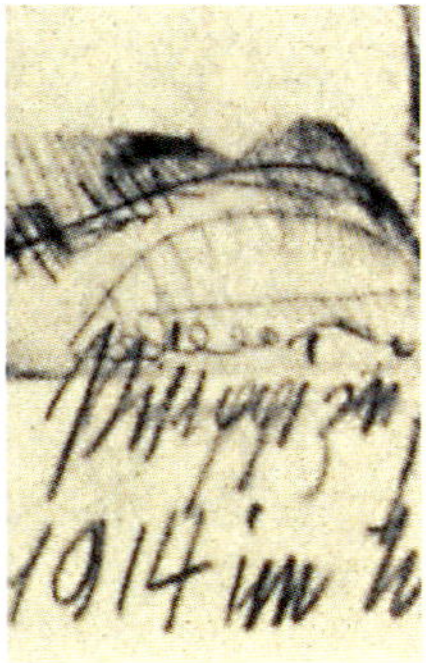

The notion of the hermaphrodite, however, also leads to the idea that Schiele is both a creator of art and a mother of all creation. He is outside the common sexual and social taboos of society and thus aligned to his fellow artists but he also contains within himself an almost mythic force and a super-sexual ability to create and procreate.

Portrait of Franz Hauer

1914
Lithograph, 13 x 11 cm
Private collection

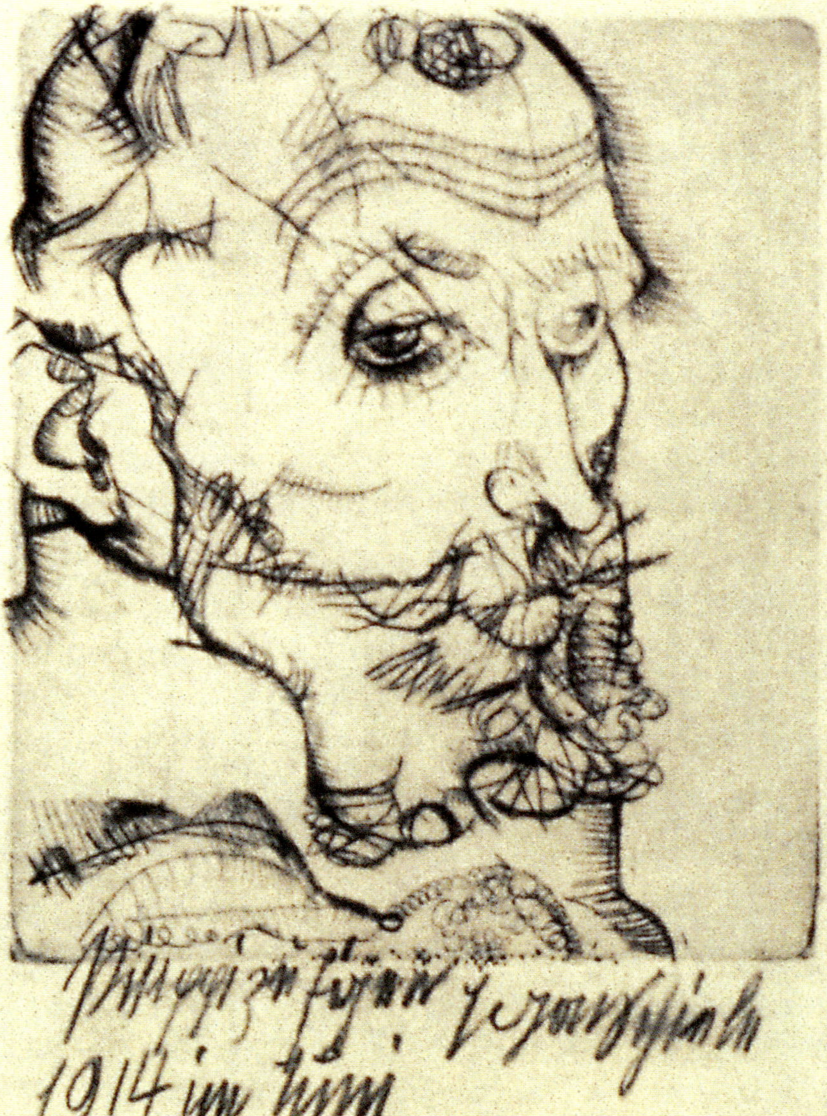

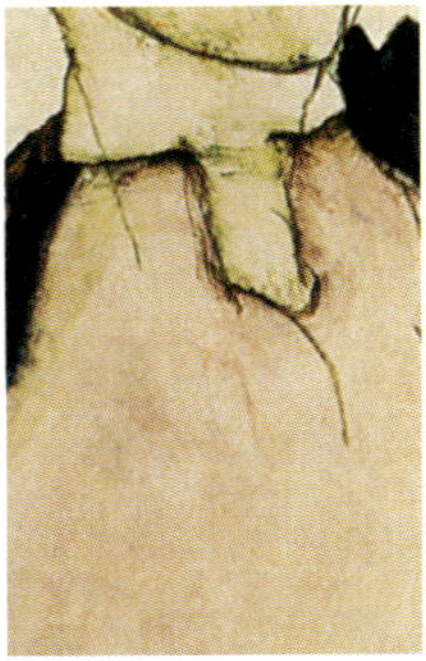

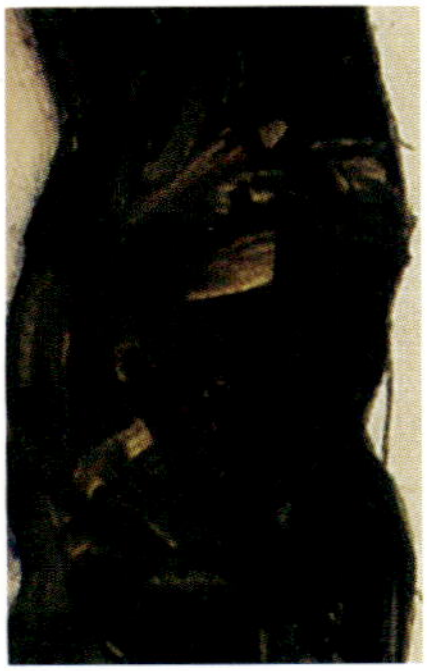

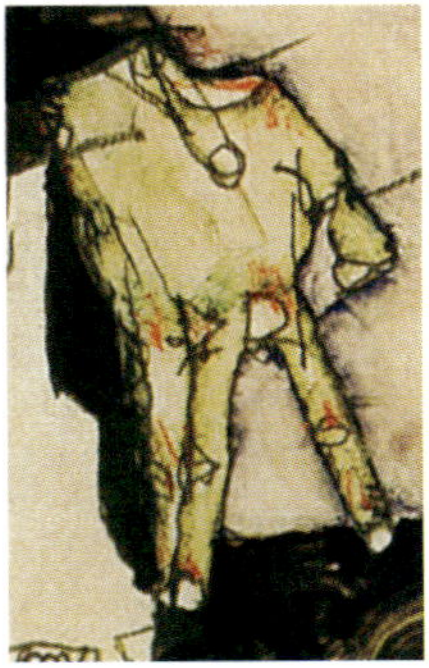

Moreover, the artist's "interior" vision is strongly suggested in several works by Schiele in which he depicts himself with eyes closed, or blind, almost eye*less* (*Preacher*, 1913). They include oil works in which he appears as a *"Selbstseher"* (*Self-Seer II*, 1911). On one level, the painting can be read as a reflection on the nature of "seeing" itself. The self-portrait genre is by definition an exercise in "self-seeing".

Self-Portrait with Lavender Shirt and Dark Suit Standing

1914
Pencil, watercolour and gouache on paper, 48.4 x 32.2 cm
Albertina, Vienna

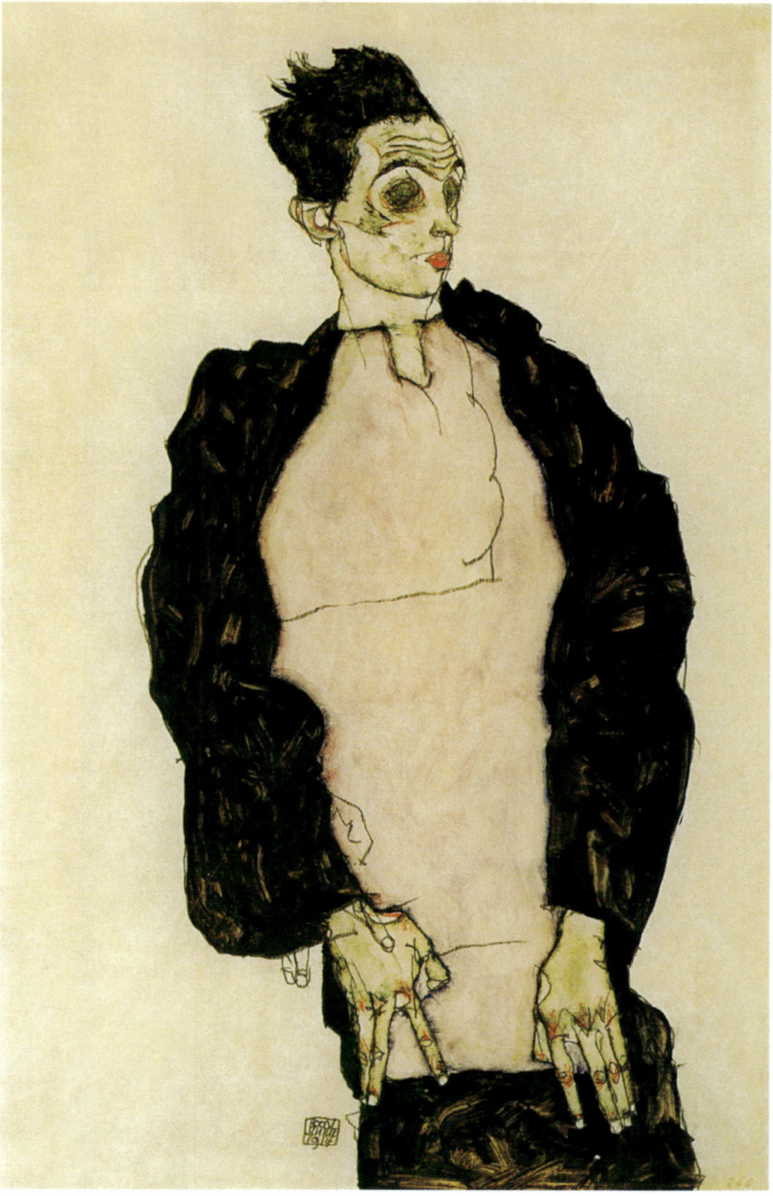

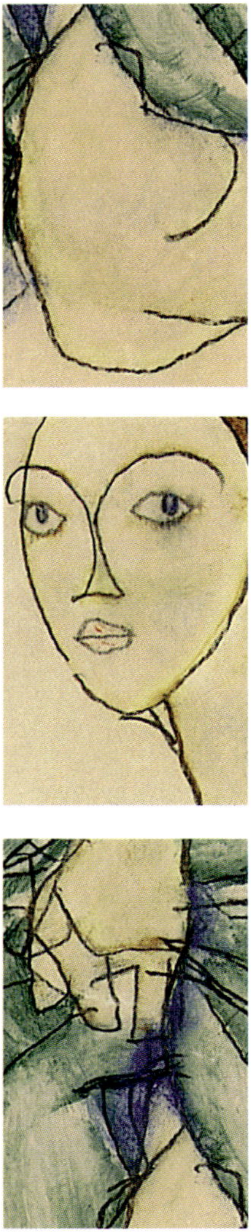

However, the conventional relationship between subject (seer) and object (what is seen), which is already destabilised in self-portraiture, since the artist takes on both roles, is *doubly* blurred here. Two kinds of "seeing" are going on. His eyes shut, as if in sleep or meditation, Schiele "sees" himself – and his mortality – in the double image, like a projection behind him. Fossil or phantom, the bleached and shrouded form is disembodied.

Standing Woman in Green Shirt

1914
Gouache, watercolour and pencil
48.2 x 32 cm
Private collection

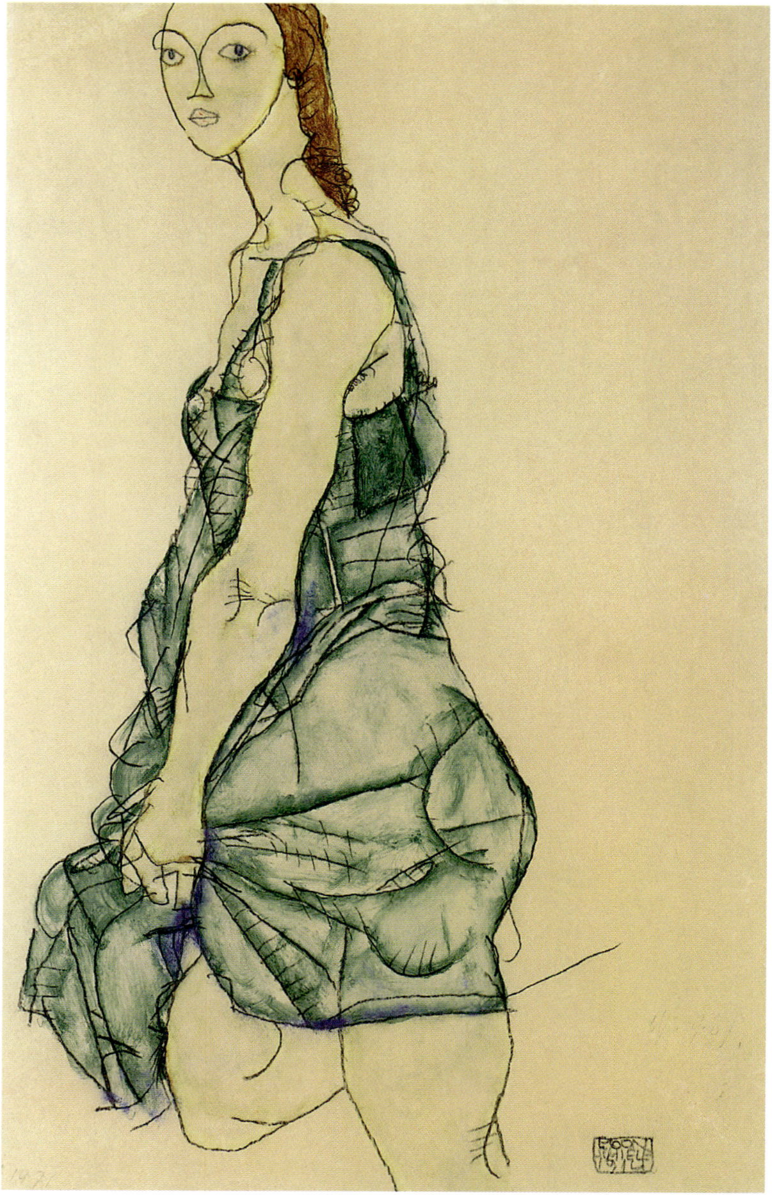

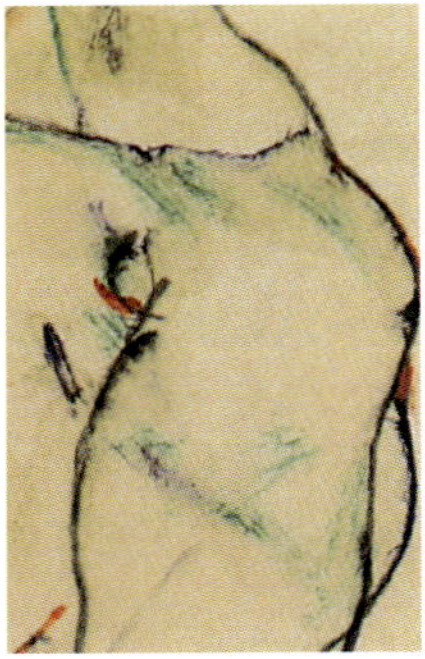

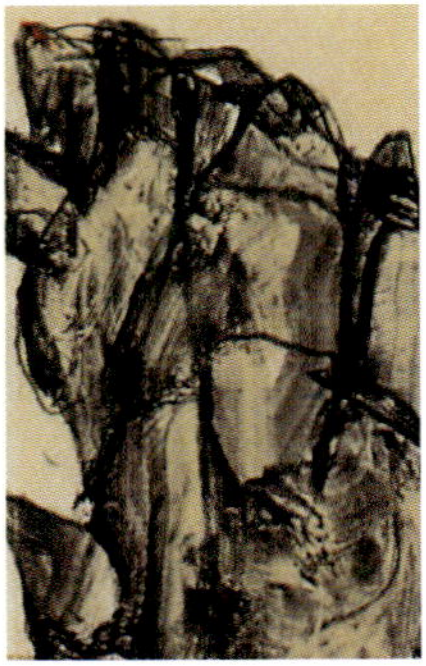

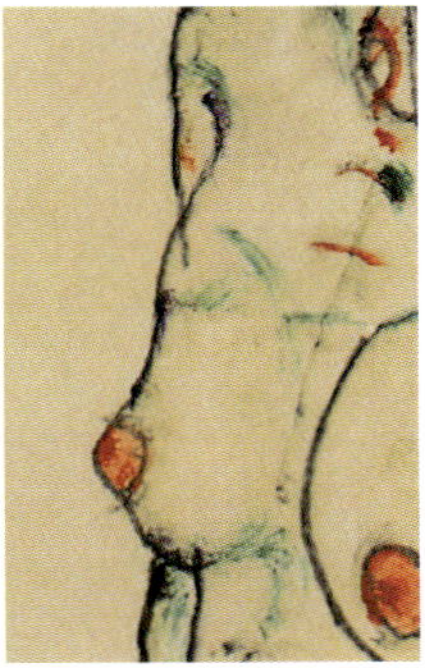

In fact, Schiele also referred to the painting as *Death and the Man*. In so doing, he created a highly original take on the traditional *vanitas* theme in art, in which the presence of death, traditionally in the shape of a skull or a skeleton, reminds us of our own transience on earth. Both themes – of vision and of mortality – are powerful and recurrent in Viennese Expressionism.

Standing Nude with Green Scarf

1914
Gouache, watercolour and pencil, 48.3 x 32 cm
Germanisches Nationalmuseum, Nuremberg

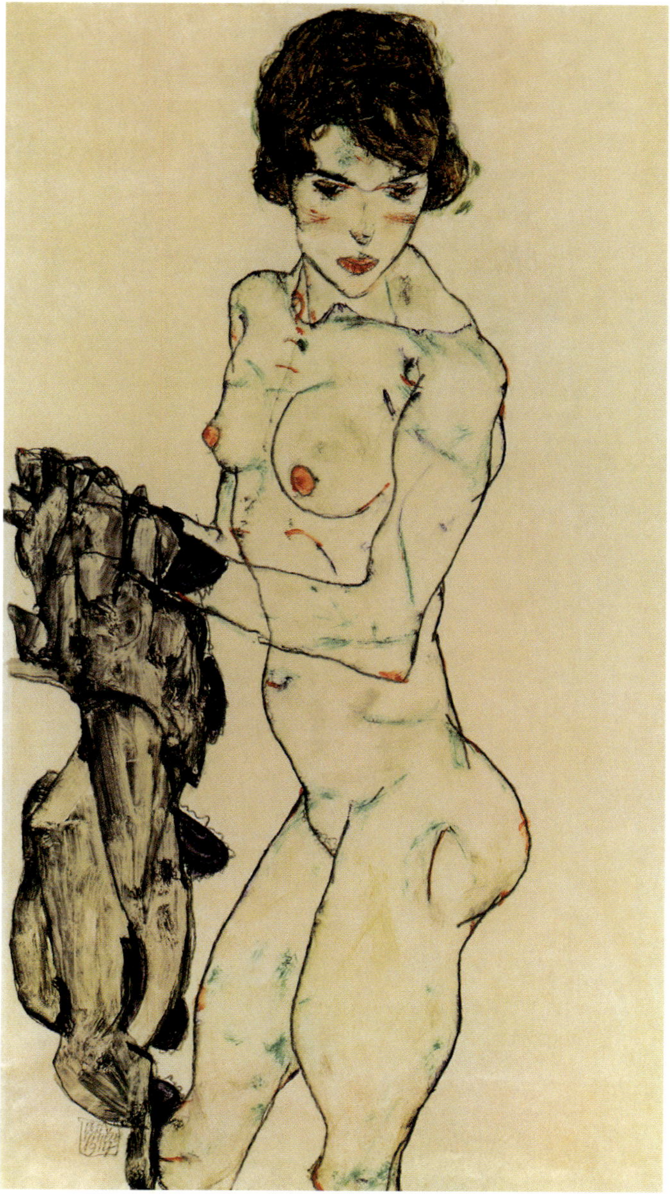

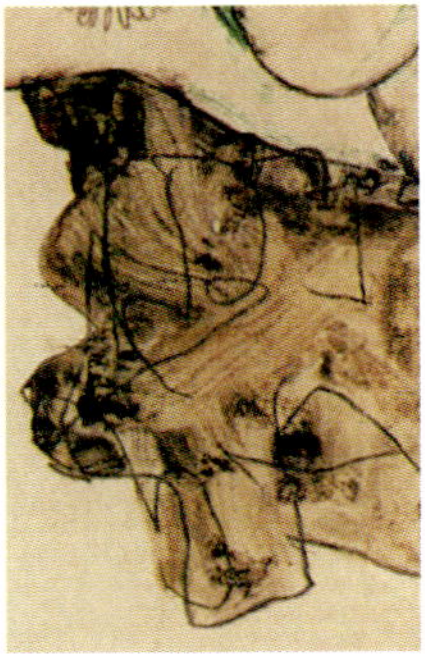
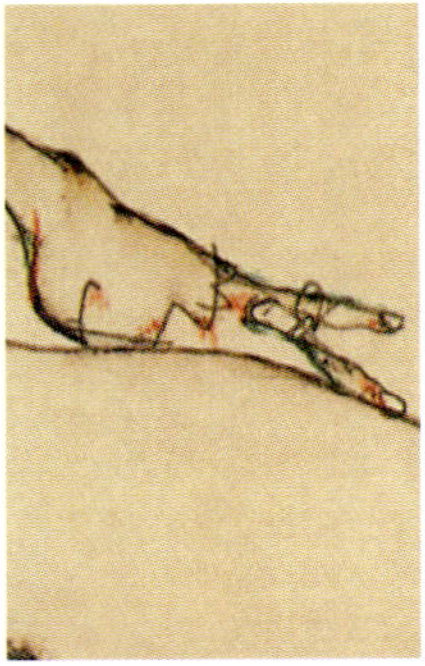
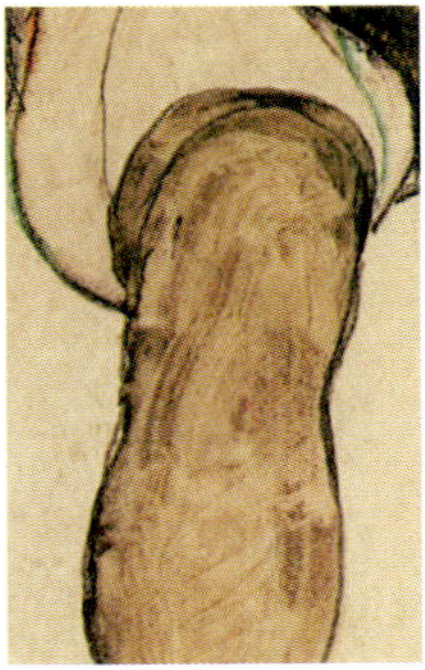

The Viennese at the turn of the century lived with a longing for death and romanticised the "beautiful corpse". "How ill everything coming into being does seem to be," wrote Trakl, who in 1914, met death at the Front.

His fascination with death led Schiele to seek its mark on exterior subjects, surpassing his own condition. Schiele shared with Osen, who had himself locked away in a Steinhof insane asylum where he might study the behaviour of the patients there, an interest in pathologic pictures of disease.

Reclining Female Nude, with Spread Legs

1914
Gouache and pencil, 30.4 x 47.2 cm
Albertina, Vienna

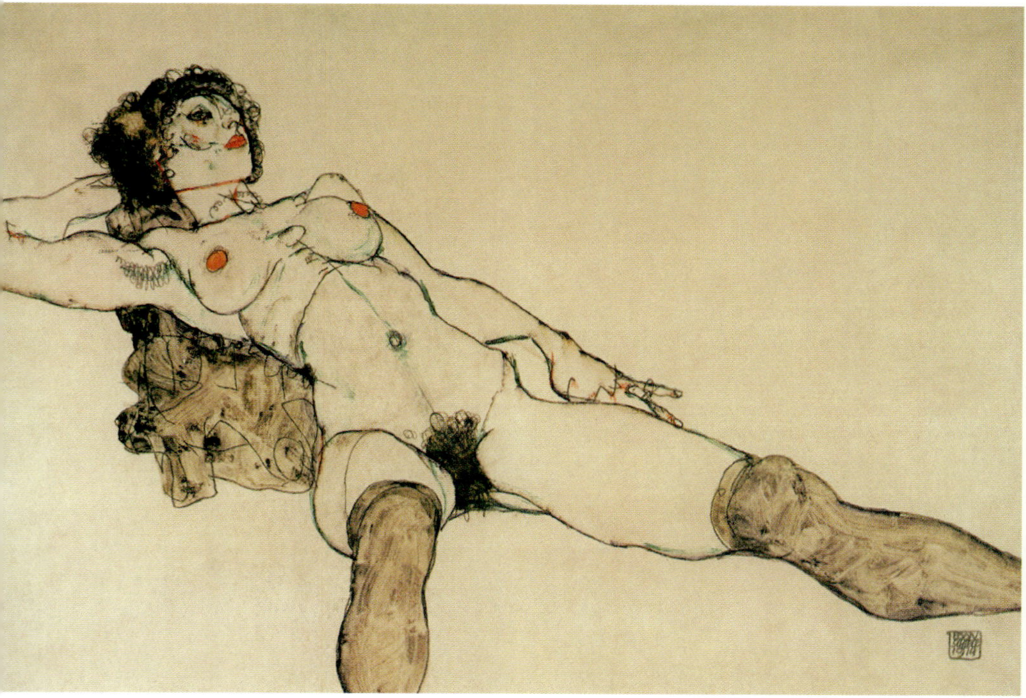

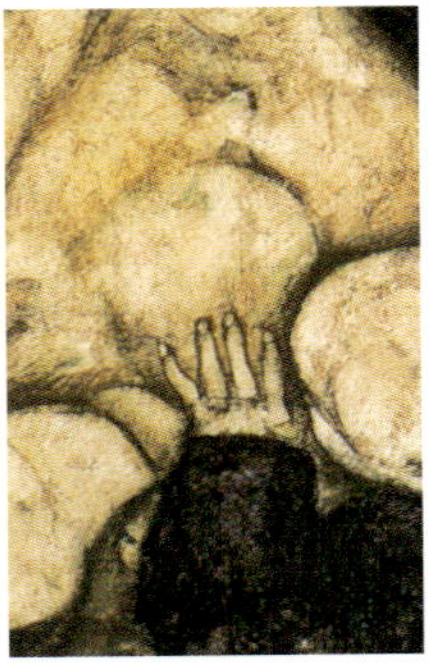

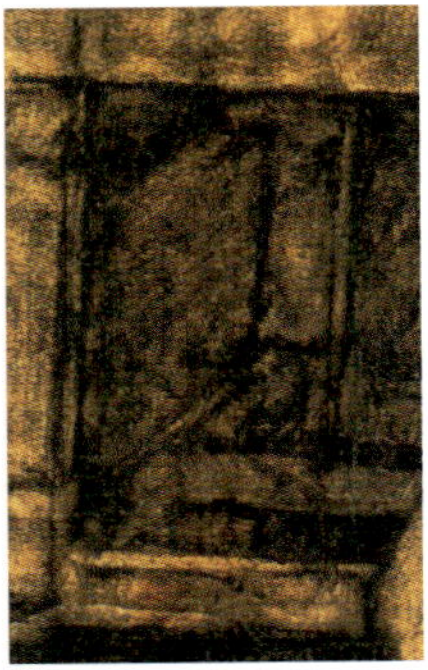

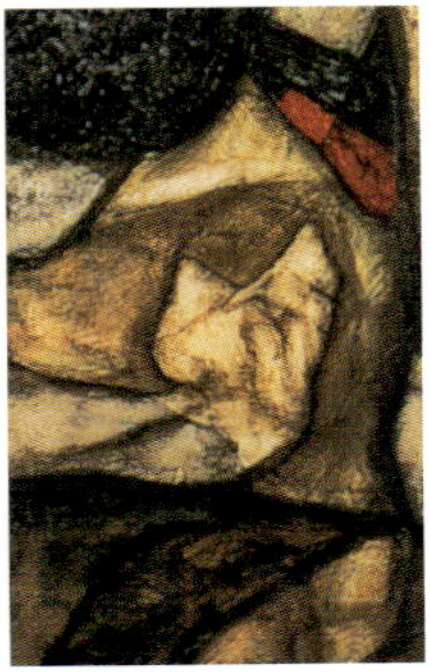

In the clinic of the gynaecologist Erwin von Graf, he studied and drew sick and pregnant women and pictures of new and stillborn infants. Schiele was "fascinated by the devastation of foul suffering, to which these innocents were exposed. Astonished, he saw unusual changes in the skin in whose sagging vessels thin, watery blood and tainted fluids trickled sluggishly, he marvelled also at light-sensitive green eyes behind red lids,

Blind Mother I

1914
Oil on canvas, 99.5 x 120.4 cm
Leopold Museum, Vienna

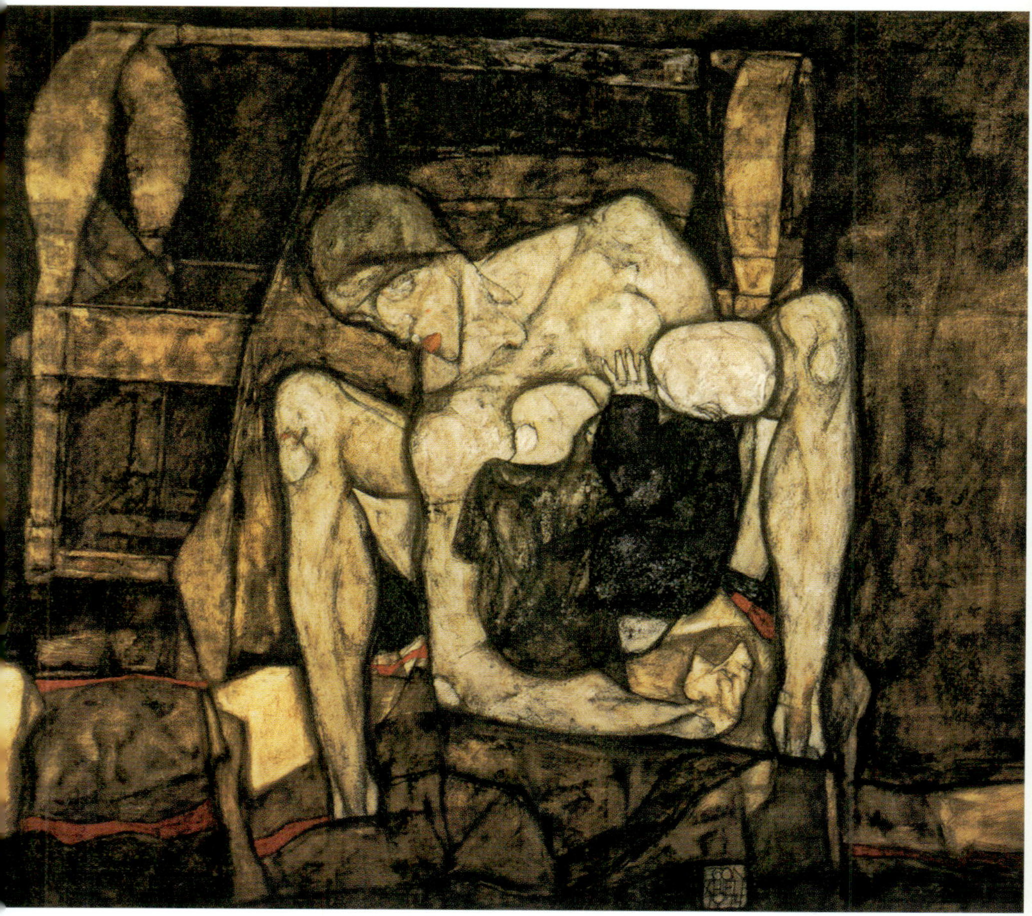

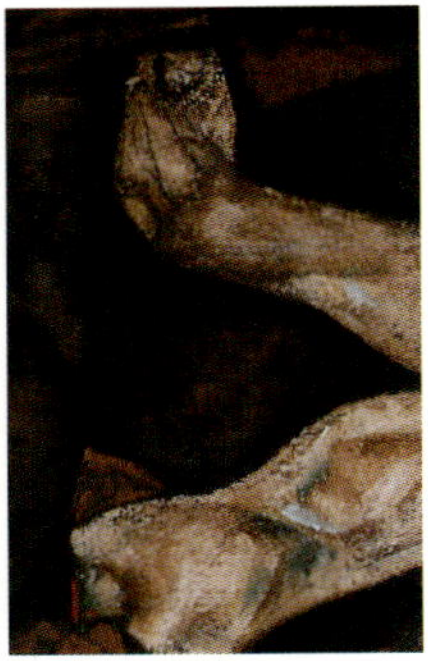

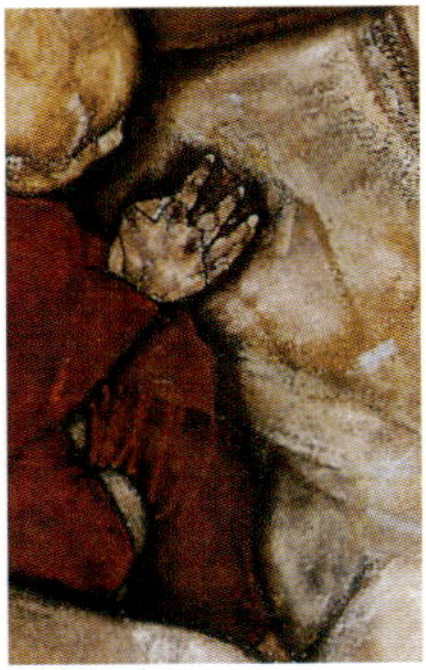

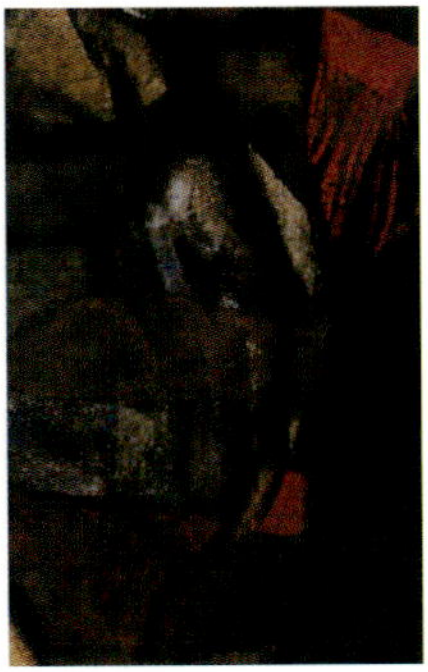

the slimy mouths and the soul in these unsound vessels,'' reports Roesseler. Therein he resembled Oskar Kokoschka, called the "soul slasher" and of whom it was said that "painting hand and head, he lay bare in a ghostly manner the spiritual skeleton of her whom he portrayed". To the colour lithograph of his drama, *Murder Hope of Women*, he commented: "The man is bloody red, the colour of life, but he lies dead in the lap of a woman, who is white, the colour of death." Man and woman in the dance of life and death.

Young Mother

1914
Oil on canvas, 100 x 110 cm
Private collection

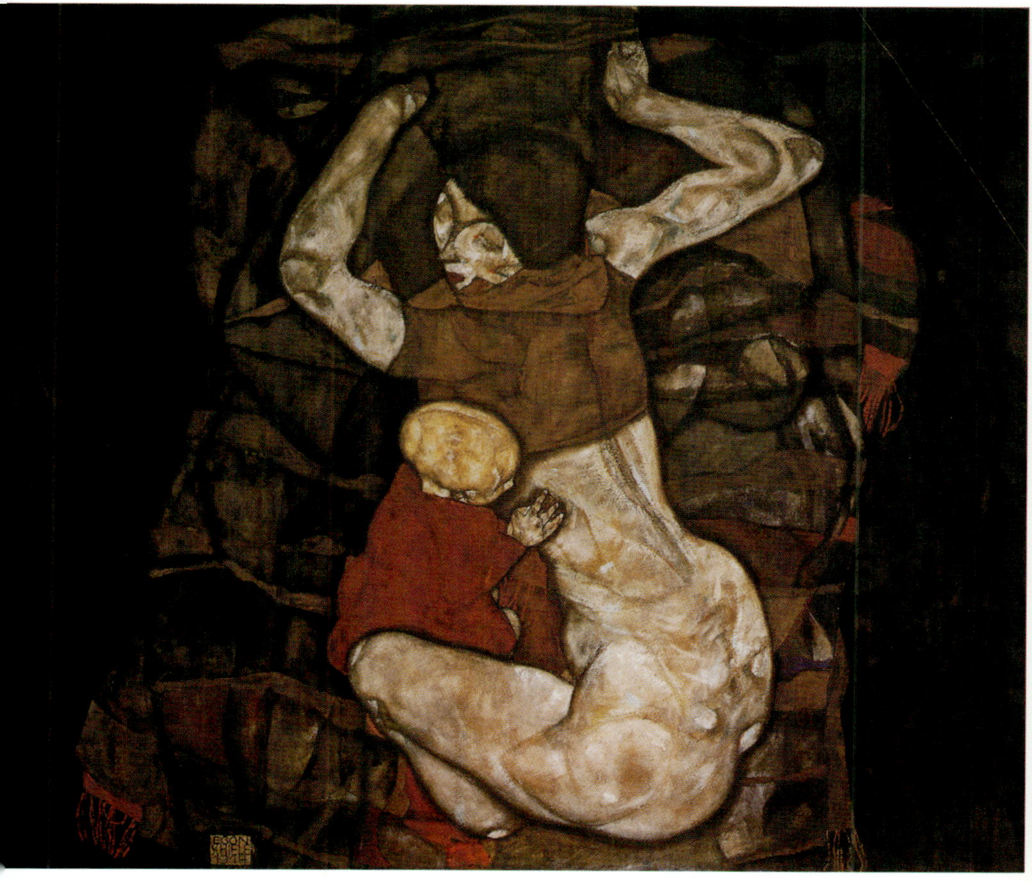

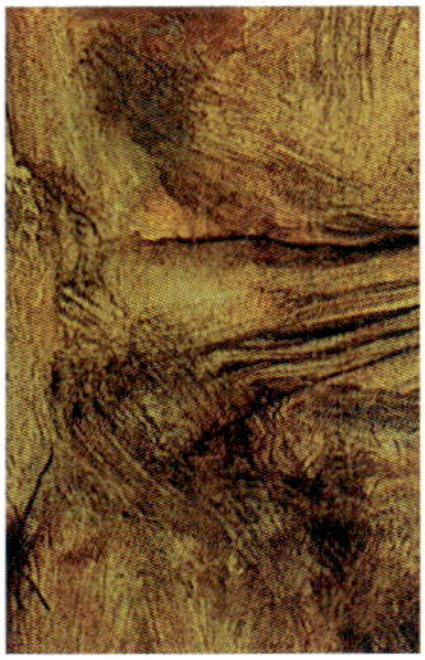

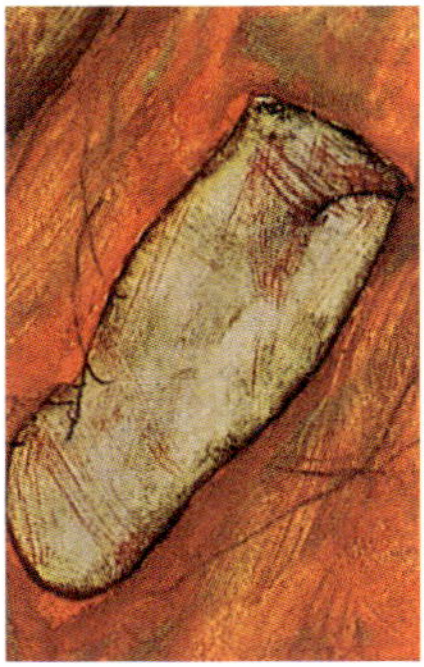

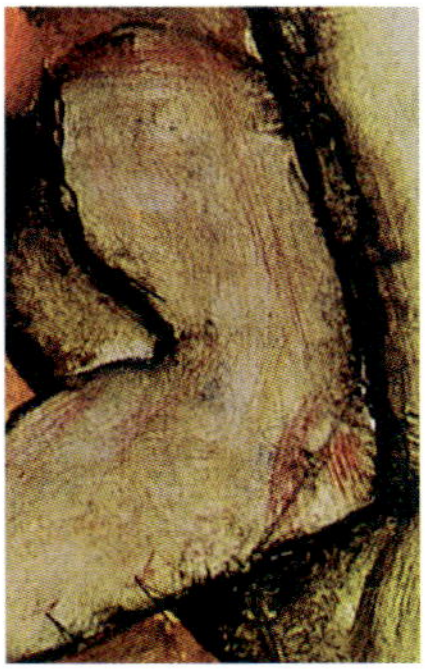

Disgust and Allure

Ulrich Brendel wrote in the periodical *Die Aktion* that Schiele captured "the vampire-like trait of the sex". His models lamented: "It is no pleasure; he always sees only the one thing." The fact that Schiele's father was syphilitic, and that his mother gave birth to several still-born children as a result, has led to much speculation around Schiele's own relationship with the body,

Mother and Child

1914
Gouache and black pencil, 48.1 x 31.9 cm
Leopold Museum, Vienna

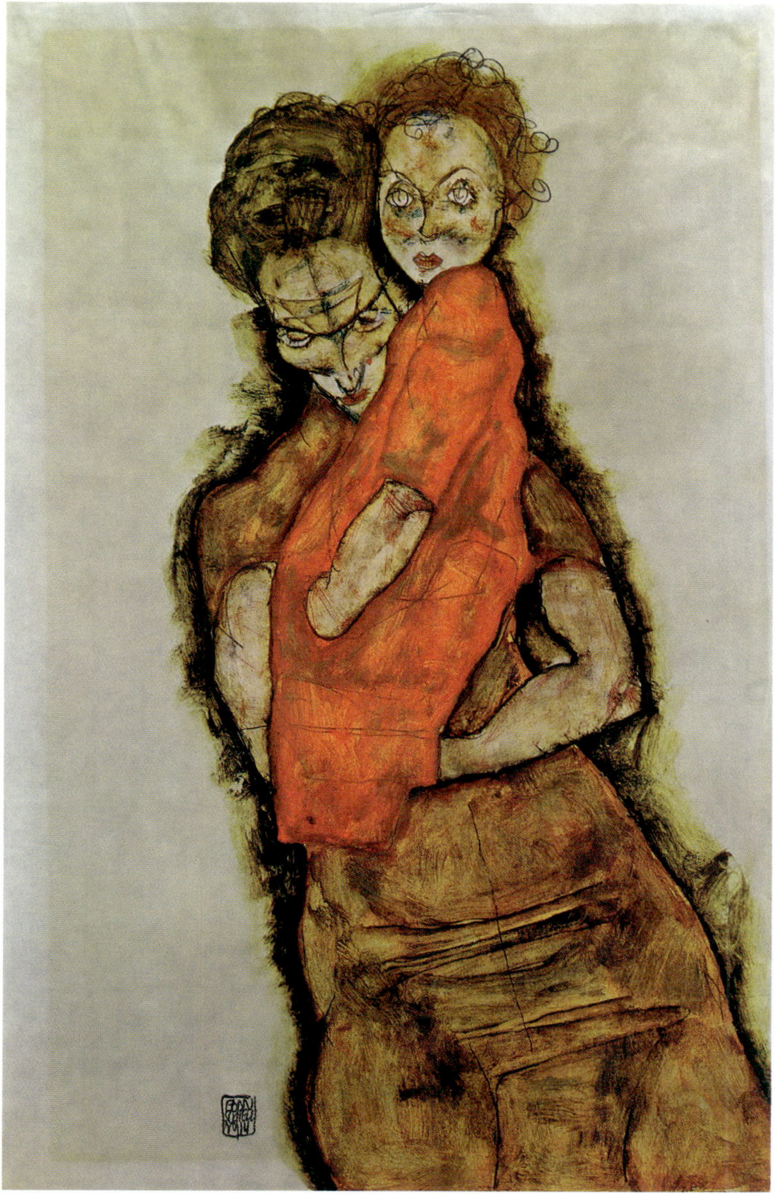

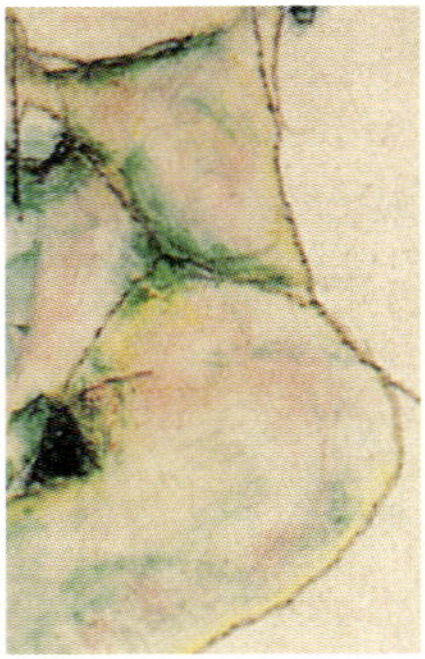

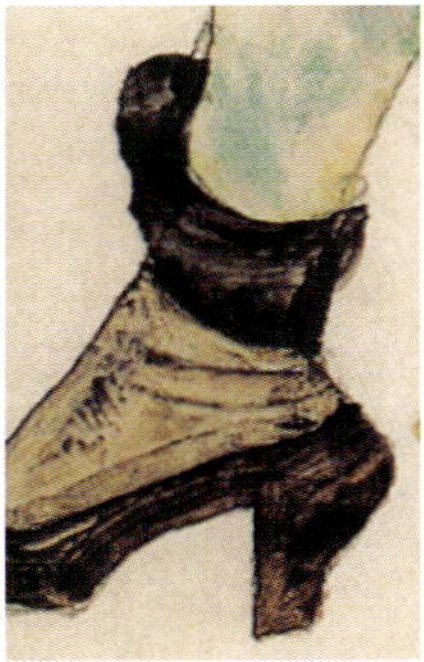

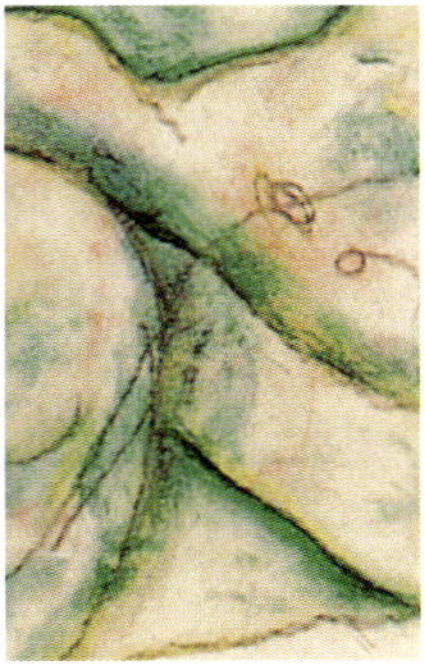

sexuality and mortality. He drew himself making love to his wife, other couples and lesbian lovers, very candid images of children and graphic visions of his own sexual fantasies. Departing from the academic nude (in which nudity is really a form of dress), his drawings convey a powerful sense of his subjects' nakedness. Almost inevitably, this is sometimes accompanied by a sense of his sitters' unease with their own physicality.

Nude with a Green Turban

1914
Gouache and pencil, 32 x 48 cm
Private collection

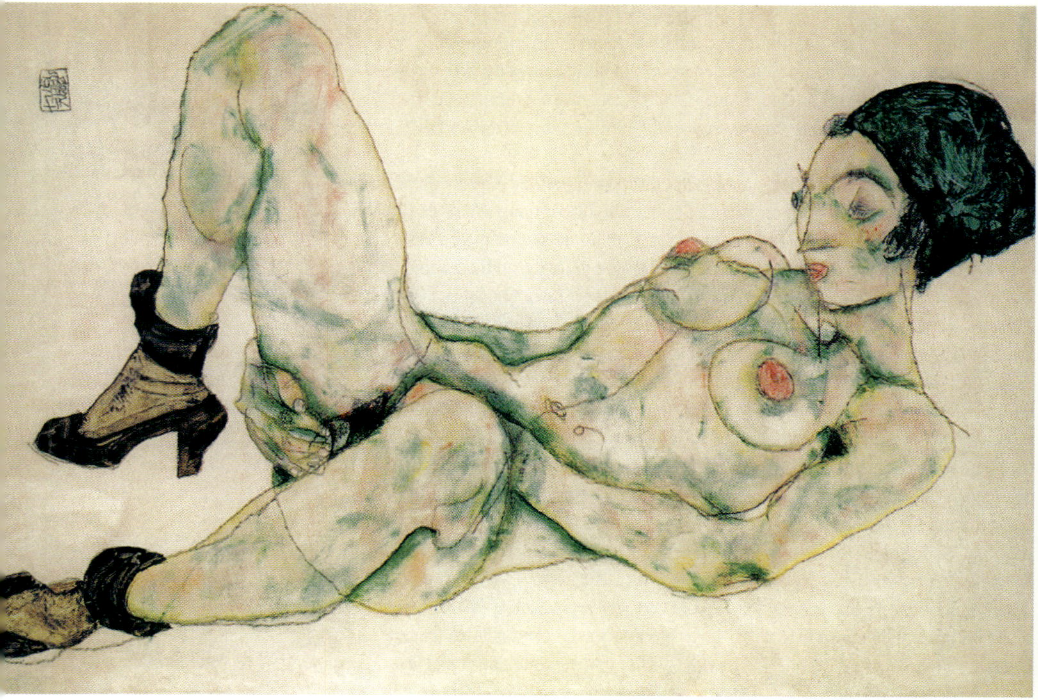

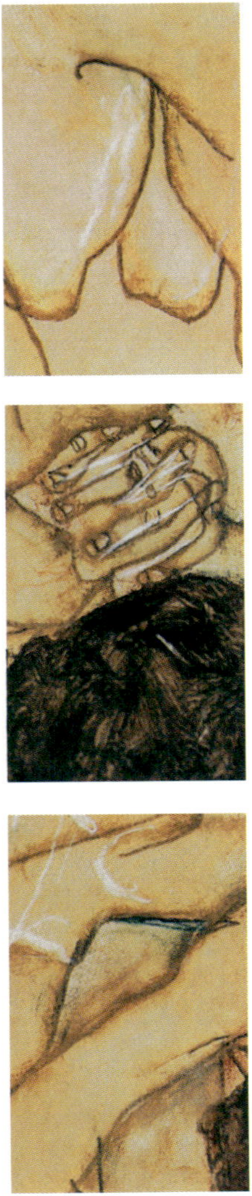

At other times, especially in some works from about 1913 onwards, his subjects are barely differentiated, coolly observed, as mortal substance.

Schiele surely profited from the high sales of pornographic photographs in direct relation to lustful consumption. In 1850, with the invention of photography, in particular the daguerreotype, pornographic photographs also came into fashion.

Two Girls (Lovers Couple)

1914
Gouache on paper, 31 x 48 cm
Private collection

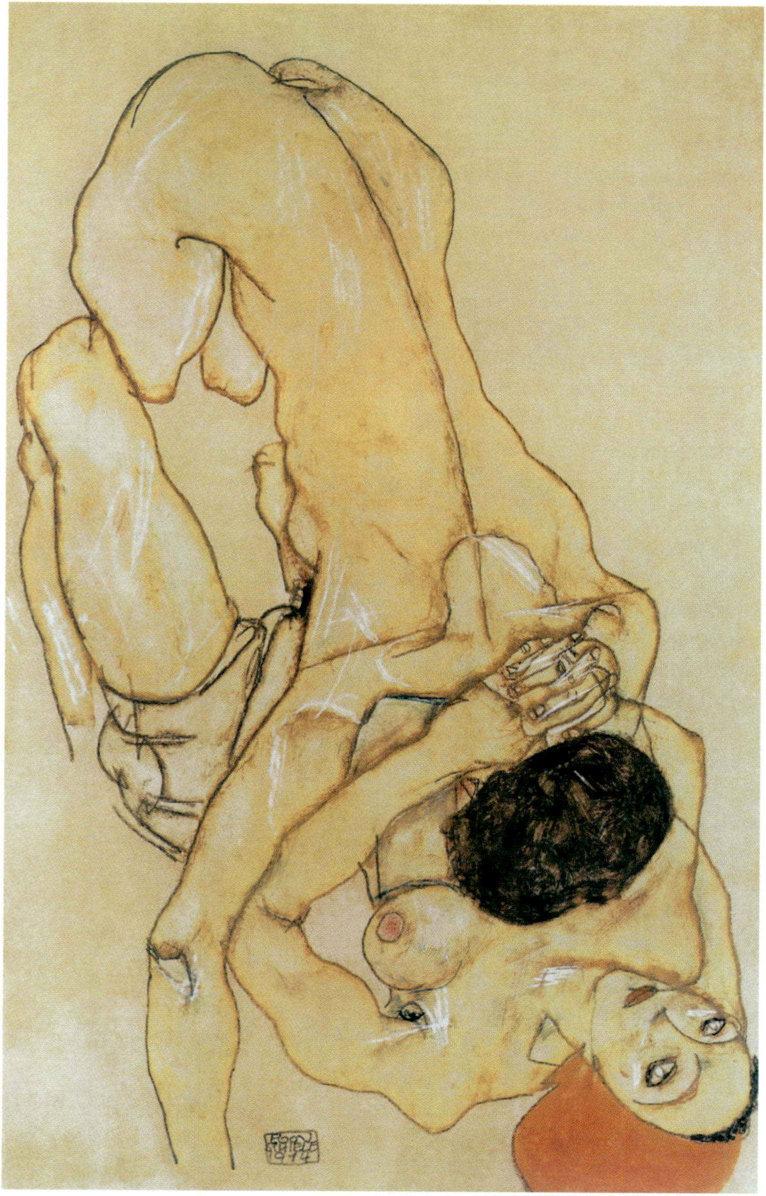

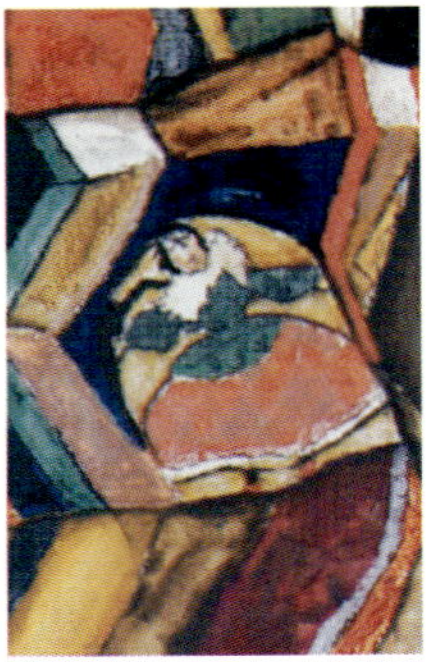

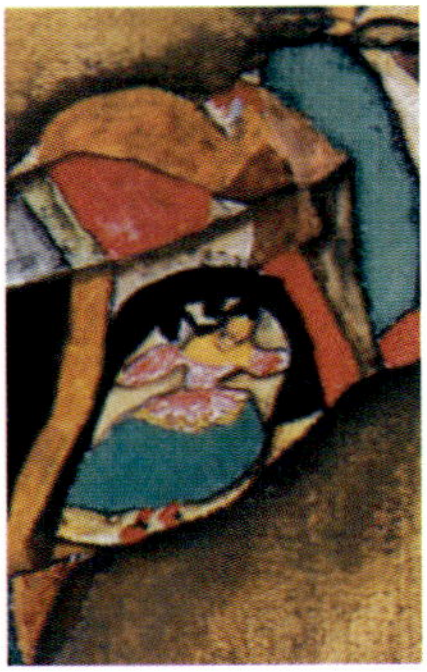

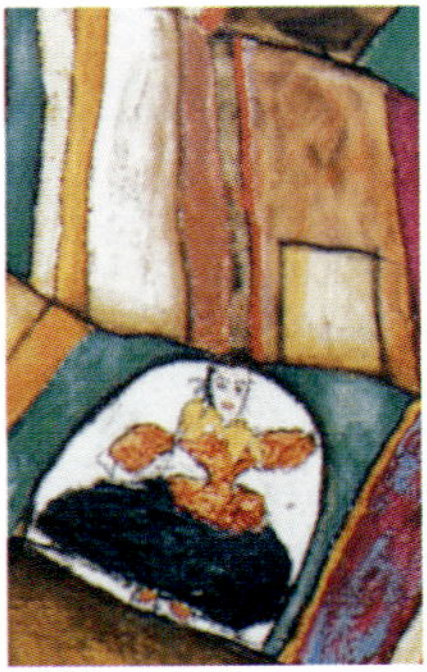

On the one hand, the photographs served as a model for artists, including Schiele, who took many photographs of his models. Around 1870, erotic postcards came into circulation. Thematic scenes from Greek and Roman mythology, heroic or Christian martyr scenes with a naked Magdalene, crucifixion of female characters and nude Greeks were portrayed. In provincial theatres, these pictures were very popular.

Portrait of Friederike Maria Beer

1914
Oil on canvas, 190 x 120.5 cm
Private collection

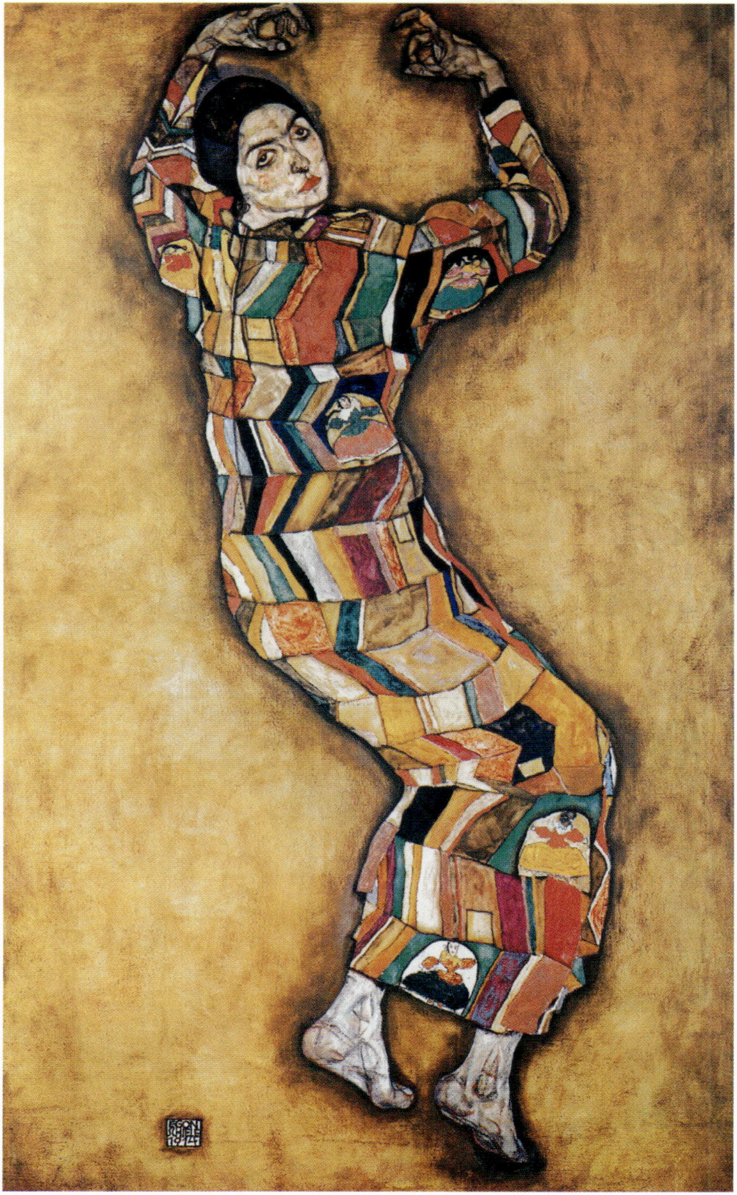

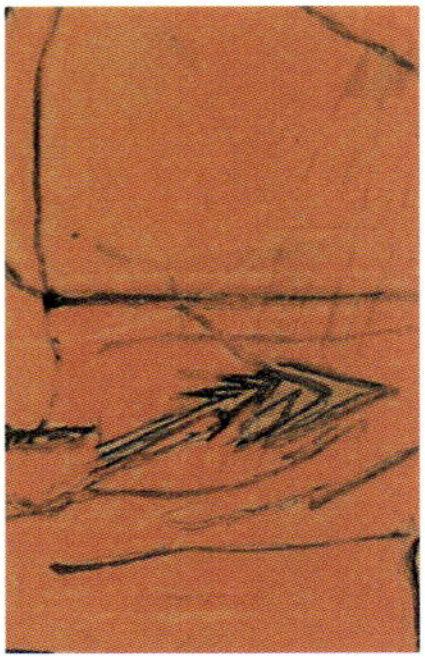

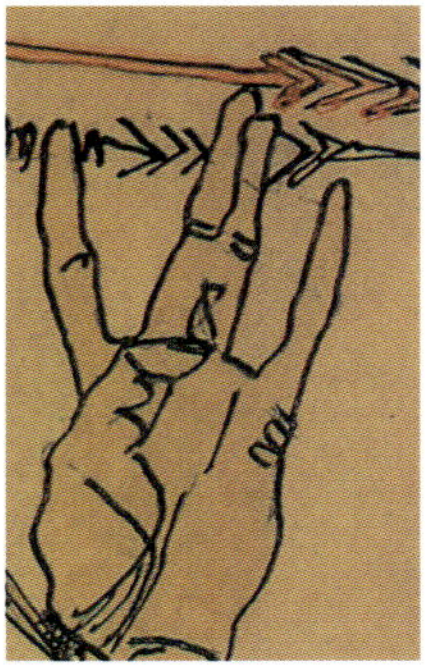

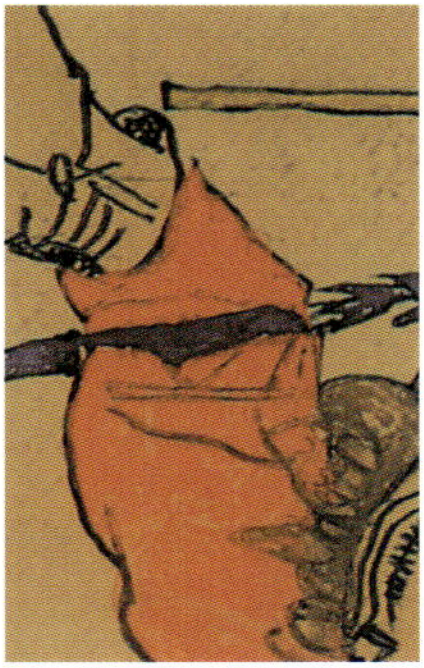

Famous collectors were the Marquis of Byros in Vienna and in Munich Doctor Kraft Ebbing. Baron von Meyer loved the "sweet girls" from Vienna. Yet, Schiele's erotic drawings testify to a personal question which in turn is embodied in this decadent epoch, namely the dialectics of carnal desire and the death instinct.

Self-Portrait as St. Sebastian (Poster)

1914-1915
Gouache, black pencil and ink
on cardboard, 67 x 50 cm
Wien Museum, Vienna

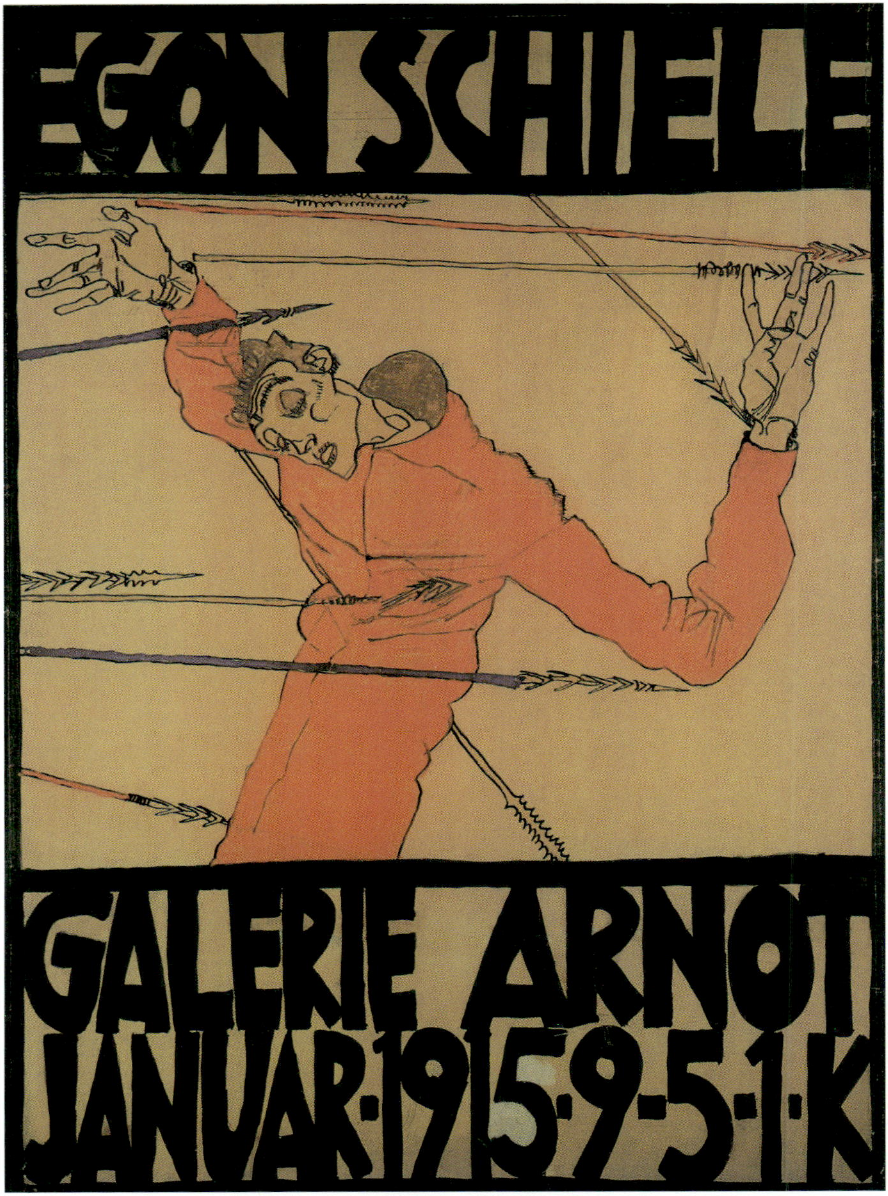
EGON SCHIELE
GALERIE ARNOT
JANUAR·1915·9-5·1·K

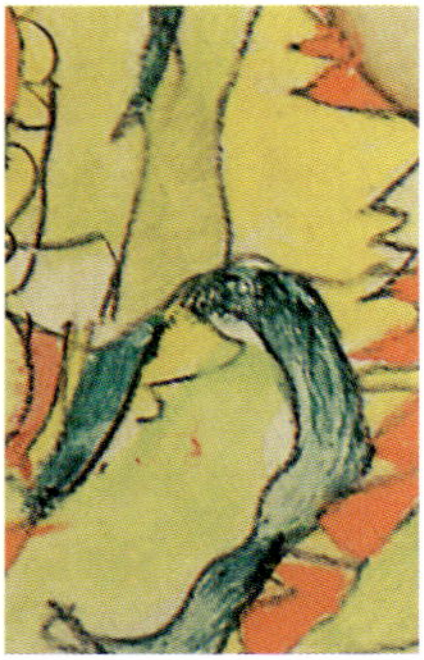

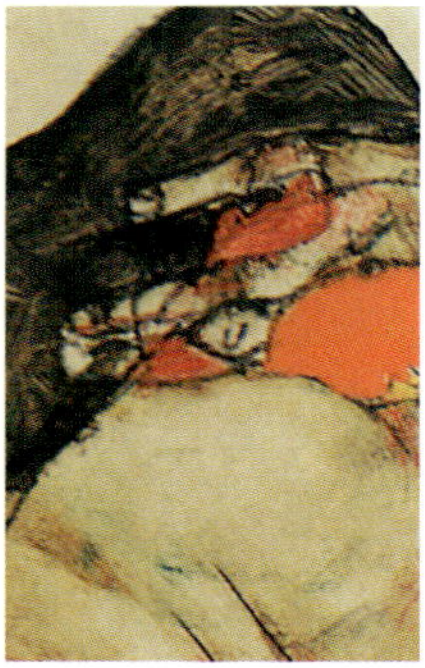

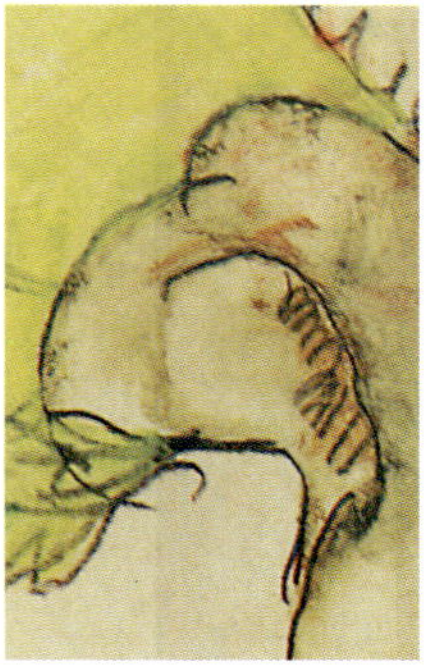

The erotic tension of his drawing does not define itself by the mere depiction of boldly lewd positions; Schiele also mingles with the colour's powerful reminiscence. A girl, her face remaining anonymously sketch-like, reclines backwards; her uplifted skirt is pleated out of which her genitals peek, becoming an inner eye slit. Again and again, Schiele discovers and sees, shows and offers the most intimate, forbidden part to the viewer.

Two Girls, Lying Entwined

1915
Gouache and pencil, 32.8 x 49.7 cm
Albertina, Vienna

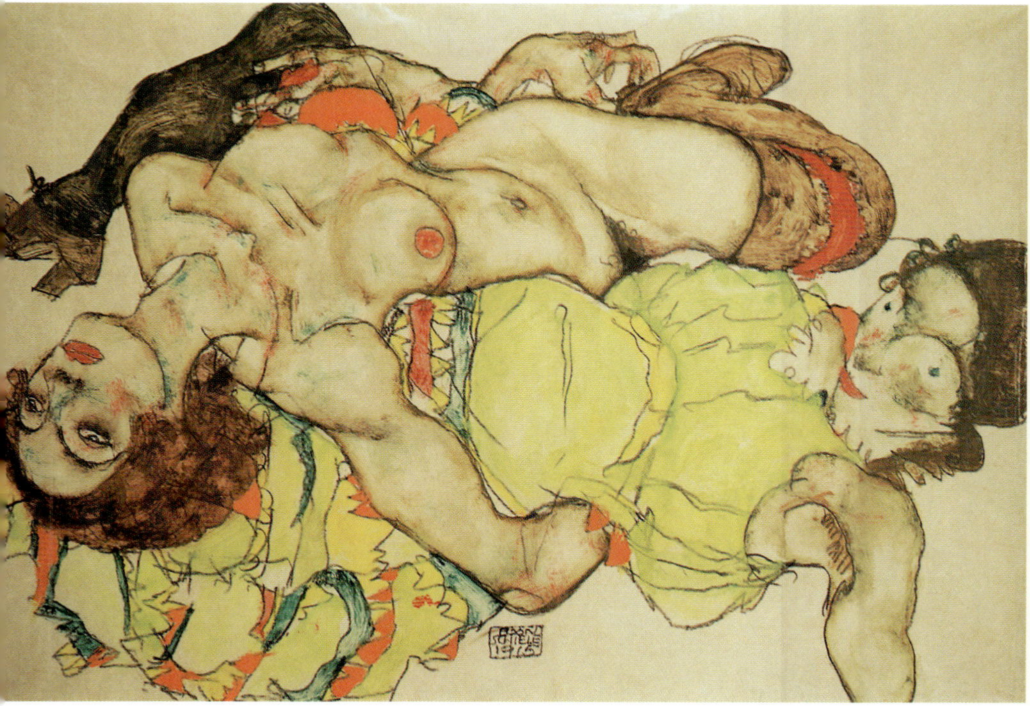

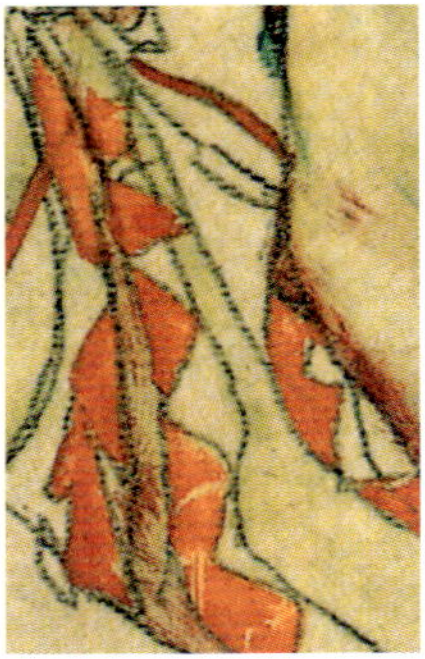
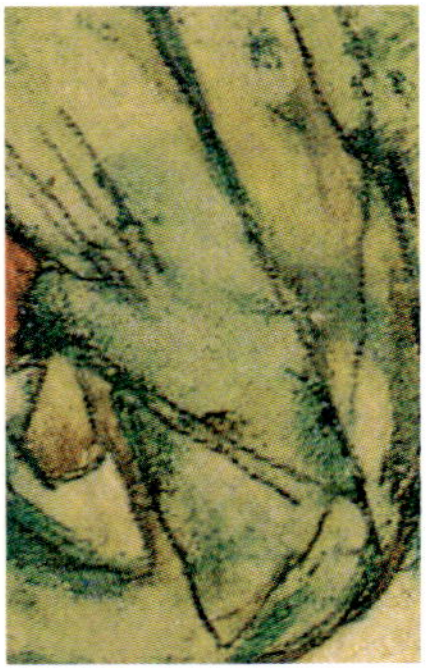
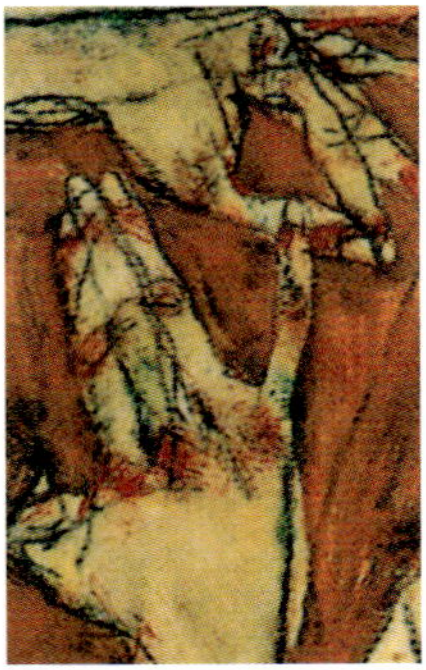

He carefully paints it in watercolours, a calyx of orange colour like a fruit. At the same time, Freud discovered the fear of castration mechanism: "the sight of Medusa's head, that is to say, that of the feminine genitalia, causes one to become rigid with fright, transforming the beholder into stone. To become rigid symbolises the erection."

Coitus

1915
Gouache and pencil, 31.6 x 49.8 cm
Leopold Museum, Vienna

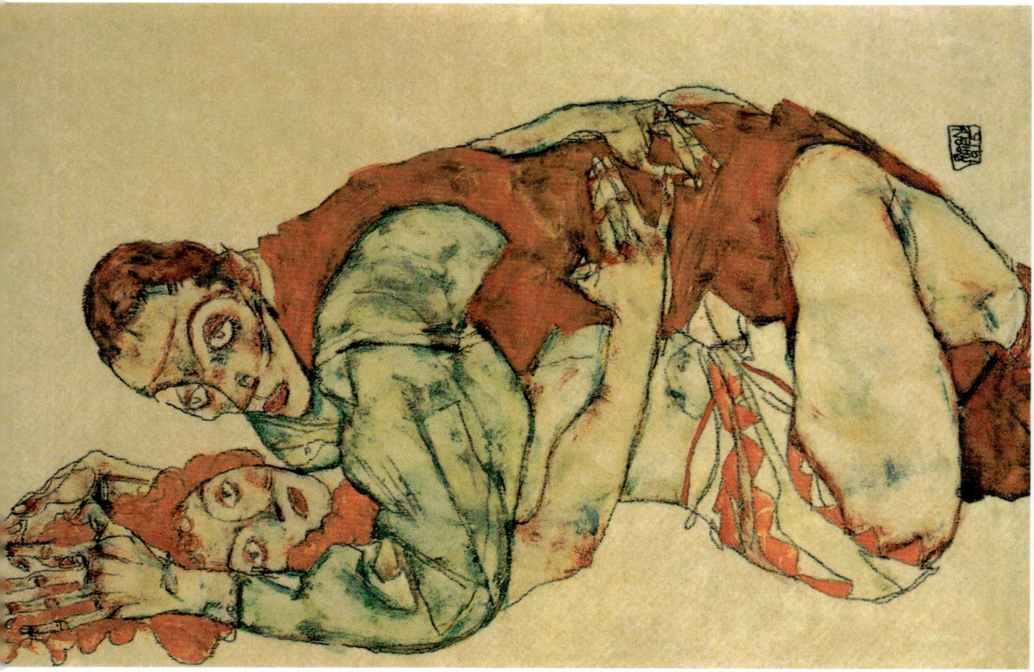

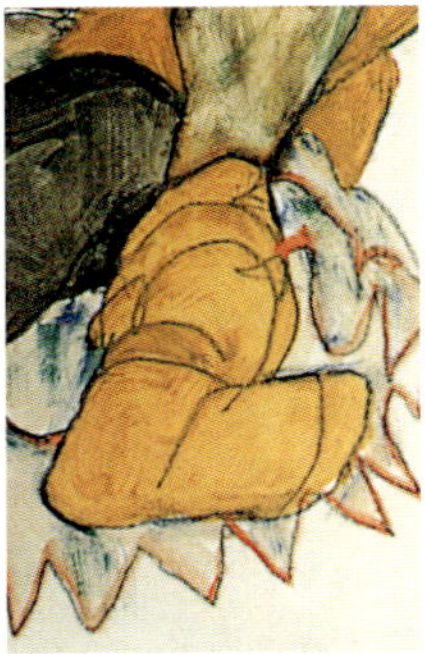

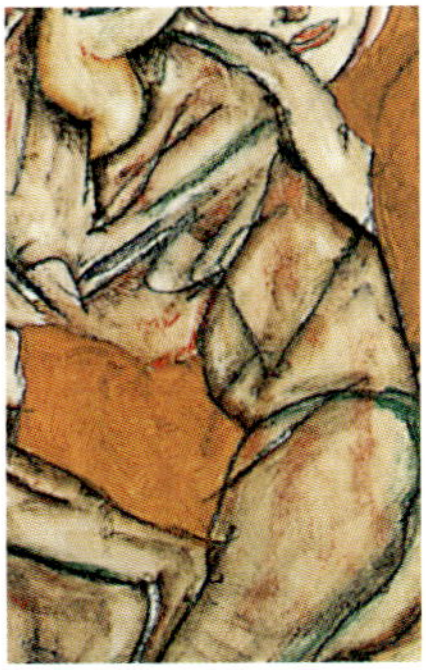

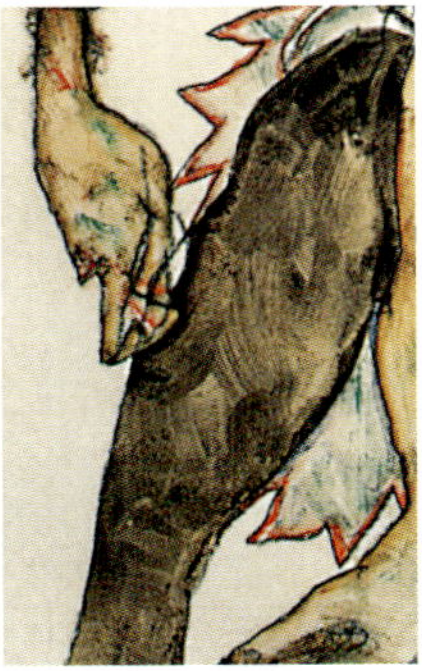

Schiele scarcely modelled the bodies he painted; only a few coloured splotches animate the white paper surface on which the body seems to lie confined by a few lines. Schiele's patron, Carl Reininghausen, whom Schiele instructed in drawing and painting, complained that he "paints so casually that the composition is no longer recognisable in places due to the splotches".

Seated Couple (Egon and Edith Schiele)

1915
Pencil and gouache on paper, 52.5 x 41.5 cm
Albertina, Vienna

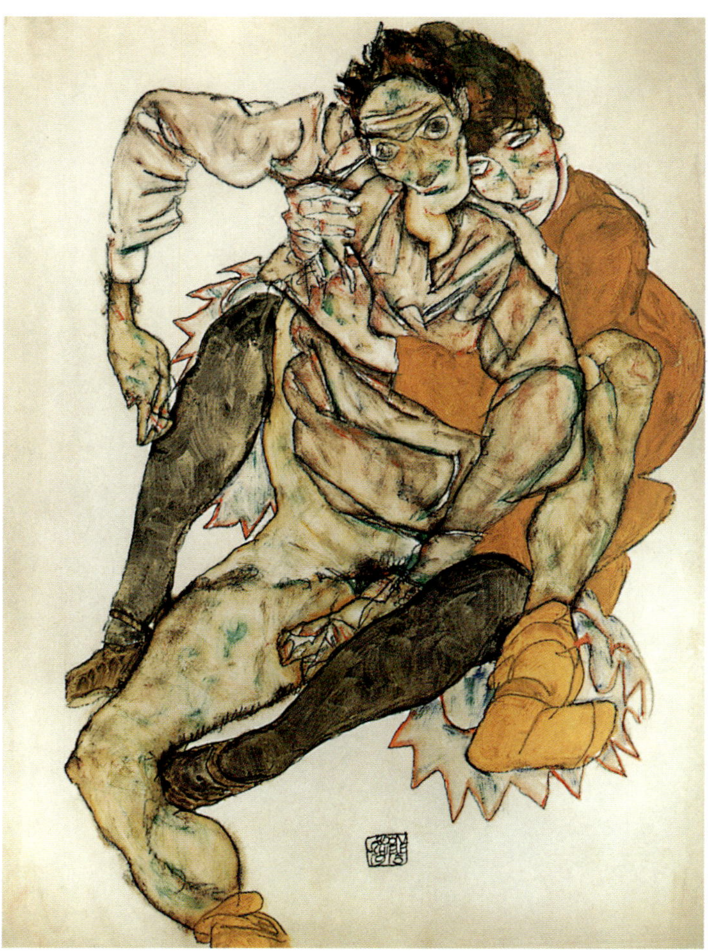

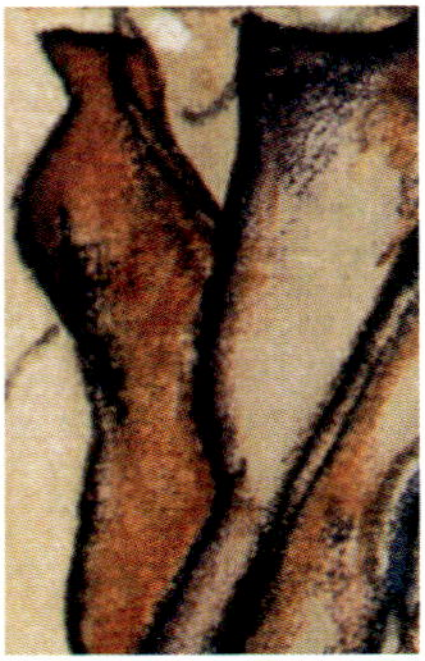

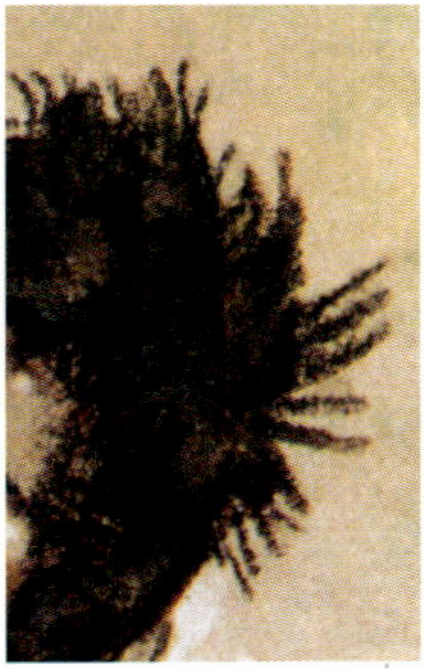

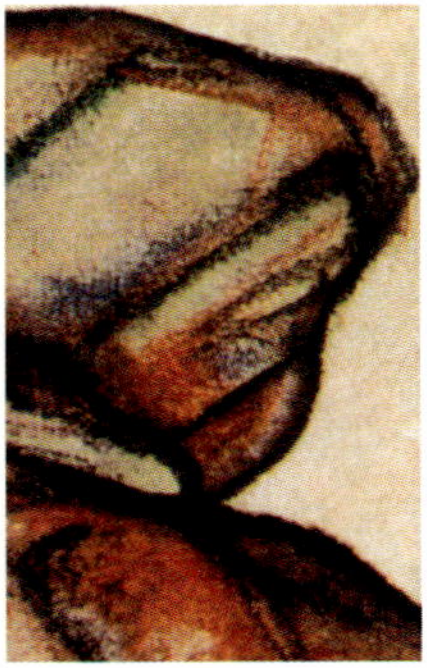

The marks on the body executed by the use of a wash are astonishing; often in contrasting colours of green and red, they create aggressive tension. In contrast to the general impression of the shape, the splotches point to a closer view, this intimacy exposes the condition of the skin. Schiele's models do not possess unblemished white, alabaster bodies; rather, he gets under their skin. "The body becomes a wound." (Werner Hofmann, Munich, 1981) Schiele turns the fleshy inner part of the vagina inside out.

Self-Portrait Arms Drawn-Back

1915
Gouache, pastel and charcoal, 32.9 x 44.8 cm
E.W. Kornfeld Collection

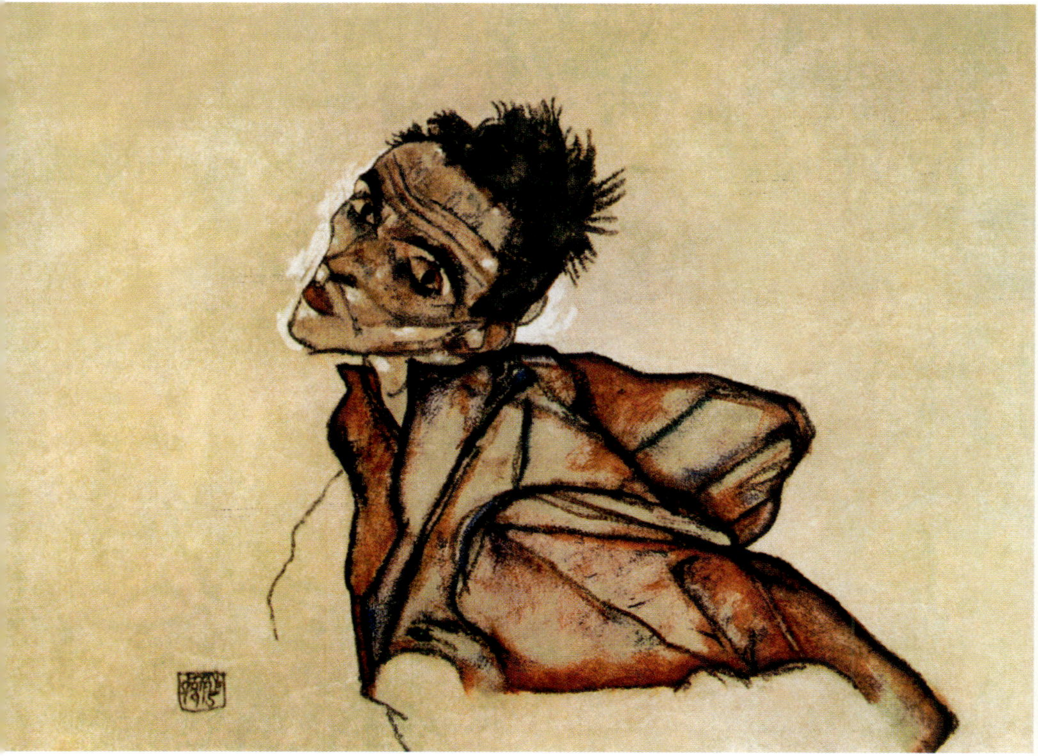

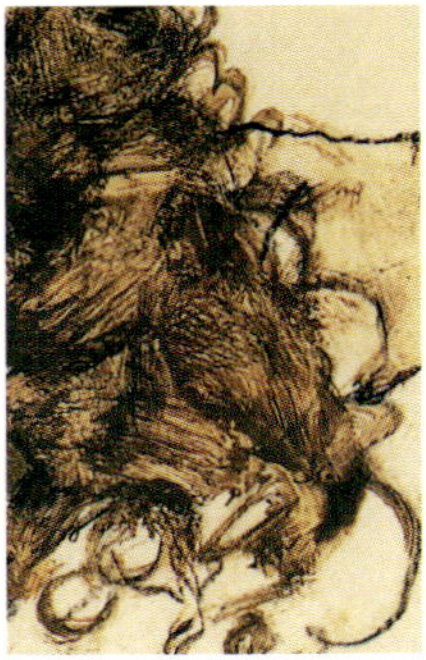

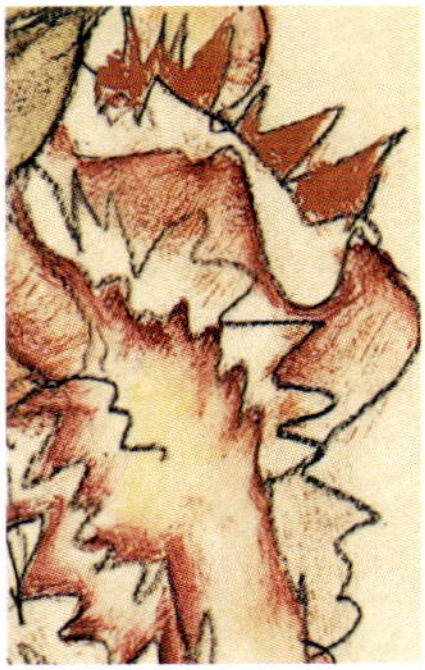

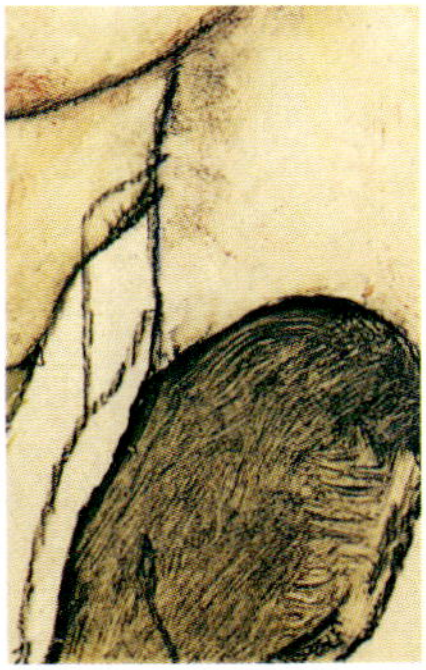

As to the aesthetics of the colour splotches which like the famous blotch paintings by Rorschach render the viewer a surface to project onto, Hugo von Hofmannstal wrote that "art is magical writing, which uses colours instead of words to portray an internal vision of the world, a puzzling one, without being". Other contemporaries, however, described Schiele's art as "manically demonic".

The Embrace

1915
Gouache, watercolour and pencil
48 x 32.7 cm
Szépmüvészeti Múzeum, Budapest

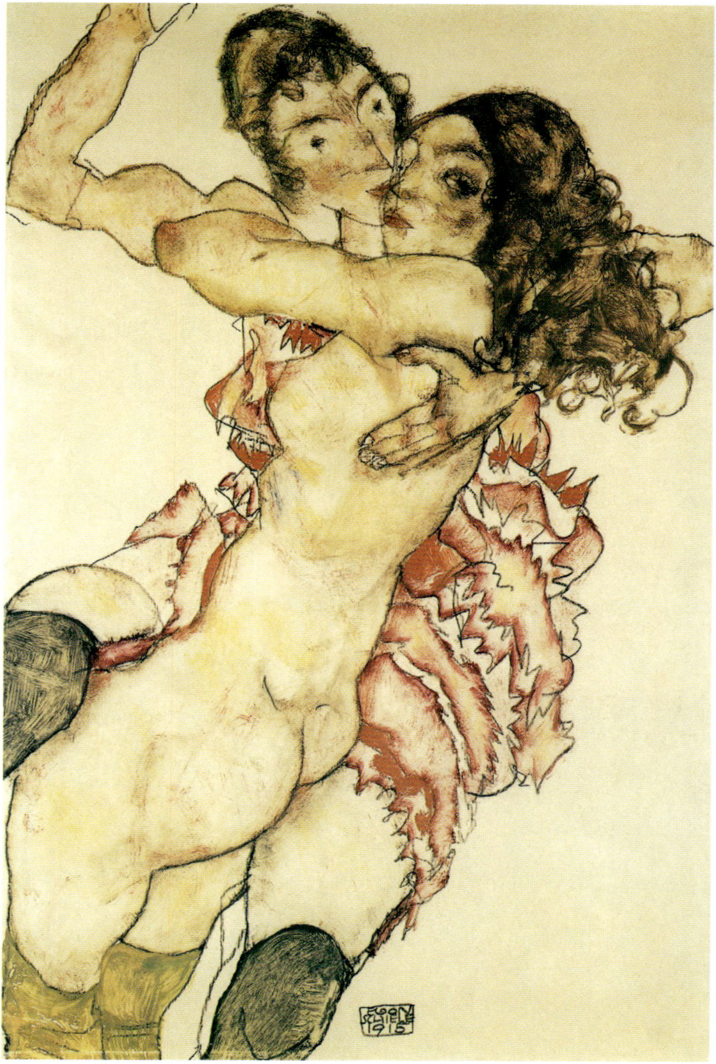
EGON
SCHIELE
1915

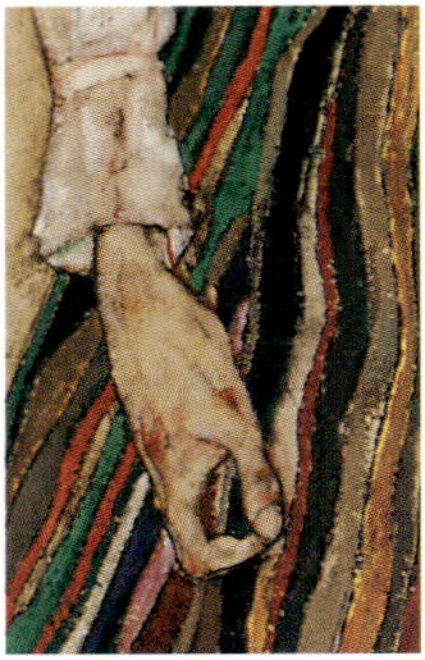

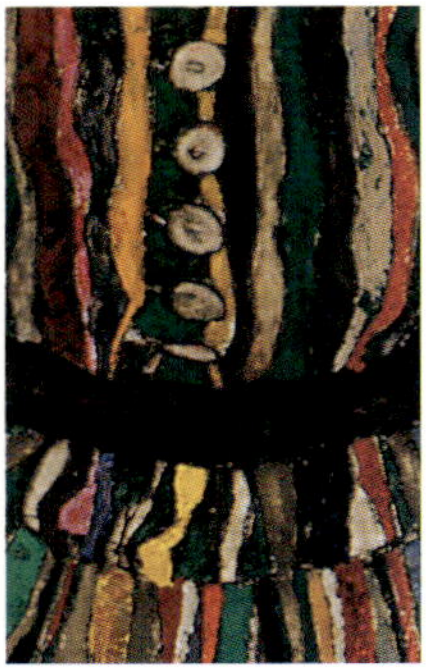

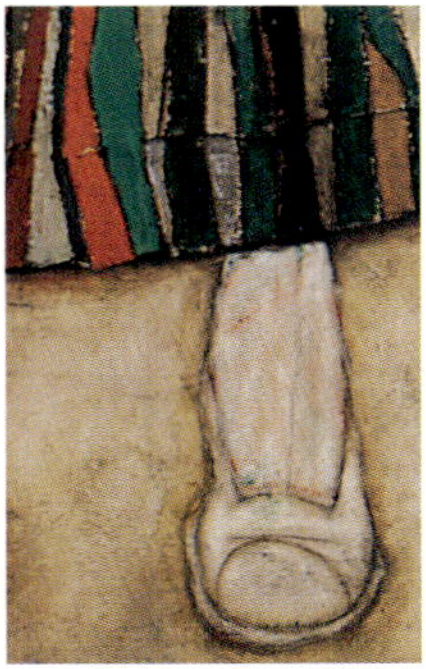

"Some of his pictures are materialisations of obscured consciousness, of apparitions grown bright." His friend Roessler in turn stressed that his face is the synthesis of inner human existence. Doubtless, the nude studies reflected the inner world of the soul's condition imposed onto the model by the artist. "I am everything at once, but never shall I do everything all at once," declared Schiele who incorporated psychological role-play into the paintings of his models. Schiele tried to capture his own psychological experience.

Portrait of the Artist's Wife Standing
(Edith Schiele in Striped Dress)

1915
Oil on canvas, 180 x 110 cm
Gemeentemuseum, The Hague

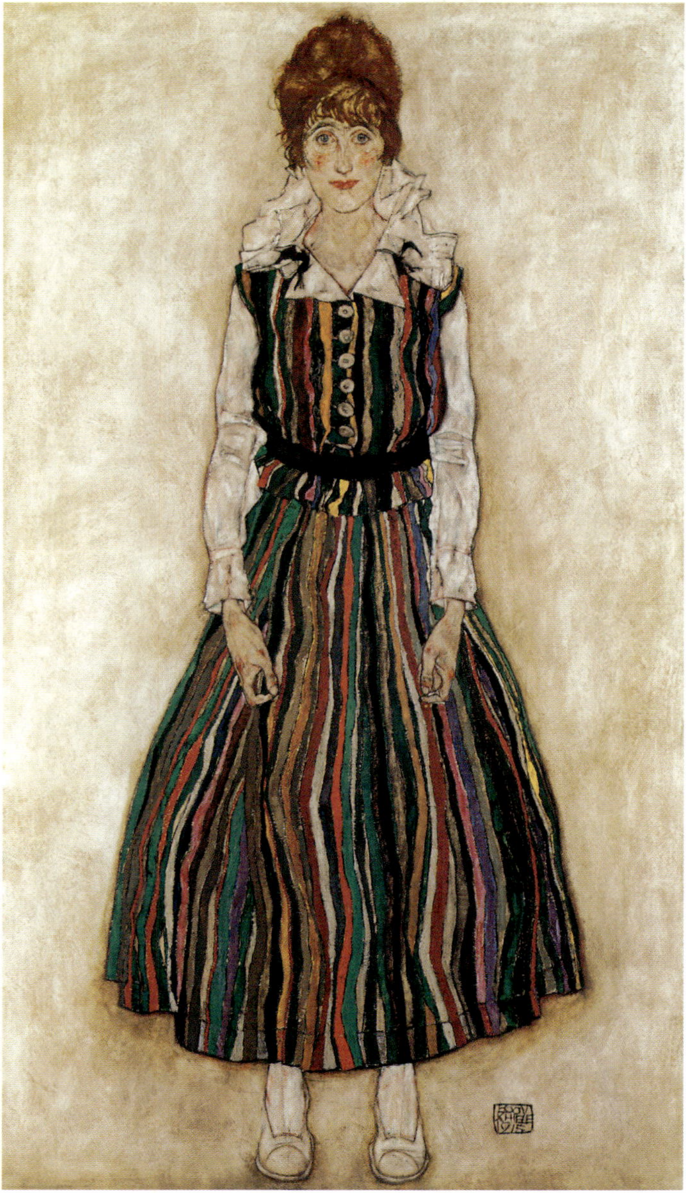

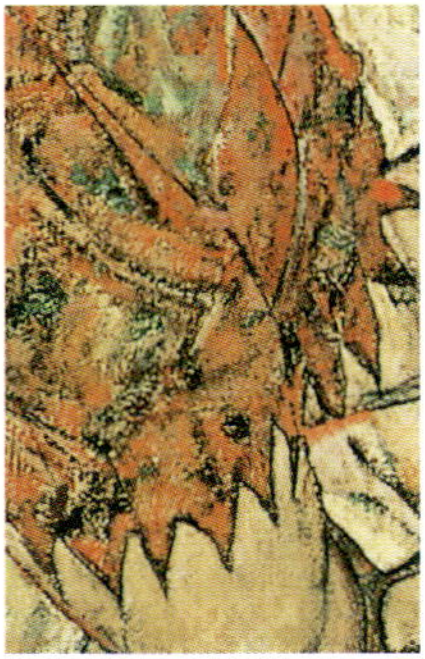

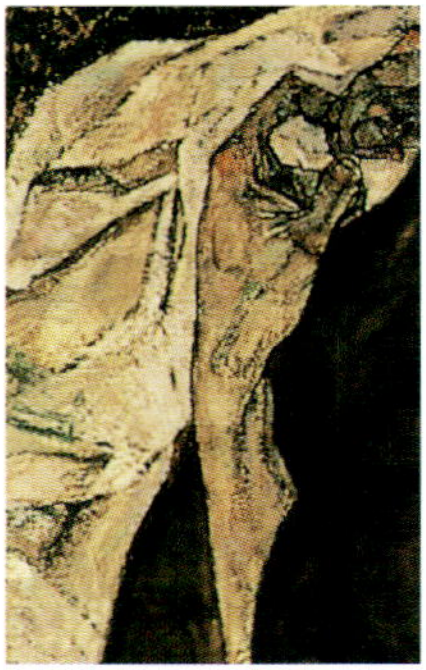

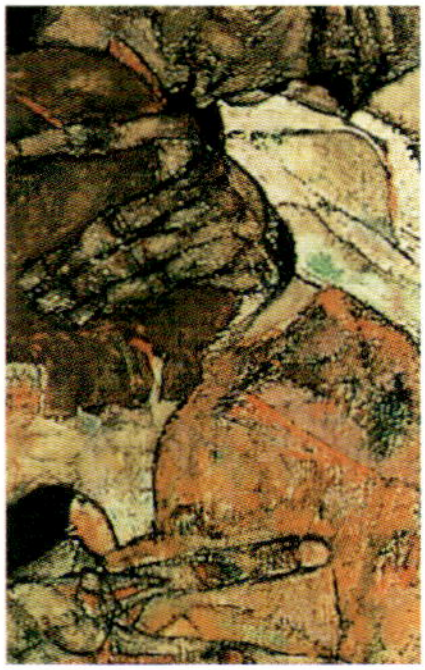

From Prison to International Recognition

In August 1911, Schiele felt impelled to relocate to Neulengbach near Vienna in Lower Austria with Wally. His retreat to the country was naïve and out of touch with reality. Inevitably, he would offend the conservative population in the countryside with his unorthodox life style. Living in sin with the still under-age Wally would rile the population of the provincial town against Schiele. For the village youth, however,

Death and the Maiden

1915-1516
Oil on canvas, 150 x 180 cm
Österreichische Galerie Belvedere, Vienna

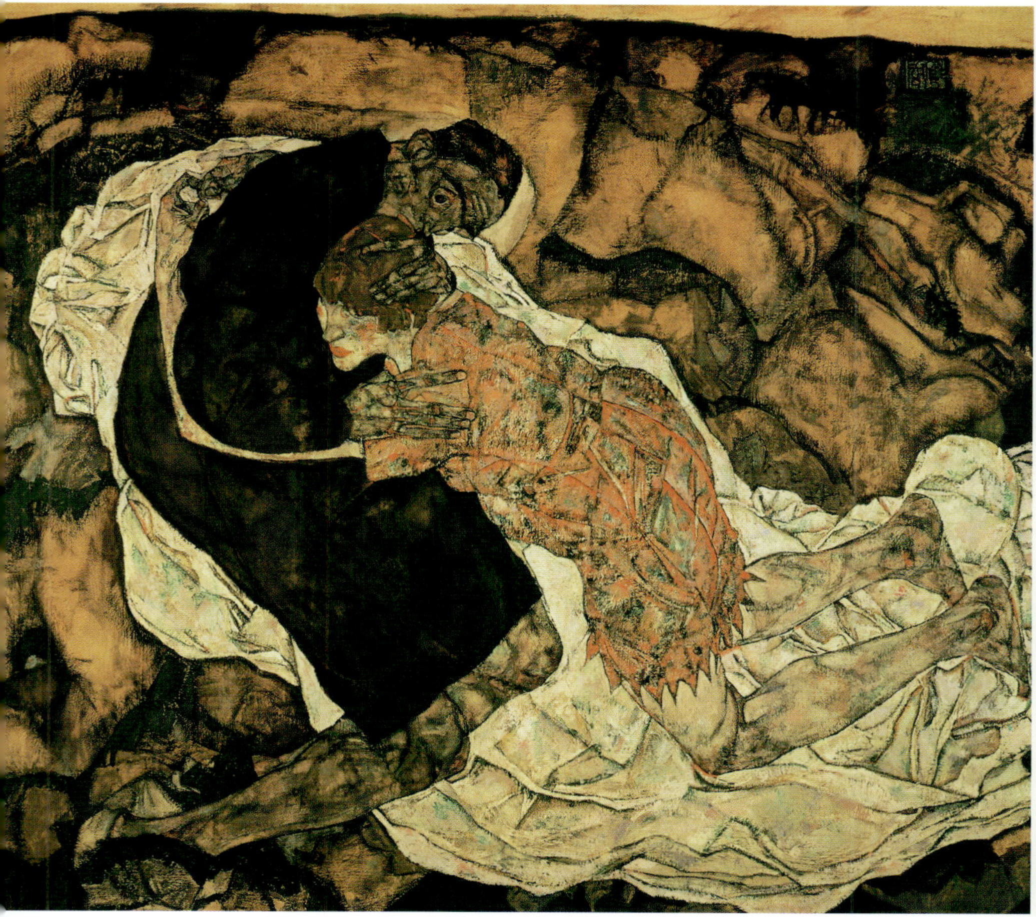

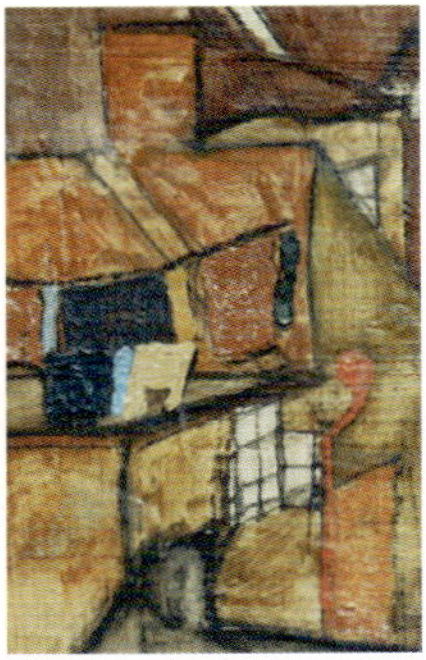

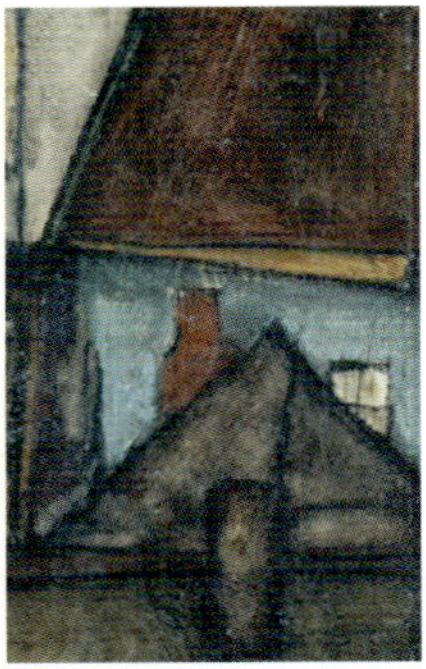

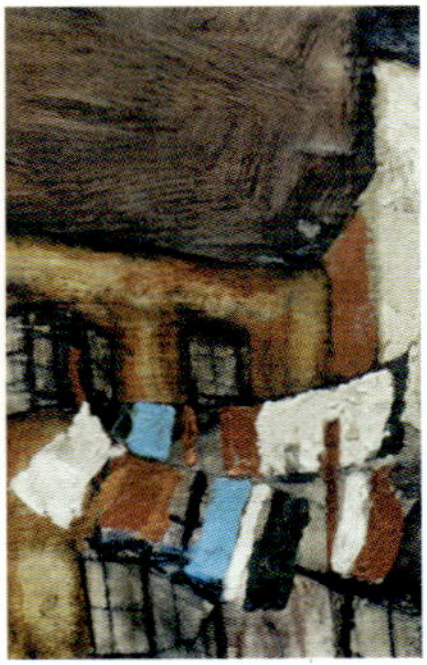

Schiele's studio was a haven of well being. Gütersloh described the free-spirited atmosphere: "Well, they slept, recuperated from parental thrashings, lazily lolled about, something they were not permitted to do at home", until 13 April, 1912, when a catastrophic incident occurred.

The father of a thirteen-year-old girl, who had run away from home and found refuge in Schiele's home, reported him for kidnapping.

A Village

1915
Oil on canvas, 109.7 x 140 cm
The Israel Museum, Jerusalem

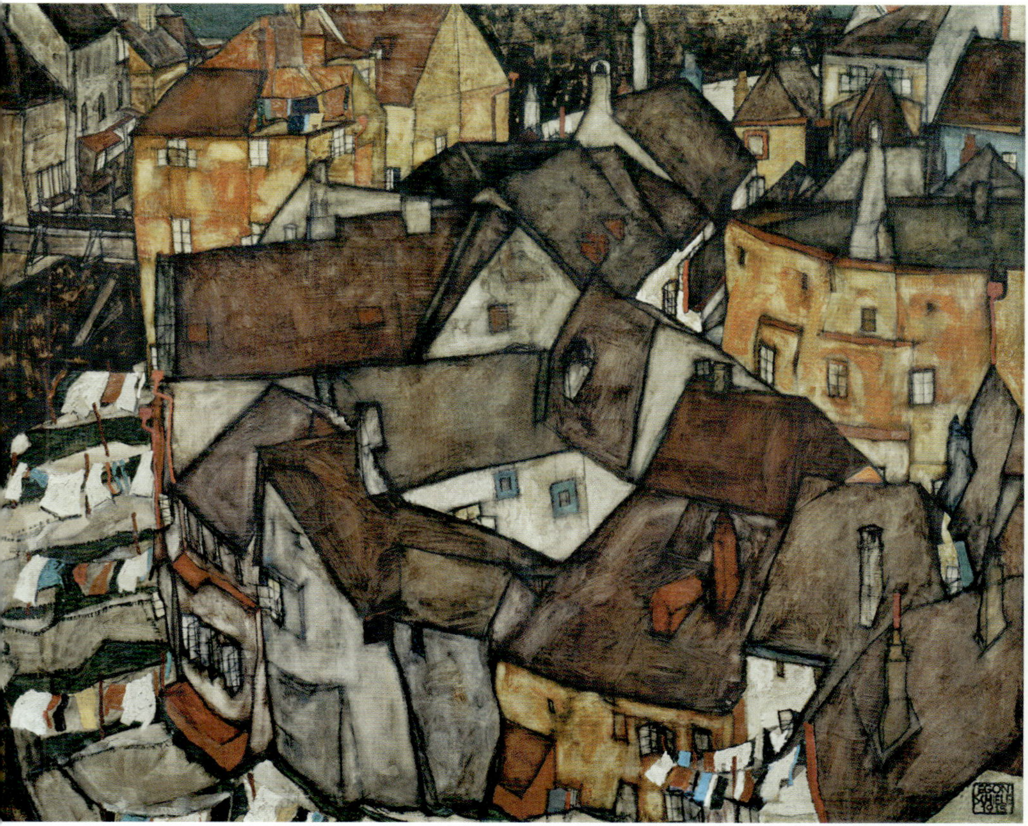
EGON SCHIELE

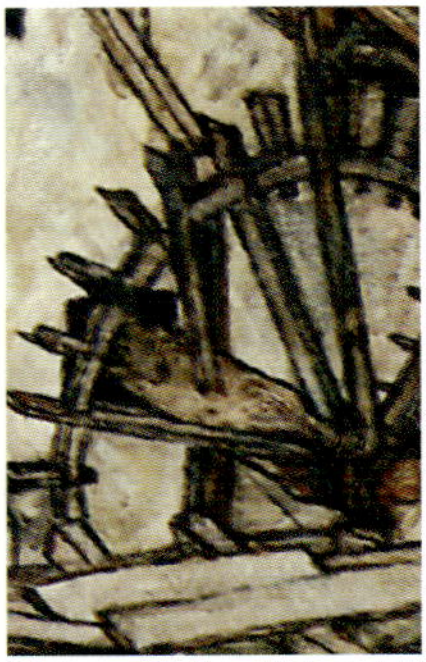

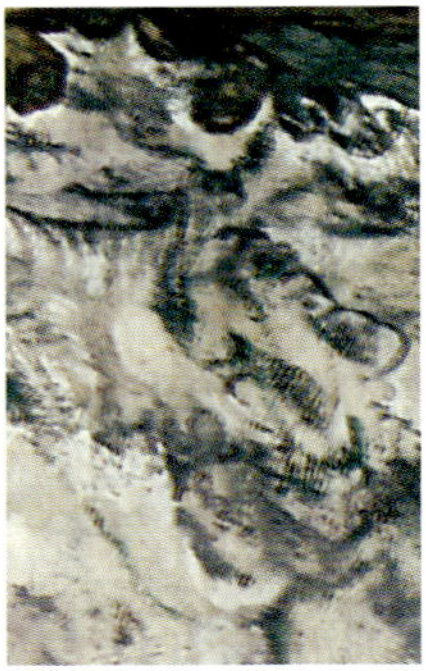

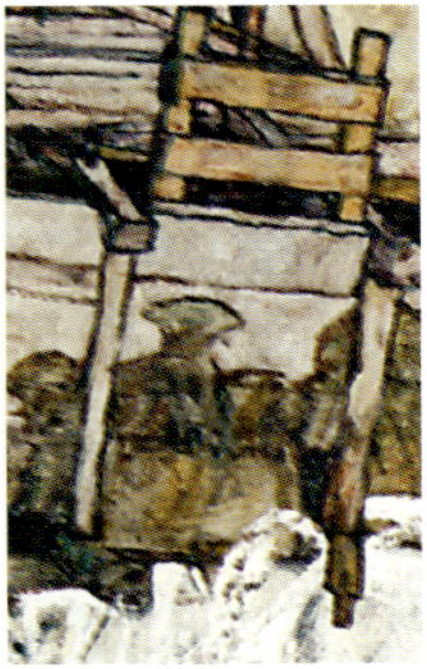

The charge was withdrawn, but Schiele was arrested and charged with endangering public morality and with circulating "indecent" drawings. Schiele's defense by Heinrich Benesch, however, was naïve. Benesch wrote: "Schiele's carelessness is responsible for the incident. Whole swarms of little boys and girls came into Schiele's studio to frolic. There, they saw the nude study of a young girl."

Mill in Ruins (Mountain Mill)

1915-1916
Oil on canvas, 110 x 140 cm
Niederösterreichisches Landesmuseum, Vienna

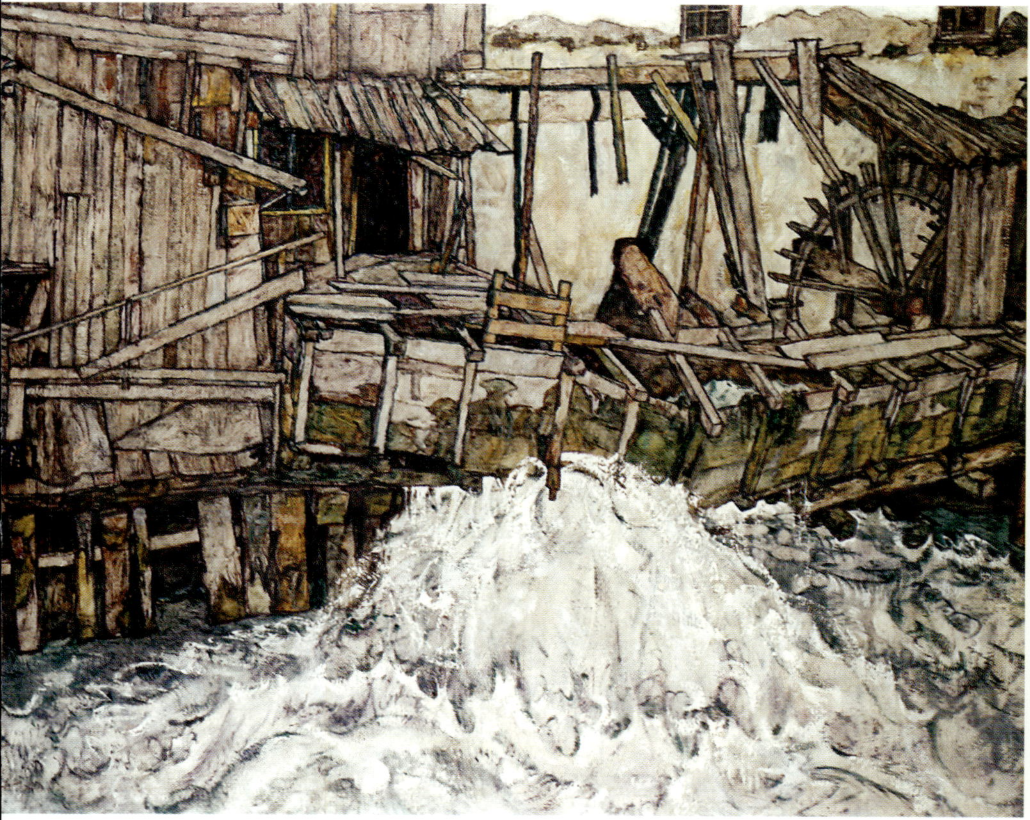

For the sake of his art, Schiele forgot all modesty, lifting the skirts of the sleeping children, and surprising two girls embracing one another. Exposure of his own private sphere as well as that of others became a confession-like, artistic expression of his own truthfulness. The private sphere and public domain became interchangeable. Schiele's influential collector Carl Reininghausen procured an attorney in Vienna for him, but at the same time,

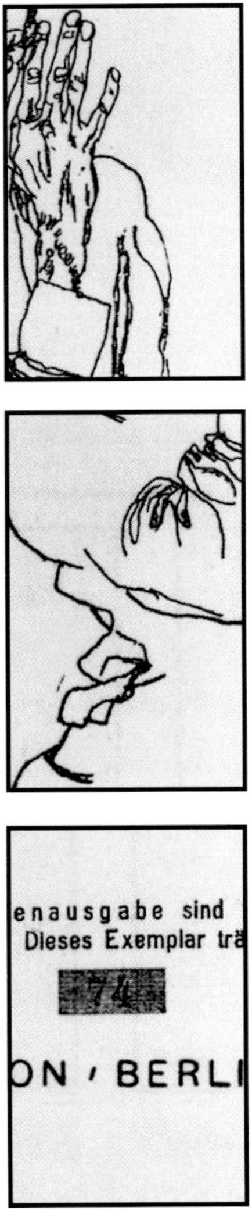

Cover of the Egon Schiele issue of *Die Aktion*

1916
Albertina, Vienna

Die Aktion

WOCHENSCHRIFT FÜR POLITIK, LITERATUR, KUNST

VI. JAHR. HERAUSGEGEBEN VON FRANZ PFEMFERT NR. 35/36

EGON SCHIELE-HEFT. INHALT: Egon Schiele: Selbstporträt (Titelzeichnung) / Professor G. F. Nicolai: Der Kampf ums Dasein / F. A. Harta: Porträt des Egon Schiele / Victor Fraenkl: Von dem Budha zu Mach / Ein unveröffentlichter Brief von Elisée Reclus / Egon Schiele: Studie / Alfred Wolfenstein: Neue Gedichte / Egon Schiele: Das Kind; Mutter und Kind (zwei Federzeichnungen) / Egon Schiele: Abendlandschaft / Wilhelm Klemm: Entsagung / Kurd Adler: Mai-Phantasie 1916 / Anton Sova: Pastorale / Egon Schiele: Studie / Arturo M. Giovannitti: Der Käfig / Egon Schiele: Bild des Malers Harta / Ulrik Brendel und Heinrich Nowak: Ueber Egon Schiele / Ich schneide die Zeit aus / Kleiner Briefkasten / Schiele: Holzschnitt

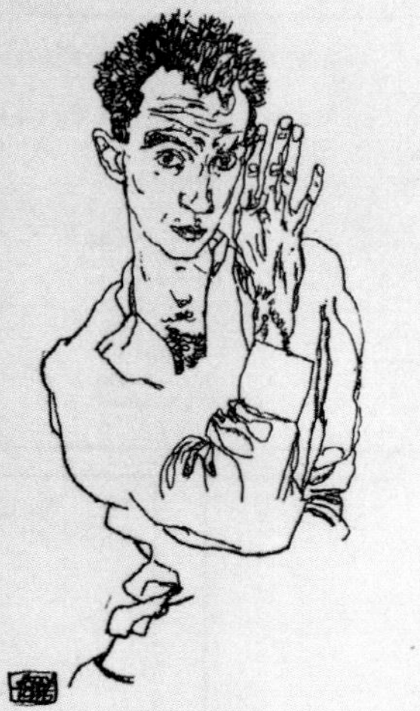

Von dieser Büttenausgabe sind 100 Exemplare gedruckt worden. Dieses Exemplar trägt die Nummer

74

VERLAG · DIE AKTION · BERLIN-WILMERSDORF

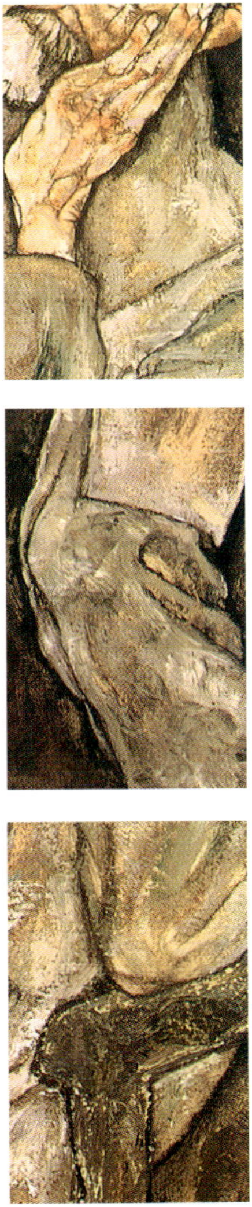

dispenses with the "cordial you" (informal) between them. In St. Pölten, Schiele spent 24 days in custody.

He pleaded: "To inhibit an artist is a crime. It is called murder of life coming into being." The prison stay validated him, the artist, in his role as an outsider. Several self-portraits of Schiele as a prisoner testify to this time. Solemnly the judge burnt one of the indecent drawings in the courtroom. Schiele's reply was: "I do not feel chastised, but cleansed."

Portrait of Johann Harms

1916
Oil on canvas, 138.4 x 108 cm
Solomon R. Guggenheim Museum, New York

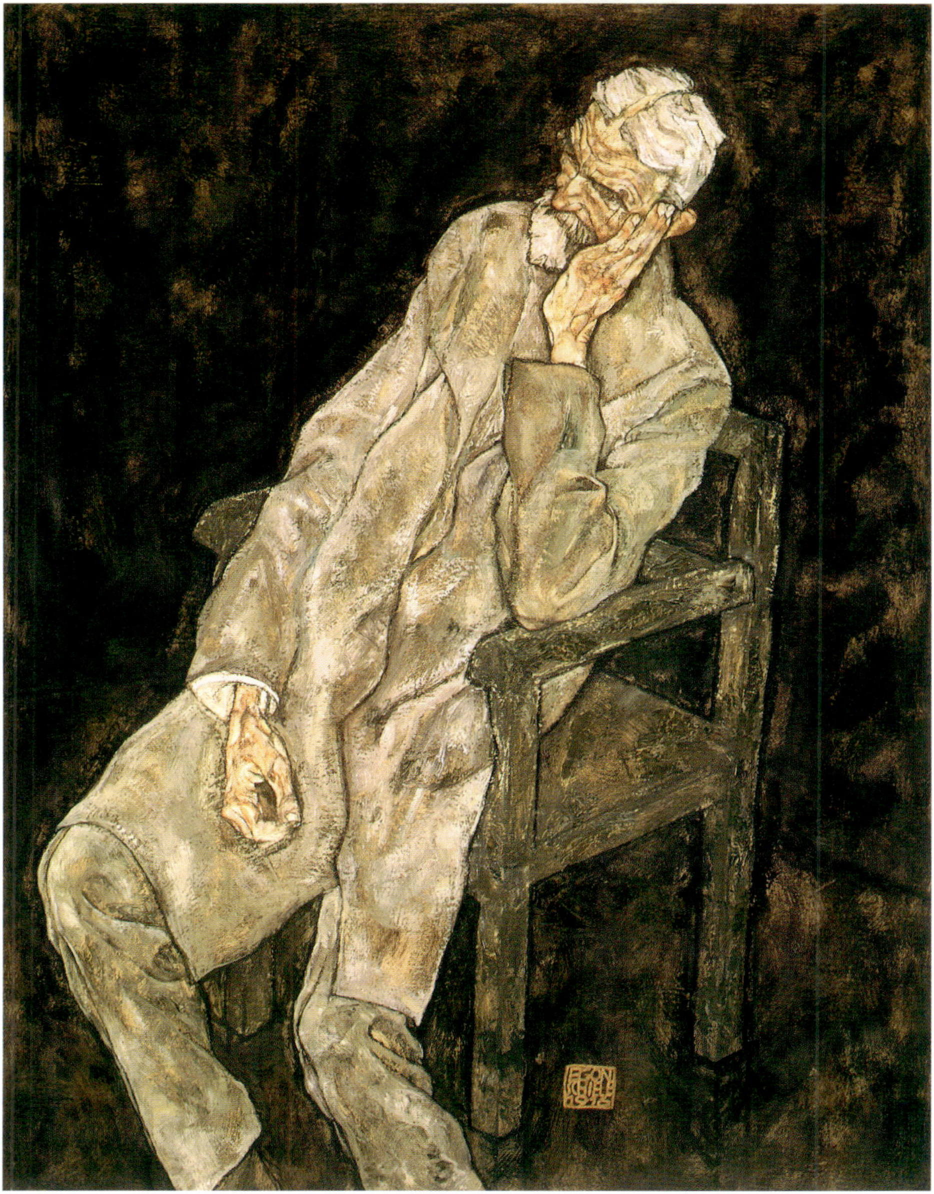

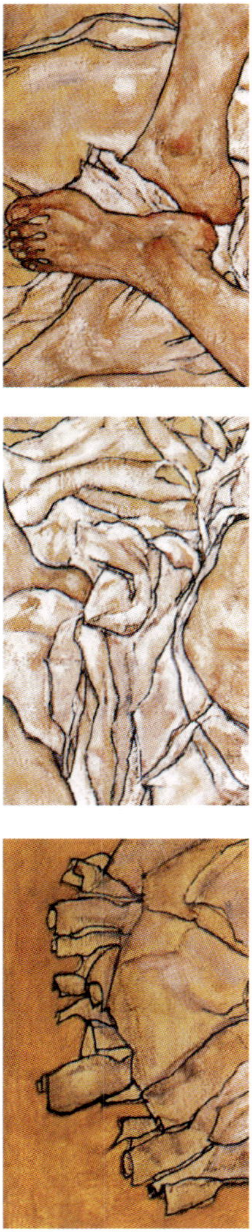

But Schiele quicky forgot this difficult trial thanks to the events that followed thereafter. In Munich, the art dealer Golz exhibited Schiele's works. 1912 was a critical year, the "New Art Group" together with the artists union displayed *Der Blaue Reiter* (The Blue Rider) in Budapest, Munich and Essen. In November, 1912, Schiele returned to Vienna and moved into an atelier in the Hiertzinger Hauptstrasse. Klimt introduced him to the collector August Lederer whose son Erich became his pupil.

Reclining Woman

1917
Oil on canvas, 95.5 x 171 cm
Leopold Museum, Vienna

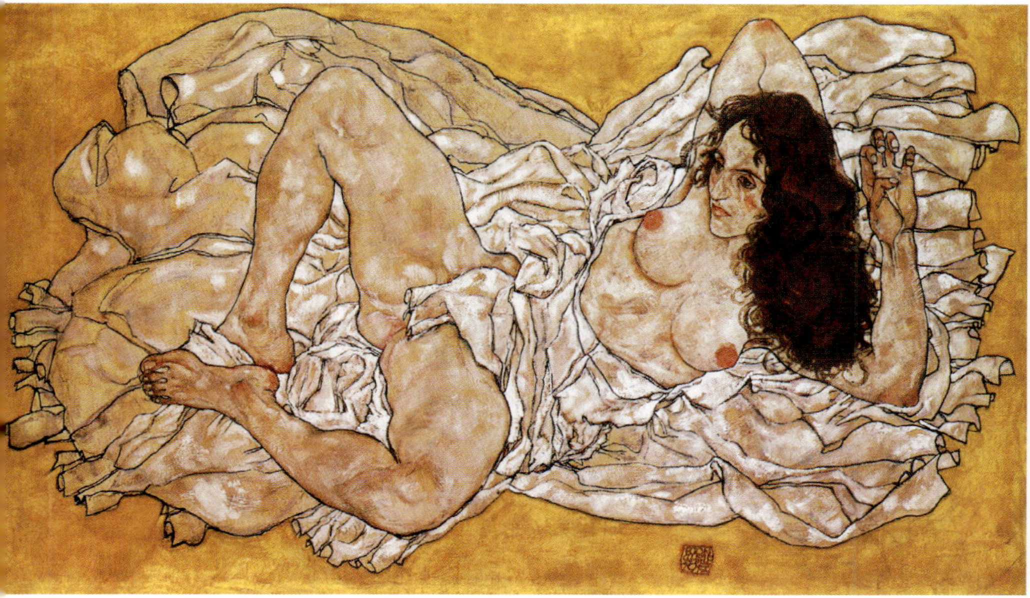

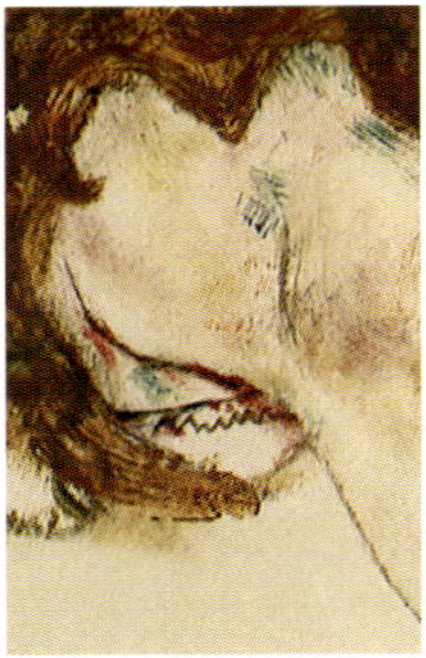

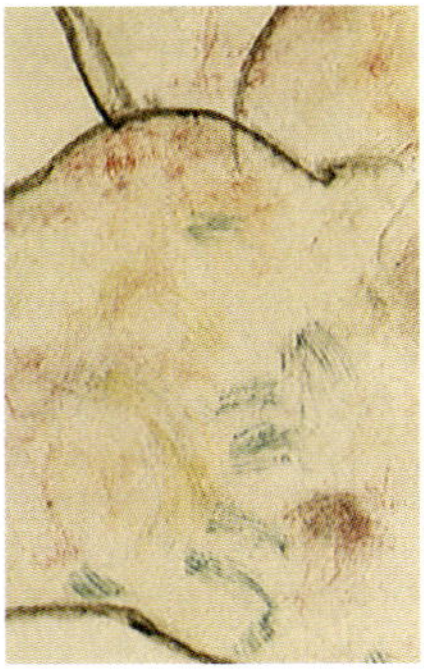

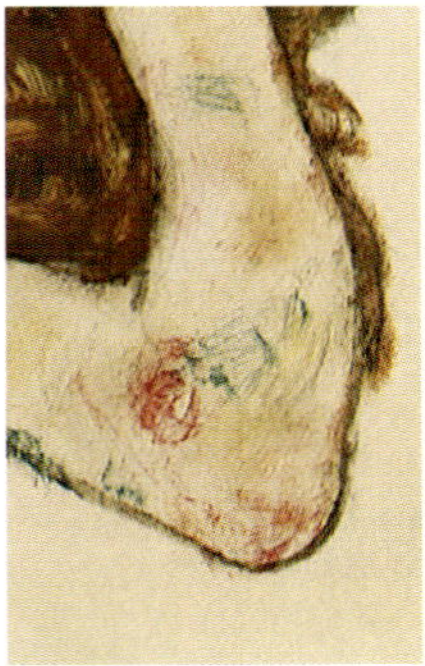

Franz Pfemfert published poems and drawings by Schiele in the Berlin periodical *Die Aktion*. Three of Schiele's works could be seen in the international special alliance exhibition in Cologne. The lithograph *Male Nude Study* appeared in the Sema-Mappe (portfolio) of the Delphin Publishing House in Munich.

In 1913, Schiele became a member of the Bund Österreichischer Künstler (federation of Austrian artists), of which Gustav Klimt was president. In the same year, he went to Munich, where he took part in a collective exhibition at the Galerie Golz.

Female Nude Lying on her Stomach

1917
Black chalk and gouache, 29.8 x 46.1 cm
Albertina, Vienna

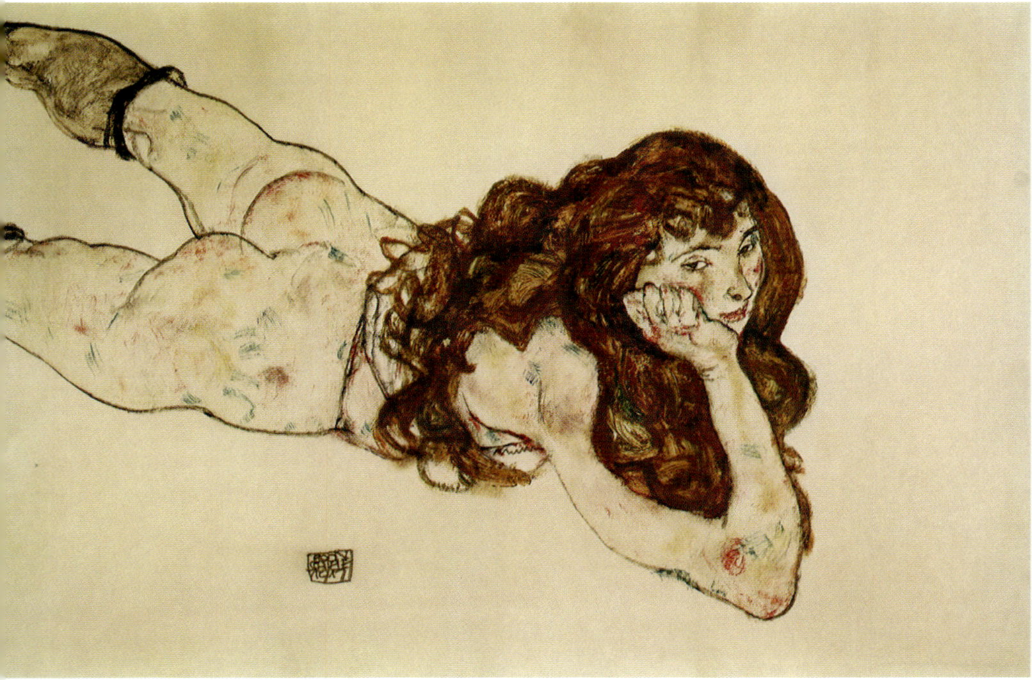

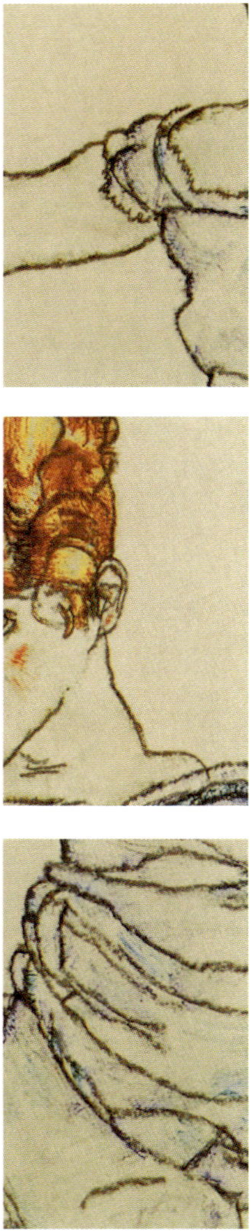

On 28 July, 1914, war was officially declared between the Austro-Hungarian Empire and Serbia. Schiele commented: "We live in the most violent time the world has ever seen. Hundreds of thousands of people perish miserably, everyone must bear his fate either living or dying; we have become hard and fearless. That which was before 1914 belongs to another world." Schiele continued with his work, he was now an internationally recognised artist who had exhibitions in Rome,

Seated Woman in Violet Stockings

1917
Gouache and black chalk, 29.6 x 44.2 cm
Private collection

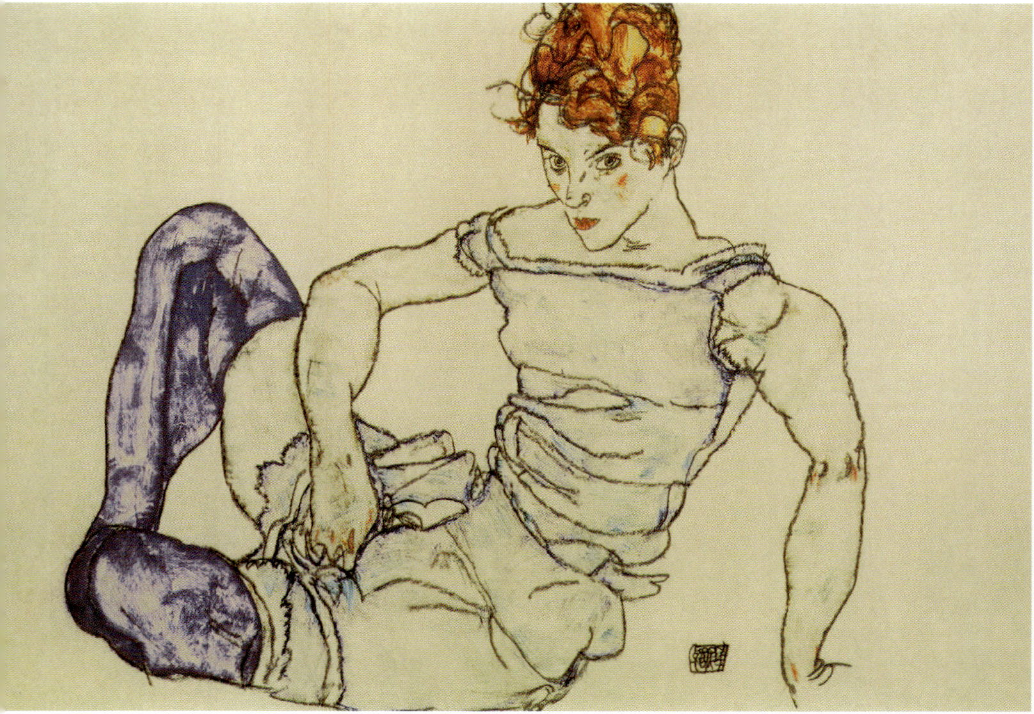

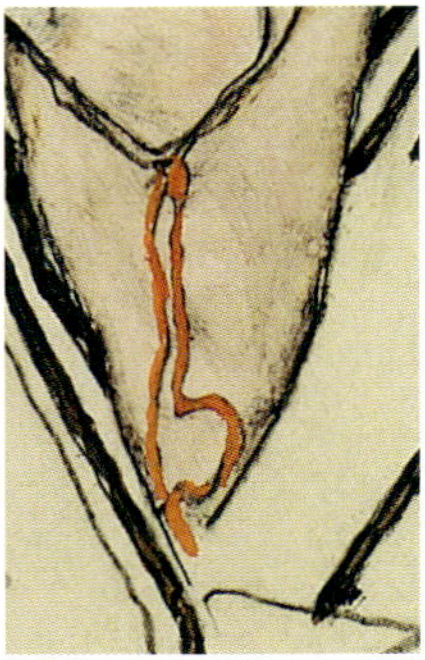

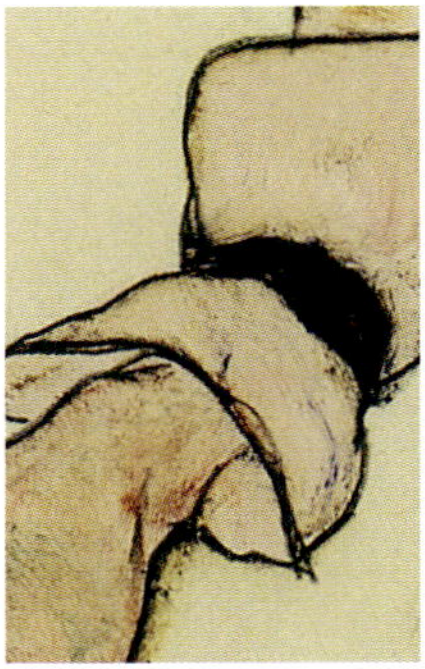

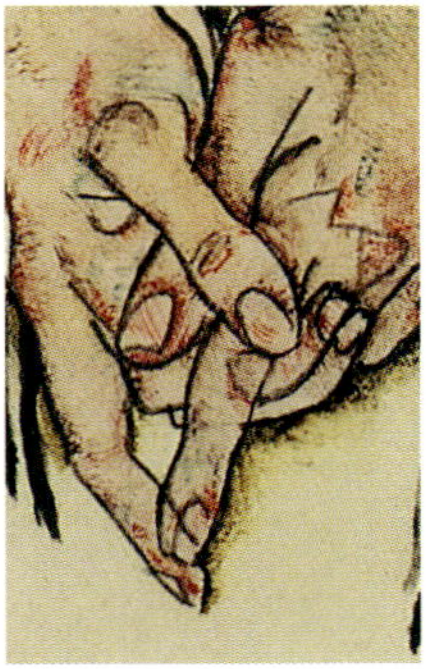

Brussels and Paris. Anton Josef Trèka (1893-1940) photographed Schiele in extravagant pantomime poses. In the Berlin periodical, *Die Aktion*, he wrote: "We are above all people of the times, in other words, such who have at the very least found the way into our present time."

As he obtained international recognition, his emotional life evolved. Schiele's beloved sister Gerti married a fellow artist, Anton Peschka;

The Artist's Sister in Law in
Striped Dress, Seated

1917
Pencil, gouache, and watercolour
on paper, 43.8 x 28.5 cm
Albertina, Vienna

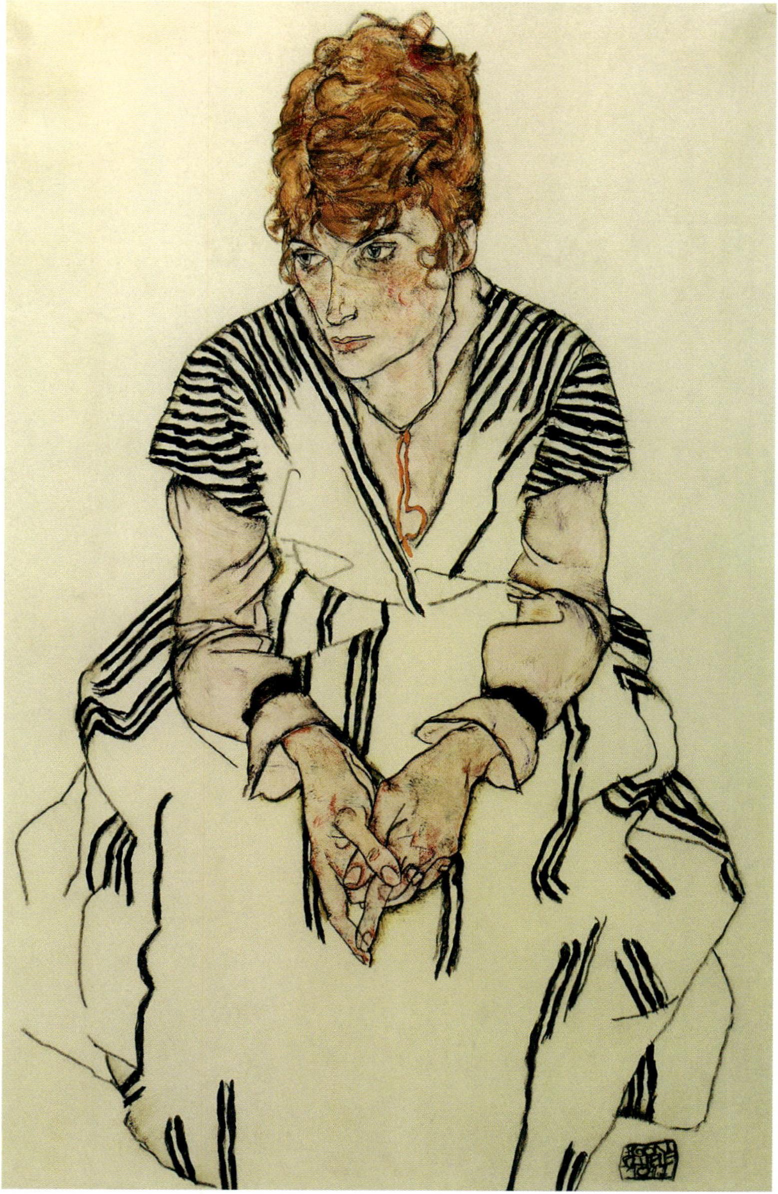

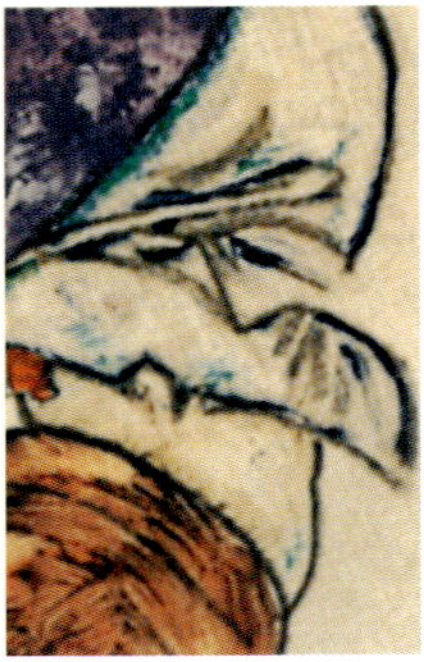

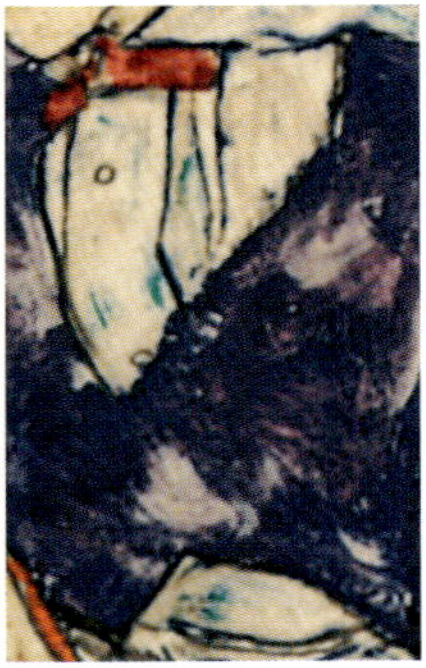

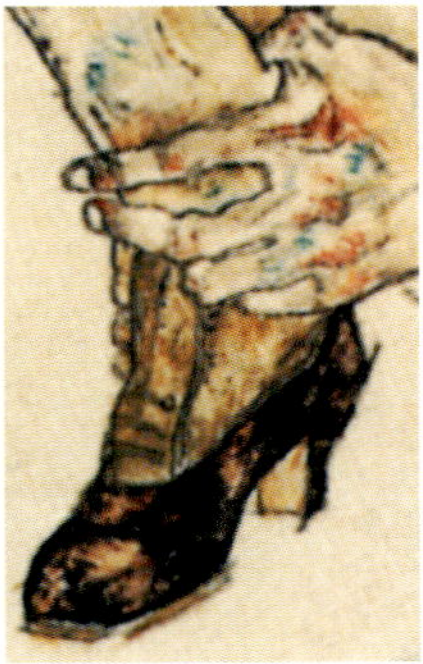

their young son often spent time with his uncle. Across from Schiele's atelier lived his landlords, the middle-class Harms family with their two young daughters. Schiele, disguised as an Apache, allowed them to see him at the window. Later, he sent Wally with an invitation to the cinema and the assurance that she too would accompany them. The two sisters modelled for Schiele and, in their vanity, competed for the favours of the young artist.

Portrait of the Artist's Wife Seated (Edith Schiele), Holding Her Right Leg

1917

Gouache and black pencil, 46.3 x 29.2 cm

The Pierpont Morgan Library, New York

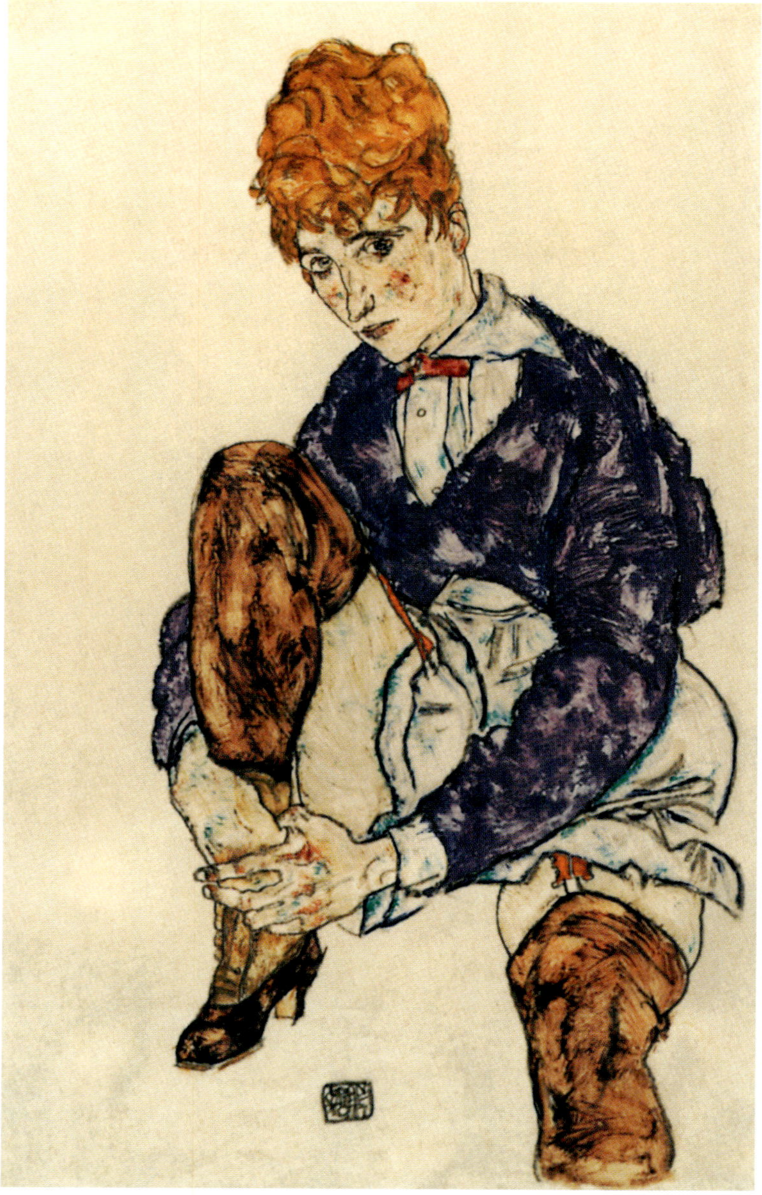

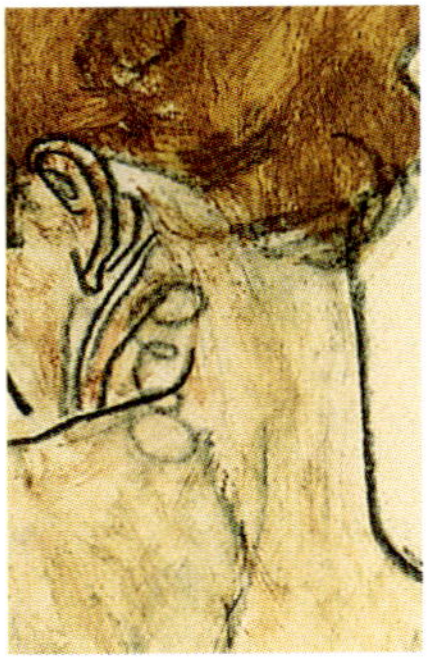

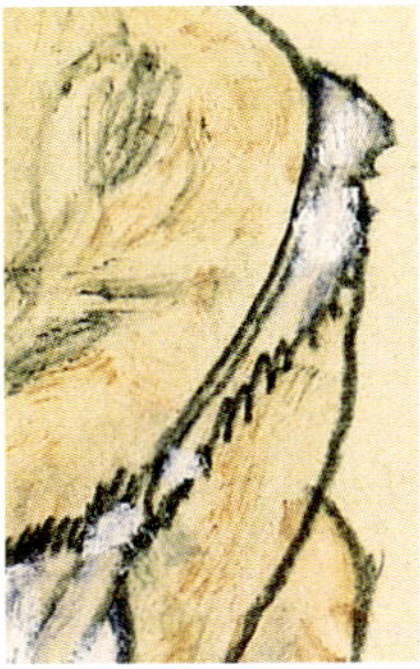

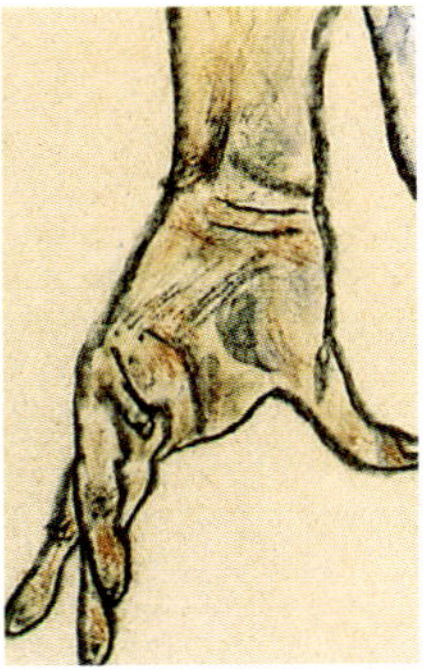

Coldheartedly, he informed Wally that he would marry Edith, a socially advantageous match for him, whereupon she joined the Red Cross as a nurse and went to the front where she would succumb to scarlet fever in 1917. In the allegorical painting *Death and the Maiden,* he came to terms with his separation from Wally. The male figure bears Schiele's features and what can be seen of the woman's face resembles Wally's features.

Seated Woman in Underwear, Back View

1917
Watercolour, gouache, black pencil and pencil, 45.9 x 29.4 cm
Serge Sabarsky Collection, New York

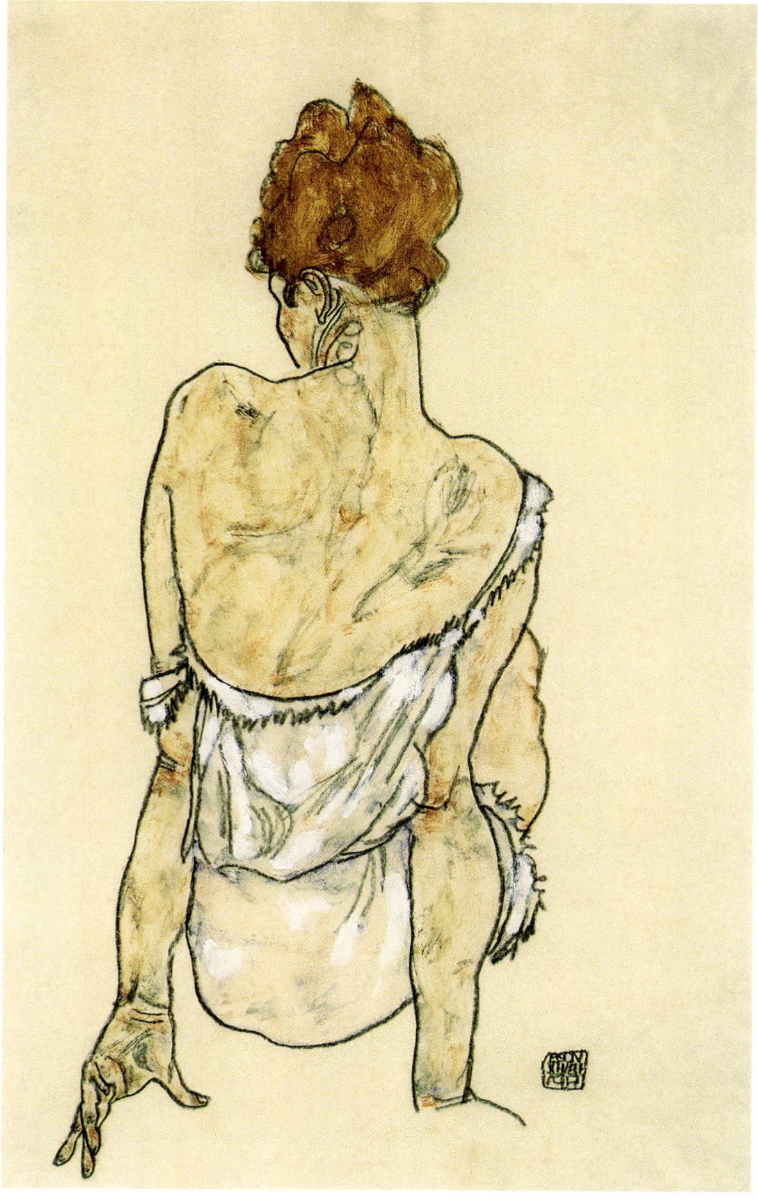

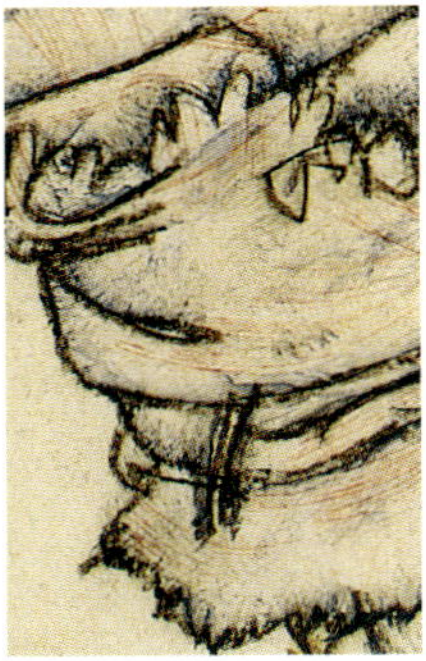
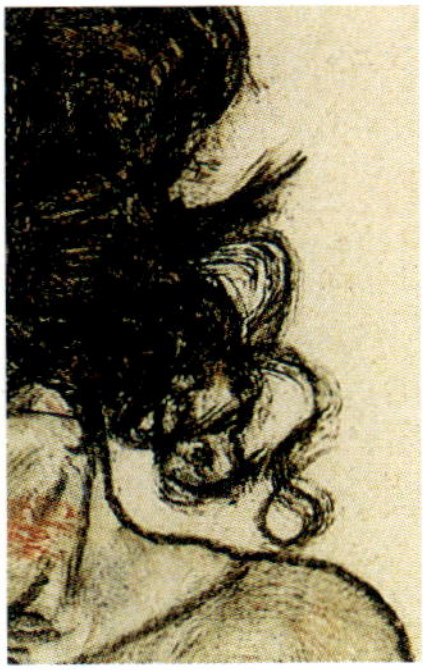
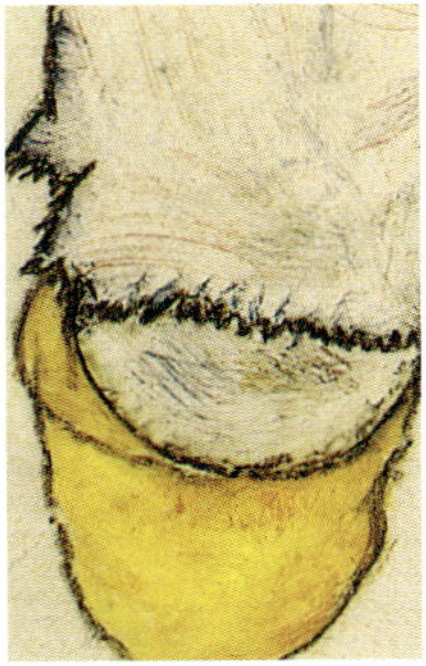

Whether we see the painting in these literal terms, or as a more universal allegory (the theme is traditionally a cautionary vanitas image), it is a haunting subject. In a bleak and barren landscape emphasising the harshness of the outside world, two lovers cling to one another on a rumpled bed sheet. Their embrace is desperate but passionless, the male figure's deadly pallor, monastic robe and sightless gaze contrasting with the flushed cheeks of the woman in a nightdress.

Kneeling Female Semi-Nude

1917
Gouache, black pencil and lead pencil
28 x 42.5 cm
Private collection

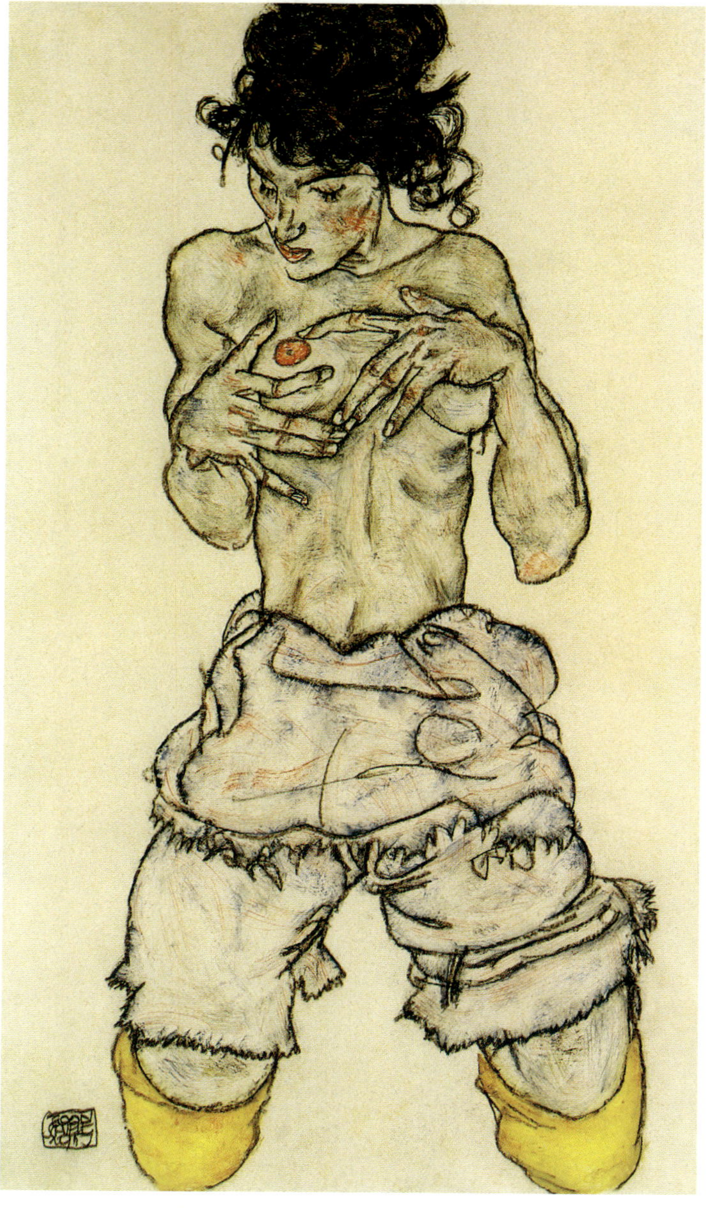

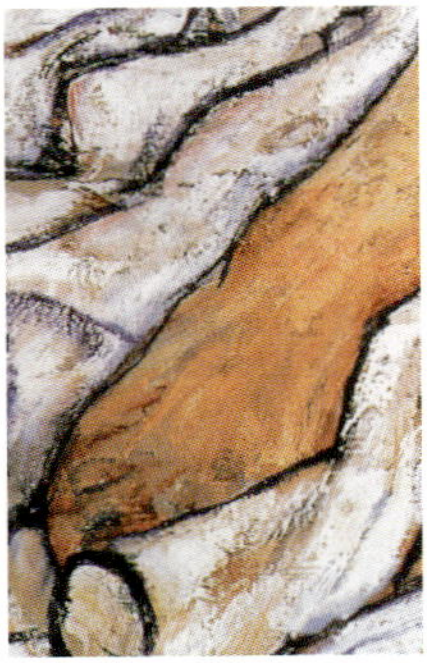

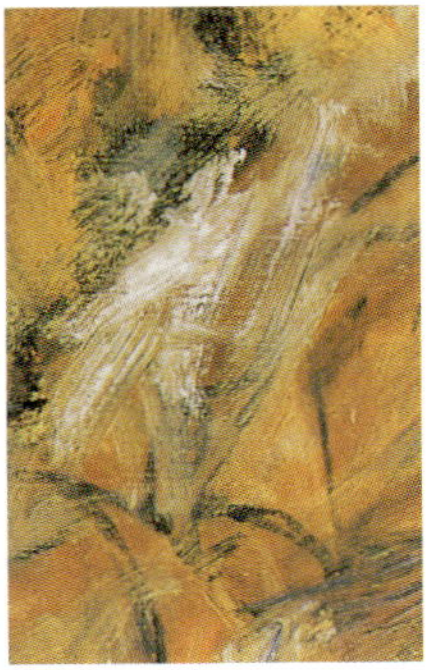

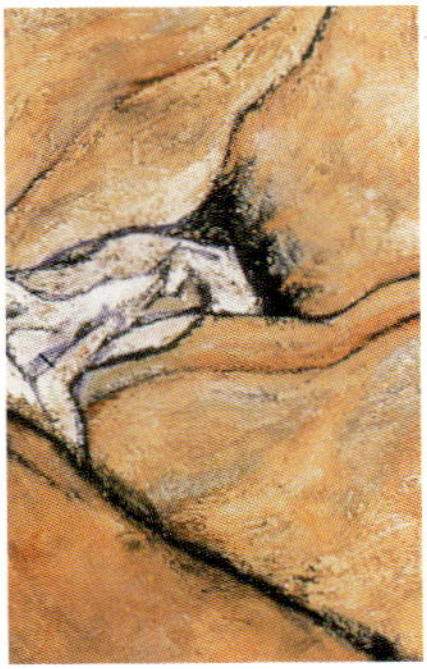

On 17 June, 1915, five days after his twenty-fifth birthday, Schiele married Edith Harms. Four days later he was inducted into military service in Bohemia. In 1916, he was held captive in the Russian prisoner of war camp located in Mühlung near Wieselburg. *Die Aktion* published two xylographs. One year later, Schiele returned to Vienna to work in the army museum.

The Embrace (Lovers II)

1917
Oil on canvas, 98 x 169 cm
Österreichische Galerie Belvedere, Vienna

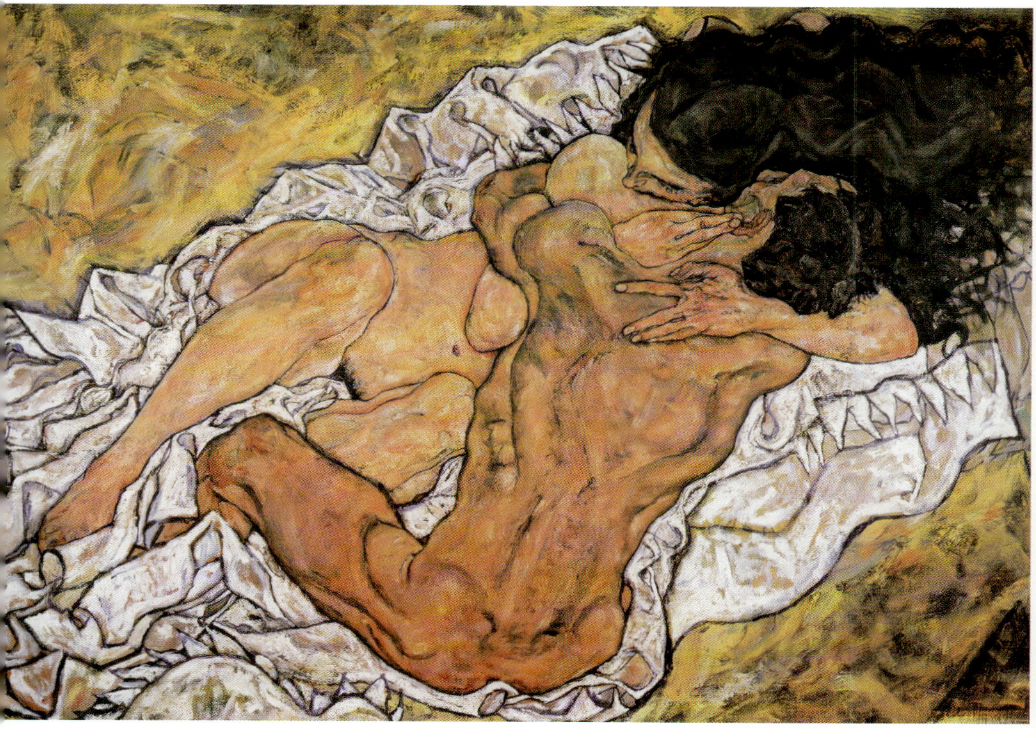

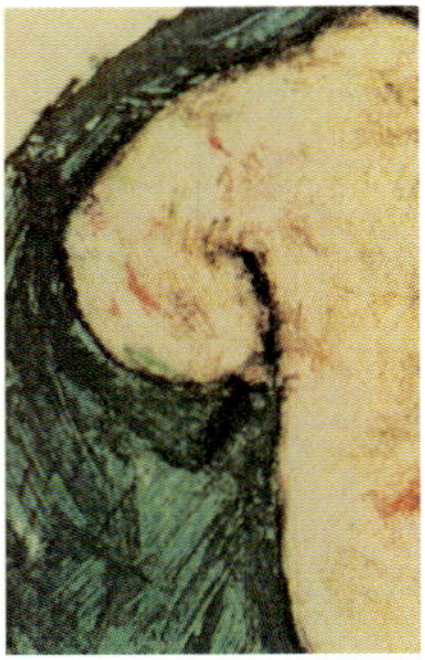

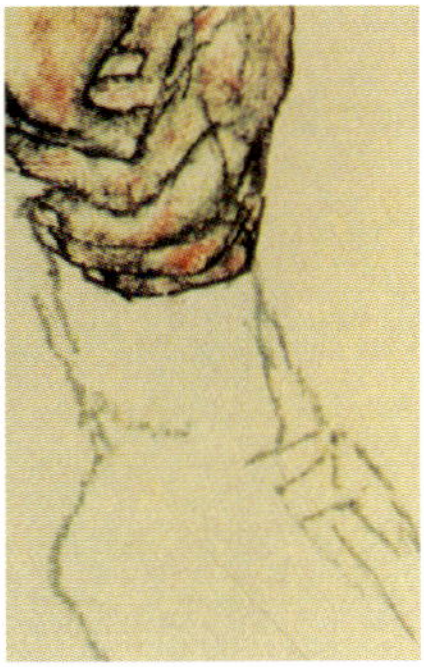

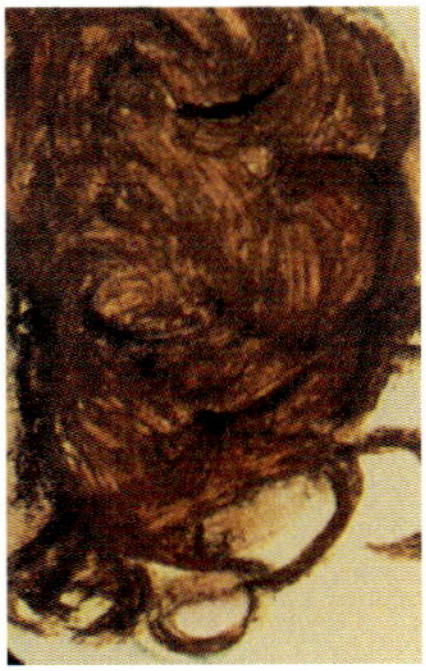

At first, his wife was his exclusive model. *Embrace* (*Lovers II*) from 1917, is one of Schiele's best known works and a culmination of his new, semi-classical style. The couple lie together affectionately grasping each other and the artist kisses his wife on the ear. At last, he is able to celebrate a union of two people as one harmonious whole. The lines are smooth; the hair of both heads is joined without distinction; the feet disappear into a single conjoined line.

Seated Woman with Bent Knee

1917
Gouache, watercolour and black pencil
46 x 30.5 cm
Národní Galerie, Prague

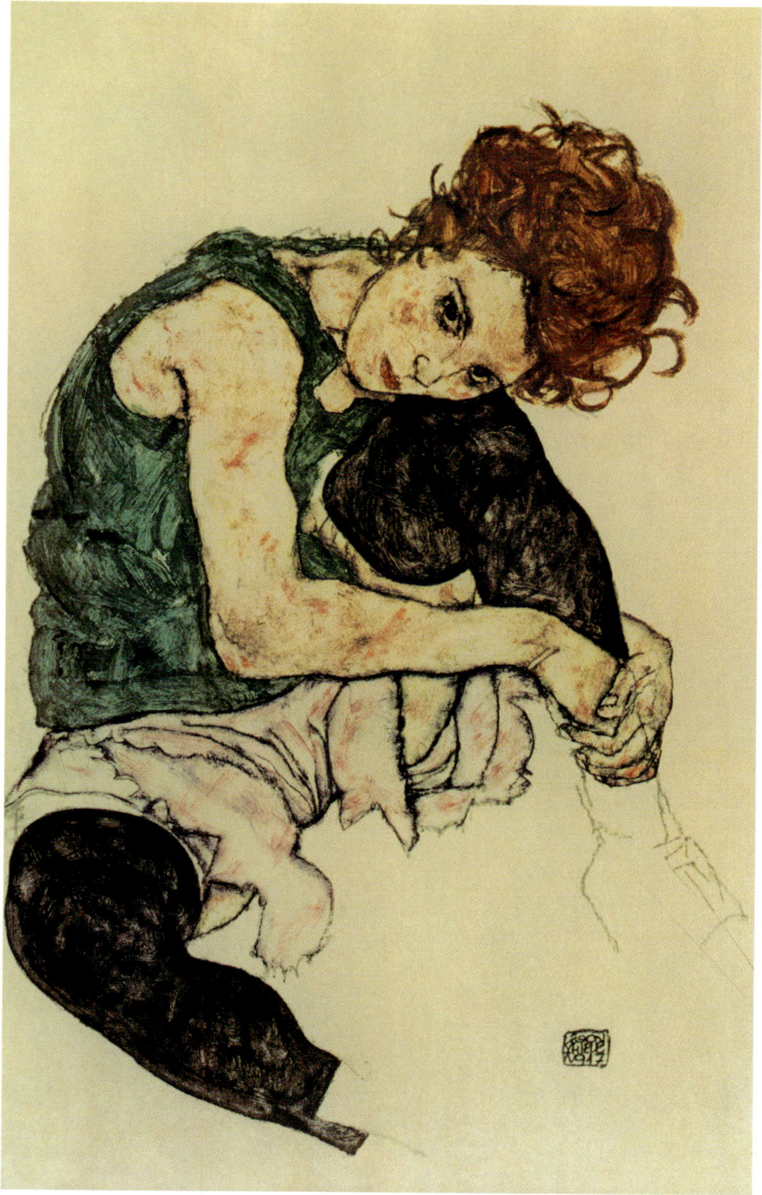

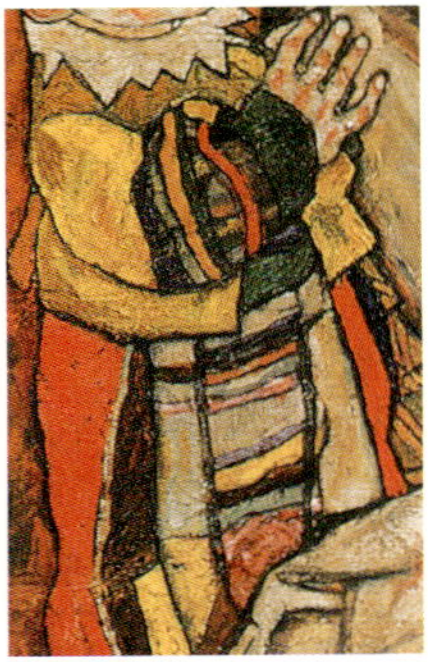

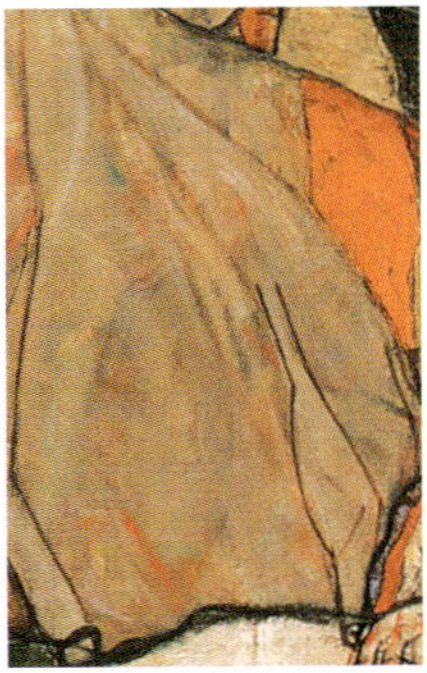

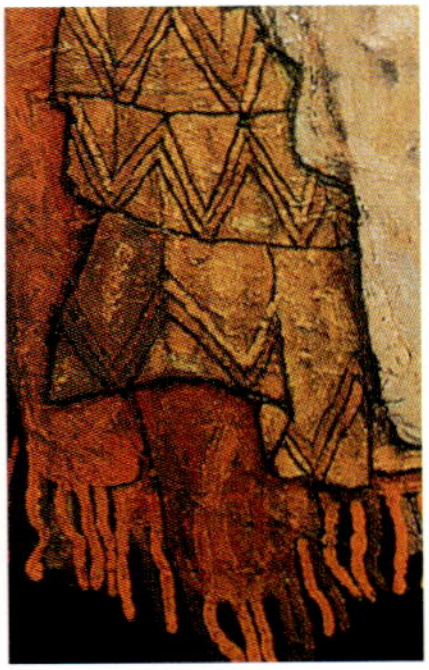

The male and female forms seem to hold each other equally and no-one is watching or aware of being watched. The sheet is still crumpled but this is now a modest device to cover the female's genitalia, rather than to expose the brutal animal truth. This is not a pornographic painting but a real image of love. It is as if Schiele is no longer hypnotically enthralled by a juvenile idea of sex and is now focused on actually learning to enjoy his relationship with his wife, Edith. They are two contented people within marriage and, unlike in former works,

Mother with Two Children III

1917
Oil on canvas, 150 x 160 cm
Österreichische Galerie Belvedere, Vienna

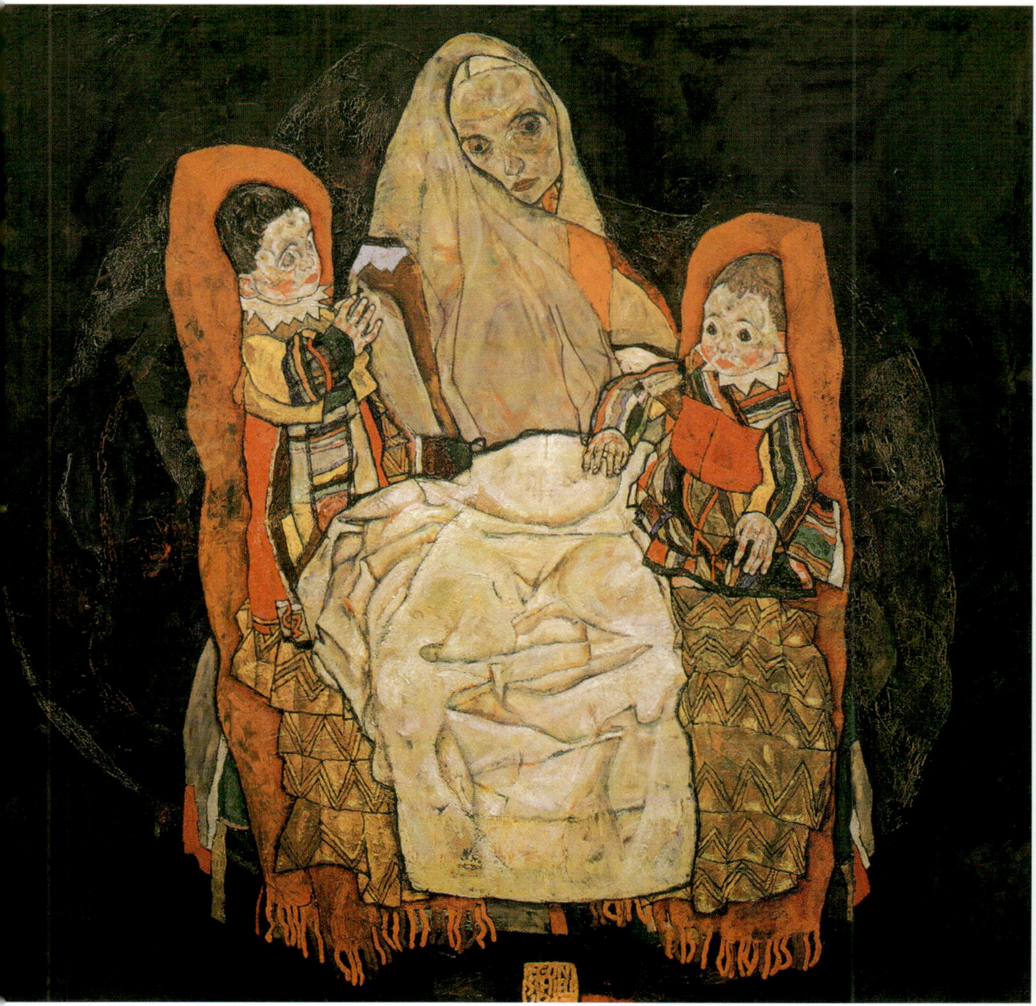

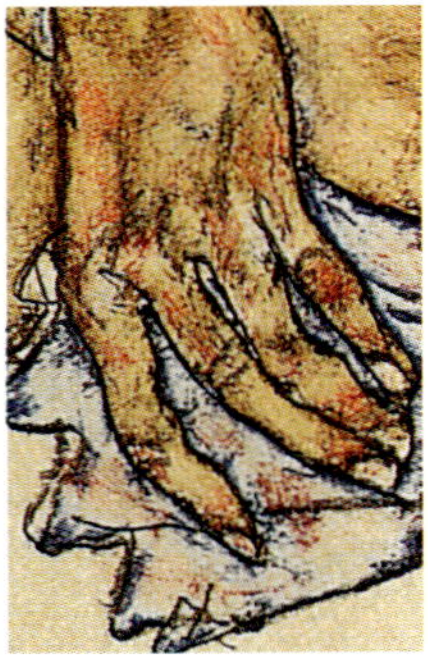

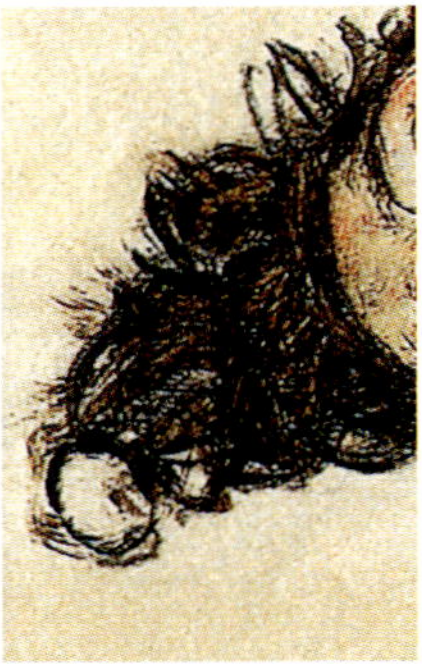

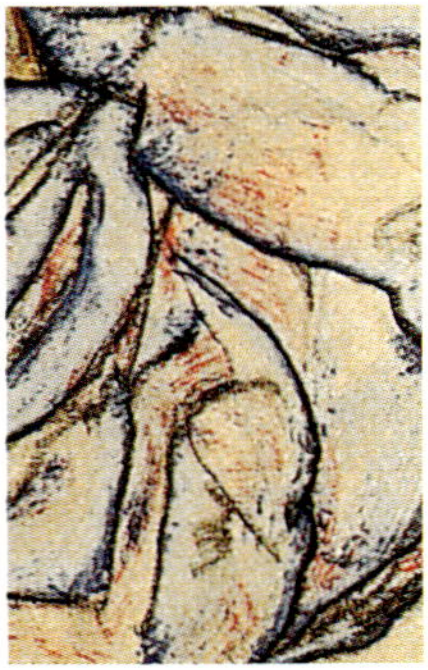

they are not actually having sex in this picture but are locked in a mutually loving embrace.

Little by little, Schiele once again began to look for models elsewhere. In 1918, 117 sessions with other models were recorded in his notebook. The Vienna book dealer Richard Lanyi published a portfolio with twelve collotypes of Egon Schiele's drawings. *Seated Woman with Bent Knee* (1917) illustrates a new advance in Schiele's technique.

Reclining Female Nude

1917
Gouache, watercolour and charcoal
29.7 x 46.3 cm
Moravská Gallery, Brno

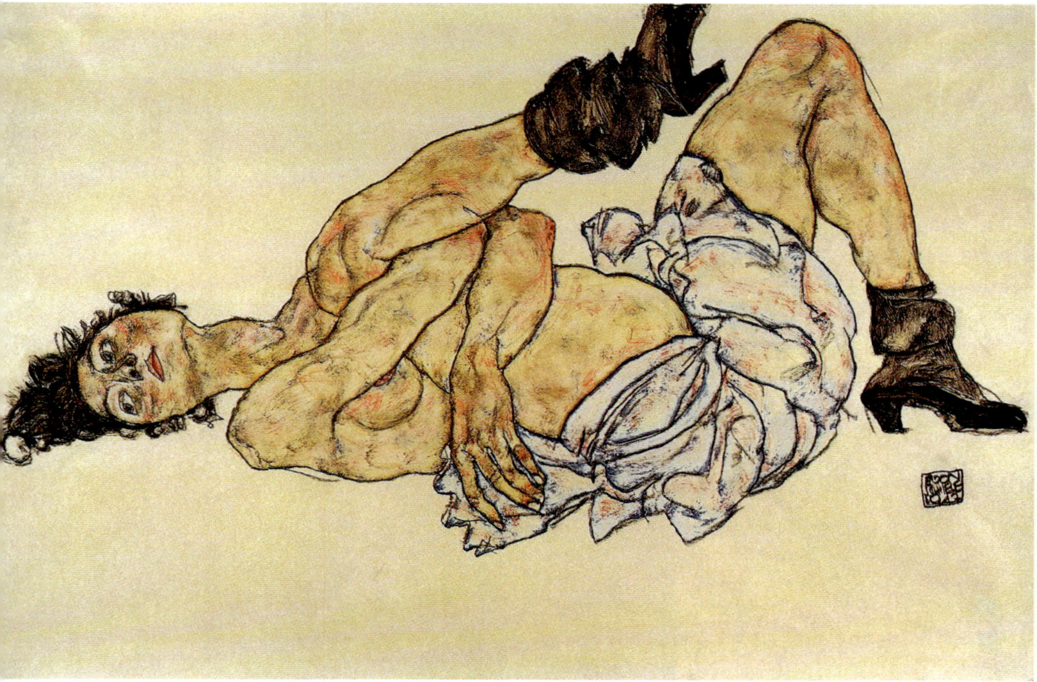

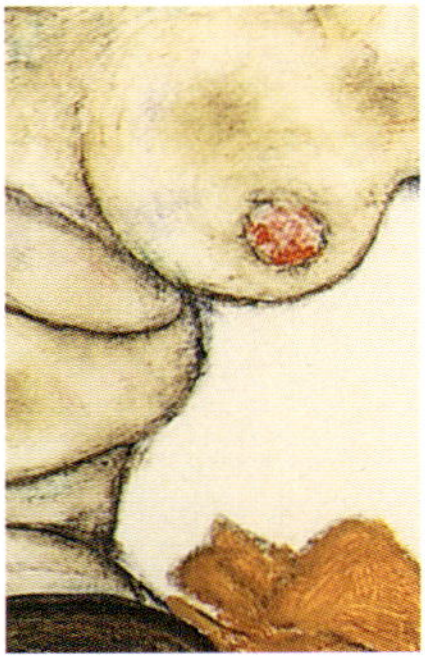

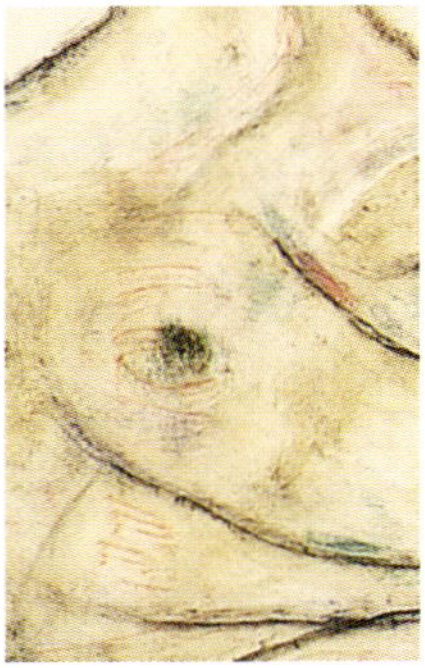

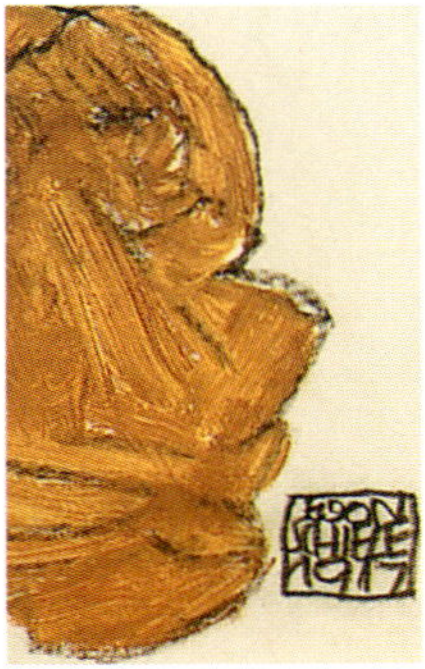

He no longer needs to draw strange proportions and novel angles to create effect. His work is simplified and he has become a more mature artist. This is one of the best known of his images from this period and, its relative fleshiness, the soft tones of the complementary greens and reds and the ease with which the model sits, all seem to point towards the work of a much more confident man. He no longer needs to shock to create effect – he can return to basic,

Reclining Nude with Yellow Towel

1917
Gouache and black pencil on paper
29 x 45.7 cm
Private collection, Richard Nagy Ltd

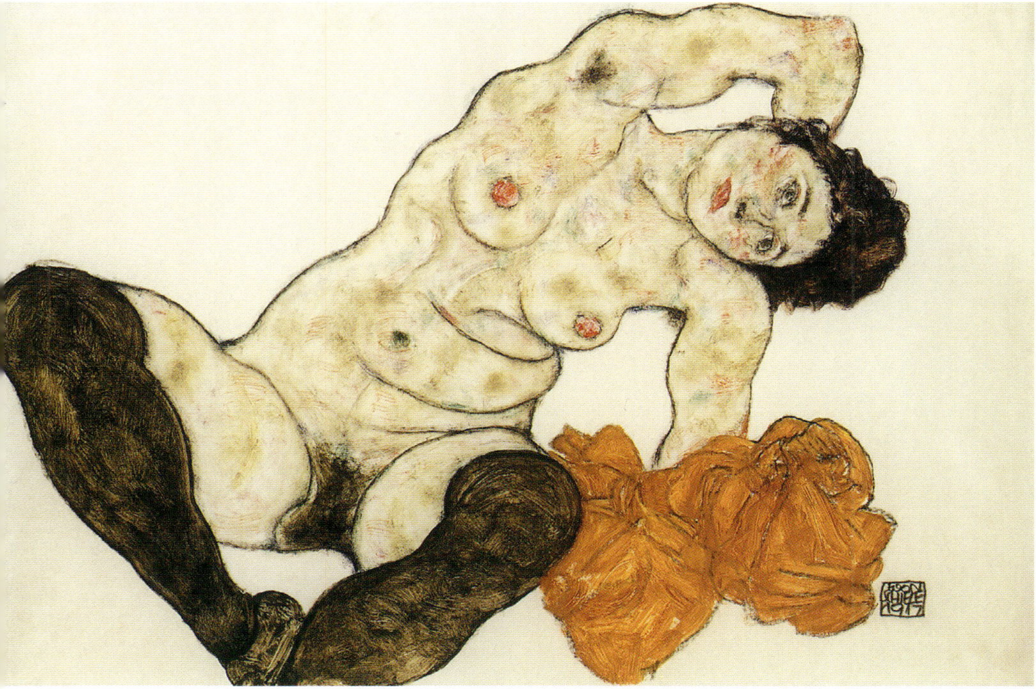

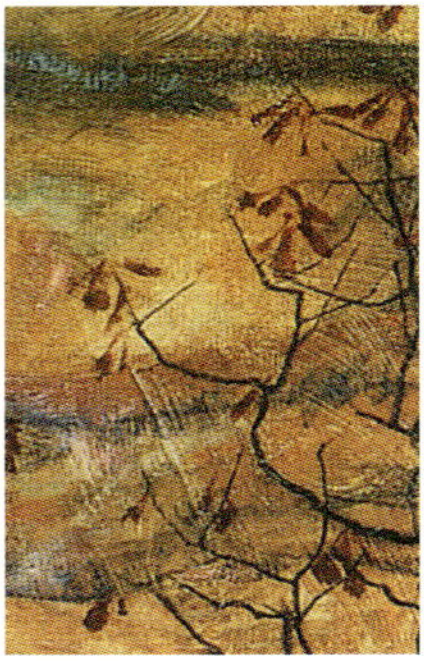

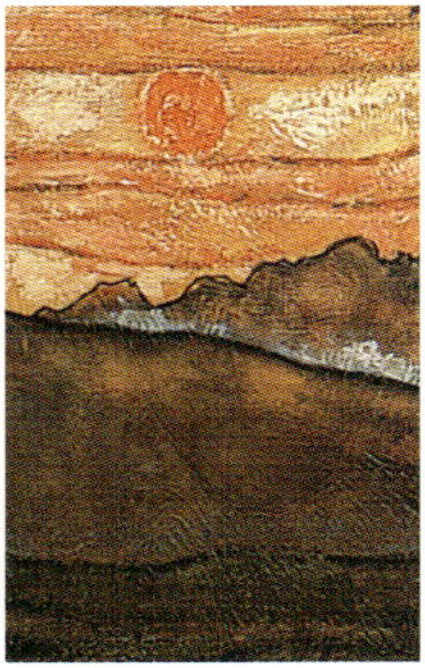

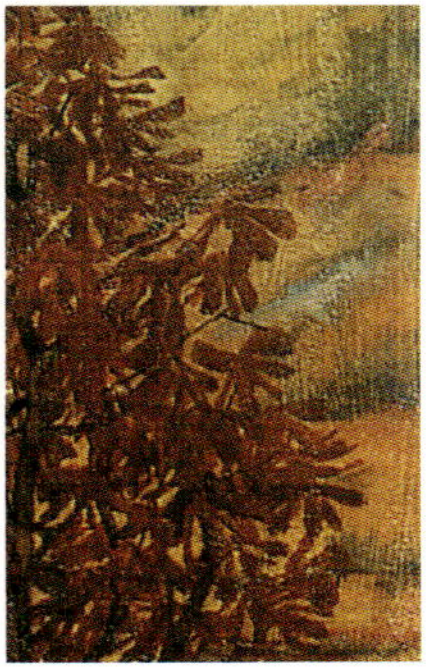

classical poses and still achieve the desired effect. Here the model sits languidly and may or may not reveal all later. This is not a woman who has madly thrown off her outer clothes at the beginning of the session but a model who has been deliberately posed and who is quite comfortable to look back at the artist since they are both warm, sentient human beings with individual personalities.

Four Trees

1917
Oil on canvas, 110.5 x 141 cm
Österreichische Galerie Belvedere, Vienna

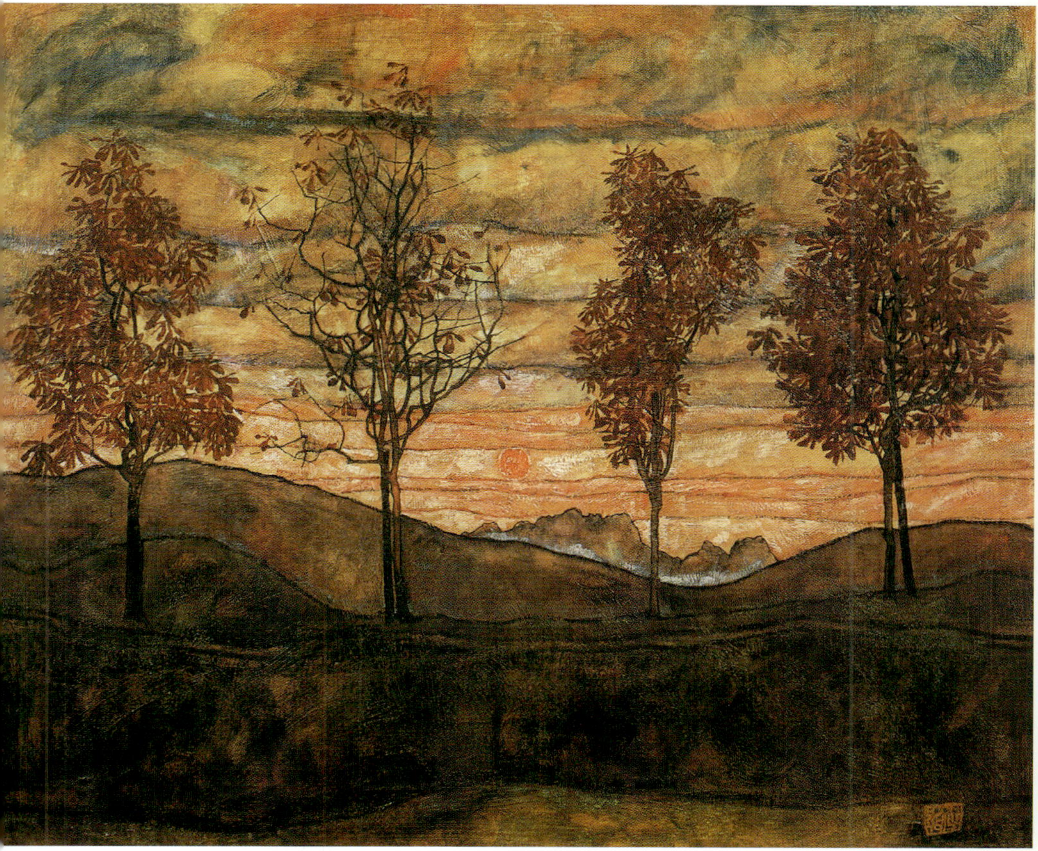

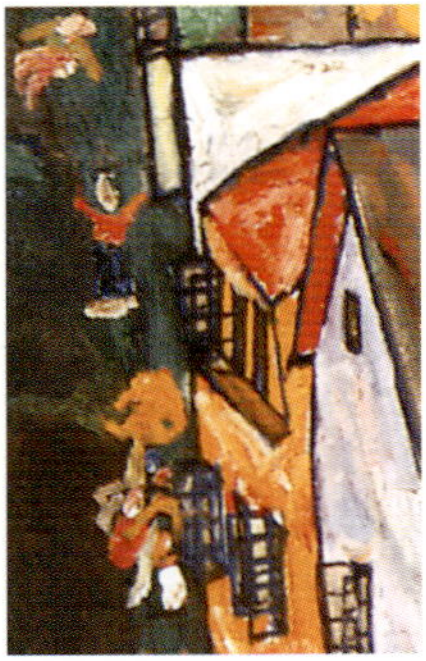

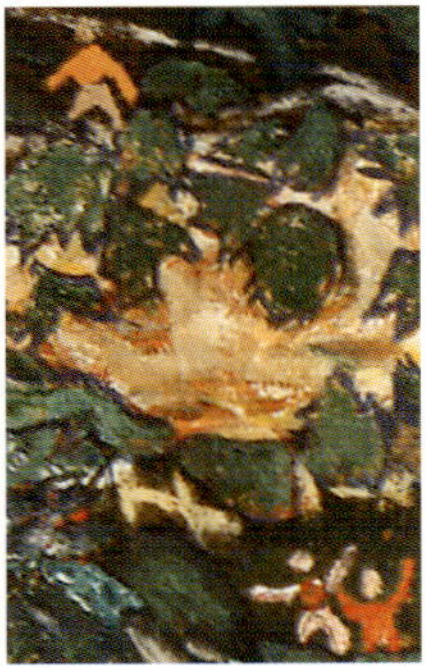

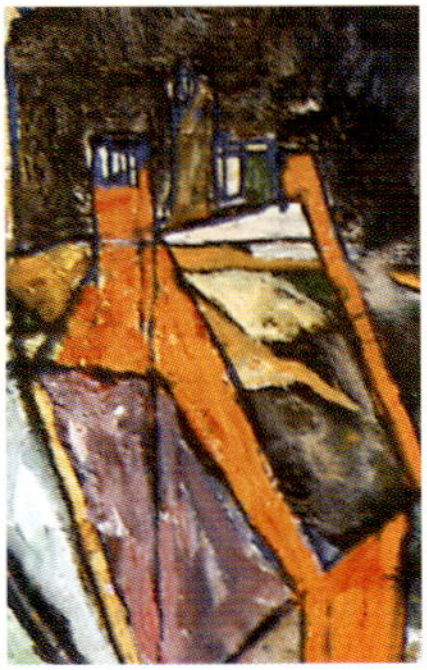

In December, Schiele worked for the periodical *The Dawn*. In a letter dated 2 March, 1917, Schiele wrote to his brother-in-law: "Since the bloody terror of world war befell us, some will probably have become aware that art is more than just a matter of middle-class luxury."

City Borders

1917-1918
Oil on canvas, 109.5 x 139.5 cm
Landesmuseum Joanneum, Graz

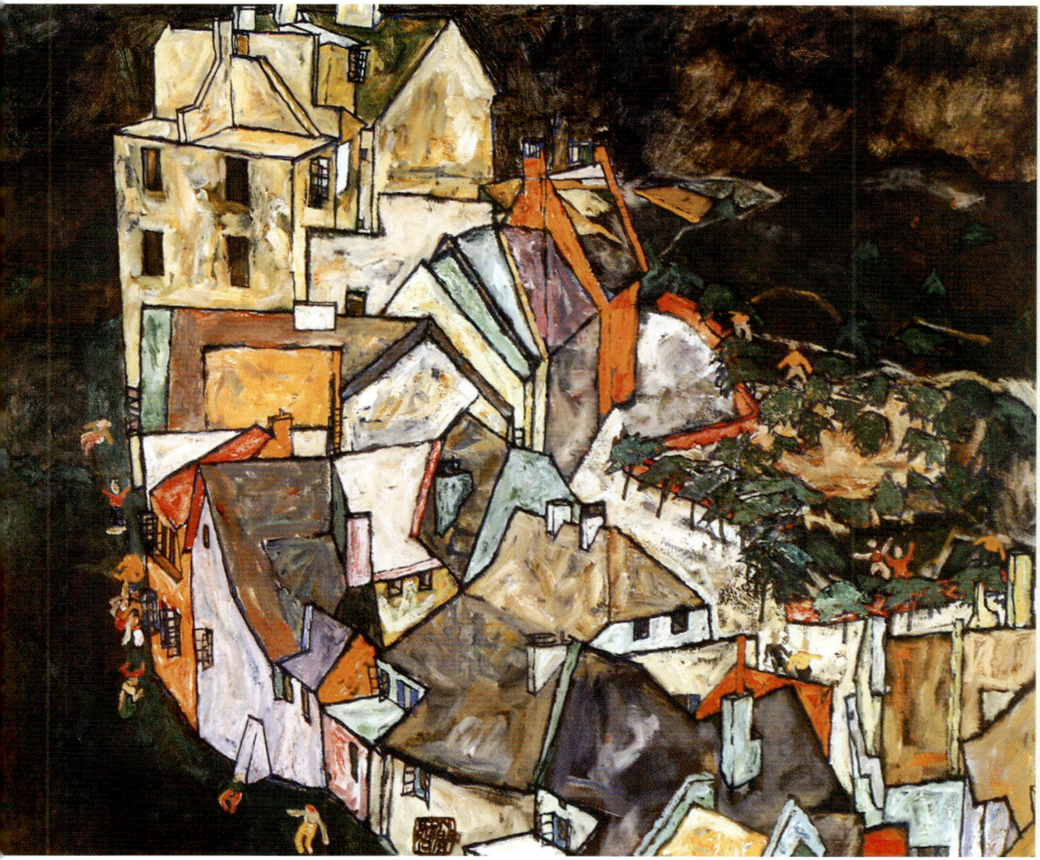

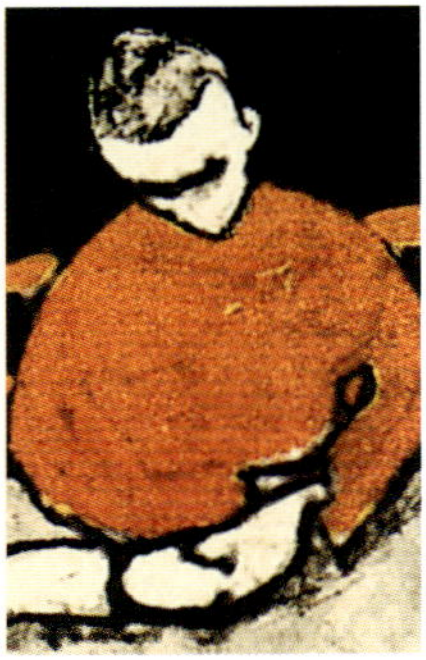

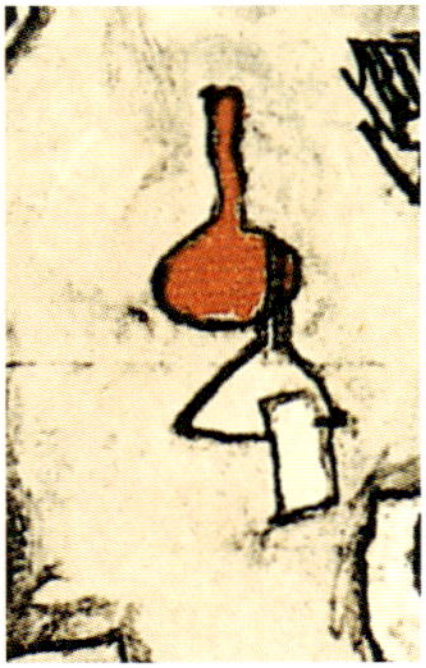

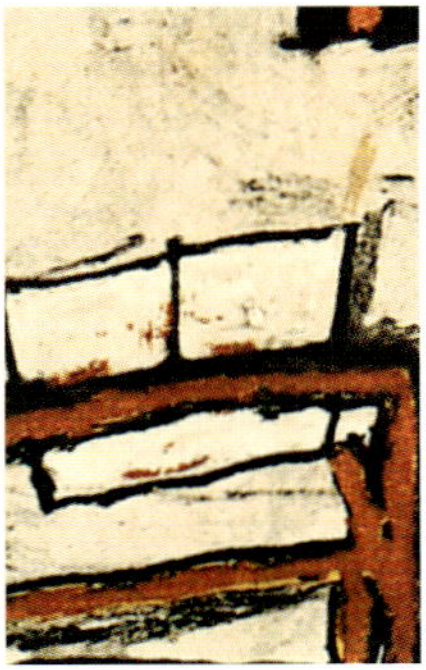

At the dawn of his short life, Schiele was an adored artist, in the midst of the viennese artistic life. At the 49th Secession Exhibition, Schiele showed over forty-five pictures and, at last, he achieved national recognition as a master painter. Only a month earlier, in February 1918, the artist's great mentor, Klimt, had died.

Poster for the 49th Secession Exhibition

1918
Lithograph, 63.5 x 48 cm
Albertina, Vienna

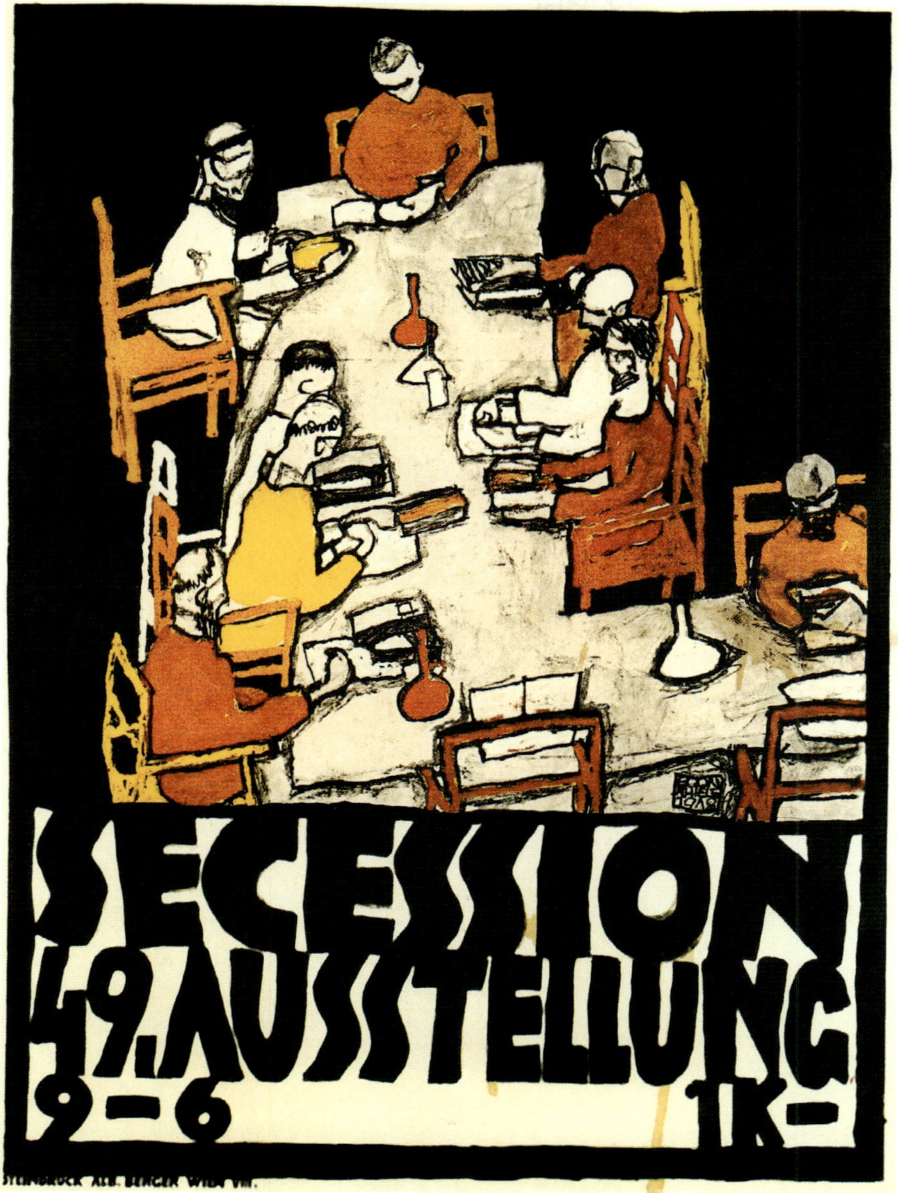
SECESSION
49. AUSSTELLUNG
9–6
1K–

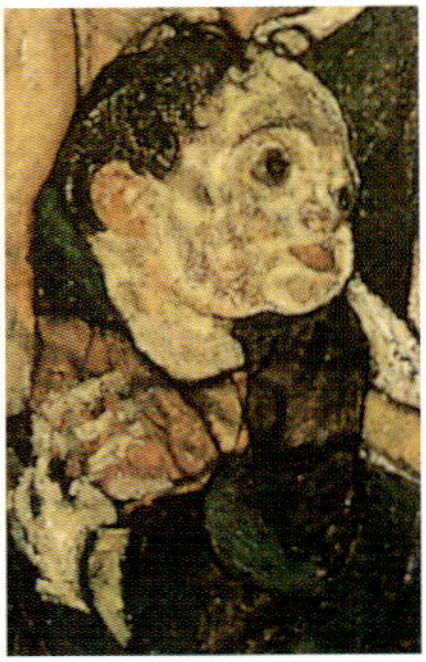

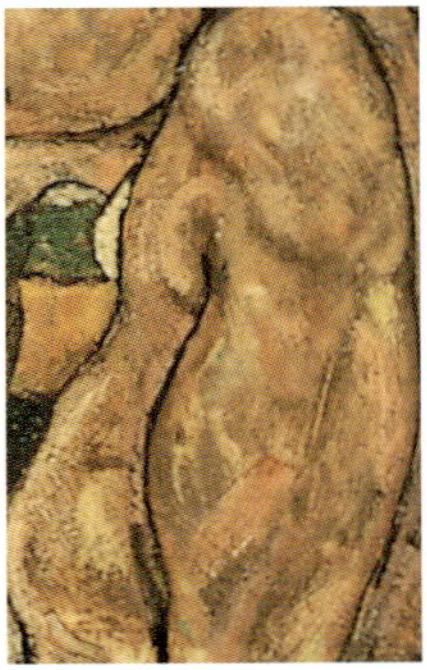

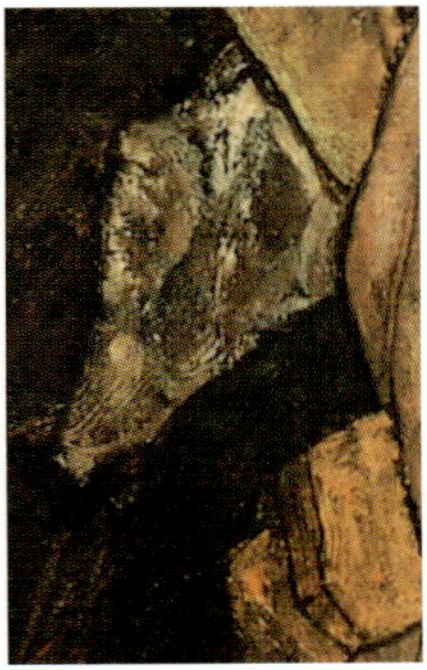

Of course, this death brought with it an entirely new role for the painter who quite suddenly found himself the figurehead of an entire artistic movement. For a number of reasons, therefore, Schiele was now on the verge of total financial and social security and it was in this frame of mind that he painted the poster for the 49th Exhibition. Here he sits at the head of a dinner party where all the other guests are his fellow artists and admirers of his work: Georg Merkel,

The Family (Squatting Couple)

1918
Oil on canvas, 152 x 162.5 cm
Österreichische Galerie Belvedere, Vienna

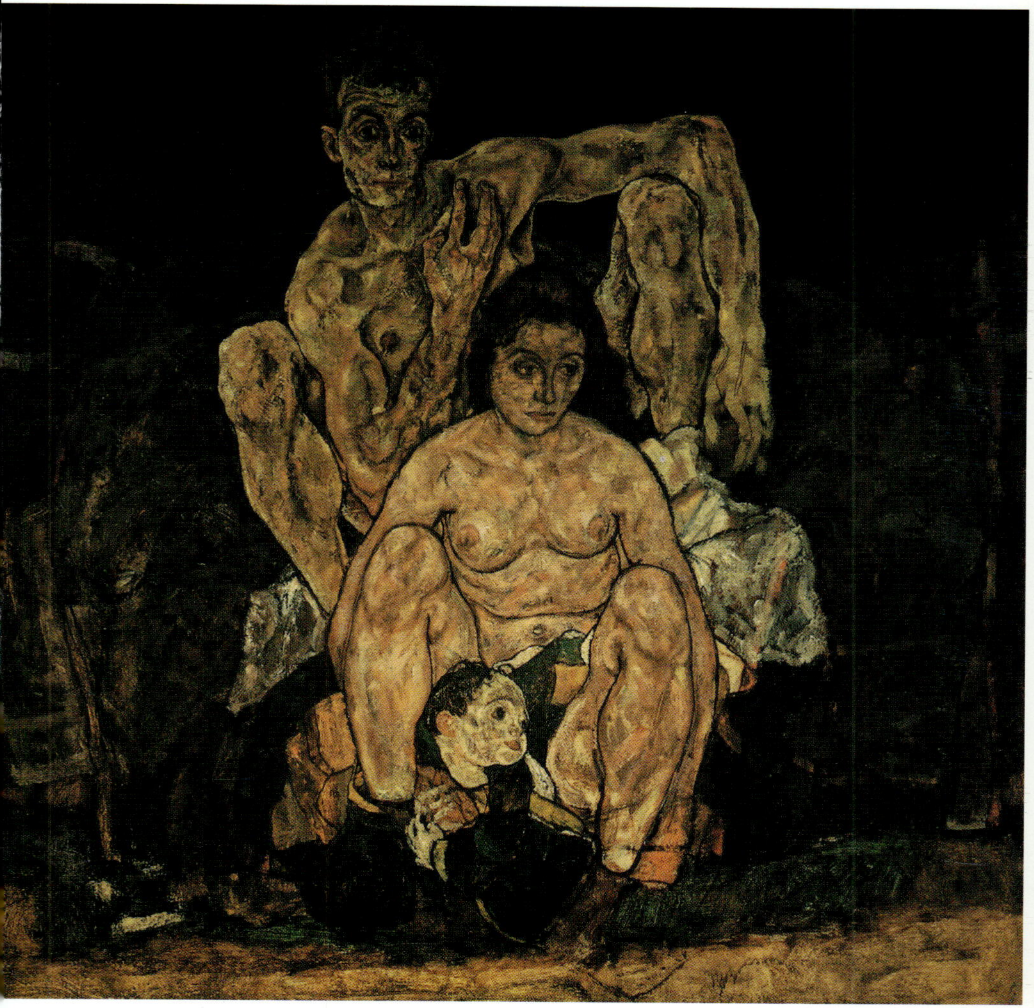

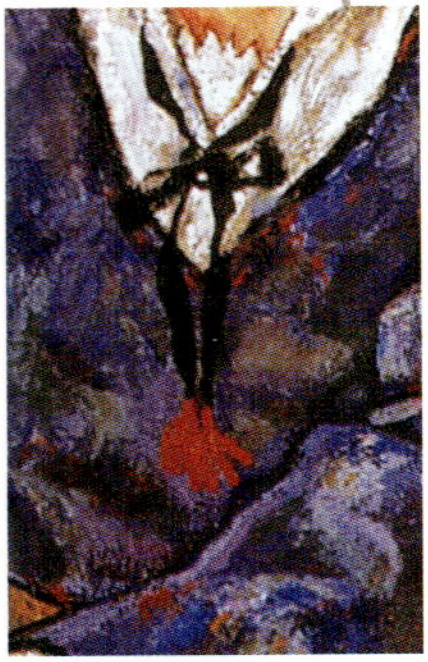
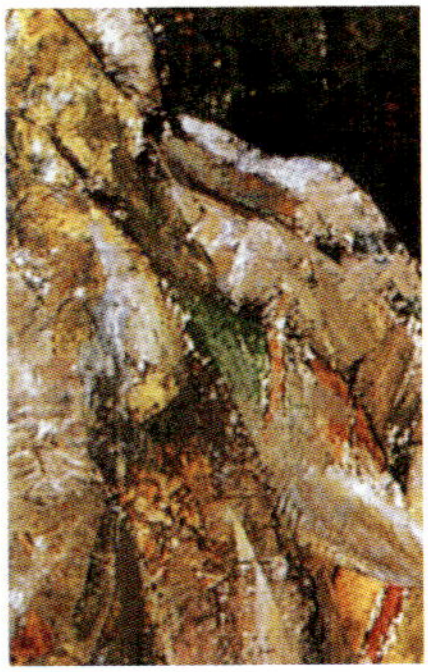
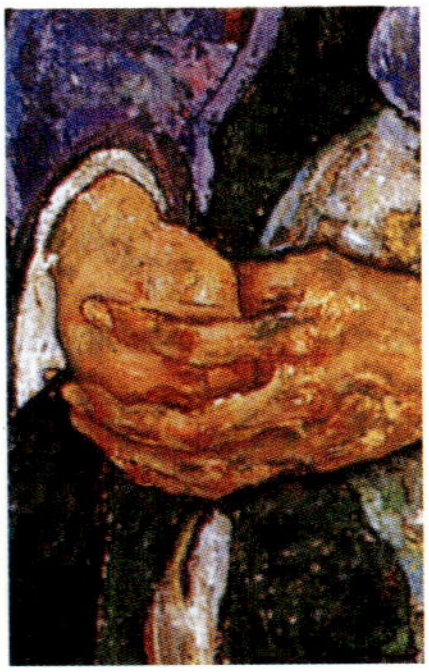

Willi Novak, Felix Harta and possibly Otto Wagner are all happily present while the foreground chair was originally occupied by an image of Klimt. By the time the poster was due to be printed, however, Klimt was dead and so, in its final version, Schiele left the seat empty. The faces are indistinct and the background anonymous – it is unimportant. The overall impression is one of a group of like-minded people, quite content in each other's company.

Portrait of Edith Schiele Seated

1918
Oil on canvas, 139.5 x 109.2 cm
Österreichische Galerie Belvedere, Vienna

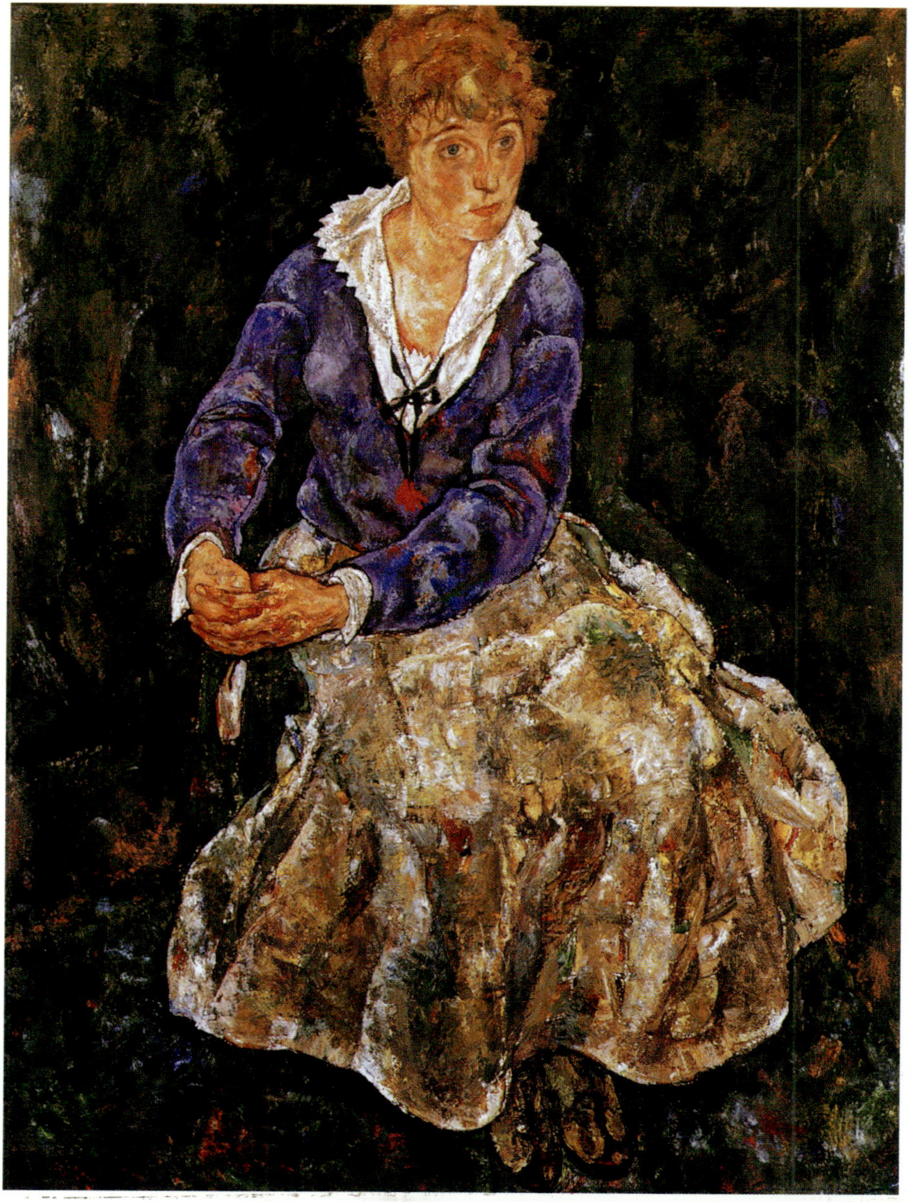

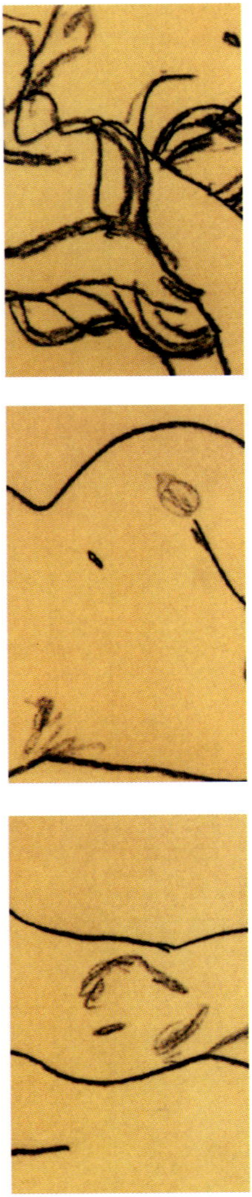

At this exhibition, Franz Martin Haberditzl purchased the *Portrait of the Artist's Wife, Seated* (1918) for the Moderne Galerie. It is the first acquisition of a painting while the Schiele was still alive. However, Schiele had to paint over the plaid skirt, as the museum's director found it too indecent. Schiele could now afford a larger atelier; the old one was to become an art school.

Nude Girl

1918
Black pencil on paper, 29.5 x 45.7 cm
Private collection, New York

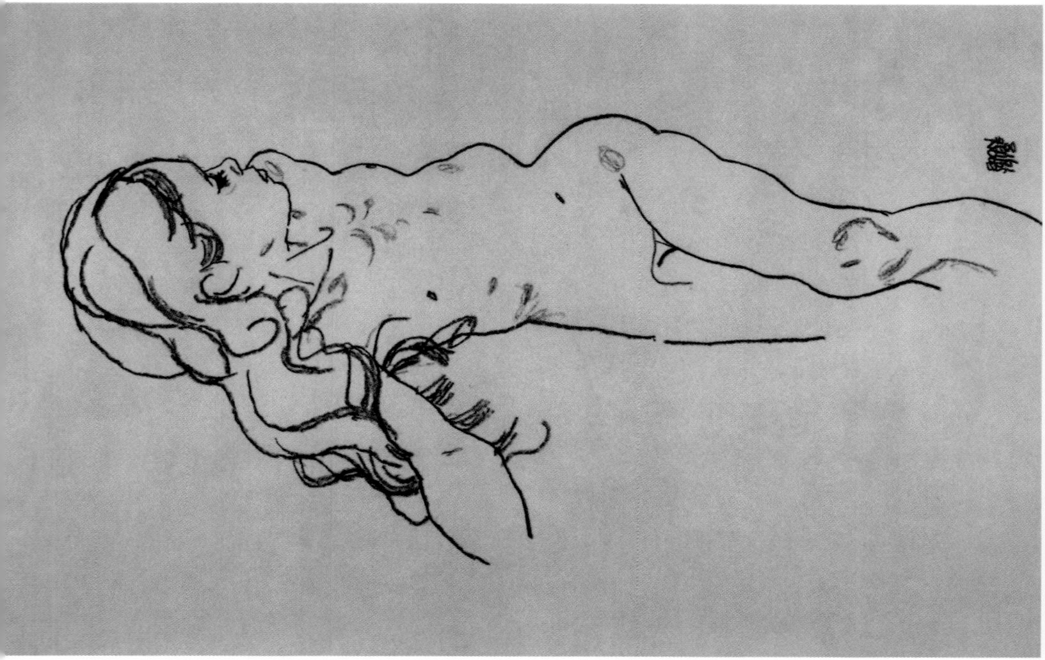

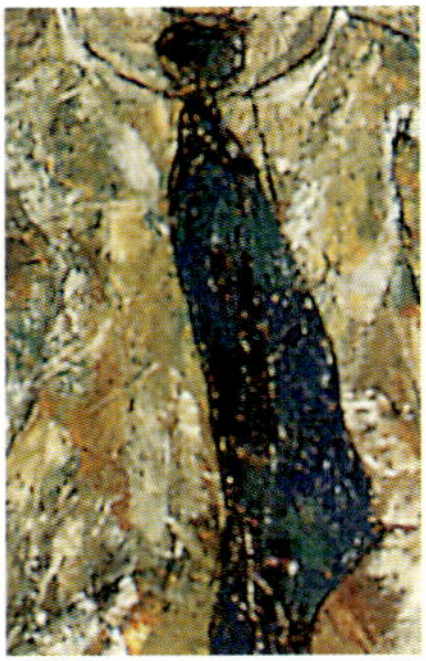

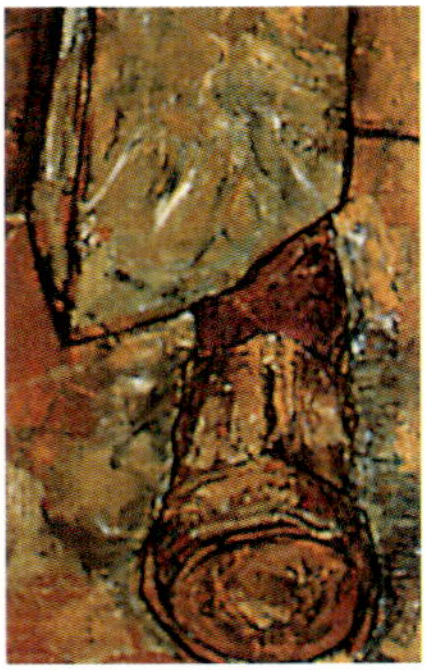

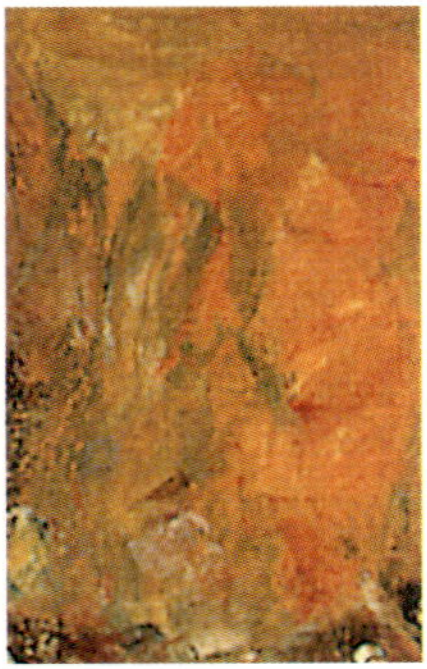

Already in 1917, Schiele had a plan for an art centre where the various disciplines of literature, music and visual art could coexist. The best-known founding members were Schönberg, Klimt, and the architect Hoffmann. Death, however, prevented these plans. On 31 October, three days after the death of his wife who was six months pregnant, Schiele also died from Spanish flu. Three days later, on 3 November, 1918, the Austro-Hungarian Empire capitulated.

Portrait of the Painter Paris von Gütersloh

1918
Oil on canvas, 140.3 x 109.9 cm
The Minneapolis Institute of Arts, Minneapolis

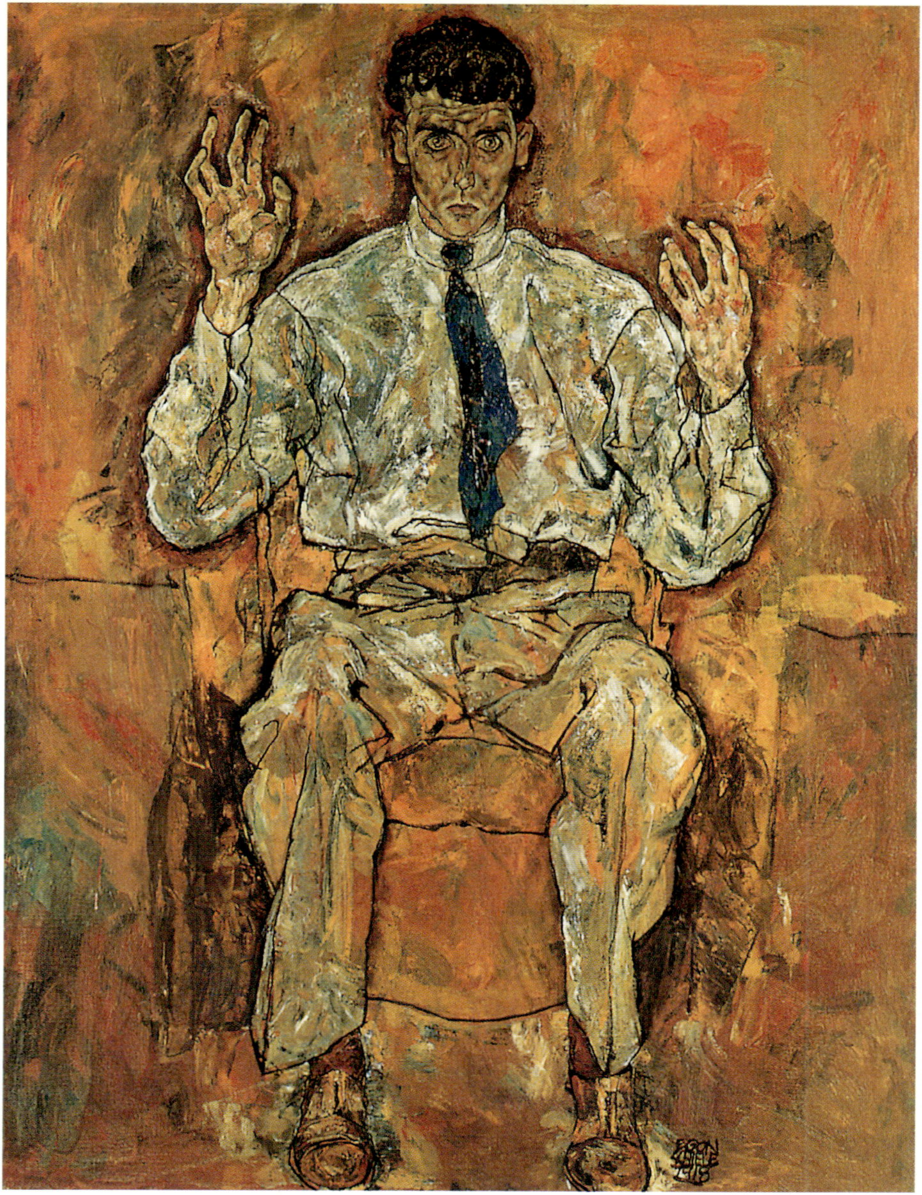

List of Illustrations